GRAMMAR
AND BEYOND

Laurie Blass
Susan Iannuzzi
Alice Savage
Deborah Gordon
with Randi Reppen

3

CAMBRIDGE
UNIVERSITY PRESS

Appendices

Introduction to *Grammar and Beyond*

Grammar and Beyond is a research-based and content-rich grammar series for beginning- to advanced-level students of North American English. The series focuses on the grammar structures most commonly used in North American English, with an emphasis on the application of these grammar structures to academic writing. The series practices all four skills in a variety of authentic and communicative contexts. It is designed for use both in the classroom and as a self-study learning tool.

Grammar and Beyond Is Research-Based

The grammar presented in this series is informed by years of research on the grammar of written and spoken North American English as it is used in college lectures, textbooks, academic essays, high school classrooms, and conversations between instructors and students. This research, and the analysis of over one billion words of authentic written and spoken language data known as the *Cambridge International Corpus*, has enabled the authors to:

- Present grammar rules that accurately represent how North American English is actually spoken and written
- Identify and teach differences between the grammar of written and spoken English
- Focus more attention on the structures that are commonly used, and less attention on those that are rarely used, in written and spoken North American English
- Help students avoid the most common mistakes that English language learners make
- Choose reading and writing topics that will naturally elicit examples of the target grammar structure
- Introduce important vocabulary from the Academic Word List

Grammar and Beyond Teaches Academic Writing Skills

Grammar and Beyond helps students make the transition from understanding grammar structures to applying them in their academic writing.

In the Student's Books

At Levels 1 through 3 of the series, every Student's Book unit ends with a section devoted to the hands-on application of grammar to writing. This section, called Grammar for Writing, explores how and where the target grammar structures function in writing and offers controlled practice, exposure to writing models, and a guided but open-ended writing task.

At Level 4, the most advanced level, the syllabus is organized around the academic essay types that college students write (e.g., persuasive, cause and effect) and is aimed at teaching students the grammar, vocabulary, and writing skills that they need in order to be successful at writing those kinds of essays.

Online

Grammar and Beyond also offers *Writing Skills Interactive*, an interactive online course in academic writing skills and vocabulary that correlates with the Student's Books. Each unit of the writing skills course focuses on a specific writing skill, such as avoiding sentence fragments or developing strong topic sentences.

Special Features of *Grammar and Beyond*

Realistic Grammar Presentations

Grammar is presented in clear and simple charts. The grammar points presented in these charts have been tested against real-world data from the *Cambridge International Corpus* to ensure that they are authentic representations of actual use of North American English.

Data from the Real World

Many of the grammar presentations and application sections in the Student's Book include a feature called Data from the Real World, in which concrete and useful points discovered through analysis of corpus data are presented. These points are practiced in the exercises that follow.

Avoid Common Mistakes

Each Student's Book unit features an Avoid Common Mistakes section that develops students' awareness of the most common mistakes made by English language learners and gives them an opportunity to practice detecting and correcting these errors in running text. This section helps students avoid these mistakes in their own work. The mistakes highlighted in this section are drawn from a body of authentic data on learner English known as the *Cambridge Learner Corpus*, a database of over 35 million words from student essays written by nonnative speakers of English and information from experienced classroom teachers.

Academic Vocabulary

Every unit in *Grammar and Beyond* includes words from the Academic Word List (AWL), a research-based list of words and word families that appear with high frequency in English-language academic texts. These words are introduced in the opening text of the unit, recycled in the charts and exercises, and used to support the theme throughout the unit. The same vocabulary items are reviewed and practiced in *Writing Skills Interactive*, the online writing skills course. By the time students finish each level, they will have been exposed several times to a carefully selected set of level-appropriate AWL words, as well as content words from a variety of academic disciplines.

Series Levels

The following table provides a general idea of the difficulty of the material at each level of *Grammar and Beyond*. These are not meant to be interpreted as precise correlations.

	Description	TOEFL IBT	CEFR Levels
Level 1	beginning	20 – 34	A1 – A2
Level 2	low intermediate to intermediate	35 – 54	A2 – B1
Level 3	high intermediate	55 – 74	B1 – B2
Level 4	advanced	75 – 95	B2 – C1

Components for Students

Student's Book

The Student's Books for Levels 1 through 3 teach all of the grammar points appropriate at each level in short, manageable cycles of presentation and practice organized around a high-interest unit theme. The Level 4 Student's Book focuses on the structure of the academic essay in addition to the grammar rules, conventions, and structures that students need to master in order to be successful college writers. Please see the Tour of a Unit on pages xvi–xix for a more detailed view of the contents and structure of the Student's Book units.

Workbook

The Workbook provides additional practice of the grammar presented in each unit of the Student's Book. The exercises offer both discrete and consolidated practice of grammar points and can be used for homework or in class. Each unit also offers practice correcting the errors highlighted in the Avoid Common Mistakes section in the Student's Book to help students master these troublesome errors. Self-Assessment sections at the end of each unit allow students to test their mastery of what they have learned.

Writing Skills Interactive

This online course provides graduated instruction and practice in writing skills, while reinforcing vocabulary presented in the Student's Books. Each unit includes a vocabulary review activity, followed by a short text that builds on the theme presented in the Student's Book and provides an additional context for the vocabulary. The text is followed by an animated interactive presentation of the target writing skill of the unit, after which students have the opportunity to practice the target skill in three different activities. Each unit closes with a quiz, which allows students to assess their progress.

Teacher Resources

Teacher Support Resource Book with CD-ROM

This comprehensive book provides a range of support materials for instructors, including:

- Suggestions for applying the target grammar to all four major skill areas, helping instructors facilitate dynamic and comprehensive grammar classes
- An answer key and audio script for the Student's Book
- A CD-ROM containing:
  - Ready-made, easily scored Unit Tests
  - PowerPoint presentations to streamline lesson preparation and encourage lively heads-up interaction

Class Audio CD

The class audio CD for each level provide the Student's Book listening material for in-class use.

Teacher Support Website

www.cambridge.org/grammarandbeyond

The website for *Grammar and Beyond* contains even more resources for instructors, including:

- Unit-by-unit teaching tips, helping instructors plan their lessons
- Downloadable communicative activities to add more in-class speaking practice
- A monthly newsletter on grammar teaching, providing ongoing professional development

We hope you enjoy using this series, and we welcome your feedback! Please send any comments to the authors and editorial staff at Cambridge University Press, at grammarandbeyond@cambridge.org.

About the Authors

Laurie Blass has more than 25 years' experience teaching and creating materials for ESL students in the United States and abroad. She is currently a full-time materials developer with a special interest in ESL for academic success and educational technology. Laurie is co-author of *Writers at Work: From Sentence to Paragraph*, published by Cambridge University Press, among many other titles.

Susan Iannuzzi has been teaching ESL for more than 20 years. She has trained English teachers on five continents and consulted on the national English curricula for countries in Africa, Asia, and the Middle East. She has authored or co-authored more than 10 English courses in use today. *Grammar and Beyond* is her first publication with Cambridge University Press.

Alice Savage is an English Language Teacher and Materials Writer. She attended the School for International Training in Vermont and is an author on the *Read This!* series, published by Cambridge University Press. She lives in Houston, Texas with her husband and two children.

Deborah Gordon, creator of the Grammar for Writing sections, has more than 25 years' experience teaching ESL students and training ESL teachers in the United States and abroad. She is currently an ESL instructor at Santa Barbara City College and a TESOL Certificate instructor at the University of California, Santa Barbara Extension. Deborah is coauthor of *Writers at Work: From Sentence to Paragraph*, published by Cambridge University Press, among many other titles.

Randi Reppen is Professor of Applied Linguistics and TESL at Northern Arizona University (NAU) in Flagstaff, Arizona. She has over 20 years' experience teaching ESL students and training ESL teachers, including 11 years as the Director of NAU's Program in Intensive English. Randi's research interests focus on the use of corpora for language teaching and materials development. In addition to numerous academic articles and books, she is the author of *Using Corpora in the Language Classroom* and a co-author of *Basic Vocabulary in Use*, 2nd edition, both published by Cambridge University Press.

Advisory Panel

The ESL advisory panel has helped to guide the development of this series and provided invaluable information about the needs of ESL students and teachers in high schools, colleges, universities, and private language schools throughout North America.

Neta Simpkins Cahill, Skagit Valley College, Mount Vernon, WA

Shelly Hedstrom, Palm Beach State College, Lake Worth, FL

Richard Morasci, Foothill College, Los Altos Hills, CA

Stacey Russo, East Hampton High School, East Hampton, NY

Alice Savage, North Harris College, Houston, TX

Acknowledgments

The publisher and authors would like to thank these reviewers and consultants for their insights and participation:

Marty Attiyeh, The College of DuPage, Glen Ellyn, IL

Shannon Bailey, Austin Community College, Austin, TX

Jamila Barton, North Seattle Community College, Seattle, WA

Kim Bayer, Hunter College IELI, New York, NY

Linda Berendsen, Oakton Community College, Skokie, IL

Anita Biber, Tarrant County College Northwest, Fort Worth, TX

Jane Breaux, Community College of Aurora, Aurora, CO

Anna Budzinski, San Antonio College, San Antonio, TX

Britta Burton, Mission College, Santa Clara, CA

Jean Carroll, Fresno City College, Fresno, CA

Chris Cashman, Oak Park High School and Elmwood Park High School, Chicago, IL

Annette M. Charron, Bakersfield College, Bakersfield, CA

Patrick Colabucci, ALI at San Diego State University, San Diego, CA

Lin Cui, Harper College, Palatine, IL

Jennifer Duclos, Boston University CELOP, Boston, MA

Joy Durighello, San Francisco City College, San Francisco, CA

Kathleen Flynn, Glendale Community College, Glendale, CA

Raquel Fundora, Miami Dade College, Miami, FL

Patricia Gillie, New Trier Township High School District, Winnetka, IL

Laurie Gluck, LaGuardia Community College, Long Island City, NY

Kathleen Golata, Galileo Academy of Science & Technology, San Francisco, CA

Ellen Goldman, Mission College, Santa Clara, CA

Ekaterina Goussakova, Seminole Community College, Sanford, FL

Marianne Grayston, Prince George's Community College, Largo, MD

Mary Greiss Shipley, Georgia Gwinnett College, Lawrenceville, GA

Sudeepa Gulati, Long Beach City College, Long Beach, CA

Nicole Hammond Carrasquel, University of Central Florida, Orlando, FL

Vicki Hendricks, Broward College, Fort Lauderdale, FL

Kelly Hernandez, Miami Dade College, Miami, FL

Ann Johnston, Tidewater Community College, Virginia Beach, VA

Julia Karet, Chaffey College, Claremont, CA

Jeanne Lachowski, English Language Institute, University of Utah, Salt Lake City, UT

Noga Laor, Rennert, New York, NY

Min Lu, Central Florida Community College, Ocala, FL

Michael Luchuk, Kaplan International Centers, New York, NY

Craig Machado, Norwalk Community College, Norwalk, CT

Denise Maduli-Williams, City College of San Francisco, San Francisco, CA

Diane Mahin, University of Miami, Coral Gables, FL

Melanie Majeski, Naugatuck Valley Community College, Waterbury, CT

Jeanne Malcolm, University of North Carolina at Charlotte, Charlotte, NC

Lourdes Marx, Palm Beach State College, Boca Raton, FL

Susan G. McFalls, Maryville College, Maryville, TN

Nancy McKay, Cuyahoga Community College, Cleveland, OH

Dominika McPartland, Long Island Business Institute, Flushing, NY

Amy Metcalf, UNR/Intensive English Language Center, University of Nevada, Reno, NV

Robert Miller, EF International Language School San Francisco – Mills, San Francisco, CA

Marcie Pachino, Jordan High School, Durham, NC

Myshie Pagel, El Paso Community College, El Paso, TX

Bernadette Pedagno, University of San Francisco, San Francisco, CA

Tam Q Pham, Dallas Theological Seminary, Fort Smith, AR

Mary Beth Pickett, Global-LT, Rochester, MI

Maria Reamore, Baltimore City Public Schools, Baltimore, MD

Alison M. Rice, Hunter College IELI, New York, NY

Sydney Rice, Imperial Valley College, Imperial, CA

Kathleen Romstedt, Ohio State University, Columbus, OH

Alexandra Rowe, University of South Carolina, Columbia, SC

Irma Sanders, Baldwin Park Adult and Community Education, Baldwin Park, CA

Caren Shoup, Lone Star College – CyFair, Cypress, TX

Karen Sid, Mission College, Foothill College, De Anza College, Santa Clara, CA

Michelle Thomas, Miami Dade College, Miami, FL

Sharon Van Houte, Lorain County Community College, Elyria, OH

Margi Wald, UC Berkeley, Berkeley, CA

Walli Weitz, Riverside County Office of Ed., Indio, CA

Bart Weyand, University of Southern Maine, Portland, ME

Donna Weyrich, Columbus State Community College, Columbus, OH

Marilyn Whitehorse, Santa Barbara City College, Ojai, CA

Jessica Wilson, Rutgers University – Newark, Newark, NJ

Sue Wilson, San Jose City College, San Jose, CA

Margaret Wilster, Mid-Florida Tech, Orlando, FL

Anne York-Herjeczki, Santa Monica College, Santa Monica, CA

Hoda Zaki, Camden County College, Camden, NJ

We would also like to thank these teachers and programs for allowing us to visit:

Richard Appelbaum, Broward College, Fort Lauderdale, FL

Carmela Arnoldt, Glendale Community College, Glendale, AZ

JaNae Barrow, Desert Vista High School, Phoenix, AZ

Ted Christensen, Mesa Community College, Mesa, AZ

Richard Ciriello, Lower East Side Preparatory High School, New York, NY

Virginia Edwards, Chandler-Gilbert Community College, Chandler, AZ

Nusia Frankel, Miami Dade College, Miami, FL

Raquel Fundora, Miami Dade College, Miami, FL

Vicki Hendricks, Broward College, Fort Lauderdale, FL

Kelly Hernandez, Miami Dade College, Miami, FL

Stephen Johnson, Miami Dade College, Miami, FL

Barbara Jordan, Mesa Community College, Mesa, AZ

Nancy Kersten, GateWay Community College, Phoenix, AZ

Lewis Levine, Hostos Community College, Bronx, NY

John Liffiton, Scottsdale Community College, Scottsdale, AZ

Cheryl Lira-Layne, Gilbert Public School District, Gilbert, AZ

Mary Livingston, Arizona State University, Tempe, AZ

Elizabeth Macdonald, Thunderbird School of Global Management, Glendale, AZ

Terri Martinez, Mesa Community College, Mesa, AZ

Lourdes Marx, Palm Beach State College, Boca Raton, FL

Paul Kei Matsuda, Arizona State University, Tempe, AZ

David Miller, Glendale Community College, Glendale, AZ

Martha Polin, Lower East Side Preparatory High School, New York, NY

Patricia Pullenza, Mesa Community College, Mesa, AZ

Victoria Rasinskaya, Lower East Side Preparatory High School, New York, NY

Vanda Salls, Tempe Union High School District, Tempe, AZ

Kim Sanabria, Hostos Community College, Bronx, NY

Cynthia Schuemann, Miami Dade College, Miami, FL

Michelle Thomas, Miami Dade College, Miami, FL

Dongmei Zeng, Borough of Manhattan Community College, New York, NY

Tour of a Unit

Grammar in the Real World presents the unit's grammar in a **realistic** context using **contemporary** texts.

Notice activities draw students' attention to the **structure**, guiding their own **analysis** of form, meaning, and use.

UNIT 4 Past Perfect and Past Perfect Progressive

Nature vs. Nurture

1 Grammar in the Real World

A Have you ever reconnected with someone from your past? Read the web article about twins who lived apart for many years. What surprised the twins when they reconnected?

The Science of Twins

Twins, especially identical[1] twins, have always fascinated scientists. Identical twins develop from one egg, have identical DNA,[2] and are usually very similar in appearance
5 and behavior. There have been many studies of identical twins raised in the same family. There have also been a number of studies of identical twins separated at birth and raised in separate families. These studies have provided
10 interesting information about the impact of *nature* (genetics) and *nurture* (the environment) on the development of the individual. However, some of the studies have been controversial.[3]

Take the case of Elyse Schein and Paula Bernstein. Elyse and Paula were identical twins
15 separated at birth. Both girls knew that their parents **had adopted** them as infants, but neither girl knew about her twin. When Elyse grew up, she longed to meet her biological mother, so she contacted the agency that **had arranged** the adoption. She **had been doing** research on her birth mother when she made a surprising discovery. She had an identical twin. Even more surprising, she learned that she **had been** part of a secret scientific study. At the time of the adoption, the agency **had allowed** different families to
20 adopt each twin. The agency **had told** the families that their child was part of a scientific study. However, it **had** never **told** the families the goal of the study: for scientists to investigate nature versus nurture.

[1]**identical:** exactly the same | [2]**DNA:** the abbreviation for deoxyribonucleic acid, a chemical that controls the structure and purpose of every cell | [3]**controversial:** causing or likely to cause disagreement

---

When Elyse and Paula finally met as adults, they were amazed. They had many similarities. They looked almost identical. They **had** both **studied** film. They both loved
25 to write. Together, the twins discovered that the researchers **had stopped** the study before the end because the public strongly disapproved of this type of research.

Although that study ended early, many scientists today make a strong case for the dominant[4] role of nature. Schein and Bernstein agree that genetics explains many of their similarities. However, recent research suggests that nurture is equally important. It
30 is clear that the nature versus nurture debate will occupy scientists for years to come.

[4]**dominant:** more important, strong, or noticeable

B *Comprehension Check* Answer the questions.
1. What was surprising about the twins' adoption?
2. What characteristics and interests did Elyse and Paula have in common?
3. What is the nature versus nurture debate?

C *Notice* Underline the verbs in each sentence.
1. Both girls knew that their parents had adopted them as infants.
2. She had been doing research on her birth mother when she made a surprising discovery.
3. Even more surprising, she learned that she had been part of a secret scientific study.

Which event happened first in each sentence? What event followed? Write the verbs. What do you notice about the form of the verbs?

1. First: _____   Then: _____
2. First: _____   Then: _____
3. First: _____   Then: _____

2 Past Perfect

▶ Grammar Presentation

The past perfect is used to describe a completed event that happened before another event in the past.	*Elyse finally met her sister, Paula. Paula **had been** married for several years.* (First, Paula got married; Elyse met Paula at a later time.)

The *Grammar Presentation* begins with an **overview** that describes the grammar in an **easy-to-understand** summary.

2.1 Forming Past Perfect

Form the past perfect with *had* + the past participle of the main verb. Form the negative by adding *not* after *had*. The form is the same for all subjects.

Elyse and Paula did not grow up together. They **had lived** with different families.
They were available for adoption because their birthmother **had given** them up.
"**Had** she **talked** about the study to anyone at the time?"
"No, she **hadn't**."
"What **had** you **heard** about this study before that time?"
"**I'd heard** very little about it."

▶ Irregular Verbs: See page A1.

2.2 Using Past Perfect with Simple Past

a. Use the past perfect to describe an event in a time period that leads up to another past event or time period. Use the simple past to describe the later event or time period.

LATER TIME   EARLIER TIME
She **learned** that she **had been** part of a secret study.

LATER TIME   EARLIER TIME
The twins **discovered** that they **had** both **studied** psychology.

b. The prepositions *before, by,* or *until* can introduce the later time period.

EARLIER TIME   LATER TIME
Their mother **had known** about the study *before* her death.

EARLIER TIME   LATER TIME
Sue **hadn't met** her sister *until* last year.

EARLIER TIME   LATER TIME
Studies on twins **had become** common *by* the 1960s.

c. The past perfect is often used to give reasons or background information for later past events.

REASON
She *was* late. She **had forgotten** to set her alarm clock.

BACKGROUND INFORMATION   LATER PAST EVENT
He **had** never **taken** a subway before he *moved* to New York.

Data from the Real World 🌐

In writing, these verbs are commonly used in the past perfect: *come, have, leave, make,* and *take.*
Had been is the most common past perfect form in speaking and writing.

The twins **had not gone** to the same school as children.
The family thought that they **had made** the right decision.
Psychologists praised the study because the researchers **had been** very careful in their work.
The researchers **had not been** aware of each other's work on twins until they met.

▶ ## Grammar Application

Exercise 2.1 Past Perfect

Complete the sentences about twins who met as adults. Use the past perfect form of the verbs in parentheses.

1. Two separate Illinois families ___*had adopted*___ (adopt) Anne Green and Annie Smith before the twins were three days old.
2. When the girls met, they were fascinated by their similarities. For example, they _____ (live) near each other before the Greens moved away.
3. As children, both Anne and Annie _____ (go) to the same summer camp.
4. Anne _____ (not / go) to college, and Annie _____ (not / attend) college, either.
5. Both _____ (marry) for the first time by the age of 22.
6. Anne _____ (get) divorced and _____ (remarry). Annie _____ (not / get) divorced and was still married.
7. Both Anne and Annie were allergic to cats and dogs and _____ never _____ (own) pets.
8. Both _____ (give) the same name – Heather – to their daughters.
9. Both _____ previously _____ (work) in the hospitality industry.
10. Anne _____ (work) as a hotel manager. However, Annie _____ (not / work) in hotels; she _____ (be) a restaurant manager.

Exercise 4.2 Past Perfect Progressive, Past Perfect, or Simple Past?

A Complete the interview with a woman who found her three siblings after many years. Use the past perfect progressive, the past perfect, or the simple past form of the verbs in parentheses. Use contractions when possible. Sometimes more than one answer is possible.

Vijay Tell us how you found your family.

Paula I <u>'d been looking</u> (look) for my sister all my life. I _____
(1)   (2)

(not / have) much luck, though. Then one day, I turned on the TV. A talk show was

on. The host of the show was interviewing three siblings – two brothers and a half

sister.[1] Different families _____ (adopt) the siblings many
                                (3)

years before.

Vijay And?

Paula They _____ (talk) about me before I turned on the program.
            (4)

The siblings had recently reunited, and they _____ (search)
                       (5)

for a fourth sibling for the past several months. I called the TV station, and we all

finally _____ (meet).
        (6)

Vijay So, you _____ (look) for a sister all your life, and you found
         (7)

three siblings!

Paula Yes, it was wonderful! We all met at one of the network offices the following week.

After we _____ (speak) for a while, it was obvious to me that
        (8)

they _____ (look) for me all their lives, too.
     (9)

[1]**half sister:** a sister who is biologically related by one parent only

B *Pair Work* Discuss these questions with a partner.

- Choose a sentence in A in which you can use either the past perfect or the past perfect progressive. Why are both possible here?
- In which sentence in A is only the past perfect correct?

C *Over to You* Do an online search for twins, siblings, or other family members who reunited after many years. Write five sentences about their experiences. Use the past perfect and the past perfect progressive.

5 | Avoid Common Mistakes ⚠

1. **Use the past perfect or past perfect progressive to give background information for a past tense event.**
    had
    I have never seen my sister in real life, so I was nervous the first time we met.
    had been dreaming
    I have dreamed about meeting her, and I finally did.

2. **Use the past perfect or past perfect progressive to give a reason for a past event.**
    had been crying
    Her eyes were red and puffy because she cried.

3. **Use the past perfect (not the past perfect progressive) for a completed earlier event.**
    arranged
    They had been arranging a time to meet, but both of them forgot about it.

4. **Use the past perfect (not present perfect) to describe a completed event that happened before a past event.**
    had
    I have visited her in Maine twice before she came to visit me.

Editing Task

Find and correct seven more mistakes in the paragraphs about sibling differences.

              had
           I have never really thought about sibling differences until my own children were

born. When we had our first child, my husband and I have lived in Chicago for just a few

months. We have not made many friends yet, so we spent all our time with our child. Baby

Gilbert was happy to be the center of attention. He depended on us for everything.

5   By the time our second son, Chase, was born, we have developed a community of

friends and a busier social life. We frequently visited friends and left the children at home

with a babysitter. As a result of our busy schedules, Chase was more independent. One

day I had just been hanging up the phone when Chase came into the room. Chase picked

up the phone and started talking into it. I thought he was pretending, but I was wrong. He

10 had been figuring out how to use the phone!

      When my husband came home, he was tired because he worked all day. When I

told him about Chase's phone conversation, though, he became very excited. Gilbert has

never used the phone as a child. At first, we were surprised that Chase was so different

from Gilbert. Then we realized that because of our busy lifestyles, Chase had learned to be

15 independent.

Writing Task

1 *Write* Use the paragraph in the Pre-writing Task to help you write about different conditions that influence people's behavior. Give examples from events and situations you have observed to support your opinion.

2 *Self-Edit* Use the editing tips to improve your paragraph. Make any necessary changes.
1. Did you use the past perfect to give background information and provide reasons?
2. Did you use time words and time clauses to clarify the time periods in your sentences or emphasize that some events happened earlier than others?
3. Did you avoid the mistakes in the Avoid Common Mistakes chart on page 59?

6 Grammar for Writing

Using Past Perfect to Provide Background Information and Reasons

Writers use the past perfect to provide background information and reasons for past situations and actions. Read these examples:

I had always thought that I was an only child, but I recently discovered that I have a sister. My parents had given me up for adoption. When I was 15, I decided to find my biological parents.

Pre-writing Task

1 Read the paragraph. What does the writer believe about the influence of the environment on relationships? What example does the writer use to explain this?

The Effects of Friends on Sibling Relationships

I believe that the experiences that a person has outside the home can be as influential as experiences inside the home. Examples of this are siblings who start out very similar but become very different from one another as they grow older. For example, Andy and Frank are two brothers who are only two years apart. They did everything together
5 and were best friends until they started junior high. After Andy had been in seventh grade for a little while, he started to change. He had made new friends at school, so he and Frank did not see each other much during the day. Frank had made new friends, too. In fact, Andy's new friends did not like Frank very much, so Andy did not feel comfortable asking Frank to spend time with them. By the time Andy and Frank were in high school, they had
10 grown very far apart. They had made different friends and they had developed different interests. They had been similar when they were young, but Andy and Frank had very little in common as young adults.

2 Read the paragraph again. Underline the sentences that contain both simple past and past perfect verbs. Double underline the sentences with verbs only in the past perfect. Circle the time clauses. Notice how the time clauses help clarify the earlier time period.

Simple Present and Present Progressive

First Impressions

1 | Grammar in the Real World

A When you meet someone for the first time, what do you notice about the person? Read the article about first impressions. What influences your first impressions?

First Impressions

Here is an interesting fact: The average person **forms** a first impression of someone in less than 30 seconds. *First impressions* **are** the opinions someone **has** about you when
5 you **meet** for the first time. What **is** your smile **telling** the other person? What **is** the way you dress **saying** about you? These factors can make a difference in the way the person **thinks** about you.

10 Handshakes, facial expressions, and general appearance **help** to create first impressions. People are constantly **forming** these impressions of others. We do not make these impressions consciously.[1] They **are** largely subconscious.[2] However, they **tend**[3] to be extremely difficult to change.

Some psychologists today **are researching** the factors that influence how
15 people react to others. For example, psychologist Brian Nosek **is** currently **using** a collection of tests known as the IAT, or Implicit Association Test, for his research. These tests **are helping** to reveal our thinking processes, both conscious and subconscious, as we form our impressions of others. Specifically, Nosek is **investigating** our use of stereotypes and attitudes about others in
20 forming first impressions.

Each test **measures** what happens while people **are making** judgments. The results **demonstrate** that people have stereotypes, and that these stereotypes **influence** their first impressions. For example, both young and old people **tend** to associate the word *good* with pictures of young people.
25 Since first impressions **influence** what a person **thinks** about you to a great degree, it **is** important to always do your best to make a good first impression.

[1]**consciously:** aware of what is happening | [2]**subconscious:** existing in the mind but not in one's awareness | [3]**tend:** be likely

B *Comprehension Check* Answer the questions.

1. How long does it take to form a first impression?

2. What is the collection of tests known as the IAT helping to reveal?

3. What is one stereotype that young and old people share?

C *Notice* Find the sentences in the article and complete them. Circle the correct verbs. Then check (✓) the box that best describes the function of each verb.

1. The average person **forms / is forming** a first impression of someone in less than 30 seconds.

   ☑ general fact or habit   ☐ temporary action

2. Handshakes, facial expressions, and general appearance **help / are helping** to create first impressions.

   ☐ general fact or habit   ☑ temporary action

3. Some psychologists today **research / are researching** the factors that influence how people react to others.

   ☐ general fact or habit   ☐ temporary action

4. Specifically, Nosek **investigates / is investigating** our use of stereotypes and attitudes about others in forming first impressions.

   ☑ general fact or habit   ☐ temporary action

What do the verbs in the simple present describe? What do the verbs in the present progressive describe?

2 | Simple Present vs. Present Progressive

▶ Grammar Presentation

The simple present and the present progressive both describe present time. The simple present describes things that are more permanent, such as general facts or habits. The present progressive describes things that are temporary, such as things in progress now or around now.

*The average person **forms** a first impression in less than 30 seconds.*

*Psychologists **are researching** the factors that influence how people react.*

2.1 Simple Present

a. Use the simple present for general facts and permanent situations.	People **form** a first impression within 30 seconds. First impressions **influence** what a person thinks about you. I **dress** conservatively at work.
b. Use the simple present to describe routines and habits.	The manager **asks** a lot of questions. We **work** for eight hours every day.
You can use time expressions such as *always, usually, often, sometimes, never, on Mondays, once a week, two days a week,* and *twice a month.*	The hiring manager <u>always</u> **writes** a report after an interview. We <u>usually</u> **follow** her recommendations. She **doesn't** interview candidates <u>on Mondays</u>. We **discuss** the manager's reports <u>once a week</u>.
c. Use the simple present for routines, scheduled events, and timetables.	The office **opens** at 9:00 a.m. The train to Boston **departs** from platform 11 at 2:00 p.m. "**Does** the meeting always **begin** at noon?" "Yes, it **does**."

▶▶ Irregular Verbs : See page A1.

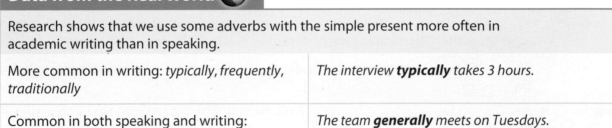

Data from the Real World

Research shows that we use some adverbs with the simple present more often in academic writing than in speaking.

More common in writing: *typically, frequently, traditionally*	The interview **typically** takes 3 hours.
Common in both speaking and writing: *generally, usually, normally*	The team **generally** meets on Tuesdays. How do you **normally** handle complaints?

2.2 Present Progressive

a. Use the present progressive to describe what is in progress now or around the present time.	Mr. Rask **is interviewing** a candidate at the moment. (The interview is happening now.) We **are interviewing** candidates all month. (Interviews may not be in progress now, but they are in progress during this month.)
b. Use the present progressive to describe temporary events or changing situations.	I **am studying** stereotypes in the workplace. (My studies will end in the future.)

Data from the Real World

Research shows that we often use the present progressive for habits that are noteworthy or unusual. This is sometimes, but not always, because these habits are not desirable. You can use *always* or *constantly* for emphasis. *Constantly* is more formal than *always*.

*She **is always disturbing** me when I am trying to study.*
*My boss **is constantly asking** me to stay late at work.*

The present progressive form is also common with verbs that describe changing or temporary situations.

*The workers at that store **are constantly changing.** Every week there is someone new.*
*We **are always looking** for new ideas and people with special talents.*

▶ Grammar Application

Exercise 2.1 Simple Present

Complete the sentences with the simple present of the verbs in the box.

give   have   have   help   make   meet   show   start   teach   videotape

1. According to many studies, most people __make__ judgments about others in only a few seconds.

2. Communication trainer Mary Hernandez _____ job seekers make a good first impression.

3. Ms. Hernandez _____ a course called Making a Good First Impression at the community college.

4. The class _____ on Mondays and Wednesdays.

5. At the first class meeting, Ms. Hernandez typically _____ students a self-assessment test.

6. The self-assessment test _____ how the students judge themselves.

7. Students almost always _____ a positive impression of themselves.

8. After the self-assessment, Ms. Hernandez usually _____ the students in mock interviews.

9. On the last day of class, students _____ real interviews with a representative from a local company.

10. Ms. Hernandez's class _____ at 6:30 p.m. and ends at 9:00 p.m.

Exercise 2.2 Simple Present or Present Progressive?

Complete the questions about Josh and Rachel with the simple present or present progressive form of the words in parentheses. Then write answers using the information in the picture.

1. Where *are Josh and Rachel working* (Josh and Rachel / work) this summer?
   Josh and Rachel are working at the Bursar's Office this summer.

2. How often _____ (Josh and Rachel / work)?
   _____

3. When _____ (Josh / start his job) in the mornings?
   _____

4. _____ (Rachel / talk) to a student right now?
   _____

5. How many _____ (students / wait) in Josh's line?
   _____

6. _____ (who / make) a better first impression on the
   students who need help?
   _____

7. When _____ (Rachel / finish) work in the afternoons?
   _____

8. _____ (who / not help) students at the moment?
   _____

Exercise 2.3 More Simple Present or Present Progressive?

A Complete the sentences from a brochure that participants received at a job fair. Use the simple present or present progressive form of the verbs in parentheses.

> ### Welcome to the State Employment Agency Job Fair!
>
> Representatives from over 30 big regional corporations _are participating_ (1) (participate) in today's state job fair. The job fair _____ (take) place (2) every year. Every year, interviews _____ (begin) at 9:00 a.m. and (3) _____ (continue) throughout the day until 6:00 p.m. The long list of (4) participating companies is on the back of this brochure. This year, companies A–G _____ (interview) candidates in room 245 on the second floor. (5) Companies H–Z _____ (meet) candidates in room 252. (6)
>
> **Tips for Job Seekers**
>
> Interviews generally _____ (take) about 30 minutes. An interviewer (7) usually _____ (spend) a few minutes reading your résumé. He or she (8) sometimes _____ (ask) you to fill out an application. An interview (9) typically _____ (end) with a question-and-answer period. The average (10) employer _____ (expect) you to know a lot about the company – this (11) is an opportunity to demonstrate your knowledge. Also, employers _____ always (12) _____ (look) for new ideas, and these ideas may come from you! (12)

B *Pair Work* Compare your answers with a partner. Discuss the reason for each of your answers.

A *I used the present progressive in number 1 because the phrase* today's job fair *tells me that the sentence is about something that is happening now.*

B *I agree with you. For number 2, I used . . .*

3 Stative Verbs

▶ Grammar Presentation

Stative verbs describe states and conditions. Generally, they do not describe actions.	That **sounds** like a great project. We **don't have** two chances to make a first impression.

3.1 Non-action or Stative Verbs

Use the simple present with stative verbs. Here are some common stative verb categories:

Description: *appear, be, exist, look, seem, sound*

Measurement: *cost, weigh*

Knowledge: *believe, forget, know, remember, think*

Emotions: *feel, hate, like, love, prefer*

Possession / Relationship: *belong, contain, have, need, own, want*

Senses: *hear, see, smell, taste*

Perception: *notice, see, understand*

She **seems** like a hard worker.

It **doesn't cost** anything to send your application.

He **doesn't believe** that first impressions are true.
I **know** stereotypes aren't true.

Employers **prefer** motivated workers.

I **don't have** a good impression of him.
I **need** a challenging career.

Can you **see** the water from your office?

When you explain the problem in that way, I **see** your point. I **understand** your viewpoint.

▶▶ Stative (Non-Action) Verbs: See page A2.

3.2 Verbs with Stative and Action Meanings

Some verbs have both stative and action meanings. You can use the present progressive with the action meanings of these verbs. Examples of verbs with stative and action meanings include *be, have, see, taste, think,* and *weigh.*

SIMPLE PRESENT (STATIVE MEANING)	PRESENT PROGRESSIVE (ACTION MEANING)
I **think** first impressions are important. (*think* = believe)	I **am thinking** about how to make a good first impression. (*think* = use the mind)
Do you **have** an interesting career? (*have* = own)	**Are** you **having** trouble at work? (*have* = experience)
She **is** the new manager. (*be* = description)	She **is being** difficult. (*be* = act)
He noticed that he doesn't **see** very well anymore. (*see* = view with the eyes)	He **is seeing** the eye doctor for an exam next week. (*see* = meet with)

▶ Grammar Application

Exercise 3.1 Verbs with Stative and Action Meanings

A Complete the article from a college newspaper. Circle the correct form of the verbs.

A Study on Stereotypes

Lisa James is majoring in psychology here at Carlson College. This semester, she **thinks/is thinking** about participating in a study on stereotypes in Professor Green's
(1)
Psychology 101 class. According to Dr. Green, many people **have/are having** fixed
(2)
ideas about members of their own and other cultures. This is true even when they
know/are knowing that the stereotypes they **have/are having** are false.
(3)   (4)

Dr. Green **believes/is believing** that when most people make generalizations
(5)
about other cultures, they **don't seem/are not seeming** to make these judgments
(6)
on observation. Instead, they **appear/are appearing** to base their judgments on
(7)
ideas that they grew up with in their own cultures.

This semester, Dr. Green **has/is having** an interesting time giving his students
(8)
two tests: a self-assessment test and a personality test. In the self-assessment test,
students describe the traits they **think/are thinking** members of their own culture
(9)
have. The personality test gives basic information about what a person is really like.
Dr. Green **believes/is believing** the results of the personality test will conflict with
(10)
the results of the cultural self-assessment test. Here's an example: People from one
culture in the study **believe/are believing** that they are hostile and argumentative.
(11)
However, when these people take the personality test, they usually **get/are getting**
(12)
very high scores for kindness and helpfulness.

The results of studies such as Dr. Green's **appear/are appearing** to show
(13)
that cultural stereotypes are almost always mistaken. Lisa is looking forward to
discovering what the tests say about her. Although she believes that she does not
have stereotypes about people, she knows that Dr. Green **believes/is believing** that
(14)
almost everyone has stereotypes of some people.

B *Pair Work* Compare your answers with a partner. Discuss the reason for each of your answers.

I used the present progressive with the verb think in number 1 because the action is happening now.

Exercise 3.2 Stative or Action Meaning?

Complete the conversation about stereotypes at work. Use the simple present or present progressive form of the verbs in parentheses. Use contractions when possible.

Alan   Claudia, how are your interview follow-up reports going? Are you still

working on them?

Claudia   I ___think___ (think) they're going well. I'm almost finished.
(1)

Alan   That's wonderful news. How many reports _____ you
(2)

_____ (have)?
(2)

Claudia   Eight. I have three more to do.

Alan   Oh, I see. So you're just a little more than half finished. Our meeting

_____ (be) always at 4:30 on Wednesdays. Why are you still
(3)

working on them?

Claudia   I don't usually take this long, but this time I'm spending a lot of time on the

reports because I _____ (be) very careful. I interviewed a lot
(4)

of people from many different cultures, both young and old, and from cities as

well as from the countryside.

Alan   So?

Claudia   Some of the reports _____ (be) finished, but I don't want to base
(5)

my judgments on only partial information. I _____ (think) that
(6)

the information would be useful if it's not complete.

Alan   I _____ (know) what you mean.
(7)

Claudia   This time, I _____ (have) a hard time separating things like
(8)

culture and appearance from people's actual abilities.

Alan   Well, it's good that you _____ (be) aware of this. Let's discuss
(9)

it later.

Exercise 3.3 More Stative or Action Meaning?

A 🔊 Listen to the interview about first impressions. Write the missing words.

Reporter When you ___meet___ someone for the first time, how does
(1)
the person's appearance affect your judgment? Today, we
_____ people to describe how they make
(2)
judgments about others.

Marta I know I _____ unfair stereotypes when I meet someone
(3)
new. To me, older people always _____ like they need
(4)
help. When I meet an older person, I ___am thinking___
(5)
about my grandparents. I speak slowly and clearly, in case the person
can't hear. I _____ it's wrong to think all older people are
(6)
like that, but I can't help it.

Marc I feel that I _____ always very fair when I meet a
(7)
new person. I _____ people's appearances don't
(8)
always say who they really are. For example, if I meet a person who
___is___ sloppy,[1] I _____ that he
(9)   (10)
or she is a lazy person.

Bin For me, it depends on the situation. When I am interviewing
people at work, I take their appearance very seriously. For example,
I always notice how a person dresses for an interview. If a person's
appearance ___very___ sloppy or careless in an interview,
(11)
I ___judge___ he or she will be a sloppy and careless worker.
(12)

[1]**sloppy:** messy, not tidy

B *Pair Work* Discuss these questions with a partner: Which person in A are you most like? How much do stereotypes affect the judgments you make about people when you first meet them? Give an example.

I think I'm like Marc. I don't like to judge someone right away. For example, my landlord seems somewhat reserved when you meet him, but he's actually a really nice guy.

4 Special Meanings and Uses of Simple Present

▶ ## Grammar Presentation

The simple present is frequently used for summarizing and reviewing as well as for explaining procedures or giving instructions.	Malcolm Gladwell's book Blink **persuades** the reader to believe in first impressions. Participants **follow** strict procedures for the Implicit Association Test.

4.1 Special Meanings and Uses of Simple Present

a. Use the simple present to summarize scientific writing or review artistic works such as books, plays, and movies.	The Implicit Association Test **measures** people's responses. Malcolm Gladwell's book Blink **discusses** the importance of first impressions. He **argues** that first impressions **are** often accurate, even if the mind **doesn't realize** it.
b. Use the simple present to explain procedures or instructions.	To administer the test, we always **follow** the same procedures. First, we **seat** participants in every other chair. We **don't** usually **put** them next to each other.
Commonly used expressions that show sequencing include *first, then, next, after that,* and *finally.*	When you arrive at the job fair, <u>first</u> you **go** to the desk and **sign** in. <u>Then</u> you **take** a look at the list of companies and **plan** which companies you **want** to see.

▶ ## Grammar Application

Exercise 4.1 Uses of Simple Present

Read the sentences. Then label each sentence *R* (book reviews), *P* (procedures and instructions), or *O* (other uses – facts, routines, schedules) according to where the text comes from.

1. First, students write their names at the top of the paper. _____P_____

2. The authors end with a set of tips for always creating good first impressions. _____

3. The class meets on Tuesdays and Thursdays from 11:30 a.m. to 1:00 p.m. _____

4. This book helps readers understand the difference between how they see themselves and how other people see them. _____

5. The required reading for this course is *Making a Good Impression* by Dr. Al Stone. _____

6. *Making a Good Impression* includes summaries of many of the latest studies on how people make first impressions. _____

7. To complete the online test, students select their answers and click "Submit." _____

Exercise 4.2 Summarizing an Article

Use the words to write sentences that describe the main points from an article on the problems with personality tests.

1. personality tests / always / not be / accurate

   Personality tests are not always accurate.

2. job candidates / sometimes / not tell / the truth

   _____

3. a job candidate's score / always / not reflect / the candidate's personality

   _____

4. candidates who take some personality tests twice / sometimes / get / different scores

   _____

   _____

5. these tests / not match / people to jobs well

   _____

Exercise 4.3 Giving Instructions

Pair Work Choose a situation with a partner in which it is important to make a good first impression, such as a job interview or a first meeting with an important person. Describe the scene and how the person makes a good first impression. Remember to use sequencing words such as *First, . . .*; *Then . . .*; *After that, . . .*; and *Finally, ...*

On the first day of work: First, the new employee shakes hands and makes eye contact with the people he or she meets.

5 | Avoid Common Mistakes ⚠

1. Use the simple present with stative verbs.

               matter
First impressions ~~are mattering~~ when you want to establish a relationship.

2. Use the simple present to express facts, routines, or habits unlikely to change.

           require
Sessions ~~are requiring~~ 10 to 15 minutes to complete.

3. Use the present progressive to show that something is in progress or temporary.

    isn't interviewing   is still studying
He ~~doesn't interview~~ for jobs this year because he ~~still studies~~.

4. Use the *-ing* form, not the base form of the verb, when using the present progressive.

    working
He is ~~work~~ as a store clerk.

Editing Task

Find and correct eight more mistakes in the paragraphs about first impressions.

Without a doubt, first impressions are important. Current research ~~is showing~~ *shows* that a first impression can last a long time. These days it seems that everyone talks about the significance of the first 30 seconds of a job interview or a meeting with a client. However, I am believing there is another side to this story.

5 Some people are having the ability to make a good first impression, but the impression may be false. I believe that time and experience are telling the truth about a person's character. Whenever I talk with someone who smiles at me and seems completely charming, I am getting suspicious. I think that the person is not sincere, and that he or she wants something from me. On the other hand, I often find that quieter,
10 more reserved people are more willing to help me when I ask. My colleague Jim is a good example. This fall he is work on a special project, so he is very busy, and sometimes he appears unfriendly. However, he usually stops and helps me when I ask. My friendlier colleagues usually smile, but when I ask them for help, they are making excuses.

In short, I am not believing that everyone who makes a good first impression
15 deserves my trust. Maybe I am too suspicious with friendly people, but I will always give awkward or shy people a second chance. After all, I think that I may be one of them.

6 | Grammar for Writing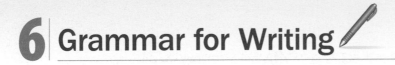

Using Simple Present and Present Progressive to Write About Present Time Situations

Writers use the simple present to discuss facts and give general information. They use the present progressive to describe scenes or temporary situations. Read these examples:

People are often nervous at job interviews.
Most people worry about job interviews.
These days, many people are looking for jobs.

Pre-writing Task

1 Read the paragraph. Which days are best for a job interview?

Best Interview Times

Most people worry about making a good impression at a job interview. They generally think about what to wear and what questions to prepare. One thing that people usually do not think about is the day of the appointment. However, some job experts believe that the actual day makes a difference. For example, some say that normally

5 the worst days are Monday and Friday, whereas Tuesday and Wednesday are the best. Monday is not ideal because on that day the interviewer is probably still thinking about the weekend, and on Friday, the interviewer is usually watching the clock and waiting for the weekend to start. On the other hand, Tuesday and Wednesday are typically much better because the interviewer does not feel as much stress as later in the week. There

10 are others who believe that any day is good, but morning appointments are better than afternoon ones because interviewers still feel relaxed in the morning. People who want to have a successful job interview might want to choose the right interview day in addition to the perfect outfit.

2 Read the paragraph again. Circle the simple present verbs. Underline the present progressive verbs. Why did the writer choose to use the present progressive for these verbs and not the simple present? <u>Double underline</u> the stative verbs.

Writing Task

1 *Write* Use the paragraph in the Pre-writing Task to help you write a good job interview tip or a tip for making a good first impression.

2 *Self-Edit* Use the editing tips to improve your paragraph. Make any necessary changes.

1. Did you use the simple present to express factual situations, routines, and habits?
2. Did you use the present progressive to express situations that are in progress or temporary?
3. Did you avoid the mistakes in the Avoid Common Mistakes chart on page 13?

Simple Past and Past Progressive;
Used To, Would
Global Marketing

1 Grammar in the Real World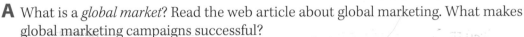

A What is a *global market*? Read the web article about global marketing. What makes global marketing campaigns successful?

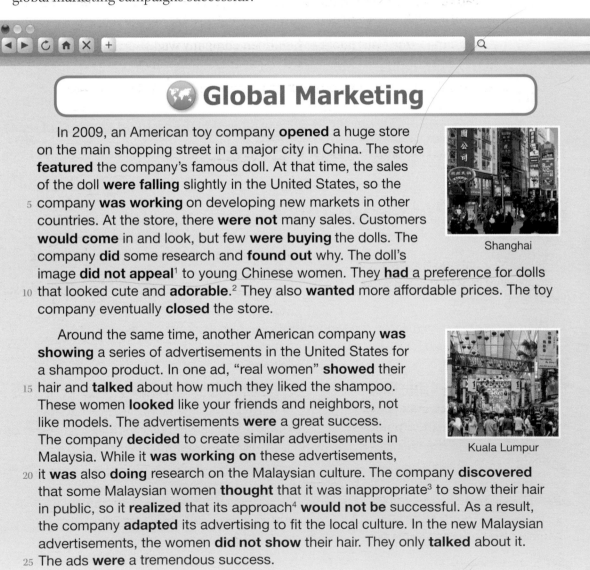

🌐 Global Marketing

In 2009, an American toy company **opened** a huge store on the main shopping street in a major city in China. The store **featured** the company's famous doll. At that time, the sales of the doll **were falling** slightly in the United States, so the
5   company **was working** on developing new markets in other countries. At the store, there **were not** many sales. Customers **would come** in and look, but few **were buying** the dolls. The company **did** some research and **found out** why. The doll's image **did not appeal**[1] to young Chinese women. They **had** a preference for dolls
10 that looked cute and **adorable.**[2] They also **wanted** more affordable prices. The toy company eventually **closed** the store.

Around the same time, another American company **was showing** a series of advertisements in the United States for a shampoo product. In one ad, "real women" **showed** their
15 hair and **talked** about how much they liked the shampoo. These women **looked** like your friends and neighbors, not like models. The advertisements **were** a great success. The company **decided** to create similar advertisements in Malaysia. While it **was working on** these advertisements,
20 it **was** also **doing** research on the Malaysian culture. The company **discovered** that some Malaysian women **thought** that it was inappropriate[3] to show their hair in public, so it **realized** that its approach[4] **would not be** successful. As a result, the company **adapted** its advertising to fit the local culture. In the new Malaysian advertisements, the women **did not show** their hair. They only **talked** about it.
25 The ads **were** a tremendous success.

Shanghai

Kuala Lumpur

[1]**appeal:** interest or attract someone │ [2]**adorable:** attractive and easy to love │ [3]**inappropriate:** unsuitable, especially for the particular time, place, or situation │ [4]**approach:** a method or way of doing something

In the past, companies **would create** one advertisement and one product for all markets. Today's markets include places all over the world, and the success of global marketing campaigns depends on two simple rules: understand the local culture and adapt the marketing and product to that culture.

B *Comprehension Check* Answer the questions.

1. What are some reasons customers in China did not buy the dolls at first? *for dolls that looked cute and adorable they had a preference*
2. Why was the campaign in Malaysia successful?
3. How are advertising campaigns different today from in the past? *the sucess of global marketing compaigns depends on two simple rules*

C *Notice* Read the sentences from the article. Check (✓) the sentence that describes an action that continued for a period of time in the past. Does the verb end in *-ing* or *-ed*?

_____ ✓ 1. Around the same time, another American company **was showing** a series of advertisements in the United States for a shampoo product.

_____ 2. As a result, the company **adapted** its advertising to fit the local culture.

2 | Simple Past vs. Past Progressive

▶ Grammar Presentation

The simple past and the past progressive describe actions in the past.	*American consumers* ***wanted*** *affordable prices.* *While the company* ***was working*** *on these advertisements, it* ***was*** *also* ***doing*** *research on the Malaysian culture.*

2.1 Simple Past

Use the simple past to describe actions, situations, or events that are completed. Use the simple past for actions that happened once or repeatedly in the past.	*Company executives* ***decided*** *to market the dolls in China in 2009.* *The dolls* ***weren't*** *popular in China a few years ago.* *What* ***did*** *the company* ***market*** *in Malaysia?* *The company executives* ***visited*** *Malaysia a few times.*
Past time markers, such as *yesterday, last week, two months ago,* and *in 2011* can be used with the simple past.	*A company* ***studied*** *Malaysian culture last year.* ***Did*** *it* ***get*** *good local advice last time?* *Who* ***gave*** *the company advice last week?*

▶▶ Irregular Verbs: See page A1.

2.2 Past Progressive

Use the past progressive to describe an activity or event in progress over a period of time in the past.	The company **wasn't selling** dolls in China at that time. Why **weren't** many people **buying** them? What **was happening** during that period?

2.3 Simple Past and Past Progressive Contrasted

a. Use the past progressive to describe background activities. These activities were in progress at the same time as the main event in the sentence. Use the simple past for the main event.	BACKGROUND ACTIVITY They **were planning** a new advertising campaign MAIN EVENT in the country, so they **did** some research on the culture.
b. Use the simple past, not the past progressive, with stative verbs.	The company **understood** the culture. NOT The company ~~was understanding~~ the culture.

▶ Grammar Application

Exercise 2.1 Simple Past and Past Progressive

A Underline the past forms of the verbs in this paragraph about early American advertising.

Benjamin Franklin is one of the fathers of American advertising. He was an early American politician and inventor. In the early 1700s, Franklin was working in Philadelphia, Pennsylvania, as a publisher and inventor. He published a variety of books, and he was also the publisher of the newspaper *The Pennsylvania Gazette*. He used *The Pennsylvania Gazette* to advertise his inventions. Franklin filled the newspaper with ads. He also advertised books, both his own and other people's. Because of the ads in his newspaper, Franklin was making a lot of money and was selling a lot of books. These were among the first advertisements in America.

B *Pair Work* Compare your answers with a partner. Discuss which verbs are simple past and which are past progressive.

Exercise 2.2 Simple Past or Past Progressive?

A Read the paragraphs about a successful advertising campaign.[1] Circle the simple past or past progressive form of the verbs. Sometimes more than one answer is possible.

In the years after World War II, the U.S. government **promoted** / **was promoting**
(1)
milk as a health product. In the 1960s, however, soft-drink[2] companies began to market
their products very aggressively. As a result, people **soon drank** / **were soon drinking**
(2)
more soft drinks and less milk. The California Milk Advisory Board (CMAB) realized that
the old health-focused advertising **didn't work** / **wasn't working**.
(3)

Beginning in the mid-1970s, milk sales **went** / **were going** down in the United
(4)
States, and the CMAB **decided** / **was deciding** to do something to increase sales. The
(5)
CMAB members **learned** / **were learning** that the majority of people believed that
(6)
milk was good for them, but they weren't drinking it.

In 1993, a new board was formed, the California Milk Processor Board (MilkPEP).
This new board **hired** / **were hiring** an advertising agency to design a new
(7)
advertisement for milk. The agency **designed** / **were designing** a very original ad. The
(8)
ad showed a person eating something sweet or sticky (like cake or peanut butter). The
ad was funny because the person really needed milk to drink, but he or she didn't have
it. This **became** / **was becoming** the very successful "Got milk?"[3] campaign. In 1994,
(9)
milk sales **increased** / **were increasing** by over 10 million gallons a year. This was a
(10)
clear indication that the new campaign was a success.

[1]**campaign:** series of advertisements | [2]**soft-drink:** a carbonated, nonalcoholic drink, also known as "pop," "soda," or "cola" |
[3]**Got milk?:** an informal way of saying "Do you have milk?"

B *Pair Work* Compare your answers with a partner. Then ask and answer questions about the information in A. Use the simple past and the past progressive.

- A *What was happening in the United States beginning in the mid-1970s?*
  B *Milk sales were going down.*

3 Time Clauses with Simple Past and Past Progressive

▶ Grammar Presentation

<table>
<tr>
<td>

The simple past and past progressive are used with time clauses to show the order of two past events.

</td>
<td>

We **changed** our minds about the product **after we saw the ads for it**.

While he was presenting the product, the audience **listened** attentively.

</td>
</tr>
</table>

3.1 Using Time Clauses with Simple Past

<table>
<tr>
<td>

a. Use time clauses beginning with the time words and phrases *after*, *as soon as*, *before*, *once*, *until*, and *when* to show the order in which two events happened.

When the time clause comes first in the sentence, use a comma.

</td>
<td>

*We found out that the ad wasn't appropriate for consumers **when we were doing research on the market**.*

***When we were doing research on the market,** we found out that the ad wasn't appropriate for consumers.*

</td>
</tr>
<tr>
<td>

b. Use *after* to introduce the first event.

</td>
<td>

FIRST EVENT   SECOND EVENT
***After the store opened,** people didn't buy the dolls.*

</td>
</tr>
<tr>
<td>

c. Use *before* to introduce the *second* event.

</td>
<td>

FIRST EVENT
The company worked with an advertising team
                    SECOND EVENT
***before it marketed the shampoo**.*

</td>
</tr>
<tr>
<td>

d. Use *as soon as* or *once* to introduce the first event when the second event happens immediately after.

</td>
<td>

                              FIRST EVENT
As soon as the company made prices
                    SECOND EVENT
***affordable,** sales improved.*

SECOND EVENT   FIRST EVENT
*Women bought the shampoo **once the ad fit the local culture**.*

</td>
</tr>
<tr>
<td>

e. *Until* means "up to that time." Use *until* to indicate the second event.

</td>
<td>

FIRST EVENT   SECOND EVENT
*There were not many sales **until the company changed its advertising**.*

</td>
</tr>
<tr>
<td>

f. Use *when* to introduce the first event. *When* means "at almost the same time."

</td>
<td>

              FIRST EVENT   SECOND EVENT
***When we thought about the low sales,** we got a little worried.*

</td>
</tr>
</table>

3.2 Using Time Clauses with Simple Past and Past Progressive

a. Use the past progressive to describe an ongoing action. Use *while* or *when* to introduce the ongoing action.	ONGOING EVENT ***While we were developing** an advertising* **campaign,** INTERRUPTION *I got sick.*
Use the simple past to describe an action that interrupts the ongoing action. Use *when* to introduce the interruption.	ONGOING EVENT *evento en desarrollo* *We were discussing the new ad campaign* INTERRUPTION **when we heard about the low sales.**
b. Use the past progressive in both clauses to talk about two actions in progress at the same time.	***While they were studying** Malaysian* **culture,** *they **were developing** an advertising campaign.*

Data from the Real World

In formal writing, *when* is more common than *while*.

when	
while	

▶ Grammar Application

Exercise 3.1 Time Clauses with *After, Before, Once,* and *When*

Read the sentences about marketing milk. Circle the time words. Underline the time clauses. Label the earlier event with *1* and the later event with *2*.

1. *1*   *2*
    (After) World War II ended, the milk companies in the United States wanted people to drink milk. They marketed milk as a health drink.

2. People drank more milk than soft drinks *1* (before) soft-drink companies started marketing *2* their drinks as "fun."

3. *1* (When) soft-drink companies began marketing their drinks as "fun," the California Milk Advisory Board (CMAB) realized it needed to market milk differently.

4. The CMAB learned that people thought milk was boring *2* (after) the board completed its *1* market research.

5. (When) the CMAB discovered that 70 percent of Californians already drank milk, it

   decided to create a campaign to persuade them to drink more milk.

6. (Before) it started a new ad campaign, the new California Milk Processor Board, MilkPEP,

   learned that most people drink milk at home with foods like cookies and cake.

7. (When) the new milk ads appeared, they immediately became famous.

8. MilkPEP created a successful Spanish-language milk ad (once) it had success with the

   "Got milk?" campaign.

Exercise 3.2 Time Clauses with *As Soon As*, *Before*, *Until*, and *While*

Read the facts about the history of advertising. Combine the sentences with the time words in parentheses. Sometimes more than one answer is possible.

1. First event: Advertising already existed in Europe.

   Second event: Europeans came to the Americas in the 1400s.

   (before) <u>Before Europeans came to the Americas in the 1400s, advertising</u>
   <u>already existed in Europe./Advertising already existed in Europe before</u>
   <u>Europeans came to the Americas in the 1400s.</u>

2. First event: Europeans were exploring the world from the fifteenth to the seventeenth centuries.

   Second event: They found new and interesting kinds of food and spices.

   (while) <u>while Europeans were   , they found</u>

   _____

3. First event: European explorers came home.

   Second event: They introduced the items to the people from their countries.

   (as soon as) <u>As soon as European   , They</u>

   _____

4. First event: Europeans didn't know anything about coffee.

   Second event: They read the ads that explained what it was.

   (before) <u>Europeans   before They read</u>

   <u>t</u>_____

5. First event: Early advertisements had no words because most people couldn't read.

   Second event: Literacy became widespread in the eighteenth century.

   (until) _Early_ " " " " " _until Literary_ "
   _____

6. First event: Newspapers were the most common form of advertising.

   Second event: Radio was invented in the 1920s.

   (before) _Newspapers were_ " " - _before Radio_ " "
   _____

Exercise 3.3 Using Time Clauses with *When* and *While*

Complete the sentences from a report on a global marketing lecture. Use the simple past and past progressive forms of the verbs in parentheses.

1. The head of marketing of a restaurant chain _was speaking_ (speak) when
   I _arrived_ (arrive).

2. When his company _was considering_ (consider) opening new restaurants, they
   realized (realize) that they needed some vegetarian food items.

3. The market researchers _did_ (do) research on the vegetarian
   consumer when the managers _were deciding_ (decide) they needed a new,
   healthy menu.

4. The managers _learned_ (learn) that they had to eliminate
   many ingredients with eggs and dairy products when the market researchers
   were interviewing (interview) vegan[1] customers.

5. While they _were listening_ (listen) to customers explain how busy they
   were, the market researchers _got_ (get) the idea that the
   company should offer delivery service.

6. The head of marketing _was thinking_ (think) about opening up
   restaurants in Chicago when he _learned_ (learn) that more people
   ordered take-out food in New York City than in Chicago.

7. While the managers _was contemplating_ (contemplate) the idea of
   opening up a place in New York City, a restaurant in a busy location
   became (become) available, and the company bought the place
   immediately.

[1]**vegan:** a vegetarian who eats no animal or dairy products

Exercise 3.4 More Using Time Clauses with *When* and *While*

A *Over to You* Think about important decisions you have made in your life. Write an answer to one of these questions. Use *when* and *while*.

- What were you doing when you decided to study here?
- What were you doing when you made an important decision about your life?

  I was working in two different jobs when I decided to take classes here.

B *Pair Work* Discuss your sentences with a partner.

4 Used To and Would

▶ Grammar Presentation

Used to and *would* describe past routines or repeated actions. *Used to* expresses states or habits that existed in the past, but do not exist now. *Would* can only express repeated actions.	*Our company **used to sell** shampoo around the world. We **would study** the local customs. Then we **would create** local marketing campaigns.*

4.1 Used To

a. *Used to* is followed by the base form of the verb. It can be used for actions or states.	*Some companies **used to ignore** local customs.* (But they don't do that now.) *This building **used to be** a TV studio.* *I **used to know** the manager's name, but I've forgotten it.*
Use *use to* not *used to* in questions with *did*.	*Where **did** you **use to go** to school when you were young?*
The negative is *didn't use to* + the base form.	*Our company **didn't use to ask** for advice from the local markets.* (But our company does now.)
b. Use the simple past, not *used to*, to talk about completed actions in the past.	*The company **made** its sales goals last year.* NOT *The company* ~~used to make~~ *its sales goals last year.* *The company made its sales goals for a decade.* NOT *The company* ~~used to make~~ *its sales goals for a decade.* *The company made its sales goals three times.* NOT *The company* ~~used to make~~ *its sales goals three times.*

4.2 *Would*

a. *Would* is followed by the base form of the verb.	In the past, companies **would create** one advertisement for all markets.
A time expression, such as *in the past*, shows the context for the action.	*In the past*, we **would meet** for an hour every Friday to talk about marketing techniques. (But we don't do that now.)
b. *Would* is only used for actions, not states.	Twenty years ago, many smaller companies **wouldn't do** a lot of marketing in other countries. Usually, the president of our company **would not attend** our weekly meetings. In the past, companies **were not** sensitive to local customs. NOT *In the past, companies ~~wouldn't be~~ sensitive to local customs.*
c. Use the simple past, not *would*, to talk about completed actions in the past.	The sales team **attended** a conference last week. NOT *The sales team ~~would attend~~ a conference last week.*

▶ Grammar Application

[handwritten: I'd = I would / you'd = you would. / He'd = He would]

Exercise 4.1 *Would*

Complete part of a lecture on the history of radio and TV advertising. Use *would* and the correct verbs in the boxes.

appear	not use	~~produce~~	read

TV commercials developed from radio commercials. In the early days of radio, radio stations sold advertising time to support themselves. Many companies ___*would produce*___ entire radio programs in order to advertise their products.
(1)
Famous Hollywood stars of the day ___*Would appear*___ on these
(2)
programs. In the early days of radio, radio stations ___*Wouldn't use*___
(3)
ads that were on tape.[1] Instead, people performed the ads live. That is, an announcer
___*Would read*___ an advertisement on the air.[2] Today, some radio ads are
(4)
still live, but many ads are also prerecorded.

[1]**on tape:** prerecorded | [2]**on the air:** while broadcasting

advertise	buy	create	match

When television appeared, advertisers ___would buy___ time
(5)
during a TV program for their commercials. They ___would create___
(6)
short, 10-second advertisements to show during these programs. They
___would match___ a program with viewers who were likely to buy their
(7)
product. For example, they ___would advertise___ laundry soap to housewives
(8)
who stayed home and watched serial dramas ("soap operas") during the day.

Exercise 4.2 *Used To, Would,* or *Simple Past?*

A 🔊 Listen to an interview about how TV advertising has changed. Write the correct
form of the verbs that you hear.

Zach How has TV advertising changed over the years?

Dave In the past, we ___used to create___ commercials with very direct messages.
(1)
Commercials ___used to tell___ the consumer exactly what to do. We never
(2)
___used to be___ vague[1] about the message at all. In addition,
(3)
commercials ___didn't used to try___ to entertain the viewer.
(4)

Zach So, how ___would___ you ___create___ an advertising message in the old
(5)   (5)
days?

Dave A commercial for our product ___would say___: "Drink Fruity Juice."
(6)
We ___show___ the product several times in a commercial. We
(7)
___didn't use to hide___ the product.
(8)

Zach What changed?

Dave We ___saw___ some research a few years ago. It ___showed___
(9)   (10)
that people no longer pay attention to commercials like those. As a result,
we ___decided___ to change our style. Now we are producing
(11)
"mystery ads." Mystery ads don't show the product until the very end of the
commercial. They entertain the viewer because the viewer has to figure out
what the product is.

[1]**vague:** unclear

B 🔊 Listen again and check your answers.

Exercise 4.3 Using *Used To*, *Would*, and Simple Past

Group Work Describe your TV viewing habits in the past and in the present. In groups, discuss your answers to the following questions. Use affirmative and negative forms of *used to* and *would*.

- When you were younger, what types of TV shows did you use to watch?
- How much TV did you use to watch as a child?
- Would your family watch TV together, or did people in your family watch different programs?
- Did you use to believe everything you saw on TV? Do you believe what you see now? Why or why not?
- Did you use to pay attention to TV commercials in the past? Do you pay attention now? Why or why not?

A *When I was younger, I used to watch a few sitcoms[1] and sports games. What about you?*

B *I didn't use to watch TV much at all. But I would always watch cartoons on Saturday mornings.*

[1]**sitcom:** a situation-comedy show

5 | Avoid Common Mistakes ⚠

1. Use the base form of the verb after *would* and *used to*.

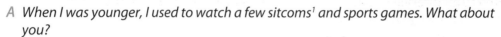

He used to ~~living~~ *live* in Bangladesh, where he studied economics.

2. Use *was* or *were* with the verb + -*ing* to describe actions in progress in the past, including in sentences with two clauses.

The new dolls were selling well, and the company ∧*was* making a lot of money.

3. Use the simple past when describing specific events in the past.

She knew that she ~~has~~ *had* a problem in one of her markets.

4. Use the past progressive to provide background information for an event.

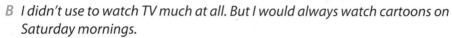

I ~~studied~~ *was studying* business administration in Malaysia when I got my first job.

Editing Task

Find and correct eight more mistakes in the transcript from a meeting.

> Hello, everyone! Welcome to the meeting.
>
> As many of you know, this past year [was] disappointing for many companies.
>
> However, we ended up doing quite well here at ABC Cell Phones. At the beginning
>
> of the year, things [were] looking bad. In fact, our sales fell [were falling] when I started here. However,
>
> 5 our excellent marketing team did their research, and they create [were creating] new and
>
> extremely successful advertisements after they discover two shifts in consumer
>
> spending.
>
> The first shift they saw was a shift to green marketing. Last year we noticed
>
> that consumers would paid [pay] more for environmentally friendly products. Therefore,
>
> 10 our first advertisement of last year showed how good our cell phone batteries are
>
> for the environment.
>
> The second shift was in who advertised our products. While we wrote [were writing] our most
>
> recent advertisement, research arrived that showed that celebrities sell products
>
> better. In October we began showing famous actors and actresses using our
>
> 15 phones, and last month alone, our sales rise [rose] by 25 percent.
>
> In short, while some businesses were struggling, we [were] increasing our profits.

6 Grammar for Writing

Using Past and Present Forms to Write About Changes

Writers use both past forms and present forms of verbs to describe changes. They use past forms to express background information about what something was like in the past. They use present forms to describe what the subject is like now. Read this example paragraph:

Years ago, most companies used to hold focus groups to find out what consumers wanted. They asked consumers questions and gave them products to review. These days, companies still employ techniques like focus groups. However, many companies use the Internet to find out what people want. Advertisers collect information about consumers based on the websites they look at.

Pre-writing Task

1 Read the paragraph. What kind of music did advertisers use to use? What kind of music are advertisers using these days?

[handwritten: musica en Publicidad]

Music in Advertising

[handwritten: atravez de   etapas a lo largo de]

Music in advertising has gone through different stages throughout the years. In the 1950s and 1960s, every product used to have a jingle, a short piece of music that is appealing and singable. A product would have several different advertisements, but the jingle was always the same. Jingles used to be effective because consumers would *[handwritten: ellos mismos]* sing them at different times to themselves, and the songs would remind them about the product. In the 1980s, advertisers stopped using jingles and started using hit songs. Nike was the first to do this. It successfully used the Beatles's song "Revolution" in its advertisements. Other companies followed Nike. Today, an interesting thing is happening. Companies are creating jingles for their products again. However, the jingles of today are
10 different because they have to compete with the short, snappy songs on MP3 players and the songs used as ringtones. They simply don't stand out as being different from regular songs anymore.

2 Read the paragraph again. Underline *used to* + verb and circle *would* + verb. Double underline the simple past verbs. Why did the writer sometimes choose to use present forms instead of a past form?

Writing Task

1 *Write* Use the paragraph in the Pre-writing Task to help you write about a change in advertising. How did it use to be? How is it now? Why did it change? You can write about one of these topics or use your own ideas.

- advertising on the Internet
- advertising on the sides of cars and buses
- billboard advertising
- changes in advertising because of DVRs or watching TV on the Internet

2 *Self-Edit* Use the editing tips to improve your paragraph. Make any necessary changes.

1. Did you use the simple past to focus on completed actions?
2. Did you use *used to* + the base form of verb and *would* + the base form of verb to write about the way things were in the past?
3. Did you use the present to write about the current situation and to highlight the differences between now and how it used to be?
4. Did you avoid the mistakes in the Avoid Common Mistakes chart on page 27?

[handwritten: gone = pasado]

1 | Grammar in the Real World

A What are the characteristics of a successful person? Read the article about Mahatma
Gandhi and Bill Gates. What qualities do they have in common?

The Making of Success

Some people **have said** that a successful person is like a sore thumb: The person
sticks out[1] wherever he or she goes. People always seem to notice something special
about the person. **Have** you ever **wondered** why? What makes someone successful?

For some time, researchers **have been trying** to answer this question. They **have**
5 **been looking** closely at people who **have achieved** success in their lives, and they
have discovered some very interesting traits.[2]

Mahatma Gandhi is one person the researchers
have studied. Gandhi was born in India in 1869.
Although he **died** in 1948, his life and principles **have**
10 **been inspiring**[3] people all over the world since then.

Gandhi **believed** in nonviolence, and he **used** this
principle to help India gain independence from the
British. His example **has been guiding** movements
for civil rights[4] and freedom around the world ever
15 since. In spite of great personal risk, he never **gave up**
on his goals to help the poor and the underprivileged,
such as ethnic minorities. Additionally, he always **aimed**
to live a simple life. At the time of Gandhi's death, the
prime minister of India **announced** on the radio: "The
20 light **has gone out**[5] of our lives, and there is darkness
everywhere."

[1]**stick out:** be easily noticed │ [2]**trait:** a characteristic, especially of a personality │ [3]**inspire:** fill someone with confidence
and the desire to do something │ [4]**civil rights:** the rights of every person in a society, including equality under law │
[5]**light goes out:** an idiom meaning joy and hope disappear

Many people consider Bill Gates one of the most successful people in the world, and certainly one of the richest. Gates **founded** the Microsoft Corporation
25 in 1975. In 1994, he **formed** the Bill and Melinda Gates Foundation. Through this foundation, he **has contributed** billions of dollars to organizations and programs working in global health, including public-health organizations, and he continues to work for
30 world health and education.

The secret of the success of Gandhi, Gates, and other successful people is strikingly similar. They **have found** a purpose in life and are not afraid to take action, to take risks, or to work hard. Sometimes they **have**
35 **failed**, but they **have** always **gone on** to reach their goal.

B *Comprehension Check* Answer the questions.

1. What principle did Mahatma Gandhi support?
2. What does the Bill and Melinda Gates Foundation do?
3. What is the secret of successful people?

over the world since then.
He had been inspiring people all
contributed billions of dollars
to organizations and programs
working in global health

C *Notice* Find the sentences in the article and complete them. Circle the correct verb forms.

1. Although he died in 1948, his life and principles __C__ people all over the world since then.
   a. inspired   b. have inspired   (c.) have been inspiring

2. His example __C__ movements for civil rights and freedom around the world ever since.
   a. guided   b. has guided   (c.) has been guiding

3. Gates __a__ the Microsoft Corporation in 1975.
   (a.) founded   b. has founded   c. has been founding

Which verbs describe actions that are still happening now?

1 - have been inspiring
2 - has been guiding } *Present Perfect*

2 Present Perfect

Completed before → *Time*

▶ Grammar Presentation

The present perfect is used to describe an event that happened at an unspecified time in the past. This event may be completed, or it may not be completed and may continue into the future.	Winners of the Gandhi Peace Prize **have contributed** to world peace. Sociologists **have studied** the definition of success for a long time.

2.1 Using Present Perfect

a. Use the present perfect to describe an action or event that happened at an unspecified time in the past.	Researchers **have discovered** similar traits in successful people.
The adverbs *already, ever, never,* and *(not) yet* can be used with the present perfect. *Ever* means "at any time in the past."	**"Has** she **received** an award <u>yet</u>?" "Yes, she **has** <u>already</u> **received** two awards." "No, she **has**<u>n't</u> **received** one <u>yet</u>." **"Have** you <u>ever</u> **thought** about the meaning of success?" "I**'ve** <u>never</u> **thought** about it."
b. Use the present perfect for actions or events that started in the past and continue into the present.	How long **has** she **been** a successful businessperson?
For, since, so far, and *still* help link between the past and the present. Other common expressions are *all day, all my life,* and *all year*.	She**'s owned** a successful business <u>for</u> 15 years. They**'ve worked** here <u>since</u> May. <u>So far</u>, he **hasn't changed** jobs. I <u>still</u> **haven't learned** to relax on weekends. They**'ve been** in the lab <u>all day</u>. He **has lived** here <u>all his life</u>.
c. Use the present perfect to describe a recent action.	Breaking news: The judges **have awarded** the Nobel Peace Prize.
The adverbs *just* and *recently* emphasize the recent past time.	I **have** <u>just</u> **discovered** the answer. He **has** <u>recently</u> **given** money to the foundation.

2.2 Present Perfect with *For* and *Since*

a. Use *for* to show the duration of time of an event that continues into the present moment.	She **hasn't worked** here <u>for</u> several years.
b. In negative sentences, the preposition *in* may replace *for*.	She **hasn't seen** her <u>in</u> several years.
c. Use *since* with specific dates or times to show the start of an event that continues into the present moment.	He **has lived** here <u>since</u> last year. She **hasn't worked** here <u>since</u> 2008.

▶ Grammar Application

Exercise 2.1 Uses of Present Perfect

Read about Blake Mycoskie, a businessperson and a humanitarian. Label the bold and underlined verbs *U* (unspecified time in the past), *C* (time that continues to the present), or *R* (recent action) according to the use of the present perfect.

Blake Mycoskie is an American businessperson. He started a shoe company called TOMS in 2006. He sells a special type of shoe, the *alpargata*. He discovered the shoe in Argentina.

Argentinean farmers **have worn** alpargatas for over 100 years.

5 Recently, experts **have discovered** a link between children going barefoot and getting certain diseases. Mycoskie **has** always **wanted** to help children stay healthy. Therefore, every time someone buys a pair of TOMS shoes, his company gives a free pair of new shoes to a child who needs shoes. Since he started TOMS, Mycoskie **has given** over a million pairs of alpargatas to children in South Africa, Ethiopia,

10 Rwanda, Argentina, Guatemala, Haiti, and the United States.

Not long ago, Mycoskie **started** a shoe factory in Ethiopia. He **has** also **created** a special shoe that helps prevent a serious foot disease. Mycoskie's favorite quote comes from Gandhi: "Be the change you wish to see in the world."

Exercise 2.2 Using Present Perfect

A Complete the interview about success. Use the present perfect form of the verbs in parentheses. Use contractions when possible.

Reporter Today, we are asking a few people about success. Are you successful? Do you know anyone who is successful? What makes someone successful?

Carlos My friend Marta is successful. She _'s wanted_ (want) to
(1)
own a restaurant for years, and now she _'s achieved_____
(2)
(achieve) her goal. Three years ago, she bought a restaurant.
She _has had_____ (have) a successful business ever
(3)
since.

Reporter How long _have_ you _known_____ (know) Marta?
(4)   (4)

Carlos I _'ve known_____ (know) her for 10 years.
(5)

Reporter _has_ she always _been_____ (be) interested in
(6)   (6)
food?

Carlos So far, that _has been_ (be) her only interest!
that's   (7)

Annie Well, I think my parents are very successful people. They
_haven't had_____ (not/have) any problems in
(8)
years. They _have raised_ (raise) five happy, successful
(9)
children. In fact, my youngest brother _has_ just
(10)
graduated (graduate) from college, and my older sister
(10)
has recently _gotten_ (get) married.
(11)   (11)

Ian You know, I _have_ never _thoght_ (think) about it.
(12)   (12)
I guess I _haven't achieved_ (not/achieve) anything
(13)
yet. I'm very happy, though! That's my idea of success!

B *Group Work* Read the definitions of success. Choose one definition and give examples of it using your experiences or those of someone you know. Use the present perfect and *already*, *never*, *yet*, *for*, *since*, *so far*, *still*, *just*, and *recently*.

Definitions

Success is having a goal and then achieving it.   *lograr*

Success is doing work that you love.

Success is having a lot of money.

Success is having good relationships with family and friends.

I think that success is having a goal and achieving it. My brother has always wanted to climb Mount Everest. He hasn't done it yet, but he has climbed several other mountains.

Exercise 2.3 *For* or *Since*?

Complete the sentences about successful people. Circle *for* or *since*.

1. Blake Mycoskie has started five businesses **since** / **for** he graduated from college.

2. Bill Gates has worked part-time for Microsoft and part-time for the Bill and Melinda Gates Foundation **since** / **for** the past several years.

3. Bill Gates has given over $28 billion to charity **since** / **for** 2007.

4. Oprah Winfrey has helped poor people **since** / **for** many years.

5. **Since** / **For** the last several years, the actor George Clooney has spent a great deal of time trying to help end the conflict in Darfur, Sudan.

Exercise 2.4 More *For* or *Since*?

Use the words to write sentences about successful people. Use the present perfect and *for* or *since*.

1. Joe and Ling have a successful marriage. They / be married / more than 30 years.
   They have been married for more than 30 years.

2. They / have / only / one fight / they first met
   They have only had one fight

3. They / not spend / a night apart / 1980
   they haven't spent a night apart since 1980

4. Mark and Amy have a successful friendship. They / be friends / high school
   they've been friends since high school

5. They / speak / on the phone every day / the past 10 years
   they have spoken on the phone every day for the past 10 years

6. Verónica / be / a successful single parent / many years
   Veronica has been a successful single parent for many years

7. She / raise / her three children by herself / her divorce
   she's raised her three children since her divorce

3 | Present Perfect vs. Simple Past

▶ Grammar Presentation

The present perfect can refer to events that began in the past, continue until now, and may continue in the future. The simple past expresses completed events.	*"**Have** you **read** any books about successful people?"* *"Yes. I **read** one about Raul Julia last week."*

3.1 Present Perfect and Simple Past Contrasted

a. Use the present perfect to refer to events or repeated actions that continue into the present moment.	*Gandhi **has inspired** people all over the world.* (Gandhi inspired people for many years, and his ideas still inspire people now.)
Use the simple past to refer to completed actions.	*Gandhi **promoted** nonviolence against British rule.* (Gandhi did this while he was alive.)
b. Use the present perfect to refer to an action completed at an unspecified time in the past that has an effect in the present.	*The Gates Foundation **has supported** health care in poor countries.* (Poor countries are benefiting from this care now.)
Use the simple past to refer to a completed action in the past that doesn't have an effect in the present.	*Bill Gates **founded** the Microsoft Corporation in 1975.* (This is a fact about Bill Gates's past.)

Data from the Real World 🌐

In informal speaking, people sometimes use the simple past with *already* and *yet* instead of the present perfect.	*We **haven't finished** yet.* *We **didn't finish** yet.* (informal speaking)
In academic writing, always use the present perfect with *already* and *yet*.	*The foundation **has** already **given** millions of dollars to charities this year.*

- ■ with present perfect
- ■ with simple past

▶ Grammar Application

Exercise 3.1 Present Perfect or Simple Past?

A Complete the online interview about the actress Marlee Matlin. Circle the correct form of the verbs.

Marlee Matlin is a successful actress, writer, and producer. She is also hearing impaired. She cannot hear, but she is able to communicate in spoken English. She won an Oscar for Best Actress and has received other acting awards as well.

Kate I really admire Marlee Matlin. She didn't let her disability stop her from achieving her dreams.

Alex I don't know that much about her.

Kate Well, she began acting at a very young age. She **played**/**'s played** Dorothy in *The Wizard of Oz* when she was seven years old.
(1)

Alex Wow. **Did she use**/**Has she used** sign language in that role?
(2)

Kate Yes, she **did**/**has**. That play was produced by a hearing-impaired
(3)
children's organization. In 1986, she **played**/**'s played** a hearing-impaired
(4)
woman in *Children of a Lesser God*, and she won an Oscar.

Alex Has she ever played a hearing person?

Kate So far, she **performed**/**'s performed** mostly hearing-impaired roles,
(5)
but in 1994, she **played**/**'ve played** a hearing woman in the television
(6)
movie *Against Her Will*.

Alex What else **did she do**/**has she done** besides acting?
(7)

Kate In 1999, she **produced**/**'s produced** a television movie. In addition,
(8)
she **was**/**'s been** very busy raising four children! Her oldest child
(9)
was/**has been** born in 1996. She **had**/**has had** her last child in 2003.
(10)   (11)

B *Pair Work* Compare your answers with a partner. Discuss the reason for each of your answers.

I chose the past for number 1 because the action happened at a specific time in the past – when she was seven years old.

Exercise 3.2 More Present Perfect or Simple Past?

A Read the time line about Diane, a successful clothing designer. Complete the sentences with the present perfect or simple past.

1999	Come to the United States; not speak English
2000	Move to Florida; study English at a school for fashion design
2002	Finish college; work as a seamstress in Miami
2003	Move to New York; get a job at Smith Designs
2005	Become a designer at Smith Designs
2006	Leave Smith Designs; start a company, Sorel Designs
2006 to present	Work at Sorel Designs
2009 to present	Make movie costumes

1. In 1999, *Diane came to the United States. She did not speak English* ~~fashion desing~~
2. In 2000, *She moved to Florida, she studied English at school for*
3. In 2002, *She finished college. She worked as a seamstress in Miami*
4. In 2003, *She moved To New York. she got a job at Smith Designs*
5. In 2005, *She became a designer at Smith Designs* .
6. In 2006, *She left Smith Designs. She started a Company Sorel designs*
7. Since 2006, *She has worked at Sorel Designs* .
8. Since 2009, *She has made movie costumes* .

B *Over to You* Think about a successful person you know: a friend, a relative, or a famous person. On a separate piece of paper, write five facts about that person's life and accomplishments. Use the simple past and present perfect. Then share your sentences with a partner.

4 | Present Perfect vs. Present Perfect Progressive

▶ Grammar Presentation

The present perfect and present perfect progressive can sometimes have similar meanings. However, the present perfect progressive focuses on the ongoing nature of the activity. The present perfect often suggests that the action is finished.	*I've worn / I've been wearing* glasses all my life. *I've been writing* an article about the meaning of success. (I haven't finished it yet.) *I've written* an article about the meaning of success. (I've already finished it.)

4.1 Similar Meaning: Habitual and Ongoing Actions

a. Use either the present perfect or present perfect progressive for habitual actions that began in the past and continue up to the present. Some verbs that show habitual action are *live, study, teach, wear,* and *work*.	Bill Gates **has worked** hard all his life. Bill Gates **has been working** hard all his life.
b. Use *how long* to ask about the duration of habitual actions.	"How long **have** you **lived** / **have** you **been living** here?" "I**'ve lived** / I**'ve been living** here for 4 years."

4.2 Different Meanings: Completed vs. Ongoing Actions

a. Use the present perfect for an event that was completed at an unspecified time in the past.	She **has read** a biography of Gandhi. (She finished it. She is no longer reading it.)
Use the present perfect progressive for an event that began in the past and is still ongoing. It emphasizes the duration of the activity.	She **has been reading** a biography of Gandhi. (She is still reading it.)
Stative verbs are usually in the present perfect (not the present perfect progressive). Stative verbs include *be, have, like,* and *see*.	They**'ve been** good friends for ages. He**'s had** a lot of experience in this business. I**'ve** always **liked** learning about successful people.
b. Use the present perfect to express *how much/how many.* = cuantos cuanto	A friend of mine **has painted** at least 100 paintings. (at least 100 paintings = how many)
Use the present perfect progressive to express *how long.* Cuanto tiempo	She **has been painting** for more than 10 years. (more than 10 years = how long)

▶ Grammar Application

Exercise 4.1 Completed or Ongoing Actions?

Read the sentences. Check (✓) whether the action is completed or ongoing. *en desarrollo*

		Completed	Ongoing
1.	Lara has learned Spanish very well. =My bien	✓	☐
2.	Michelle has also been studying French and Japanese this semester.	☐	✓
3.	Enrico has been learning a lot of languages.	☐	✓
4.	Tony has been working as a chef for the past 8 years.	☐	✓
5.	Alex has been running his own business since he was 19.	☐	✓
6.	Joe has lived in Madrid.	✓	☐
7.	Ron has been living in California since 2010.	☐	✓
8.	We've already eaten dinner.	✓	☐
9.	Sasha and Janet have been working there since 2008.	☐	✓
10.	Raymond has won three prizes for his poetry.	✓	☐
11.	I've been traveling for four weeks.	☐	✓
12.	Bryn has been dancing since she was a child.	☐	✓
13.	My mother has been cooking since she was 12.	☐	✓
14.	Luisa has written four letters to her senator.	✓	☐

Exercise 4.2 Simple Past, Present Perfect, and Present Perfect Progressive

A Complete the following podcast transcript with the correct forms of the verbs in parentheses. Sometimes more than one answer is possible.

Zaha Hadid is an architect. She _has designed_ (design)
(1)
many famous buildings around the world, including the
Rosenthal Center for Contemporary Art in Cincinnati. Hadid
was born in Iraq, and she ___studied___ (study)
(2)
architecture in London in the late 1970s. Since the 1980s, she 's worked
has been working (work) at a design company,
(3)
and she 's been teaching (teach) architecture at   she's taught
(4)
several universities.

Richard Branson is one of the world's most successful
businesspeople. He was born in England. He
___had___ (have) a hard time in school because
(5)
he had a learning disability.[1] Reading was difficult for him. As
a result, he __left__ (leave) school at age 16.
(6)
After that, he __started__ (start) his first business.
(7)
Later, he __opened__ (open) a record shop called
(8)
Virgin Records. Since then, he 's started (start)
(9)
new businesses in many different industries, including
transportation, entertainment, and communications.

[1] **learning disability:** a condition that affects a person's ability to learn

B *Pair Work* Compare your answers with a partner. Discuss the reason for each of your answers.

In number 1, I wrote has designed *because the action continues into the present, but the action seems complete. So, I didn't choose* has been designing.

C ◀)) Listen to the podcast and check your answers.

D *Over to You* Think about your life story. Write answers to these questions on a separate piece of paper. Use the simple past, the present perfect, and the present perfect progressive. Share your answers with a partner.

- Have you accomplished something important (for example, learned a language, graduated from high school, saved money for an important purchase)? How did you do it?
- What are some things that you have done recently that make you feel happy? How long have you been doing them?
- What have you been doing recently that makes you feel successful?

5 | Avoid Common Mistakes ⚠

1. Use correct subject-verb agreement when forming the present perfect.

have
Young (people) ~~has~~ always gone to college with high expectations.

2. Use the present perfect (not the present perfect progressive) for a time period that starts in the past and is completed.

finished
He has ~~been finishing~~ two books since last week.

3. Remember to include *been* for the present perfect progressive.

been
The definition of success has ˄ changing over the years.

4. Use the present perfect progressive (not the present progressive) for actions that began in the past and are still continuing.

has been
He ~~is~~ studying for six hours, and he refuses to stop.

Editing Task

Find and correct eight more mistakes in the paragraphs about a student's success in his job.

I am a college student by day and a sous-chef[1] by night. My studies are important,

has
but my restaurant job ~~have~~ taught me what I really need to know about success. I am *have been*

working in the kitchen of Da Lat, a French-Vietnamese bistro, for three years, and the job

has been a wonderful experience for me because I have learned many new skills.

[1]**sous-chef:** the head chef's assistant

5 First, I have been becoming a much better planner since I started working at Da Lat.

6 Planning and preparation are very important in a kitchen. If the chef have not prepared

7 the ingredients well beforehand, it will take too long to make each dish, and customers

8 will complain. We start our preparation early each day, and by the time the first customer

9 comes, we have working for 6 hours.

10 Second, I have developing better interpersonal skills. For example, I have been

11 receiving two promotions in the last two years. Last year, I became a line cook because

I had learned to pay attention to what others might need before they ask. I think that for

the past few months, I am paying better attention in other areas of my life as well.

My college education is important, but I will always be grateful for my job at Da Lat.

15 This job have given me mental and social skills for my future.

6 | Grammar for Writing

Using Present Perfect, Present Perfect Progressive, and Simple Past to Describe a Series of Events

When writing about a living person, writers use the simple present, the simple past, the present perfect, and the present perfect progressive to talk about different points in the person's life:

- Use the simple present or present progressive to describe the person's current (situación actual) situation.
- Use the simple past to describe actions that were completed at a specific time in the past.
- Use the present perfect to describe situations or actions that occurred at unspecified times in the past or that continue into the present.
- Use the present perfect progressive to focus on the ongoing nature of something that began in the past.

Read this example paragraph:

Shakira Isabel Mebarak Ripoll is a Colombian musician. She recorded her first album at the age of 13, and since then she has sold more albums than any other Colombian recording artist in history. For the past few years, she has been working with several charities, including an organization that she helped create.

became =

Complain = Quejarse   beforehand = de antemano

Pre-writing Task

1 Read the paragraph. What was the first important achievement of the person in the paragraph? Why was it so special? What has she done since that accomplishment?

An Artist or an Architect?

Maya Lin is an incredible American architect and artist. Her career began when she won a national competition to design the Vietnam Veterans Memorial in 1981. Lin was just 21 years old and was still an undergraduate in college at that time. This memorial became famous almost immediately. Millions of people have traveled to Washington,

5 D.C., to see it over the years. Since then, Lin has accomplished many more things. She completed her master's in architecture in 1986, and she has been designing monuments, parks, and other important structures ever since. She has designed many of her structures to draw people's attention to nature, to the environment, and to social issues. Recently she has been creating a lot of landscape art. Because Lin is both an artist and an architect, she

10 combines both of her interests in her designs. People have been questioning whether her work is art or architecture for many years. Lin likes to think of her work as a combination of both. Lin has won awards and honorary degrees throughout her career. Not all of Lin's designs have been popular, but Maya Lin has been a very successful architect and artist since she was a very young woman.

2 Read the paragraph again. Underline the present perfect verbs that are used to show a time period that extends up to now. Double underline the present perfect progressive verbs that are used to show duration up to now. Circle the simple past verbs.

Writing Task

1 *Write* Use the paragraph in the Pre-writing Task to help you write about the achievements of a person you admire. Describe specific events in the person's life, and include current activities the person is involved in.

2 *Self-Edit* Use the editing tips to improve your paragraph. Make any necessary changes.

1. Did you use the present perfect to write about events that happened at an unspecified time in the past?
2. Did you use the present perfect and present perfect progressive to describe situations that started in the past but are still ongoing in the present?
3. Did you use the simple past to write about actions that happened at specified times in the past?
4. Did you use the simple present or present progressive to write about the person's current activities?
5. Did you avoid the mistakes in the Avoid Common Mistakes chart on page 42?

Past Perfect
and Past Perfect Progressive

Nature vs. Nurture

1 | Grammar in the Real World

A Have you ever reconnected with someone from your past? Read the web article about twins
who lived apart for many years. What surprised the twins when they reconnected?

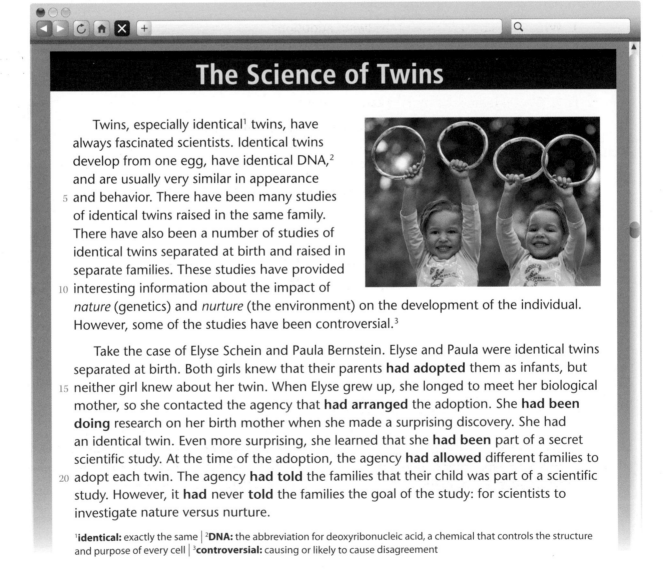

The Science of Twins

Twins, especially identical[1] twins, have
always fascinated scientists. Identical twins
develop from one egg, have identical DNA,[2]
and are usually very similar in appearance
5 and behavior. There have been many studies
of identical twins raised in the same family.
There have also been a number of studies of
identical twins separated at birth and raised in
separate families. These studies have provided
10 interesting information about the impact of
nature (genetics) and *nurture* (the environment) on the development of the individual.
However, some of the studies have been controversial.[3]

Take the case of Elyse Schein and Paula Bernstein. Elyse and Paula were identical twins
separated at birth. Both girls knew that their parents **had adopted** them as infants, but
15 neither girl knew about her twin. When Elyse grew up, she longed to meet her biological
mother, so she contacted the agency that **had arranged** the adoption. She **had been
doing** research on her birth mother when she made a surprising discovery. She had
an identical twin. Even more surprising, she learned that she **had been** part of a secret
scientific study. At the time of the adoption, the agency **had allowed** different families to
20 adopt each twin. The agency **had told** the families that their child was part of a scientific
study. However, it **had** never **told** the families the goal of the study: for scientists to
investigate nature versus nurture.

[1]**identical:** exactly the same | [2]**DNA:** the abbreviation for deoxyribonucleic acid, a chemical that controls the structure
and purpose of every cell | [3]**controversial:** causing or likely to cause disagreement

When Elyse and Paula finally met as adults, they were amazed. They had many similarities. They looked almost identical. They **had** both **studied** film. They both loved
25 to write. Together, the twins discovered that the researchers **had stopped** the study before the end because the public strongly disapproved of this type of research.

Although that study ended early, many scientists today make a strong case for the dominant[4] role of nature. Schein and Bernstein agree that genetics explains many of their similarities. However, recent research suggests that nurture is equally important. It
30 is clear that the nature versus nurture debate will occupy scientists for years to come.

[4]**dominant:** more important, strong, or noticeable

B *Comprehension Check* Answer the questions.

1. What was surprising about the twins' adoption?
2. What characteristics and interests did Elyse and Paula have in common?
3. What is the nature versus nurture debate?

C *Notice* Underline the verbs in each sentence.

1. Both girls knew that their parents had adopted them as infants.
2. She had been doing research on her birth mother when she made a surprising discovery.
3. Even more surprising, she learned that she had been part of a secret scientific study.

Which event happened first in each sentence? What event followed? Write the verbs. What do you notice about the form of the verbs?

1. First: _____ Then: _____
2. First: _____ Then: _____
3. First: _____ Then: _____

2 Past Perfect

▶ Grammar Presentation

The past perfect is used to describe a completed event that happened before another event in the past.	*Elyse finally met her sister, Paula. Paula **had been** married for several years.* (First, Paula got married; Elyse met Paula at a later time.)

2.1 Forming Past Perfect

Form the past perfect with *had* + the past participle of the main verb. Form the negative by adding *not* after *had*. The form is the same for all subjects.	*Elyse and Paula did not grow up together. They **had lived** with different families.* *They were available for adoption because their birthmother **had given** them up.* *"**Had** she **talked** about the study to anyone at the time?"* *"No, she **hadn't**."* *"What **had** you **heard** about this study before that time?"* *"I**'d heard** very little about it."*

▶▶ Irregular Verbs: See page A1.

2.2 Using Past Perfect with Simple Past

a. Use the past perfect to describe an event in a time period that leads up to another past event or time period. Use the simple past to describe the later event or time period.	LATER TIME EARLIER TIME *She **learned** that she **had been** part of a secret study.* LATER TIME EARLIER TIME *The twins **discovered** that they **had** both **studied** psychology.*

b. The prepositions *before*, *by*, or *until* can introduce the later time period.	EARLIER TIME LATER TIME
	*Their mother **had known** about the study before her death.*
	    EARLIER TIME LATER TIME
	*Sue **hadn't met** her sister until last year.*
	        EARLIER TIME LATER TIME
	*Studies on twins **had become** common by the 1960s.*

c. The past perfect is often used to give reasons or background information for later past events.	REASON *She was late. She **had forgotten** to set her alarm clock.* BACKGROUND INFORMATION LATER PAST EVENT *He **had** never **taken** a subway before he moved to New York.*

Data from the Real World

In writing, these verbs are commonly used in the past perfect: *come, have, leave, make,* and *take*. *Had been* is the most common past perfect form in speaking and writing.	The twins **had not gone** to the same school as children. The family thought that they **had made** the right decision. Psychologists praised the study because the researchers **had been** very careful in their work. The researchers **had not been** aware of each other's work on twins until they met.

▶ Grammar Application

Exercise 2.1 Past Perfect

Complete the sentences about twins who met as adults. Use the past perfect form of the verbs in parentheses.

1. Two separate Illinois families ___had adopted___ (adopt) Anne Green and Annie Smith before the twins were three days old.

2. When the girls met, they were fascinated by their similarities. For example, they ___had lived___ (live) near each other before the Greens moved away.

3. As children, both Anne and Annie ___had gone___ (go) to the same summer camp.

4. Anne ___hadn't gone___ (not / go) to college, and Annie ___hadn't attended___ (not / attend) college, either.

5. Both ___had married___ (marry) for the first time by the age of 22.

6. Anne ___had gotten___ (get) divorced and ___had remarried___ (remarry). Annie ___hadn't gotten___ (not / get) divorced and was still married.

7. Both Anne and Annie were allergic to cats and dogs and ___had___ never ___owned___ (own) pets.

8. Both ___had given___ (give) the same name – Heather – to their daughters.

9. Both ___had___ previously ___worked___ (work) in the hospitality industry.

10. Anne ___had worked___ (work) as a hotel manager. However, Annie ___hadn't worked___ (not / work) in hotels; she ___had been___ (be) a restaurant manager.

Exercise 2.2 Past Perfect and Simple Past

A Read the article about a famous twin study. Underline the simple past forms. Double underline the past perfect forms.

> The University of Minnesota is the birthplace of one of the most important twin studies in the world. It <u>started</u> in 1979. Thomas J. Bouchard <u>had</u> already <u>been</u> on the faculty[1] of the university for some time when he <u>began</u> his study of identical twins. Bouchard read an article about a set of twins who <u>had been</u> separated at birth. The twins <u>had</u> recently <u>met</u> and <u>had found</u> many similarities. They <u>found</u> out that they <u>had lived</u> near each other for years. Bouchard <u>was</u> amazed by the twins' story and <u>decided</u> to start the Minnesota Twins Reared Apart Study. Bouchard <u>began</u> to study sets of twins that <u>had been</u> separated at birth. Over the years, the Minnesota Twins Reared Apart Study has <u>studied</u> more than 8,000 sets of twins. The study continues today.
>
> [1]**faculty:** the people who teach in a department in a school

B *Pair Work* Compare your answers with a partner. Discuss the reason for each of your answers.

In line 2, had been *refers to the first event. Dr. Bouchard joined the faculty before the twin study. The twin study began later. The study is the second event, so* started *is in the simple past.*

Exercise 2.3 More Past Perfect and Simple Past

A 🔊 Listen to an interview with twins who are actors. Complete the sentences with the verbs you hear.

Claudia Today, I'm interviewing Alex and Andrew Underhill. They appear in the *Spy Twins* movie series based on the books of the same name. How did you get the part in the first *Spy Twins* movie?

Alex A friend __*had seen*__ the advertisement
          (1)
in the newspaper and later

_____ us about it. We
          (2)
_____ any acting before
          (3)
then, but we _____ to
                              (4)
try out anyway.

Claudia How many twins were at the audition?

Andrew When we got there, we _____ (5) that about five other sets of twins _____ (6) for the audition.

Alex We also noticed that all the twins were wearing matching outfits. Until that audition, we _____ (7) never _____ (7) the same clothes in our whole lives. We decided to run out to the nearest shopping mall to buy some matching clothes. The audition _____ (8) just _____ (8) when we _____ (9) .

Claudia _____ (10) you _____ (10) the *Spy Twins* novels before your audition?

Andrew Yes. The third book _____ (11) when we _____ (12) to the first audition.

Claudia What's it like being twins? Are you two close? Do you do the same things?

Alex Yes, in lots of ways.

Andrew We definitely think the same way.

Alex Right! Once, we took the same test in school. Of course, we were in the same grade, but we had different teachers. We had exactly the same answers correct, even though we _____ (13) in the same classroom!

Claudia Wow! I guess you're a lot alike in many ways! Well, thanks, Alex and Andrew. It's been great talking with you.

B 🔊 Listen again and check your answers.

C Use the time line to complete the sentences about Alex and Andrew. Use the past perfect form of the verbs in the box.

build	decide	graduate	~~make~~	record	start

1986	The twins are born.
1993	The twins audition for the first *Spy Twins* movie.
1995	They record their first pop song and make a TV movie.
1996	The twins start a fashion company for young men's clothing.
1997 to 2003	The twins make three more *Spy Twins* movies.
2004	They graduate from high school; they start college.
2005	The twins decide to stop acting.
2008	They graduate from college.
2008 to present	They work as fashion designers for their clothing company.

1. By 2004, Alex and Andrew _had made_ four *Spy Twins* movies.
2. Before 1995, the twins _____ (not) a pop song.
3. By 2006, the twins _____ to stop acting.
4. The twins _____ (not) a fashion company yet in 1995.
5. The twins _____ from high school by 2005.
6. They _____ a successful career before the age of 30.

D *Over to You* Make a time line about yourself from your birth to the present. Write five sentences about your life. Use the past perfect with *before*, *by*, and *until*.

3 | Past Perfect with Time Clauses

▶ Grammar Presentation

The past perfect is often used with time clauses for events that occurred in an earlier time period leading up to a later event or time period.	*By the time Elyse discovered her sister, people **had forgotten** about the twin study.*

3.1 Order of Events

a. Use time clauses to show two separate past time periods. Use the past perfect to signal an event that occurred in an earlier time period.	*Elyse **had moved** by the time the researchers called her.*
The time words *after, as soon as, before, by the time, until,* and *when* can introduce the time clauses.	*After they **had met**, they noticed their many similarities.* *Until Elyse started her research, she **hadn't known** about the twin study.*
b. With *before* and *after*, the past perfect is not always necessary because the order is clear. In this case, the past perfect emphasizes the earlier time period.	*Elyse **moved** before she met her twin.* OR *Elyse **had moved** before she met her twin.*
c. In time clauses with *when*, the use of the past perfect in the main clause usually shows a good amount of time between events.	*When Paula met Elyse, she **had** already **learned** about the research.* (She learned about the research. She met Elyse some time later.)
d. The use of *as soon as* with the past perfect shows that one event happened very soon after the other.	*As soon as the researchers **had learned** about the public's reaction to the study, they **stopped** it.* (The scientists learned about the public's reaction to the study. They stopped the study very soon after that.)
The use of the simple past in both clauses shows that one event happened very soon after the other.	*When Paula met Elyse, she **learned** about the research.* (She learned about the research very soon after she met Elyse.)

▶ Grammar Application

Exercise 3.1 Order of Events

A Read the blog entry about twin studies. Underline the past perfect form of the verbs.

Twin World by Cory Daniels

   Before her twins were born, Kim Lee had read a lot about twin studies. After she
had done a little research, Kim found an early reading study for twins. She contacted
the researchers and learned that she had to wait until the twins were four years old.
When she enrolled the twins in the study, she hadn't known that the twins needed to
give a DNA sample. As soon as Kim learned this, she took the twins out of the study.
Kim thought that taking a DNA sample was an invasion of her children's privacy.

B *Pair Work* Discuss why the past perfect is used in each case in A. Then find a
sentence with a time clause that describes two events that happened at the same time
or almost the same time. What is the form of the verbs in this sentence?

Exercise 3.2 Time Clauses

Complete the article about siblings[1] who were separated as children. Circle the correct
time word. Write the simple past or past perfect form of the verbs in parentheses.
Sometimes more than one answer is possible.

There are many stories of non-twin brothers and sisters
who are separated for one reason or another and meet
again as adults. Here are a couple.

Glenn Mint and Bruce Mathews are brothers. They had
never met (until)/after Glenn _started_ (start) working
       (1)   (2)
at the same company as Bruce. Bruce was surprised
because the new employee looked just like him. They
started asking each other questions. Before/After they
                                          (3)
met, each man _had known_ (know) that he
                 (4)
had a sibling. Before/As soon as Glenn _had discovered_ (discover)
                       (5)   (6)
Bruce's birth date, he knew Bruce was his long-lost brother.

Quin Mara, 82, knew that she was adopted and that she had siblings, but she had
never met them. After/Until a relative _had found_ (find) a family tree,[2] Quin
                     (7)   (8)
learned the names of her siblings and started looking for them. Until/By the time
                                  didn't know   (9)
she saw the family tree, she _hadn't known_ (not/know) that she was
                                  (10)
the youngest of nine children. As soon as/Before she _had discovered_
                                    (11)   (12)
(discover) that, she began to look for her brothers and sisters. She was very happy
because five of her siblings were still alive. Before/After she _had met_
                                                     (13)   (14)
(meet) them, she didn't know that they had spent the last several decades looking for
each other.

[1]**sibling:** a brother or sister | [2]**family tree:** a drawing that shows all the members of a family, usually over a long
period of time, and how they are related to each other

Exercise 3.3 Combining Sentences

Read the story about how environment affects personality. Combine the sentences with the time words in parentheses. Use the past perfect for the earlier event and the simple past for the later event.

1. Diego and Shannon were married for a few years. Then they decided to have a baby.

   (when) _When Diego and Shannon had been married for a few years, they decided to have a baby._

2. Diego and Shannon did not think much about the nature versus nurture debate. Then their first child, Mario, was born.

   (until) _Diego and Shannon hadn't thought much about the nature versus nurture debate until their first child Mario had been born_

3. Diego and Shannon didn't have much experience with music. Then they became parents.

   ~~(before)~~ (had) _they hadn't had much experience with music, before became parents._

4. Three-year-old Mario saw an electronic keyboard in a shop. Then he asked his parents to buy him one.

   (after) _three year old Mario had seen an electronic keyboard in a shop, he asked his parents to buy him one._

5. Diego and Shannon heard Mario playing the keyboard. Then they realized their son's musical talent.

   (as soon as) _Diego and Shannon had heard Mario playing the keyboard, they realized their son's musical talent_

6. Diego and Shannon realized Mario's talent. Then they enrolled him in piano classes.

   (as soon as) _Diego and Shannon had realized Mario's talent, they enrolled him in piano classes_

7. Diego and Shannon enrolled Mario in piano classes. Then Mario became an excellent musician.

   (after) _Diego and Shannon had enrolled Mario in piano classes, he became an excellent musican_

8. Mario took a few years of piano classes. He started composing music.

   (by the time) _Mario had taken a few years of piano classes, he started composing music._

realize=(darse cuenta)

4 | Past Perfect Progressive

▶ Grammar Presentation

The past perfect progressive emphasizes the ongoing nature of a past activity or situation leading up to a more recent past time.	*Living with a roommate was hard for me in the beginning. I **had been living** alone for years.*

4.1 Forming Past Perfect Progressive

Form the past perfect progressive with *had + been + -ing* form of the verb. Form the negative by putting *not* between *had* and *been* or using the contraction *hadn't*.	*She knew Boston well when I visited her. She'**d been living** there for years.* *When my brother visited me, I **had not / hadn't been living** there long.*

4.2 Using Past Perfect Progressive

a. Use the past perfect progressive for an action or situation that continued up to an event or situation in past time. This can show a reason or give background information.	*He looked tired because he **had been working** all night.* *My eyes were sore because I **hadn't been wearing** my contacts.*
b. With some verbs such as *live, play, teach, wear,* and *work*, use either the past perfect or past perfect progressive. The meaning is similar.	*The twins **had lived** in different cities before they **discovered** each other.* OR *The twins **had been living** in different cities before they **discovered** each other.*

▶ Grammar Application

Exercise 4.1 Past Perfect Progressive

Complete the story about brothers who reconnected after many years. Use the past perfect progressive form of the verbs in parentheses.

Mark and Peter were brothers. Their parents could not take care of them. One family adopted Mark, and another family adopted Peter. Mark and Peter _had been dreaming_ (dream) of finding
(1)
each other since 2005. When they finally met, they were surprised by how much they had in common. For most of their adult lives, their jobs had been related, even though they _hadn't been working_ (not / work) in the (hadn't worked)
(2)
same business. Mark _had been making_ (make) furniture, and Peter
(3)
had been selling (sell) furniture. Mark _had been interviewing_
(4)   (5)
(interview) for jobs in furniture stores and decided to take a new position at Mark's store. Peter _had been talking_ (talk) to a friendly customer when he
(6)
saw a man who looked like him walk into the store. Peter quickly stopped what he _had been doing_ (do) and introduced himself. That first day, Peter and
(7)
Mark talked for hours. They found out that they _hadn't been living_ (had lived)
(8)
(not / live) in the same city, but they had attended schools in the same district for most of their childhood. They _had been crossing_ (cross) paths for many years
(9)
without ever meeting. They had never expected to have so much in common.

Exercise 4.2 Past Perfect Progressive, Past Perfect, or Simple Past?

A Complete the interview with a woman who found her three siblings after many years. Use the past perfect progressive, the past perfect, or the simple past form of the verbs in parentheses. Use contractions when possible. Sometimes more than one answer is possible.

Vijay   Tell us how you found your family.

Paula   I <u>'d been looking</u> (look) for my sister all my life. I <u>hadn't had</u>
            (1)   (2)
          (not / have) much luck, though. Then one day, I turned on the TV. A talk show was

          on. The host of the show was interviewing three siblings – two brothers and a half

          sister.[1] Different families <u>had adopted</u> (adopt) the siblings many
                                              (3)

          years before.

Vijay   And?

Paula   They <u>had been talking</u> (talk) about me before I turned on the program.
                        (4)
          The siblings had recently reunited, and they <u>'d been searching</u> (search)
                                                                 (5)
          for a fourth sibling for the past several months. I called the TV station, and we all

          finally <u>met</u> (meet).
                      (6)

Vijay   So, you <u>had been looking</u> (look) for a sister all your life, and you found
                         (7)
          three siblings!

Paula   Yes, it was wonderful! We all met at one of the network offices the following week.

We'd been
speaking   – spoke   After we <u>had spoken</u> (speak) for a while, it was obvious to me that
                                          (8)
                       they <u>had been looking</u> (look) for me all their lives, too.
                               had looked (9)

[1] **half sister:** a sister who is biologically related by one parent only

B *Pair Work*   Discuss these questions with a partner.

- Choose a sentence in A in which you can use either the past perfect or the past perfect progressive. Why are both possible here?

- In which sentence in A is only the past perfect correct?

C *Over to You*   Do an online search for twins, siblings, or other family members who reunited after many years. Write five sentences about their experiences. Use the past perfect and the past perfect progressive.

5 | Avoid Common Mistakes ⚠️

1. **Use the past perfect or past perfect progressive to give background information for a past tense event.**

   had
   I ~~have~~ never seen my sister in real life, so I was nervous the first time we met.

   had been dreaming
   I ~~have dreamed~~ about meeting her, and I finally did.

2. **Use the past perfect or past perfect progressive to give a reason for a past event.**

   had been crying
   Her eyes were red and puffy because she ~~cried~~.

3. **Use the past perfect (not the past perfect progressive) for a completed earlier event.**

   arranged
   They had ~~been arranging~~ a time to meet, but both of them forgot about it.

4. **Use the past perfect (not present perfect) to describe a completed event that happened before a past event.**

   had
   I ~~have~~ visited her in Maine twice before she came to visit me.

Editing Task

Find and correct seven more mistakes in the paragraphs about sibling differences.

    had
I ~~have~~ never really thought about sibling differences until my own children were
had been living
born. When we had our first child, my husband and I ~~have~~ lived in Chicago for just a few
hadn't
months. We ~~have~~ not made many friends yet, so we spent all our time with our child. Baby
Gilbert was happy to be the center of attention. He depended on us for everything.

5   By the time our second son, Chase, was born, we *had* ~~have~~ developed a community of
friends and a busier social life. We frequently visited friends and left the children at home
with a babysitter. As a result of our busy schedules, Chase was more independent. One
hung
day I had just ~~been hanging~~ up the phone when Chase came into the room. Chase picked
up the phone and started talking into it. I thought he was pretending, but I was wrong. He
figured
10 had ~~been figuring~~ out how to use the phone!

    When my husband came home, he was tired because he *had been working* ~~worked~~ all day. When I
had
told him about Chase's phone conversation, though, he became very excited. Gilbert ~~has~~
never used the phone as a child. At first, we were surprised that Chase was so different
been learning
from Gilbert. Then we realized that because of our busy lifestyles, Chase had ~~learned~~ to be
15 independent.

6 | Grammar for Writing

Using Past Perfect to Provide Background Information and Reasons

Writers use the past perfect to provide background information and reasons for past situations and actions. Read these examples:

I had always thought that I was an only child, but I recently discovered that I have a sister. My parents had given me up for adoption. When I was 15, I decided to find my biological parents.

Pre-writing Task behavior = comportamiento

1 Read the paragraph. What does the writer believe about the influence of the environment on relationships? What example does the writer use to explain this?

The Effects of Friends on Sibling Relationships

I believe that the experiences that a person has outside the home can be as influential as experiences inside the home. Examples of this are siblings who start out very similar but become very different from one another as they grow older. For example, Andy and Frank are two brothers who are only two years apart. They did everything together

5 and were best friends until they started junior high. After Andy had been in seventh grade for a little while, he started to change. He had made new friends at school, so he and Frank did not see each other much during the day. Frank had made new friends, too. In fact, Andy's new friends did not like Frank very much, so Andy did not feel comfortable asking Frank to spend time with them. By the time Andy and Frank were in high school, they had

10 grown very far apart. They had made different friends and they had developed different interests. They had been similar when they were young, but Andy and Frank had very little in common as young adults.

2 Read the paragraph again. Underline the sentences that contain both simple past and past perfect verbs. Double underline the sentences with verbs only in the past perfect. Circle the time clauses. Notice how the time clauses help clarify the earlier time period.

Writing Task

1 *Write* Use the paragraph in the Pre-writing Task to help you write about different conditions that influence people's behavior. Give examples from events and situations you have observed to support your opinion.

2 *Self-Edit* Use the editing tips to improve your paragraph. Make any necessary changes.

1. Did you use the past perfect to give background information and provide reasons?
2. Did you use time words and time clauses to clarify the time periods in your sentences or emphasize that some events happened earlier than others?
3. Did you avoid the mistakes in the Avoid Common Mistakes chart on page 59?

UNIT 5

Be Going To, Present Progressive, and Future Progressive

Looking Ahead at Technology

1 Grammar in the Real World

A How is technology used today? Read the web article about technology use in the future. What is one way that technology use will develop?

Looking Ahead at Technology

Technology has become an essential part of everyday life for many people. We depend on the Internet, for example, for easy access to information and communication. Computers, cell phones, and other handheld gadgets provide constant
5 entertainment. No one knows for sure what technology **is going to bring** us in the future. However, there is no doubt that it **will continue** to drastically affect how we live and work.

Market research[1] suggests that in the future we **will be depending** on the Internet even more than we are now.
10 According to British writer Tim Walker, the world **will be** "blanketed[2] by Wi-Fi."[3] This **will allow** us to connect to the Internet almost anywhere. However, people **will not want** to carry around bulky laptops. Instead, computers **will be** wearable. Computers **will be** combined with watches, glasses, shirts, or backpacks. Some people are already using glasses which project the Internet onto the glass lenses. People **will be** able to see the Internet but also
15 see the rest of the world. Combining computers and glasses **is going to become** even more popular in the future.

Other people **will use** fabric-based computers. This technology, called "smart clothing," **will combine** computers with clothing. With smart clothing, people **will be** able to look at their shirt sleeve and see the news or the weather, which people **will download**
20 directly from the Internet. Researchers predict that the use of laptops and computers **will decrease** as the availability of smart clothing increases.

In the future, there **will be** many advances in technology and many changes in the ways technology affects our lives. As technology changes, devices such as smart clothing **will become** more and more popular. In short, it is clear that almost everything we do **will**
25 **happen** with the help of technology.

¹**market research:** the study of consumer behavior | ²**blanket:** cover | ³**Wi-Fi:** a system of wireless networks, especially used for the Internet

B *Comprehension Check* Answer the questions.

1. What are some ways technology will change in the future? *1-throught the development of fabric based computers.*
2. How will people in the future access the Internet? *2- woold blanketed w/wi-fi computers)*
3. What is "smart clothing"? *Combination of computers + clothing*

C *Notice* Find the sentences in the article and complete them.

1. Market research suggests that in the future we *will be depending* on the Internet even more than we do now.

2. Combining computers and glasses *is going to become* even more popular in the future.

3. Other people *will use* fabric-based computers.

How many different verb forms in items 1–3 did the author of the reading use to talk about the future?

2 | *Be Going To*, Present Progressive, and Simple Present for Future

▶ Grammar Presentation

Be going to and the present progressive are used to describe future plans. The simple present is used to describe a scheduled future event.	I **am going to buy** a new smartphone. The store **is offering** free Wi-Fi all next week. The new movie **comes out** next week.

2.1 *Be Going to* vs. Present Progressive for Future Plans

a. Use *be going to* + base form of the verb to express general intentions and plans for the future.	I**'m going to buy** a 3D TV someday.
You can use expressions like *probably, most likely, I think*, and *I believe* with this form.	My parents probably **aren't going to buy** one. I think they **are going to save** their money for a trip instead.
b. Use the present progressive to express definite plans and arrangements for the future, especially when a time or place is mentioned.	I**'m buying** a 3D TV tomorrow. The class **is taking** a trip to the science museum next week.
c. In many cases, both forms can be used to express the same idea.	I**'m watching** a movie this evening. I**'m going to watch** a movie this evening.

2.2 Simple Present for Scheduled Events

Use the simple present for scheduled events in the future and for timetables. Some common verbs for this use include *arrive, be, begin, finish, leave,* and *start*.	The conference **begins** on Monday and **ends** on Friday. Beginning June 10, all trains to New England **leave** from platform 14.

▶ # Grammar Application

Exercise 2.1 *Be Going To* or Present Progressive?

A Complete the conversation about e-readers. Use *be going to* or the present progressive and the verbs in parentheses. Sometimes more than one answer is possible.

Mei   I <u>'m going to buy</u> (buy) an e-reader one of these days. Any suggestions?
(1)

Kyle Look at this ad. Big Buy <u>is going to have</u> (have) a sale on the iRead next week.
(2) is having

Mei   How much is it?

are lowering
Kyle They <u>are going to lower</u> (lower) the price to $69.
(3)

Mei   That's great. I'<u>m visiting</u> (visit) a friend near that area <u>next week</u>.
(4)

I'll stop by.

Kyle That's a great price.

Mei   Yes, it's quite a deal. You know, I think companies <u>are going to give</u> (give)
(5)

e-readers away someday. They're getting less and less expensive. Soon they'll

be free!

am going to meet
Kyle I've got to go. I'<u>m meeting</u> (meet) some friends for dinner. What
(6)

are doing
<u>are</u> you <u>going to do</u> (do) tonight?
(7)   (7)

Mei   I'<u>m going to go</u> (go) straight home. I'm tired.
(8)
I'm going

B *Pair Work* Compare your answers with a partner. Discuss the reason for each of your answers.

In the first sentence, one of these days *made the plan seem like an intention because he wasn't really sure, so* be going to *is correct.*

Exercise 2.2 *Be Going To*, Present Progressive, or Simple Present?

Look at the clues. Then complete the sentences about a new phone. Use *be going to*, the present progressive, or the simple present form of the verbs in parentheses.

1. Clue: definite plan

   BestProduct _is launching_ (launch) a new YouPhone next week.

2. Clue: scheduled event

   The new YouPhone ___becomes___ (become) available in stores on Friday, January 15.

3. Clue: definite plan

   All employees ___are preparing___ (prepare) for a busy first day of sales.

4. Clue: definite plan

   All stores ___are openning___ (open) at 8:00 a.m. that day.

5. Clue: definite plan

   The stores ___are giving___ (give) away water and free coffee to customers in line.

6. Clue: scheduled event

   School ___closes___ (close) early that day because of a holiday.

7. Clue: future intention

   The newspaper ___are going to interview___ (interview) Anne Green, a representative from BestProduct.

8. Clue: future intention

   Ms. Green ___is___ probably ___going to speak___ (speak) for a few minutes and then answer some questions.

Exercise 2.3 More *Be Going To*, Present Progressive, or Simple Present?

A Complete the article about a social networking site. Use *be going to*, the present progressive, or the simple present form of the verbs in parentheses. Sometimes more than one answer is possible.

Changes Ahead for Youth Network

Youth Network, Inc., announced today that it ___is buying___ (buy)
(1)
FacePlace, the popular social networking website. FacePlace
has already accepted Youth Network's offer of $3.1 billion. The
company has not made any definite plans, but it ___is___ probably
(2)
___starting___ (start) asking people to pay for the
(2)
site. It won't be free anymore. In addition, some people think that the
network ___puts___ (put) ads on the site. Another
(3)
possibility is that Youth Network ___is showing___ (show)
(4)
its TV programs on FacePlace. Next week, FacePlace technicians
___are going to meet___ (meet) with Youth Network technicians
(5)
to help with the changes. They ___are planning___ (plan) to
(6)
shut down the old FacePlace website at 1:00 a.m. on Saturday,
August 10. The new Youth Network site ___is going to go___ (go)
(7)
live at 6:00 a.m. the next day.

B *Pair Work* Compare your answers with a partner. Discuss the reason for each of your answers.

In item 1, the plan seems definite because the company made an announcement to the press, so the company arranged the action. The present progressive is correct.

3 | *Will* and *Be Going To*

▶ Grammar Presentation

Will and *be going to* can both express future plans and predictions. They can also be used in other ways, for example, to make a promise or to express an expectation.	Wi-Fi **will allow** us to connect to the Internet almost anywhere. Technology **is going to become** easier to use. I**'ll help** you with your computer.

3.1 *Will* and *Be Going to* for Predictions and Expectations

a. Use *will* and *be going to* for predictions, expectations, or guesses about the future.	People **will connect** to the Internet from almost anywhere. I**'m not going to** have Internet access while I'm on vacation.
b. You can use *certainly, definitely, likely, maybe, perhaps,* and *probably* to show degrees of certainty.	Technology **will** <u>certainly</u> **be** more sophisticated in the future.
Use *certainly, definitely, likely,* and *probably* after *will* or after *be.*	There **will** <u>probably</u> **be** many people at the concert next week. People **are** <u>definitely</u> **going to wear** computers in the future.
Use *maybe* and *perhaps* at the beginning of sentences.	<u>Maybe</u> I**'ll get** an e-reader this year.
c. Use *be going to* to predict the future when there is present evidence.	My computer is behaving strangely. I think it**'s going to crash**.
d. Generally, in speaking, *be going to* is used for intentions and plans. However, in academic writing, *will* is used much more frequently.	By 2020, people throughout the world **will access** the Internet.

3.2 *Will* for Requests, Offers, and Promises

Use *will* for requests, offers, and promises.	**Will** you **help** me buy a computer? I**'ll research** the best buys for you.

3.3 *Will* for Quick Decisions

Use *will* for decisions made at the time of speaking.	*"We need someone to take notes for our group."* *"I'll do it."* (quick decision)
The same verb with *be going to* expresses a previous decision.	*"Bob is going to do it."* (previous decision)

▶ Grammar Application

Exercise 3.1 *Will* or *Be Going To?*

A Complete the phone conversation between an employee and a technician in the tech department. Circle *will* or *be going to*. If both are possible, circle both.

Bill　Tech Department, Bill speaking.

Kate　Hi, Bill. This is Kate in Business Development. My laptop is behaving very strangely this morning. It **will / 's going to** crash at any minute. **Will you / Are you going to**
(1)　　　　　　　　　　　　　　　　　　　　　　　　　(2)
send someone to look at it?

Bill　Of course. I **will / am going to** .
(3)

Kate　Soon?

Bill　I promise. **I'll / 'm going to** send Dave in five minutes.
(4)

Kate　Bill, **will you / are you going to** send Silvia instead, please? She's fixed this same
(5)
problem before.

Bill　Oh, OK. Then Silvia **will / is going to** be there in about 5 minutes.
(6)

Kate　Thanks, Bill. Bye.

A few minutes later:

Silvia　Hi, Kate. Are you having problems with your laptop again?

Kate　Uh-huh. This is the fourth time! I think **I'll / 'm going to** ask for a new computer.
Prediction　　　　　　　　　　　　　　　　(7)

Silvia　**I'll / 'm going to** look at it for you.
(8)

Kate　Thanks, Silvia.

B *Pair Work*　Compare your answers with a partner. Discuss the reason for each of your answers.

I chose be going to *for item 1 because the speaker is making a prediction based on evidence. She said her computer was behaving strangely. That's evidence that it might be crushing.*

Exercise 3.2 More *Will* or *Be Going To*?

A 🔊 Listen to a discussion about education and technology. Complete the sentences with the form of the verbs you hear.

Ms. Ng   __Will__ (1) everyone please __be__ (1) quiet? The noise __is gonna make__ (2) it hard to hear our speaker. And __Will__ (3) someone please __will open__ (3) the windows? The air conditioner isn't working well.

Alex   I __'ll do__ (4) it.

Ms. Ng   Thanks. And __Will__ (5) you all please __turn off__ (5) your cell phones? I promise I __won't ask__ (6) you   *Prediction*   to do anything else except enjoy today's presentation. OK, today,   *Prediction*   we __'re going to hear__ (7) from an expert on education, Dr. Paul Bell. I'm sure you __'ll__ (8) all __find__ (8) him very interesting.

Dr. Bell   Thank you. Well, it's clear that the world of the college student   *Prediction*   __is going to be__ (9) very different in a matter of a few years. For example, we already know that colleges __will offer__ (10) *are gonna offer* more courses online. This __will save__ (11) money for schools and for students. Students __will save__ (12) money on transportation costs because they can learn anywhere. Online learning also means that schools and individuals __will you__ (13) fewer resources such as paper and fuel. But what __will__ (14) the consequences of online education __be__ (14)?

B Find an example of each meaning, and write the number of the item next to it.

__1__ a request   _____ a promise

_____ a prediction based on evidence   _____ an offer

C *Group Work*   Make predictions or share expectations about the future of phones, TVs, movies, schools, cars, or something else. As a group, write five sentences. Use *will* and *be going to*. Share your sentences with the class.

4 | Future Progressive

▶ Grammar Presentation

The future progressive emphasizes an action that will be in progress at a specific time in the future. *[handwritten: énfesais]*

We **will be reading** most books electronically in five years. *[handwritten: moust / iláctronicly]*
Everyone **is going to be using** computers to watch TV in 2020.

4.1 Forming Future Progressive

a. Form the future progressive with *will* or *be going to* + *be* + verb + *-ing*.

People **will be working** on smartphones instead of laptops in 10 years.
Consumers **are not going to be using** coins and paper money by the year 2025.

b. Use the future progressive to describe or ask about an action in progress at a time in the future.

Will you **be working** tomorrow at noon?

Use *certainly, definitely, likely,* and *probably* after *will* or *be going to* to show degrees of certainty. Use them before *won't.*

I **definitely won't be watching** TV tonight.
I**'ll probably be working** on my project all afternoon.

c. Sometimes *will* + base form and future progressive are very similar in meaning, especially when the future event will occur at an indefinite time.

I think the computer specialist **will arrive** later. I don't see her.
I think the computer specialist **will be arriving** later. I don't see her.

4.2 Future Progressive and *Be Going To* Contrasted

The future progressive and *be going to* can both express plans and intentions.
Use the future progressive for a more formal tone.
Use *be going to* for a less formal tone. *[handwritten: menos]*

Mr. Lee, **will** you **be coming** with me to the lecture on technology tomorrow? (more formal)
Marie, **are** you **going to come** with me to the lecture tomorrow? (less formal) *[handwritten: menos formal]*

▶ Grammar Application

Exercise 4.1 Future Progressive

Complete the interview about the future of TV. Use the future progressive form of the verbs in parentheses.

Claire Mr. Reyes, you've been involved in the television industry for well over 30 years. We know that the TV industry is changing rapidly. Tell us about its future.

Mr. Reyes Certainly. The television industry __will be creating__ (create) its own
                                                              (1)

shows in the future. It __is going to be saving__ *ahorrar* (save) a lot of money
                                  (2)

this way because it __won't be buying__ (not / buy) the shows from
                            (3)

other producers. In addition, people __will be watching__ (watch)
                                              (4)

TV using many different types of media.

Claire What do you mean? *que quieres decir?*

Mr. Reyes I mean that we __will be ~~be~~ using__ (use) computers, phones,
                                        (5)

e-readers, and other gadgets to watch TV shows more and more. People

__won't be watching__ (not / watch) by themselves, either. They
              (6)

__will be socializing__ (socialize) through social networks as they
              (7)

watch TV.

Claire How will that work?

Mr. Reyes *el espectador* Viewers __are going to be sending__ (send) or texting messages, and they
                                                (8)

__will be chating__ (chat) with others while they watch. In fact,
            (9)

they have already started to do so. This will affect marketing, too.

Claire In what way?

Mr. Reyes *anunciar* Advertisers __will be asking__ (ask) viewers to share their
                                          (10)

opinions of the things they are viewing, such as products in ads or clothes

worn by actors.

Claire It sounds as though advertising will become interactive.

Mr. Reyes Exactly.

Claire Thank you very much, Mr. Reyes, for taking the time to talk to us.

Exercise 4.2 Future Progressive or *Be Going To*?

A Complete the formal announcement of a lecture on the future of movies. Use the future progressive form of the verbs in parentheses. Sometimes more than one answer is possible.

The Future of Movies
Presented by Dr. Maria Sanderson
Michaels Hall
8:00 p.m., Friday, January 7

What __will__ people __be seeing__ (see) at the movies 10 years from
⁽¹⁾   ⁽¹⁾
now? __are__ we __going to be watching__ (watch) only 3D movies? __Will__
        ⁽²⁾   ⁽²⁾   ⁽³⁾

are people going to people __be viewing__ (view) movies in theaters, or will theaters
                                  ⁽³⁾

disappear? Dr. Sanderson __will be discussing__ (discuss) the future
                          is going ⁽⁴⁾ *to be*

of the movie industry and the movie-going experience in general. She *is gonna be*

__will be giving__ (give) examples of past, present, and future film
        ⁽⁵⁾

technology, and she __will be taking__ (take) questions from the audience.
                    is going ⁽⁶⁾ *to be taking*

B Complete the conversation between two students about the lecture in A. Use *be going to* or the future progressive and the verbs in parentheses. Sometimes more than one answer is possible.

Chao   __Are__ you __going to go__ (go) to the lecture?
         ⁽¹⁾   ⁽¹⁾   *be attending*

Verónica Yes, I __am__ definitely __gonna attend__ (attend). What about you?
                  ⁽²⁾   ⁽²⁾

'm not gonna to go ← Chao No, I __'m not going to going__ (not / go). I'm not interested. Why __Will__ you
I won't be going   ⁽³⁾   ⁽⁴⁾

__be going__ (go)? *are you going – are you gonna go*
    ⁽⁴⁾

Verónica I'm taking film history, so it will help me with my class. I __'m going to take__ (take)
                                                                          ⁽⁵⁾
          'm gonna ask   *will be taking*
notes. I __am__ also __going to be asking__ (ask) questions. *am gonna be taking*
          ⁽⁶⁾   ⁽⁶⁾
          will *be asking*

Exercise 4.3 More Future Progressive

Over to You What will you be doing 20 years in the future? Where will you be living? What will you be doing for entertainment? Write five sentences about the way you imagine the future. Use the future progressive. Share your sentences with a partner.

5 | Avoid Common Mistakes ⚠️

1. Use the future progressive to talk about actions that will be in progress at a future time.

                          be working

You won't see me next week because I will ~~work~~ in Seoul.

2. Use the simple present for scheduled events.

                    starts

The teleconference ~~will always start~~ at 4:00 p.m.

3. Remember to use *be* with *be going to*.

  am

I ^ going to give a presentation on the twenty-fifth of next month.

4. Use the present progressive (not *will*) when talking about definite plans.

       are traveling

We ~~will travel~~ to the home office at the end of the month.

Editing Task

Find and correct the mistakes in the e-mail about travel plans.

Hi Layla,

                                                                    be presenting

Thanks for agreeing to take this trip on short notice. Vinh can't go because he'll ~~present~~

at a conference in Chicago, and your name came up immediately as a replacement. We know

                                                      are

you are familiar with the software, so we feel confident that you going to do a great job.

5   Your first flight leaves Newark Liberty International Airport at 9:00 a.m. on the twenty-second

     Will be arriving ❤   *will be*

and arrives in London late in the afternoon. That evening you are having dinner with James

                     are

and Eleanor Wilson. They going to be driving you around during your stay.

    On Monday, your first presentation starts at 9:00 a.m. at the headquarters of Logan and

                                                             being *ocupado*

Lowe. We have scheduled three presentations that day. You are going to be very busy!

        Will be leaving

10   You leave London on the 8:00 p.m. flight to Beijing. In Beijing you won't have much free

                   ×   *is*

time because you ~~will~~ give your presentation at several companies. Alan going to send you

the details in a separate e-mail. You are flying when he sends it.

Best of luck,

Antoine

UNIT
Be Going To, Present Progressive, and Future Progressive
Writing Task
1 Write Use the paragraph in the
change. You can.....

UNIT 6

Future Time Clauses, Future Perfect, and Future Perfect Progressive

Business Practices of the Future

1 Grammar in the Real World

A What personal information do you have online? Read the web article about cloud computing. What are the pros and cons?

Smart Businesses Have Their Heads in the Cloud

More and more people are accessing their personal electronic data from their phones and other devices using cloud computing. *Cloud computing* is the term for computer work on the Internet. Instead of storing files on your own computer or mobile device, you pay a cloud services provider[1] to keep everything on a computer
5 in another location.

In addition to storing information, cloud computing sometimes offers software and management tools that can help companies cut costs. According to a recent survey on
10 cloud computing, by 2020, many companies **will have eliminated**[2] their technology departments and **saved** large sums of money because they **will have been using** the cloud. In addition, **when these businesses move**
15 **their work to the cloud**, they will not need to spend money on software updates because the cloud will provide access to the most current technology.

[1]**provider:** a business that provides access to a service, such as the Internet or the cloud | [2]**eliminate:** remove or take away

Cloud computing has risks, however. Some people say that cloud services are not secure. Also, experts say that there are a growing number of attacks by hackers[3] on
20 secure sites. Many companies will not use cloud services **until they are confident that their data will be secure**.

Nonetheless, companies will save a lot of money and will attract more customers by using the cloud. One study suggests that cloud computing **will have generated** more than $45.5 billion by 2015. However, Internet services are not always reliable,
25 and connection breakdowns are costly. Furthermore, the increasing number of hackers will pose a risk. Are these risks worth it?

[3]**hacker:** a person who breaks into computer networks and steals private information

B *Comprehension Check* Answer the questions.

1. What will happen to many technology departments in the future? Why?
2. What are some risks of cloud computing?

C *Notice* Complete these sentences from the article.

1. According to a recent survey on cloud computing, by 2020, many companies
   <u>Will have eliminated</u> their technology departments and saved large
   sums of money because they <u>Will have been using</u> the cloud.
2. Many companies <u>Will not use</u> cloud services until they are
   confident that their data will be secure.

Look at the verbs that you wrote. There are three different forms for describing the future. Which form describes completed future events?

Will have eliminated = future perfect

Will have been using = future perfect progressive

Will not use = future time clauses.

2 | Future Time Clauses

▶ Grammar Presentation

Future time clauses show the order of future events.	*Our business will increase **as soon as we improve our marketing**.* *We won't use a social networking site **until we hire someone to monitor it**.*

2.1 Using Time Clauses for Future Events

a. Use the simple present in the time clause. Use the future with *will* or *be going to* in the main clause.	*After I **buy** my new phone, I'**ll use** the cloud to store my data.* *We'**re going to research** cloud services before we **choose** one.*
You can also use the present perfect in the time clause to emphasize the completion of the event.	*Until business **has improved**, the company won't hire new employees.*
b. Use time clauses with *after*, *as soon as*, *once*, and *when* when the event in the time clause happens first.	FIRST EVENT ***As soon as/Once** they get cloud services, their* SECOND EVENT *business will improve.* SECOND EVENT FIRST EVENT *I'll find a good job **after** I graduate.*
c. Use time clauses with *before* and *until* when the event in the time clause happens second.	FIRST EVENT SECOND EVENT *I'll finish the report **before** I leave.*
Use *until* to show when the event in the main clause will stop or change.	 *I'll continue working on the report **until** she calls.*
In time clauses with *not . . . until*, the action in the time clause happens first.	SECOND EVENT *We **won't** start using the software **until** all* FIRST EVENT *employees are trained.*

2.1 Using Time Clauses for Future Events (continued)

d. The time clause can come first or last in the sentence. Use a comma when the time clause comes first.	***Once we start using the cloud,*** we'll save money. *She is going to move **as soon as she finds a better job.***

Tan Pronto
as soon as = en cuanto

2.2 Using Time Clauses with *When* and *While* for Ongoing Events

a. Use *when* or *while* with the simple present in the time clause and *will* or *be going to* in the main clause to show two events that are happening at the same time.	*I'll be taking* my vacation **while** the company **moves** to its new office.
You can also use the present progressive in the time clause to express an ongoing event.	*esperar* *The staff **is going to wait** outside **while** / **when** we're discussing our budget.* presupuesto
b. Use the simple present in the *when* clause to interrupt an ongoing event in the main clause.	*We'll be meeting when he arrives.* (The meeting will be happening. He will arrive during the meeting.)

▶ Grammar Application

Exercise 2.1 Using Future Time Clauses

A Read the sentences about cloud computing. Underline the time clauses, and circle the conjunctions in each clause. Double underline the main clauses.

1. Once a company starts using the cloud, it will have access to more customers.

2. Companies will start saving a great deal of money as soon as they move their work to the cloud.

3. Companies are going to have difficulty competing until they begin advertising on social networking sites.

4. After companies have moved to cloud computing, they will receive technological support and updates on new technology.

5. Once companies believe that the data is secure with cloud services, more companies are going to move their data to the cloud.

B Complete the sentences from a meeting about cloud computing. Circle the correct form of the verbs.

1. I think we **are going to attract** / **attract** more international customers once we **are going to start** / **start** using cloud computing.

2. I'm concerned that our data (will not be) / is safe
   once we **begin** / will begin to use cloud computing.

3. As soon as our company **will start** / (starts) using
   the cloud, we (are going to save) / save
   a lot of money. We will be able to eliminate our
   technology department.

4. We **are going to save** / have saved up to $10,000
   annually after we **will change** / (have changed)
   to using only electronic forms.

5. I'm pretty worried that the company
   (isn't going to save) / hasn't saved money until cloud services **will become** / (become)
   more reliable and secure.

6. As soon as the company marketing department **will create** / (has created) a social
   networking site, we **have** / (will have) free advertising.

7. We (won't approve) / approve using cloud services until the manager
   (has approved) / will approve the budget.   hasta
   first event

Exercise 2.2 Time Clauses with *When* and *While*

Complete the conversation about social networking and blogs in advertising. Use the
correct form of the verbs in parentheses. Sometimes more than one answer is possible.

Erin OK, everyone. We're going to have to find cheaper ways to market our

products.

Bo I'm sure that while we *'re discussing* (discuss) the new budget next week,
                               (1)
we'll think of some inexpensive ways to market our products.

Erin I think we should use social networking sites and blogs.

Bo I agree. Let's prepare a presentation. Lisa can write some descriptions of

our new products. I'll do research on the most popular social networking

sites while you _____find_____ (find) some interesting blogs.
          Suena bien   (2)   encontrar
Erin Sounds good. While we 're __doing__ (do) that, the art department
                                    (3)
will work on some drawings for our profile page.

Bo OK. I'll investigate how other food companies market themselves on social

networking sites while the art department ____works____ (work) on
                                                (4)
the drawings. dibujo

Erin Look for Dan's Imported Food. That's our biggest competitor.

Bo   Right. I'm sure that when I ___study___ (study) Dan's page, I'll get
     (5)
     some good ideas. I'll take notes while I ___'m looking___ (look) at it.
                                              (6)

Erin While you ___analyze___ (analyze) Dan's page, I'll think about how
                 (7)
      we can use blogs for marketing as well.

Bo   Great idea. While you ___re thinking___ (think) about blogs, I'll get
                           (8)
      some information on the impact e-mail can have.

Erin Good plan! Let's get moving!

Exercise 2.3 Time Clauses with *When*

Look at Jared's meeting agenda. Then complete the sentences about what is going to
happen. Pay close attention to the sequence of events. Use *will* or the future progressive
of the verbs in parentheses. Sometimes there is more than one correct answer.

Agenda

8:00—8:20	Introduce new employees
8:15	Sara arrives; introduce Sara
8:20—10:00	Brainstorm for new budget
10:00—10:20	Take break
10:00	Photocopy worksheets
10:20	Return from break; hand out worksheets; put everyone into small groups
10:20—11:30	Small-group discussions; walk around and take notes
11:30	Vice president arrives; reassemble group

1. I ___will be introducing___ (introduce) the new employees when Sara arrives.
2. When Sara arrives, I ___will introduce___ (introduce) her.
3. I ___will photocopy___ (photocopy) the worksheets when the group takes a break.
4. I ___will hand out___ (hand out) the worksheets when the group returns from the break.
5. When people return from the break, I ___will put___ (put) them into
   small groups.
6. When people work in small groups, I ___will be walking___ (walk) around and
   ___will be taking___ (take) notes.
7. When the vice president arrives, the groups ___will be finishing___ (finish)
   their discussions.
8. I ___will reassemble___ (reassemble) the group when the vice president arrives.

Exercise 2.4 More Future Time Clauses

A Combine the sentences from Marta and Aaron's "to-do" list. Note that *M* is Marta and *A* is Aaron. Use *after*, *until*, or *when* with the present perfect in the time clauses. Sometimes more than one answer is possible.

1. Jan.–Feb. (M & A): Research and plan the business
   Mar. (M): Get a loan *préstamo*

   After Marta and Aaron have researched and planned the business, Marta will get a loan./Marta will get a loan after Marta and Aaron have researched and planned the business.

2. Mar.–Apr. (M & A): Get business training *negocio*
   May–Jun. (M & A): Get management training *trainning*

   After Marta and Aaron have gotten business Trainning, they will get manag

3. Apr. (A): Think of a name for the business
   May (M): Find a location for the business *location for the*

   When Aaron has thought of a name for the business, Marta will find

4. Sept. (M): Get a tax identification number
   Oct. (M & A): Buy equipment for the business

   After Marta has gotten a tax indent. number, they will buy equipment for the bu

5. Nov. (M & A): Promote the business
   Dec. (M & A): Open the business

   they won't open the business until they have promoted the business

6. First week of Dec. (M & A): Have a sale
   Dec. 25–31: Close for one week

   When they have had a sale, they will close for one week

B *Pair Work* Compare your sentences with a partner. What are some different ways to express the same ideas?

   A *I wrote "After Marta and Aaron have done some research, they will get a loan."*
   B *I wrote "Marta and Aaron won't get a loan until they have done some research."*

3 | Future Perfect vs. Future Perfect Progressive

▶ Grammar Presentation

The future perfect is used to describe events that will be completed at a time in the future. The future perfect progressive describes events that will be in progress at a time in the future. These forms are much more common in speaking than in academic writing.	*By 2020, many companies **will have moved** their work to online servers.* *By 2020, our company **will have been using** online servers for 10 years.*

3.1 Forming Future Perfect

will + have + past participle

Form the future perfect with *will + have* + the past participle of the main verb. Form the negative by putting *not* between *will* and *have*, or use *won't have*.	*By May, we **will have opened** the new office.* ***Will** the team **have finished** the project by next week?* *By next week, the team **won't have finished** the project.*

3.2 Forming Future Perfect Progressive

Form the future perfect progressive with *will + have + been* + the *-ing* form of the main verb. Form the negative by putting *not* between *will* and *have*, or use *won't have*.	*By May, I **will have been working** here for a year.* *How long **will** you **have been working** here by next month?* *We **won't have been working** here for very long.*

3.3 Future Perfect and Future Perfect Progressive Contrasted

a. Use the future perfect for an event that will be completed by a time in the future.	*I **will have made** my decision before tomorrow.* ***Will** she **have told** you her decision by noon?*
b. Use the future perfect progressive for an event that will be in progress at a time in the future.	*How long **will** he **have been working** in the computer industry on his fortieth birthday?*
c. You can introduce a particular future time with a preposition such as *before* and *by* (*by that time, by then*) or a time clause in the simple present.	*He**'ll have been working** for us for 10 years by next June.* *They just moved to Dallas, so they **won't have been living** there long when you visit next month.*
You can use *already* to express certainty about future situations.	*We can't change the plan. The managers **will** already **have had** their meeting by Monday.* *They**'ll have** already **made** a decision by the time we get there.*

3.3 Future Perfect and Future Perfect Progressive *(continued)*

d. Use the future perfect, not the future perfect progressive, with stative verbs such as *have*, *hear*, and *know*.

She **will have known** about it by then.

NOT She ~~will have been knowing~~ about it by then.

▶ Grammar Application

Exercise 3.1 Future Perfect

Look at the schedules. Then complete the sentences with the future perfect. Use the negative when necessary.

10:45 a.m.: Katie will finish the report.
11:00 a.m.: The meeting will start.
11:15 a.m.: Kyle will arrive.

1. Katie _will have finished the report_ by the time Kyle arrives.

2. The meeting _won't have met_ _____ by the time Kyle arrives.

3. By 11:00 Kyle _____ .

12:30 p.m.: The meeting will end.
 1:30 p.m.: Kyle and Katie will go out to eat lunch.
 2:30 p.m.: Kyle and Katie will return from lunch.

4. By 12:40, the meeting _____ .

5. By 1:40, Kyle and Katie _____ .

6. By 2:15, Kyle and Katie _____ .

5:30 p.m.: Kyle's wife arrives home.
6:00 p.m.: Kyle leaves work.
7:30 p.m.: Kyle and his family will eat dinner.

7. Kyle's wife _____ before Kyle leaves work.

8. Kyle _____ by 6:15.

9. At 6:45, Kyle and his family _____ .

Exercise 3.2 Future Perfect Progressive

Read Eric's work schedule. Then complete the sentences with the information in the schedule. Use the future perfect progressive and *for*.

Tuesday	Wednesday	Thursday–Friday
8:30: Be at work 12:00: Lunch meeting with Mark at restaurant 1:00–4:00: Discuss new project 5:00: Meet with Japanese tutor; cancel tutoring sessions for Wed.– Fri. 6:15–7:15: Call from Japan	8:00: Pick up laptop from IT 9:00–5:00: Attend software training; bring lunch from home	9:00–5:00: Attend software training; bring lunch from home 6:00–8:00: Work out at the gym

1. By 4:30 on Tuesday, Eric / work / hours

   By 4:30 on Tuesday, Eric will have been working for 8 hours.

2. By 4:00 on Tuesday, Eric / discuss the new project / hours

   _____

   _____

3. By 6:45 on Tuesday, Eric / talk on the phone / hour

   _____

   _____

4. By 4:00 on Wednesday, Eric / attend a software training / hours

   _____

   _____

5. By 5:00 on Friday, Eric / attend a software training / days

   _____

   _____

6. By 7:15 on Friday, Eric / work out at the gym / minutes

   _____

   _____

Exercise 3.3 Time Clauses with Future Perfect and Future Perfect Progressive

A 🔊 A company is making its building energy-efficient and healthier for its employees. Read the time line. Then listen to questions about the time line. Circle *Yes* or *No*.

Time Line

February 2015	Approve the building plans
March 2015	Find a temporary site for workers
April 2015	Move into the temporary site
May 2015	Construction firm starts construction; installs solar heating system
October 2015	Finish all construction; "green" interior designer arrives; install new workstations
February 2016	Move back into the building
June 2016	Water department inspects water quality
August 2016	Send report on building improvements to finance department
March 2017	New law starts that requires all buildings to have energy-saving features
August 2017	OSHA[1] (Occupational Safety and Health Administration) visit

[1]**OSHA:** a U.S. government agency that inspects companies' workplaces to make sure that the companies follow health and safety laws

1. Yes (No)   3. Yes No   5. Yes No   7. Yes No
2. Yes No   4. Yes No   6. Yes No   8. Yes No

B 🔊 Listen again and check your answers.

C *Over to You* Answer the questions. Then share your answers with a partner.

- What year will it be in two years?
- What will you have accomplished by that time?
- What will you have been doing until then?

4 | Avoid Common Mistakes ⚠️

1. **Use future forms in the main clause and present forms for the time clause.**

   We will buy it after we ~~will~~ get back from our trip.

2. **Remember to use the future perfect when describing a future event that occurs before another future event.**

   will have
   They∧ left by the time we get there, so we won't see them.

   have moved
   By that time, you will ~~move~~.

3. **Make sure you do not confuse the future perfect progressive with other forms.**

   living
   In June, we will have been ~~lived~~ in Texas for 2 years.

4. **Remember to use *will* when forming the future perfect.**

   will
   By this time next year, she∧ have gotten a better job.

Editing Task

Find and correct seven more mistakes in the paragraph about the future of health care

have changed
Experts say that by 2020, the health care industry will ~~change~~ in many ways because of technology and the Internet. I plan on working in this industry, so it is fascinating for me to know that by the time I graduate, the job market has changed dramatically. One change that interests me is in the doctor-patient relationship. By that time,

5 technology will empower patients because they will have been used the Internet to gather information and discuss information with others. Also, health-care companies will have been used cloud computing for a few years, so a patient's medical files will always be available to both the patient and the doctor. This means that, for example, when a patient will arrive for his appointment, he will not have to fill out forms, and the doctor have

10 already seen the patient's information. By the time a patient decides on a treatment, the doctor and patient will have been discussed many options. The whole health-care system will have improved, so more people will live in a state of health.

5 | Grammar for Writing ✎

Using Future Perfect and Future Perfect Progressive to Write About Completed and Ongoing Events in the Future

Writers use a combination of future forms to describe something that will happen in the future. They use the future perfect for events that will be completed in the future. They use the future perfect progressive for ongoing events in the future. Read these examples:

You'll <u>have become</u> an expert in cloud computing by the time you get your degree.
Once I get my degree, I <u>will have been</u> in the program for three years.
I'll <u>have been studying</u> for a year before I really understand cloud computing.
By next May, he <u>will have been working</u> in cloud computing for eight years.

Writers also often use the words *before, by, by the time,* and *once* to indicate the time of an event. *By* can be followed only by a time or noun phrase, such as *by 1981* or *by the end of the year. Before* can be followed by a time or noun phrase or by a clause such as *before he arrives. By the time* and *once* can be followed only by a clause.

Pre-writing Task

1 Read the paragraph about getting an IT certificate. Who do you think is the writer of this paragraph? Where would you find a paragraph similar to this one?

Getting an IT Certificate

Westport City College (WCC) has become a well-respected institution in the Westport community over the past several decades. By the end of this spring, WCC will have been educating students for 50 years. Once summer break begins, we will have served over 1 million Westport residents. WCC has always offered programs in leading fields

5 of industry, and we are constantly updating our programs to teach the most up-to-date information. Right now, we have exciting news for students with an interest in computers. By next fall, WCC will have been offering a certificate program in Information Technology for over 30 years, but we are planning many important changes to the program for September. For example, we will offer a specialized certificate in cloud computing next

10 fall. Two new professors will be joining our team of excellent instructors to help make this happen. Professor Gordon Jones will be teaching several basic courses, including Cloud Computing 101. By the time he joins us, Professor Jones will have been working in cloud computing for 10 years. Professor Margaret Chan will have trained employees to use

cloud computing in over a dozen successful technology companies by the time she begins

15 teaching at WCC. If you are interested in enrolling in our new and improved IT certificate program, please send your application right away. A lot of students are interested, and at this rate, we will have received over 200 applications by the end of the month!

2 Read the paragraph again. Circle the uses of the future perfect. Underline the uses of the future perfect progressive. Which actions will be completed in the future and which will be ongoing in the future? Double underline the expressions with *by*, *by the time*, and *once*. Which expressions are followed by a time or a noun phrase? Which are followed by clauses?

Writing Task

1 *Write* Use the paragraph in the Pre-writing Task to help you write about a new program of study you might be interested in. Imagine you are writing this paragraph for a brochure. Write about what the program will offer.

2 *Self-Edit* Use the editing tips to improve your paragraph. Make any necessary changes.

1. Did you use the future perfect to write about events that will be complete at a specific time?
2. Did you use the future perfect progressive to write about events that will be ongoing at a specific time?
3. Did you use the expressions *before*, *by*, *by the time*, and *once* to indicate times? Did you use time words and clauses after the appropriate expressions?
4. Did you avoid the mistakes in the Avoid Common Mistakes chart on page 87?

Social Modals

Learning How to Remember

1 Grammar in the Real World

A Have you ever forgotten something important? Read the article about memory improvement. Which memory-improvement technique do you think works best?

How to Improve Your Memory

Some people have excellent memories, but most of us struggle to remember at times. You know the feeling: You **have to give** a class presentation,
5 and you are terrified. As you wait your turn, you repeat the information over and over in your mind, but you keep forgetting a key point. You **should have brought** your notes with you, but where
10 are they? You **can't remember**. If you are more forgetful than you would like to be, you **might want to follow** the advice of memory-improvement experts. Whether you want to memorize a speech
15 or simply remember where you left your cell phone, these experts offer tips to jumpstart[1] your brain.

Gini Graham Scott, PhD, is the author of *30 Days to a More Powerful Memory*.
20 She points out that if you want to remember something, it is necessary that you pay attention. You **must observe** what you want to learn. People often

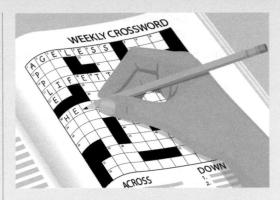

forget things simply because they weren't concentrating. Scott says that you **have** 25 **to** first **take in** information in order to save it in your memory. Other experts agree that visualization is an effective technique forgetful people **should try**. Create a mental picture – a picture 30 in your mind – of what you want to remember. The more unusual the image, the easier it will be to recall. For example, if you want to remember the due date for a final project, you **could visualize** 35 that date flashing in bold colors on a

---

[1]**jumpstart:** start something more quickly by giving it extra help

giant television screen. The scene **has to be** unusual and animated for the memory to stick. Memory specialists agree that 40 the more you exercise your brain, the better you will be able to remember information. How can you give your brain a workout?[2] You **might want to tackle** the daily crossword puzzle. Changing a 45 daily routine **is** also **supposed to work**. In addition, you **could challenge** your brain by writing with your nondominant[3]

hand or by taking a different route to school or work.

In today's multitasking[4] world, a good 50 memory is crucial. Without it, you **cannot maintain** order and priorities in your life. Fortunately, there are remedies[5] for forgetfulness. Practice careful observance, creative visualization, and mental exercise 55 to improve your memory.

---

[2]**workout:** a period of exercise | [3]**nondominant:** not as important, strong, or noticeable | [4]**multitask:** work on several tasks at the same time | [5]**remedy:** a substance or method for curing an illness, or a way of dealing with a problem or difficulty

B Comprehension Check Answer the questions.

1. What must you do to remember something, according to Gini Graham Scott?
2. What is visualization?
3. What are some ways to exercise your brain?

C Notice Find the sentences in the article and complete them.

1. You _____ _____ **give** a class presentation, and you are terrified.

2. You _____ **brought** your notes with you, but where are they?

3. Scott says that you _____ first **take in** information in order to save it in your memory.

Which sentences tell you it is necessary to do something?

(handwritten at top: past modal → modal + have + past part)

2 | Modals and Modal-like Expressions of Advice and Regret

▶ Grammar Presentation

(handwritten: try add to conclution)

The modals and modal-like expressions *could*, *had better*, *might*, *might want to*, *ought to*, and *should* can be used to express advice and regret.	You **should try** to improve your memory. I **should have** followed your advice.

(handwritten: A4 → A5)

2.1 Modals and Modal-like Expressions of Present and Future Advice

a. Use *could* and *might* to offer advice and suggestions or to give choices.	He **could do** some puzzles to improve his memory. You **might try** some tips for improving your memory.
Might (*not*) is often used with *want to* to give suggestions.	You **might not want to** start with the most difficult math problem. Try this one – it's easier.
b. Use *should* to say something is a good idea. Use *shouldn't* to say something is a bad idea.	Greg **should improve** his memory. Kate **shouldn't spend** so much time doing crossword puzzles.
Ought to is also possible, but less common. *Ought not* (*to*) is rare.	We **ought to take** a memory class together.
c. Use *had better* (*not*) only in informal conversation to give strong advice, especially as a warning.	You**'d better pay** attention now. (Or you will be in trouble.)
There is often a negative consequence if the advice or warning is not followed.	She **had better not forget** my book again tomorrow. (Or I will never lend her anything again.)
Had is almost always contracted, and often omitted, in informal conversation.	He**'d better** remember to bring his ID next time.

▸▸ Modals and Modal-like Expressions: See page A3.

2.2 Modals and Modal-like Expressions of Past Advice and Regret

a. Use *ought to have* or *should have* + the past participle for past events or situations that were advisable but did not happen.	She **ought to have been** at the lecture, but she was sick. (Being at the lecture was a good idea, but she wasn't there.) You **should have made** an effort to improve your memory. (Improving your memory was a good idea, but you didn't do it.)

2.2 Modals and Modal-like Expressions of Past Advice and Regret *(continued)*

b. Use *shouldn't have* + the past participle for past situations in which bad decisions were made. It is often used to express regret.	He **shouldn't have taken** that difficult class. (But he did, and now he's frustrated.) *We* **shouldn't have listened** to him. (But we did, and now we're sorry.)
c. *Should (not) have* may be used to criticize.	You **should have followed** his advice. (But you didn't, and now look at the trouble you're in.)

▶ Grammar Application

Exercise 2.1 Present and Future Advice

A Complete the class discussion about improving memory. Circle the correct words or expressions.

Ms. Yost So, let's review our discussion about improving memory. What advice do experts give students? Sara?

Sara You (**should**)/ **'d better not** pay
(1)
attention to what you're learning.

Ms. Yost Right. So, for example, what's one good way to pay attention?

Sara Um, you **'d better / could** take notes
(2)
while you're reading.

Manuel Or you **might / 'd better** take notes during lectures.
(3)

Ms. Yost Right. Do you have any other advice?

Manuel I think students **'d better / shouldn't** use a computer to take notes. They
(4)
might not / should use a pen and a piece of paper.
(5)

Ms. Yost Good idea. In fact, studies show that writing information by hand – instead of using a keyboard – helps you remember it better.

B *Pair work* Compare your answers with a partner. Discuss the reason for each of your answers.

I use had better not *for warnings. This isn't a warning. It's advice. So I chose* should *in number 1.*

Exercise 2.2 More Present and Future Advice

A Read the study tips from a web article. Then complete the e-mail to a friend. Use the tips and the modals in parentheses.

Study Tips

1. Try visualizing to remember dates and names.
2. Read your textbook two or three times.
3. Try teaching someone else the material.

4. Don't wait until the last minute to study.
5. Get plenty of sleep before a test.

Send   Attach   Save Draft   Spelling ▾   Cancel

Hi _____ ,

I know you're having trouble studying for tests. I just read some study tips online. Here's some advice:

1. (could) _You could try visualizing to remember dates and names._

2. (ought to) _____

3. (might) _____

4. (should not) _____

5. (had better) _____

I hope this helps! Talk to you soon.

Best,

_____

B *Pair Work* Tell a partner which tips you use. Then think of two more study tips and share them with another pair.

Exercise 2.3 Past Advice and Regret

A Complete the conversation about Phoebe, a student who plagiarized. Use the correct form of the words in parentheses.

Jake What happened to Phoebe? I heard she left college.

Sofia She committed plagiarism. She really

<u>shouldn't have copied</u> those articles from the
(1. not / should / copy)
Internet.

Jake I know. She _____
(2. should / take)
notes on the web articles. Then she

_____ _____ _____ her notes.
(3. ought to / summarize)

Sofia You're right. She _____
(4. should / give)
credit to the sources of the ideas, too. Why do you think she did this, anyway?

Jake Maybe she was under pressure or waited too long to start her paper. She

_____ _____ earlier.
(5. ought to / start)

Sofia I agree. She _____ _____ until the last minute.
(6. should / not / wait)

Jake Or she ___ _____ _____ to the teacher if she was
(7. should / talk)
having problems. Maybe we _____ her.
(8. should / help)

Sofia Yes, let's try to be more helpful the next time a classmate is stressed!

B *Pair Work* Compare your answers with a partner. Do you agree with the students' advice about Phoebe? What other advice would you give Phoebe?

C *Group Work* Think about a time when you made a decision you regret, or a time when a friend made a bad decision. What should you (or your friend) have done to make the situation better? Write five sentences with *should not have* + the past participle.

3 | Modals and Modal-like Expressions of Permission, Necessity, and Obligation

▶ Grammar Presentation

| The modals and modal-like expressions *be allowed to, be required to, be supposed to, can, have to,* and *may* are used to express permission, necessity, and obligation in the present, past, and future. | We **weren't supposed to see** the answers for the memory test.
They **will have to take** the test again.
Students **may not take** the memory improvement class more than once. |

3.1 Modals and Modal-like Expressions of Permission

a. Use *can (not)* and *may (not)* to talk about permission in the present and future.	Students **can register** for the class now. You **may wait** until next week to register. I **can't miss** more than two classes. You **may not join** after the first class.
Use *could (not)* as the past form of *can (not)*.	We **could ask** questions at the end of the lecture, but we **couldn't interrupt** the lecture.
b. You can also use *be (not) allowed to* for permission in the present, past, and future. For the future, add *will* before *be (not) allowed to*.	We **aren't allowed to talk** during the test. He **was allowed to talk** during the test, but he **was not allowed to use** his books. They **will be allowed to use** their notes tomorrow. She **won't be allowed to use** her notes.
You can use *permitted* instead of *allowed* in formal speech and writing.	Students **are not permitted to refer** to notes during examinations.

3.2 Modals and Modal-like Expressions of Necessity and Obligation

a. Use *be required to, be supposed to, have to, must,* and *need to* to express necessity or obligation in the present and future. *Must* and *be required to* are more formal and are not often used in speaking.	You **are required to take** the class. Teachers **are supposed to hand out** the syllabus on the first day of class. Everyone **is required to work** hard. Applicants **must have** experience for this job.
Use *will be required to, will have to,* and *will need to* for future time.	You **will need to write** an essay for this course.

3.2 Modals and Modal-like Expressions of Necessity and Obligation (continued)

b. Use *be not supposed to* or *must not* for the present and future to say that something is inappropriate or to express prohibition.

Students **are not supposed to take** their books into the exam room. (It is inappropriate.)
You **must not talk** during the exam. (There is no choice.)

c. Use *were required to*, *were supposed to*, or *had to* to describe necessity and obligation in the past.

The applicant **was required to take** a test.
I **was supposed to stay** after class last week.
We **had to arrive** at 7:00 a.m. for the exam.

There is no past form of *must*. Use *had to* instead.

He **had to** reschedule his exam yesterday.
NOT He ~~must~~ reschedule his exam yesterday.

d. The negative forms of *be required to*, *have to*, and *need to* describe choices or options.

You **are not required to show** your ID. (It is optional.)
You **didn't have to remain** in the exam room after you finished. (It was your choice.)
Students **won't need to bring** their own pencils next time. (It will be your choice.)

▶ Grammar Application

Exercise 3.1 Present and Future Permission

A Complete the rules for a college Spanish class. Use the present or future form of the words in parentheses. Sometimes more than one answer is possible.

Spanish 101: Classroom Rules

Dictionaries

Students _can bring_ monolingual dictionaries along to class, but they
(1. can / bring)

_____ any bilingual dictionaries at all. Students
(2. not / may / use)

_____ print dictionaries during tests. However, they
(3. can / use)

_____ online dictionaries during tests.
(4. not / be allowed to / access)

Laptops

You _____ laptop computers to class for note taking
(5. be allowed to / bring)

only. You _____ laptops for web browsing during class.
(6. not / must / use)

Computer Lab

Students _____ the lab until they have purchased
(7. not / may / use)

the book.

Exercise 3.5 Past Necessity and Obligation

A Complete the story about an older person's learning experience. Use the correct forms of the words in parentheses.

When my grandmother was in high school, she _had to follow_ a lot of rules

(1. have to / follow)
and regulations, and she _____ very hard. There

(2. have to / work)
were no computers, so she _____ notes by hand. She

(3. have to / take)
_____ hundreds of textbook pages a week and write

(4. be required to / read)
several papers each semester. She _____ any classes. She

(5. not / be supposed to / miss)
_____ class every day in order to pass. Of course, there was

(6. have to / attend)
no Internet then, so she _____ to the library to do research.

(7. have to / go)
High school in her time was very different from how it is today!

B *Over to You* Write five sentences about some rules and regulations that you remember in a learning environment in the past, for example, in another school you attended. Share your sentences with a partner and discuss this question: How did the rules and regulations help you to learn?

4 | Modals and Modal-like Expressions of Ability

▶ Grammar Presentation

| The modals *be able to* and *can* are used to express ability in the present, past, and future. | *I **couldn't** remember anything the professor said. I **won't be able to** pass the test. She **can** remember dates well.* |

4.1 Modals and Modal-like Expressions of Present and Future Ability

| **a.** Use *be able to* and *can* to describe ability in the present. | *I **am able to remember** faces well, and I **can** usually **remember** names as well.* |
| Use *be not able to* and *can't / cannot* for negative statements in the present. *Be not able to* is more formal than *can't*. | *He **isn't able to meet** us today.* |

4.1 Modals and Modal-like Expressions of Present and Future Ability *(continued)*

b. Use *can* and *will be able to* to describe ability in the future.	*We **can meet** the professor at noon tomorrow. He **will be able to see** us then.*
Use *can't* and *will not / won't be able to* for negative statements in the future. Notice that *not* comes before *be* in the future form.	*I **can't go** to the lecture on Friday. We **won't be able to take** the memory test until next month.*

4.2 Modals and Modal-like Expressions of Past Ability

a. Use *could* (*not*) to describe general ability in the past. *Was / were* (*not*) *able to* is also possible, especially to talk about a particular ability or talent.	*When I was younger, I **could be** very persuasive. I **could understand** the lecture, but I **couldn't remember** all of the information. She **was able to read** by the time she was four.*
Use *was / were able to*, not *could*, to describe ability on a particular occasion in the past.	*Once, I **was able to** convince my friend to memorize 100 new words in a week.* NOT *Once, I ~~could~~ convince my friend to memorize 100 new words in a week.*
b. Use *could have* + the past participle to describe situations in which a person had the ability to do something but did not do it.	*I **could have taken** the memory test last Saturday, but I didn't sign up for it.*
Use *couldn't have* + the past participle to describe situations in which a person didn't have the ability to do something.	*Eric **couldn't have known** the answer to that question. He didn't study at all.*

▶ Grammar Application

Exercise 4.1 Past, Present, and Future Ability

Complete the story about memory loss. Use the past, present, or future form of the words in parentheses.

A few years ago, Alicia was a successful physician. She was very popular with her

patients because she ___*could diagnose*___ their problems quickly and accurately.
                       (1. can / diagnose)

Alicia's favorite pastime was riding her bike. She _____
                                   (2. can / ride)

her mountain bike for hours in the hills around her town. Then one day last year, a car

came up behind Alicia while she was riding on a narrow road, and it hit her. The accident

caused a serious brain injury, even though she was wearing a helmet.

Alicia is in full-time therapy now. Today, she _____

(3. be able to / do)

many things. However, when she finishes therapy, she _____

(4. not / be able to / return)

to her old job because of her memory loss. Therefore, Alicia is planning to help other people

with her condition. Once Alicia is ready, she _____ of other

(5. be able to / take care)

patients.

Exercise 4.2 Past Ability

Complete the sentences about Diana. Use *could have* and the correct form of the verbs
in parentheses.

1. Diana had an accident like Alicia's. She was riding
   a bike in the hills when a car hit her. The driver
   could have avoided (avoid) hitting her, but he was
   driving too fast.

2. She went to a doctor, but he didn't think her
   injuries were serious. Diana didn't think the doctor
   _____ (make) a mistake
   about her diagnosis.[1]

3. Diana went to work after the accident, and
   her behavior seemed normal. Her co-workers
   _____ (not / imagine)
   that she had a brain injury.

4. The first clue that Diana was not well was when she
   went to a nearby store. She forgot how to get home.
   A neighbor had to help her. She _____ (not / remember)
   the way without help.

5. Finally, Diana found a specialist, Dr. Lee, who diagnosed her correctly and helped her
   get a service dog. Diana probably _____ (manage) fine
   by herself, but she was very thankful for the service dog because it made her life easier.
   Now she is in a memory rehabilitation program and doing well.

[1]**diagnosis:** when a doctor says what is wrong with someone who is ill

5 | Avoid Common Mistakes ⚠

1. **When talking about advice and regret in the past, remember to use *have* + the past participle after a modal, not the simple past form of the verb.**

   have
   I should ︿remembered her name, but I didn't expect her to be at the party, and I got confused.

2. **Remember to use a form of *be* in *be allowed to* and *be supposed to*.**

   was
   The president ︿supposed to attend the 2 o'clock meeting, but he didn't show up.

3. **Use *did not have to* when talking about a choice in the past.**

   did not have to e-mail
   I ~~must not have e-mailed~~ the office manager, but I wanted to be sure he was aware of the problem.

Editing Task

Find and correct six more mistakes in the paragraphs about multitasking.

is
Technology ︿supposed to simplify life; however, in reality, it has led to people trying to do too many things at once. One example is driving while texting or talking on a cell phone. After an accident, drivers who are caught by the police admit that they should turned off their phones when they got in the car, but they did not. They must not have called someone
5 while driving, but they did.

Another issue is multitasking in the classroom. Many of my teachers have had a difficult time dealing with students who surf the Web while listening to lectures. One of my instructors said he ought to required a password last semester to log onto the Internet during class. Students must not have gone online, but they sometimes checked e-mail or
10 visited websites instead of listening to the lecture. As a result, students were often distracted.

In contrast, my friend had an instructor who had the opposite view. My friend did not worry about taking notes because students not allowed to – even on paper! The professor thought all note taking was a form of multitasking; instead, he handed out worksheets with highlights of his lecture. At the end of the semester, some students
15 complained. They argued that the professor should not banned computers in class because students today are used to multitasking.

6 | Grammar for Writing ✎

Using Modals to Write About Problems and Solutions

Writers often use modals and modal-like expressions of ability (*be able to, can, could*) to discuss the possible effects of a problem or difficult situation. They use modals of advice to give suggestions for helping someone deal with the situation. Read this example paragraph:

Studies show that students who sleep well before taking tests get better grades. When students do not get enough sleep after studying, their brains <u>cannot</u> process the information they read. Therefore, students <u>should</u> study over a period of a few days and get a good night's sleep before a test.

Pre-writing Task

1 Read the paragraph. What are the effects of stress on academic achievement? What advice does the writer give to solve this problem?

Memory and Stress

Research shows a strong relationship between high levels of stress and low levels of academic achievement. Stress causes the body to produce high levels of the hormone cortisol. This hormone can limit the brain's ability to process information. Therefore, high levels of stress can have a negative effect on memory and could lead to poor test scores.

5 For this reason, colleges and universities should address the problems of stress in their new-student orientations. First, they should teach new students to recognize the signs of stress, such as headaches, anxiety, and trouble sleeping. The orientation schedule might include relaxation classes and deep-breathing lessons. Counselors could also tell students about the importance of exercise. In addition, colleges and universities should provide

10 stress reduction workshops for students during the school year. Students who learn how to manage their stress will remember what they learn, and will therefore have a better chance at success in their studies.

2 Read the paragraph again. Underline the modals and modal-like expressions that are used to describe the possible effects of stress. <u>Double underline</u> the modals and modal-like expressions that are used to describe ways of dealing with stress.

Writing Task

1 *Write* Use the paragraph in the Pre-writing Task to help you write about the effects of a problem or difficult situation that students may encounter. Explain the causes of the problem and suggest possible solutions. You can write about one of these topics or use your own ideas.

- difficulties with class participation
- problems understanding the teacher
- problems with homework
- trouble with tests or quizzes

2 *Self-Edit* Use the editing tips to improve your paragraph. Make any necessary changes.

1. Did you use modals and modal-like expressions of ability to describe possible effects of the problem?
2. Did you use different modals and modal-like expressions to give strong and less strong advice?
3. Did you avoid the mistakes in the Avoid Common Mistakes chart on page 103?

1 | Grammar in the Real World

A How do you protect personal information like computer passwords? Read the web article about hacking. What are some ways to prevent hackers from stealing personal information?

Hacking: A Computer Crime on the Rise

Cyber[1] hacking **may be** the most common computer crime today. Cyber hacking occurs when a person accesses someone else's computer without permission and steals
5 information. It **can happen** to anyone. It **might** even **have happened** to someone you know.

The truth is that hacking is not difficult to learn. In fact, it **might be** too easy. Young adults tend to be skilled at using computers, so it **may not be** surprising to learn that a large number of computer hackers are teenagers. They **might hack** into other computers
10 for the challenge – to see if they can do it and get away with it. There are other hackers, however, who **must have** more malicious[2] intentions because they steal credit card numbers and other personal information.

Severe[3] penalties for these cyber crimes **should have stopped** hacking by now, but they have had little effect. It does not look like cyber hacking **will go** away
15 anytime soon. For protection against hacking, anyone who uses a computer or other technological device **should be** aware of hackers and **should be using** antivirus software. Another safety measure is to use complex[4] passwords, which **could prevent** attacks from being successful.

In short, if you act safely and responsibly, hackers **will** likely **have** a hard time
20 breaking into your computer. However, even these safety measures cannot guarantee that your information is safe.

[1]**cyber:** related to computers | [2]**malicious:** intended to harm or upset other people | [3]**severe:** extreme | [4]**complex:** having many connected parts, making it difficult to understand

B *Comprehension Check* Answer the questions.

1. What age are many hackers?
2. What information do some hackers steal?
3. Is anyone's computer completely safe from hackers?

C *Notice* Read the sentences. Check (✓) the box next to each sentence to show if the action or situation is possible or very certain.

	Possible	Very Certain
1. Cyber hacking **can** happen to anyone.	☐	☐
2. In fact, it **might be** too easy.	☐	☐
3. There are other hackers who **must have** more malicious intentions because they steal credit card numbers and other personal information.	☐	☐
4. In short, if you act safely and responsibly, hackers **will** likely **have** a hard time breaking into your computer.	☐	☐

Which bold words in the sentences tell you that an action or situation is possible?

2 | Modals of Present Probability

▶ Grammar Presentation

Modals of present probability are used to express how likely it is that something is happening now.	*Your computer **may be** at risk of being hacked.* *He **must not be** worried about data security.*

2.1 Modals of Present Probability

a. Choose a modal depending on how certain you feel about something.

most certain ↑	can't, couldn't, have to, must (not)	*Hackers **can't be** interested in my data.* *Your password **must not be** secure.*
certain	ought to, should (not)	*Antivirus software **should protect** you.* *It **shouldn't be** difficult to find good software.*
least certain ↓	could, may (not), might (not)	*Good antivirus software **could cost** a lot.* *That software **might not be** good enough.*

2.1 Modals of Present Probability (continued)

b. Use *can't* and *couldn't* when you are almost certain something is not likely or not possible.	He **can't be** online now. His computer is broken. *Meg* **couldn't be shopping** *for a new laptop. Her old computer works perfectly.*
You can also use *can't* and *couldn't* to express disbelief or surprise.	*Your brand-new computer is broken? You* **can't be** *serious!*
c. Use *have to* and *must* (*not*) when you are mostly certain or when you think there is only one logical conclusion.	*As a lawyer, he* **has to know** *that hacking into computers is illegal!* *Large companies* **must worry** *about the security of their data.*
In formal speaking and writing, *must* is much more common than *have to*.	*People without antivirus software* **must believe** *they are not at risk.*
d. Use *ought to* and *should* (*not*) when you have an expectation based on experience or evidence. *Should* is more common than *ought to. Ought not to* is rare.	*That computer* **should be** *available in the store because I saw it on the store's website.* *You* **shouldn't have** *trouble figuring out my password because it's an easy one.*
e. Use *could*, *may* (*not*), and *might* (*not*) when you are unsure or when you don't have much evidence.	*I* **could have** *a virus on my computer because it isn't working normally.* *I* **might not buy** *a new computer this year because my old one still works fine.*

⊠ Modals and Modal-like Expressions: See page A3.

▶ # Grammar Application

Exercise 2.1 Present Probability

A Complete the interview about hacking. Use the correct modals and the information in parentheses to help you. Sometimes more than one answer is possible.

Jason Today we are asking people: How secure is your computer or smartphone? Could you be the victim of a hacker?

Emily It's impossible. Hackers __can't/couldn't__ be
(1)
interested in my computer. I don't have anything

valuable on it. (**impossible**)

Jason But you _____ have some valuable
(2)
information on your computer. Everyone does.

(**a logical conclusion**)

Emily What do you mean?

Jason I'm sure you've bought things online at some point. Your credit card information _____ be on your computer. (**a logical conclusion**)
(3)

Carlos Well, I'm certain that my phone is safe. It _____ be of interest to anyone,
(4)
especially a hacker. (**unlikely**)

Jason Oh, you _____ have GPS – global
(5)
positioning software – on your phone, then.
Because if you did, you'd feel different. (**a logical conclusion**)

Carlos But I do have GPS on my phone . . .

Jason Well, that _____ make you a little less sure, then, because GPS
(6)
is one of the things that hackers are interested in. It lets them see where you go every day. (**expectation based on evidence**)

Carlos My GPS? That _____ be true! (**surprise**)
(7)

Belén You know, my computer _____
(8)
be of interest to a hacker for some reason,
I guess. (**unsure**)

Jason I'm afraid that's true.

B *Pair Work* Compare your answers with a partner. Take turns saying the sentences with other modals that have the same meaning.

Hackers can't be interested in my computer.

Exercise 2.2 More Present Probability

A *Over to You* Read the statements. Then respond with information that is true for you. Use modals of present probability to show how certain you feel that the statements are true for you. Explain why.

1. A person can hack into your computer or smartphone at any time.

   That can't be true. I have excellent security software.

2. It is very likely that a thief will steal your identity.

   _____

3. Your credit card number is not safe.

_____

4. Your home is very safe. It's unlikely that a burglar can enter and take valuable items from you.

_____

5. The downtown area of your city or town is dangerous at night. It's a bad idea to walk there alone at night.

_____

6. It's very safe for children to walk to school alone in your neighborhood.

_____

B *Pair Work* Take turns asking questions about each other's statements.

You say that it can't be true that a person can hack into your computer because you have good security, but good security is sometimes not enough. For example, banks tend to have good security, but hackers get into their computers.

3 | Modals of Future Probability

▶ Grammar Presentation

Modals of future probability with *could*, *may*, *might*, *ought to*, *should*, and *will* express the probability of something happening in the future.	*Your new computer **should be** here next week.* *I **won't buy** a new computer next year because my current one is still fairly new.*

3.1 Modals of Future Probability

a. Choose a modal depending on how certain you are about something.

most certain	*will (not)*	*Hackers **will be** interested in our company's financial data.*
certain	*should (not), ought to*	*Our new website **should be** ready by next week.* *The secure web page **ought to be** available soon.*
least certain	*may (not), might (not), could*	*She **could learn** a lot about Internet security in her course next month.*

b. Use *will* and *won't* to express strong certainty. | *The company **will hire** very few people this year.*

You can add words like *probably* and *likely* to weaken the certainty. | *The company* <u>probably</u> ***won't hire*** *any students.*

3.1 Modals of Future Probability *(continued)*

c. Use *should* (*not*) and *ought to* when you have an expectation based on experience or evidence.	The software **should be** ready by Friday. (Because it is almost ready now.) *We **shouldn't expect** new passwords until Monday.* (Because it usually takes a few days.)
d. Use *could, may* (*not*), and *might* (*not*) when you are unsure or when you don't have much evidence.	The company **could start** storing personal data as early as next month. *A manager **might join** us next week.*
You can also use these modals with a progressive form of the verb.	The class **may be starting** soon. There are a lot of students in the room.

▶ Grammar Application

Exercise 3.1 Future Probability

A Complete the ad with *will* and the verbs in parentheses.

I-safe Home Security System

The home of the future ___will be___ (be) safer.

(1)

Homeowners _____ (be) able

(2)

to control everything in the home with the new

I-safe Home Security System.

Here are just a few of I-safe's features:

- You _____ (not / need) to worry about the new babysitter. I-safe

  (3)

  _____ (let) parents use their computers or smartphones at work to

  (4)

  watch the babysitter.

- I-safe _____ (allow) you to control appliances and heating and cooling

  (5)

  systems from wherever you are.

- I-safe _____ (lock) the doors to your home for you.

  (6)

- The I-safe Home Security System _____ (be) available this spring.

  (7)

B Complete the conversation about the I-safe. The speakers are not very certain about the claims in the ad. Circle the correct words.

Customer Are you going to sell the I-safe system next spring?

Sales clerk It (will likely)/ will be available next spring, but the manager isn't sure.
(1)

Customer Can I use the I-safe to control the TV from my smartphone?

Sales clerk You **will / should** be able to control the TV, but I'm not really sure.
(2)

Customer I have a babysitter. If I install I-safe cameras to watch her from time to time,

she **should / may not** be happy about being on camera.
(3)

Sales clerk You're right, there **shouldn't / could** be some concerns about privacy.
(4)

Customer I use a tablet computer while I commute to work on the train. I haven't

read anything about using the I-safe with my tablet. I-safe probably

won't / shouldn't work with it, right?
(5)

Sales clerk I'm not quite sure, but it **ought to / will** send images to your tablet.
(6)

Customer OK. Thanks for your help.

C *Pair Work* Imagine that the I-safe company is going to give away its product for free for one month. Will you get an I-safe? Why or why not? Use modals in your answers.

A I probably won't get an I-safe because I'm not very worried about home security.

B I might get one. I'm not sure because there could be some privacy issues with it.

Exercise 3.2 More Future Probability

A 🔊 Listen to the conversations about future probability. Write the missing words.

Conversation 1

Anne Someone broke into the Lees' apartment, and now they're moving.

Martin That's awful. Where are they going to go?

Anne I'm not sure. *They'll* probably move to the suburbs.
(1)

Martin But Joe Lee has a good job here in the city. _____ be able to
(2)
move very far away.

Anne I know. And the children are in school in the city. _____ want to
(3)
change schools.

Martin Well, I wish them luck.

Conversation 2

Truong I spoke with Andrew Martinez yesterday. Guess what? _____
(4)

buy a home security system.

Ben I know. We went to a home security show last week. He liked the system with

the cameras that send images to your phone. _____ be the
(5)

system he's going to buy.

Truong _____ learn a lot from Andrew when he puts in his system.
(6)

Conversation 3

Reporter The airport commissioner announced today that Bay City Airport will start

using cameras with sensors that will detect heart rate and body temperature.

_____ be ready by next year.
(7)

Josh I read about the cameras online as well. In fact, I heard that

_____ start using the cameras by the end of this year.
(8)

Katie ___ _____ be interesting to see what happens.
(9)

B ◀⬥)) Listen again and check your answers.

4 Modals of Past Probability

▶ Grammar Presentation

<table>
<tr>
<td>Modals of past probability with can, could, may, might, and must are used to make inferences or guesses about the past.</td>
<td>A hacker couldn't have accessed this computer! I have the best protection available.
A hacker might have found a way to break into it.</td>
</tr>
</table>

4.1 Forming Modals of Past Probability

<table>
<tr>
<td>Form modals of past probability with modal + have + the past participle of the main verb.
Form the negative by putting not between the modal and have. Only use contractions with could and can.</td>
<td>The company may have been careless with security.
I must not have turned off my phone.
She could have changed her password, but I'm not sure.
It couldn't have been Joe's fault. He wasn't here.</td>
</tr>
</table>

4.2 Using Modals of Past Probability

a. Choose a modal depending on how certain you are that something happened.

most certain	couldn't, can't
certain	must (not)
least certain	may (not), might (not), could

You **couldn't have chosen** a strong password. Kim guessed it immediately!

Someone **must have stolen** all the passwords because hackers have gotten into every computer.

The computer **may not have had** strong antivirus software because it was older.

b. Use *can't have* or *couldn't have* when you are absolutely certain something was impossible or unlikely.

I **can't have entered** the wrong password! I've had the same one forever.

He **couldn't have hacked** our computers. He doesn't know how.

c. Use *must (not) have* when you feel certain about something or when you believe there is only one logical conclusion.

I **must not have written** the password down. I can't find it anywhere.

You **must have received** the security e-mail. Ms. Liu sent it to everyone.

d. Use *could have, may (not) have,* or *might (not) have* when there isn't much evidence or when you are guessing.

He **may not have followed** the security advice because he didn't believe it was important.

He **might have changed** his password. I don't think he is still using his old one.

Data from the Real World

May (not) have, could (not) have, and *might (not) have* are the most common modals used for speculating about the past in speaking and writing. *Must (not) have* is less common. *Cannot/can't have* is relatively rare.

may (not) have	
could (not) have	
might (not) have	
must (not) have	
cannot / can't have	

▶ Grammar Application

Exercise 4.1 Past Probability

Complete the article about credit card fraud. Use the correct form of the words in parentheses.

Credit Card Fraud: How Does It Happen?

There was a $10,000 charge from a jewelry store on Claudia's credit card

statement. She didn't buy any jewelry, so someone _must have stolen_ her credit

(1. must / steal)

card number.

Claudia said, "I _____ the victim of credit card theft."

(2. not / could / be)

However, someone obviously _____ her card information.

(3. must / obtain)

How _____ that _____ ? There are many ways a

(4)   (4. could / happen)

person _____ Claudia's credit card information. Someone

(5. might / steal)

_____ Claudia's credit card number when she used her card

(6. may / steal)

in a store or a restaurant. In addition, a thief _____ a credit card

(7. could / take)

account statement or a bill from her mailbox or her trash.

Exercise 4.2 More Past Probability

Write a response for each situation. Use the words in parentheses with modals of past probability to write guesses or logical conclusions. Sometimes more than one answer is possible.

1. Isabela can't find her wallet.

    She may / might / could have lost it.

(**guess:** she / lose / it)

2. There was a charge on Bo's bill that he didn't recognize.

    _____

(**logical conclusion:** someone / steal / his credit card number)

3. Bo paid his credit card bill, even though he didn't recognize some of the charges.

    _____

(**logical conclusion:** he / not / call / the credit card company)

4. The waiter took a long time to bring Hong's credit card back.

    _____

(**guess:** he / copy / the card number)

5. Terry threw an unopened letter from her credit card company into the trash.

    _____

(**logical conclusion:** she / not / think / it was important)

Exercise 4.3 Using Modals of Past Probability

Read the web article about tips for avoiding identity theft. Then complete the sentences about examples of identity theft. Use the tips to write logical conclusions or guesses about what has happened. Sometimes more than one answer is possible.

How to Avoid Identity Theft

1. Write to credit card companies. Tell them to remove your name from their mailing lists.

2. Check your credit card bill carefully each month. Make sure there are no incorrect charges on it.

3. Don't carry all of your credit cards with you.

4. Make photocopies of important documents, such as your passport, and keep the copies in a safe place in your home.

5. Check that e-mails from your bank and other businesses are authentic. Never give personal information in an e-mail.

1. Fred gets a lot of credit card offers in the mail. He never opens them.
    *He must not have called the companies and asked them to remove his
    name from their mailing lists.*

2. Sarah paid her credit card bill, but there were charges on it for things she did not buy.
    _____

3. A pickpocket stole Luis's wallet while he was riding the bus. Now Luis has to cancel all of his credit cards.
    _____

4. Wei went to Canada on a business trip and lost his passport. It took longer than usual for him to leave the country because he didn't know his passport number.
    _____

5. Nicole responded to an e-mail that she thought was from her bank, and now she is missing money from her account.
    _____

5 | Avoid Common Mistakes ⚠️

1. Do not use *must* to talk about future probabilities.

will/may
It ~~must~~ be even more difficult to catch cyber criminals in the future.

2. Remember to use *be* + verb + *-ing* when using the progressive with modals.

be
He might∧working.

3. Use the correct word order when using modals of probability to talk about the past.

not
He must∧have ~~not~~ locked the computer because the thief was able to get his information.

Editing Task

Find and correct four mistakes in the paragraph about computer hackers.

What happens to computer hackers who decide to stop hacking? They might find

that cyber crime can lead to interesting careers. For example, some companies hire a

computer hacker with the hope that the former cyber criminal ~~must~~ *will* become a brilliant

security consultant in the future. Although some say that these companies might taking a

5   risk by hiring these former criminals, the companies seem to believe that the risk is worth

it. Adrian Lamo was breaking into computer systems for fun in high school. However,

when he hacked into the *New York Times* in 2002, the newspaper must have not thought

it was funny, because he was arrested. He now uses his skills for a different purpose and

works as a consultant. Robert Tappan Morris might have ended his chances for a good job

10   when he created the Morris worm, a particularly bad computer virus, in 1988. However,

he is now on the faculty of the famous Massachusetts Institute of Technology (MIT).

Apparently, they believe that a reformed hacker must be able to stop future cyber crimes.

In short, while computer hackers sometimes go to prison for their crimes, these days their

career opportunities may increasing.

6 | Grammar for Writing ✐

Using Modals to Hedge

Can, *could*, and *may* (*not*) make your writing sound less certain. This is especially helpful when you are stating opinions. Using modals to sound less certain is called *hedging*. Hedging is more common in academic writing than in other kinds of writing, such as editorial pieces. Read these examples:

Strong laws <u>will</u> reduce cyber crime.
Strong laws <u>may</u> reduce cyber crime.

The first sentence expresses strong certainty. The second sentence expresses less certainty. It shows that other opinions are possible, too. The writer of the second sentence is hedging.

Pre-writing Task

1 Read the paragraph. What type of crime is the paragraph about? What is the writer's opinion of these criminals?

New Types of Criminals

Cyber crime is a serious problem throughout the world for many reasons. Cyber criminals are extremely difficult to find. They may be the hardest criminals to catch. Cyber criminals can commit their crimes from anywhere in the world. Also, it can be impossible to know if they are working alone or with other cyber criminals. They do not need to be
5 in the same place. Also, cyber criminals may be more educated and know more about computers than most other criminals. They may know more about the Internet than the police or even many computer specialists. Furthermore, no one knows how many cyber crimes have been committed. Some victims of cyber crimes may not have reported the crimes because they did not realize that a cyber crime happened to them. Another problem
10 is that the laws against cyber crimes are changing all the time. In addition, some countries may not even have any clear laws against cyber crime yet. In the future, people will make more and more purchases and do more and more business using e-mail and the Internet. This could become riskier as cyber criminals continue to get smarter and harder to catch.

2 Read the paragraph again. Circle the uses of *can*, *could*, and *may* as hedging expressions. Underline the hedging modal that refers to the past. <u>Double underline</u> the hedging modal that refers to the future.

Writing Task

1 *Write* Use the paragraph in the Pre-writing Task to help you write about why many employers read their employees' e-mails and track their Internet use. Use these sentence starters.

- Employers may read their employees' e-mail in order to _____ .

- Some employees could be _____ .

- Reading employees' e-mails could lead to _____ .

2 *Self-Edit* Use the editing tips to improve your paragraph. Make any necessary changes.

1. Did you use hedging modals to show that other opinions are possible?
2. Did you use *cannot, could not, have to, must* (*not*), *ought to,* and/or *should* (*not*) to express probability in the present when you were fairly certain?
3. Did you use *will* and other modals with time words to express probability in the future?
4. Did you avoid the mistakes in the Avoid Common Mistakes chart on page 117?

Nouns and Modifying Nouns

Attitudes Toward Nutrition

1 | Grammar in the Real World 🌐

A What makes a person healthy? Read the article about health habits today. Are people as healthy today as they were in the past?

❧ A Health Crisis ❧

Obesity has become **a major problem** in the United States. According to recent National Institutes of Health studies, less than one-third of **Americans** over the age of 20 are at a healthy weight. That means that two-thirds of the **adult population** is overweight, and one-third of all **adults** are obese.[1]

5   **Modern U.S. society** is partially responsible for this **alarming health trend**. Processed, prepared, and packaged **food** has very little nutritional value. Michael Pollan, author of *Food Rules*, argues that **many modern food products** are not truly **food** at all. They contain a great deal of **fat** and refined[2] **sugar** but very little – or no – nutrition.

One other cause of obesity is the unhealthy choices people are making in **their**
10 **lifestyles**. **Exercise** used to be part of everyday **life**. It was a necessary part of a society where work depended mostly on farming and physical labor.[3] Today, people often sit at a computer all day, watch hours of TV, use personal cars, and have little daily exercise.

Health experts have been studying ways to reduce obesity because there is a link between obesity and other serious **diseases**, such as **diabetes**[4] and **heart disease**. **One**
15 **way** is to eat more **green and brown food**, such as green **vegetables** and brown **rice** and **grains**. These foods help people use calories, and they aid digestion.[5] In contrast, people who have a **diet** of mostly fast food, white sugar, white flour, and **fat** are at greater risk of obesity. **These diets** contain calories that easily become **fat** when people do not use them for **energy** and exercise.

20   Experts recommend fewer **servings of** unhealthy food, bigger **portions of** healthy food, and a more active lifestyle.

[1]**obese:** extremely fat │ [2]**refined:** made more pure by removing unwanted material │ [3]**physical labor:** work that involves effort from the body │ [4]**diabetes:** a disease in which the body cannot control the amount of sugar in the blood │ [5]**digestion:** the ability of the body to create energy from food

B *Comprehension Check* Answer the questions.

1. Why does Michael Pollan argue that many modern food products are not truly food?
2. How did people stay active in the past?
3. What are some diseases related to obesity?

C *Notice* Look at the nouns in bold. Write *C* next to each noun that you can count and *NC* next to each noun that you can't count. Then look at the words that modify some of the nouns. Are they all adjectives? Circle the ones that are not adjectives. What part of speech are they?

1. green and brown **food**
2. heart **disease**
3. food **products**
4. the **elderly**
5. **obesity**

2 | Nouns

▶ Grammar Presentation

There are two types of common nouns in English: count and noncount.	COUNT NOUN ***Vegetables*** *are good for you.* NONCOUNT NOUN *Good* ***nutrition*** *is essential for good health.*

2.1 Count Nouns

Count nouns are nouns that you can count and make plural. Use a singular or plural verb with count nouns.	*This* ***apple*** *tastes great.* ***Vegetables*** *are very important and keep us healthy.*
Use a determiner such as *a / an, the, this*, and *his* with singular count nouns.	*Is a* ***tomato*** *a* ***vegetable***? *There's an* ***onion*** *in the* ***refrigerator***. *This* ***banana*** *doesn't taste ripe.* *His* ***sandwich*** *looks delicious.*
You can use a plural count noun with or without a determiner such as *a few, many, some, these*, and *those*.	*Some* ***diets*** *don't work very well.* ***Diets*** *often don't work very well.*

2.2 Irregular Plural Nouns

a. Some plural nouns have irregular forms. These are the most common irregular plural nouns in academic writing.	*man – men*	*woman – women*	
	child – children	*person – people*	
	foot – feet	*tooth – teeth*	
b. Some nouns have the same form for singular and plural.	*one fish – two fish*	*one sheep – two sheep*	
c. Some nouns are only plural. They do not have a singular form.	*clothes*	*headphones*	*pants*
	glasses	*jeans*	*scissors*

2.3 Noncount Nouns

a. Noncount nouns are nouns that cannot be counted. Use a singular verb with noncount nouns. Here are some common categories of noncount nouns.	
Abstract concepts: *health, nutrition*	Good **health** is very important.
Activities and sports: *dancing, exercise, swimming, tennis, yoga*	**Yoga** has been my favorite activity for years.
Diseases and health conditions: *arthritis, depression, diabetes, obesity*	**Obesity** has become a serious problem.
Elements and gases: *gold, hydrogen, oxygen, silver*	**Oxygen** is the most common element in the body by weight.
Food: *beef, broccoli, cheese, rice*	**Broccoli** isn't popular with my family.
Liquids: *coffee, gasoline, oil, tea*	**Tea** has many health benefits.
Natural phenomena: *electricity, hail, lightning, rain, thunder*	**Hail** consists of small balls of ice.
Particles: *pepper, salt, sand, sugar*	Too much **salt** isn't good for you.
Subjects: *economics, genetics, geology*	I wasn't very good at **economics** in college.
Areas of work: *construction, business, medicine, nursing*	She's studying **nursing**.
b. You can use a noncount noun with or without a determiner. Use a determiner after you have already mentioned the noun and wish to give more information.	**Cheese** is one of my favorite foods, but I don't like the **cheese** on this pizza. It's too stringy.
c. You can use *the* + certain adjectives to describe a group of people with the same characteristic or quality: *the dead, the disabled, the educated, the elderly, the living, the poor, the rich, the unemployed.* Use a plural verb.	**The elderly** sometimes don't eat well. **The poor** are often not able to buy nutritious food. **The unemployed** are especially affected by the poor economy.

▶️ Noncount Nouns and Measurement Words to Make Noncount Nouns Countable: See page A5.

Data from the Real World

Some common noncount nouns in speaking and writing are:

advice	equipment	information	music	research	stuff
bread	evidence	knowledge	news	rice	traffic
cash	fun	luck	permission	safety	water
coffee	furniture	milk	progress	security	weather
damage	health	money	publicity	software	work

▶ Grammar Application

Exercise 2.1 Count Nouns

A Complete the excerpt from a web article about nutrition. Circle the correct verbs.

A healthy diet **include / (includes)** a lot of fresh fruit and vegetables. Vegetables
(1)
is / are especially low in calories and high in nutrients such as vitamins and
(2)
minerals. Therefore, it's a good idea to add more fruit and vegetables to your diet
if you want to improve your health.

Current nutrition guidelines **suggest / suggests** eating about four or five
(3)
servings of fruit and vegetables a day. One serving **is / are** about a half cup.
(4)
Nutrition experts also **suggest / suggests** choosing fruit and vegetables by color –
(5)
dark green, yellow, red, and so on – and eating a variety of colors each day.
This is because fruit and vegetables with a lot of color often **contain / contains**
(6)
the highest amounts of nutrients. Half a cup of broccoli, for example, **has / have**
(7)
50 milligrams of vitamin C and only about 15 calories.

Low-calorie fruit, such as tomatoes and berries, **is / are** also a good choice. A
(8)
medium tomato **has / have** only about 20 calories and 15 milligrams of vitamin C.
(9)
Blueberries **has / have** 80 calories and 15 milligrams of vitamin C per cup.
(10)
Intensely colored fruit and vegetables often **contain / contains** antioxidants,
(11)
chemicals that protect cells from disease. Antioxidants also **enhance / enhances**
(12)
the effects of vitamin C and protect the heart and your health!

B *Over to You* What else do you know about the benefits of fruit and vegetables? Write five sentences about fruit and vegetables. Share your sentences with a partner.

Exercise 2.2 *The* + Adjective

Complete the statements about nutritional issues that affect different groups of people. Rewrite the words in parentheses with *the* + adjective.

1. _The wealthy_ (People who are wealthy) tend to have a better diet than poor people do because they can easily shop for and buy whatever they need.

2. _____ (People who are poor) often do not have convenient access to fresh fruit and vegetables because there are few good supermarkets in poor neighborhoods.

3. There often are free food programs for _____ (people who are homeless) in large urban areas.

4. _____ (People who are elderly) sometimes have poor nutrition because they might suffer from diseases that cause a loss of appetite.

5. _____ (People who are young) are becoming less healthy in America because of too much junk food and a lack of exercise.

6. In Minneapolis and in many other parts of the country, farmers' markets are opening in areas that are easier for _____ (people who are disabled) to access.

7. _____ (People who are unemployed) in the United States can get help buying food by applying for SNAP, the government-sponsored Supplemental Nutrition Assistance Program.

8. We usually assume that _____ (people who are educated) make wise choices when they eat, but this is not always true.

Exercise 2.3 Count or Noncount Noun?

A Complete the magazine article about health. Add plural endings to the nouns in bold where necessary. If a noun does not have a plural, write ✗ on the line.

～～～ Tips for a Healthy Life ～～～

Due to the worldwide epidemic of obesity, many people are concerned about their

health ✗ . **Specialist** _____ who study how the body works have some **advice** _____ for you:
    (1)   (2)   (3)
exercise more and eat healthier food.

The Harvard School of Public Health recommends adding more exercise to your daily life.

With the exception of some people who work in very active **occupation** _____ such as
                                                    (4)

construction _____ or landscaping, many of us simply do not move enough throughout the day.
        (5)

Exercise _____ not only helps burn calories, it also lowers the risk for many **illness** _____ such
      (6)   (7)

as **heart disease** _____ and diabetes. One way to increase activity is through aerobic exercise
          (8)

such as **swimming** _____ . Aerobic exercise increases your intake of **oxygen** _____ , which
           (9)   (10)

helps you burn fat faster. However, many physical activities count as exercise, including

dancing ✗ and **gardening** _____ .
  (11)   (12)

The next step is changing our diet. Some **research** _____ shows that a plant-based diet
                                       (13)

is a good choice. People who eat less meat tend to be healthy. They do not usually eat

processed food that is high in fat, sugar, and **salt** _____ . The Harvard School of Public
                                        (14)

Health suggests that we follow a plant-based diet. They suggest eating fresh fruit and

vegetable _____ and whole grains such as brown **rice** _____ . They also recommend preparing
     (15)   (16)

your food from fresh **ingredient** _____ .
                (17)

There is a lot of confusing **information** ✗ about nutrition, but exercise and simple,
                                   (18)

unprocessed food are all you really need to live a healthy life.

B *Pair Work* Make a list of the noncount nouns in A. Then work with a partner and identify which category the nouns in A are from: abstract concepts, activities and sports, diseases and health conditions, food, subjects, particles, or areas of work. Then think of one more noun for each category.

  A Health *is an abstract concept.*

  B Right. And kindness *is another abstract concept.*

3 Noncount Nouns as Count Nouns

▶ Grammar Presentation

When we refer to noncount nouns as individual items, they can sometimes have a count meaning. They may also be made countable with measurement words describing specific quantities.

NONCOUNT NOUN
Light makes plants grow.

MEASUREMENT+ COUNT NOUN
A bunch of **lights** were visible in the distance.

3.1 Making Noncount Nouns Countable

a. Some noncount nouns can have a count meaning when we refer to individual items within a general category.	I always put **cheese** on my pasta. (general category) English **cheeses** are very strong. (individual kinds) **Food** is essential to life. (general category) Some **foods** contain a lot of sugar. (individual food items)
b. Use measurement words to make noncount nouns countable. Here are common measurement words and expressions. Abstract concepts: *a bit of, a kind of, a piece of* Activities or sports: *a game of* Food: *a drop of, a grain of, a piece of, a serving of, a slice of* Liquids: *a cup of, a gallon / quart of, a glass of* Natural phenomena: *a bolt of, a drop of, a ray of* Particles: *a grain of, a pinch of* Subjects and occupations: *an area of, a branch of, a field of, a type of* Miscellaneous: *an article of* (clothing), *a bunch of* (people, objects), *a crowd of, a group of, a pack of* (wolves, dogs, wild animals), *a piece of* (furniture, equipment, news)	Eight glasses of **water** are on the table. There is a piece of **cake** in the refrigerator. A bit of **kindness** goes a long way. I play five games of **tennis** a week. Would you like a piece of **pie**? The recipe calls for two cups of **oil**. A few drops of **rain** are enough to ruin a picnic. A pinch of **salt** makes food taste good. Two branches of **medicine** are cardiology and neurology. There were a bunch of **people** at the store.

▸ Noncount Nouns and Measurement Words to Make Noncount Nouns Countable: See page A5.

▶ Grammar Application

Exercise 3.1 Noncount Nouns with Count Meanings

A Complete the conversation about purchasing food through the Internet. Use the correct form of the nouns in parentheses. Sometimes more than one answer is possible.

Jake Do you have any _experience_ (experience) buying food online?
(1)

Emily Yes, I've bought different kinds of imported _____ (cheese),
(2)

a variety of _____ (coffee), and different sorts of
(3)

_____ (tea).
(4)

Jake I didn't know you liked _____ (cheese) so much.
(5)

Emily I don't. I bought all of those _____ (cheese) as gifts.
(6)

Jake Anyway, how was the shopping?

Emily I've had many good _____ (experience) with online shopping.
(7)

The prices were reasonable, and the items arrived in good condition.

Jake Did it take a long _____ (time) for the items to arrive?
(8)

Emily Not usually. Two _____ (time) they were late.
(9)

Jake Do you ever buy _____ (fruit) online?
(10)

Emily I don't think that's a good idea, but I have friends who buy

_____ (fruit) like *cherimoya* and *durian* online without any
(11)

problems.

Jake It's probably safe to buy _____ (coffee) and
(12)

_____ (tea) online, right?
(13)

Emily Sure. I've also bought items like _____ (sugar) and
(14)

_____ (flour) online.
(15)

Jake Why would you do that?

Emily I buy hard-to-get _____ (sugar) such as *demerara* and
(16)

turbinado online because I can't find them in my local store.

Jake And there are special types of _____ (flour), too?
(17)

Emily Well, I have a friend who is allergic to wheat, so I get a few different

gluten-free _____ (flour) from a special diet site.
(18)

B *Pair Work* Compare your answers with a partner. Discuss the reasons for each of your answers.

I chose the noncount noun experience *in item 1 because the speaker is talking about an abstract concept.*

Exercise 3.2 Measurement Words with Noncount Nouns

Complete the sentences with the correct quantifier from the box. Add determiners and any other necessary words. Sometimes more than one answer is possible.

~~bit~~	cup	gallon	glass	piece	serving
can	drop	game	grain	pinch	slice

1. Let me give you _a bit of_ advice: Stop worrying about calories, and just eat food that's good for you.

2. Should we play _____ chess after dinner?

3. Please cut a very thin _____ bread for me.

4. _____ fruit is about a half a cup.

5. _____ tea has less caffeine than a cup of coffee.

6. Doctors recommend drinking 32 ounces of water a day, but it's hard to remember to drink four _____ water each day.

7. This sauce needs just _____ salt – not too much!

8. The cupboard is empty. There isn't even _____ rice left there!

9. Here's a bottle of soy sauce. Just put a tiny _____ soy sauce on the fish. We're trying to cut down on sodium.

10. The chocolate cheesecake that you baked looks absolutely delicious! Could you cut _____ for me?

11. I've brought you _____ chicken soup to help with your cold. It's not homemade, but I think it will help you feel better.

12. If you're going to the supermarket, could you pick up _____ milk? The children drink so much of it and we need a lot.

Exercise 3.3 More Measurement Words with Noncount Nouns

A Write the correct quantities of food in Luis's blog. Use the words in the box. Add any other necessary words.

1 / bottle / water	~~quart / olive oil~~	2 / piece / fish
1 / box / pasta	2 / loaf / bread	wedge / cheese

The Wandering Gourmet
by Luis Martinez

The highlight of my trip to San Francisco was the Ferry Plaza Farmers' Market. I spent a lot of money! My chef friend, Lisa, came with me. She made a delicious dinner from the ingredients. Here's what we bought:

1. _a quart of olive oil_   2. _____   3. _____

4. _____   5. _____   6. _____

B *Pair Work* Compare your answers with a partner. Then work together to think of more noncount nouns that you can use with each measurement word.

A *You can also say* a quart of water.

B *Or* a quart of milk.

4 | Modifying Nouns

▶ Grammar Presentation

Adjectives that modify nouns, including nouns acting as adjectives, follow a specific order.	That was a **delicious green Washington** apple! (opinion + color + origin) I saw a **shocking government** report on nutrition. (opinion + type)

4.1 Order of Modifiers

The order of modifiers is as follows:

Opinion / Evaluation	Size	Age	Shape	Color	Origin	Material	Type
delicious traditional useful	large short small tall	antique new old two-year-old young	round square triangular	black green yellow	French imaginary scientific	cotton leather metal	dog government shoulder

▶▶ Order of Adjectives Before Nouns: See page A6.

4.2 Using Modifiers

a. Do not use commas between two adjectives from different categories	OPINION ORIGIN That was a **delicious French** cake. OPINION TYPE It was a **disappointing medical** report. SIZE MATERIAL You'll need a **big metal** pan.
b. Use *and* or a comma between two adjectives of opinion.	OPINION OPINION The food has an **interesting** and **memorable** taste. The food has an **interesting, memorable** taste.
Use *and* between two colors or two materials used as adjectives.	COLOR + COLOR She bought a **red** and **yellow** dress. MATERIAL + MATERIAL The **cotton** and **silk** tablecloth is new.

▶ Grammar Application

Exercise 4.1 Order of Adjectives

Complete the sentences with the adjectives in parentheses. Remember to use the correct order.

1. Wei got a _new French glass_ (French / glass / new) coffeemaker for his 25th birthday.

2. Every other week, Mei's Kitchen will feature ___with___ (easy / Asian / new) recipes for you to try at home.

3. SNAP is a _____ (government / useful) food program for people who are out of work.

4. We went to the farmers' market in the city last Saturday and bought a lot of _____ (small / purple) potatoes.

5. The _____ (Thai / new) restaurant downtown has a _____ (rectangular / lovely) dining room area with _____ (red / beautiful) walls.

6. There were _____ (lovely / white) flowers in some _____ (glass / antique / tall) vases on the tables.

Exercise 4.2 More Order of Adjectives

A On a separate sheet of paper, write five sentences about things in the picture. Use two or three adjectives in each sentence. Choose adjectives from the box, or think of your own adjectives.

antique	large	silver
beautiful	long	small
clean	metal	square
cotton	oval	tall
delicious	rectangular	white
enormous	round	wooden

There are clean white napkins in the tall clear glasses.

B *Over to You* Think of a party or wedding that you attended. Write five sentences to describe the decorations and the food. Use two or three adjectives in each sentence.

Exercise 4.3 More Order of Adjectives

A 🔊 Listen to a restaurant review. Complete the sentences with the missing words. Pay attention to punctuation and adjective order.

Last week, we ate at Le Bambou, an _elegant new_ Vietnamese restaurant
(1)
in town. We ordered several _____ dishes. We highly
(2)
recommend the _____ spring rolls. They were
(3)
a _____ _____ appetizer, and they were perfect
(4)
for the _____ evening. The main course
(5)
was a _____ chicken dish served with
(6)
_____ vegetables.
(7)
We were especially impressed with Le Bambou's atmosphere. It has a
_____ dining room. The tables were covered
(8)
with _____ tablecloths, and they were all lit by
(9)
_____ candles in _____
(10)   (11)
holders. The walls were painted a lovely shade of blue, and the color gave the restaurant
a sense of calm. The serving dishes looked like _____
(12)
antiques. There were _____ dragons on the plates.
(13)
All in all, Le Bambou was a _____ experience.
(14)

B 🔊 Listen again and check your answers.

C *Over to You* Choose a restaurant that you know. Write a review of the restaurant similar to the review in A. Share your sentences with a partner.

Last month we went to the lovely, popular neighborhood restaurant called Buon Appetito...

5 | Avoid Common Mistakes ⚠

1. **When a noun modifies another noun and a number comes before it, use the singular form of the noun.**

   eight-year-old
   An ~~eight-years-old~~ child should be able to pronounce all of the ingredients.

2. **When a noun is followed by a prepositional phrase, the verb agrees with the noun, not the object of the preposition.**

   advertises
   The company behind these products ~~advertise~~ to young children.

3. **Do not make noncount nouns plural.**

   advice
   The author has ~~advices~~ for shoppers.

4. **Remember to use the plural form of count nouns.**

   vegetables
   These ~~vegetable~~ taste good when they are served raw with salad dressing.

Editing Task

Find and correct seven more mistakes in the paragraphs about children's eating habits.

ten-year-old
What does a ~~ten-years-old~~ child eat in a day? Specialists in nutrition is finding out that the news is not good. As a result, they are looking for ways to improve children's eating habit. They are also involved in trying to help families make healthier choice.

Most experts suggest that a few key practices can help families. One of these

5 practices are common sense: people should eat unprocessed food. When there is a choice between canned corn and fresh corn, people should choose the fresh corn. Secondly, people should read labels carefully. Because labels contain a lot of informations, people should familiarize themselves with the nutrition and calorie content of their favorite products. Finally, people can boost the health content of certain kinds of food. For

10 example, it is possible to substitute whole-grain flours for white flour in most recipes.

Parents and children live busy lives, but research shows that when a healthy child becomes a 40-years-old adult, that person can look forward to a healthy old age.

6 | Grammar for Writing ✏

Using Precise Nouns and Adjectives to Make Your Writing Clearer

Using precise nouns and precise adjectives will make your writing clearer. For example, instead of using the general noun *people* to say what type of people you are writing about, instead use *adults, children, senior citizens,* or *students*. Read these examples:

Many people aren't aware of the nutritional value of food.
Many Americans aren't aware of the nutritional value of food.

Note that an easy way to be specific is to use adjectives, such as *young adults, middle-aged people,* and *sugary desserts.*

Pre-writing Task

1 Read the paragraphs. What kinds of changes is the writer suggesting? How many suggestions does the writer give?

Small Changes for Better Health

Doctors say that most of their overweight patients know that they would benefit from some lifestyle changes. However, many of these same patients are quick to tell their doctors about their own personal reasons for not making these changes. Overweight children may prefer to play indoors rather than go outside and play. Overweight adults
5 often say they are too busy at work.

Doctors and nutritionists have studied this problem. They have found that many overweight adults and children think they need to do a lot of vigorous exercise to get any benefit. This false belief discourages them, and so they end up doing nothing at all. Recent studies show that a little light exercise can help. Some suggestions for small changes
10 include parking the car at the far end of a parking lot or getting off the bus one stop early. Another practical suggestion is taking stairs instead of elevators. Doctors also suggest that when watching TV, people walk or run in place during the commercials. Another clever idea for working adults and busy teens is to stand up and walk around when using the phone. Big changes can be scary and overwhelming, but small changes are not, so it is
15 more likely that people will try them.

2 Read the paragraph again. Underline the nouns that refer to people. Which ones seem especially precise? Circle the adjectives.

Writing Task

1 *Write*   Use the paragraph in the Pre-writing Task to help you write about a health problem or issue people have. What suggestions do you have for changes? You can write about one of these topics or use your own ideas.

- healthy or unhealthy eating habits
- healthy or unhealthy exercise habits
- healthy or unhealthy lifestyle habits (getting too little sleep, watching too much TV, etc.)

2 *Self-Edit*   Use the editing tips to improve your paragraph. Make any necessary changes.

1. Did you replace any general nouns with precise nouns?
2. Did you use adjectives to make your nouns more precise?
3. Did you avoid the mistakes in the Avoid Common Mistakes chart on page 133?

1 | Grammar in the Real World

A How does color affect your mood? Read the magazine article about the effects of color on mood. What is your favorite color? How does it affect your mood?

The Effects of Color on Mood

Research has shown that colors have **a** direct impact on our feelings. Therefore, it makes sense for people to surround themselves with colors
5 that make them feel good. Successful decorating depends on making **the** right color choices.

It is beneficial to choose colors that make people feel comfortable, happy,
10 relaxed, energized, or whatever mood is desired. Bright orange walls in **a** bedroom, for instance, may keep **a** sensitive person awake, whereas light blue seems to have **a** relaxing effect. Maya Romero of Omaha,
15 Nebraska, suffered from chronic insomnia. **A** friend suggested that **the** orange walls in her bedroom might be contributing to

the problem. Maya listened to her friend's advice and painted **the** walls light blue. Since then, she has had much less trouble 20 sleeping.

Color affects moods in **a** variety of ways. Yellow is **a** cheerful, uplifting color for **most** people. However, strong shades of yellow can be overwhelming when used 25 for **an** entire room. Light yellow, on the other hand, can lift **a** person's mood like **a** room filled with sunshine. Similarly, green can revive **the** spirit. This may be because green reminds us of nature. 30

Typically, people experience **the** color blue as comforting. However, it is better to avoid using too much blue in one room. **A** room with blue walls and blue furniture can seem cold and overly formal. 35 Christopher and Marie Wang of Duvall, Washington, moved into **a** new home and painted **the** walls in their living room blue. Then they filled **the** room with furniture of varying shades of blue. They loved it, 40 but they noticed that conversation died when they sat in **the** room with guests. They asked advice from **a** decorator to see if **the** problem was related to **the** decor.

⁴⁵ **The** decorator suggested that they replace their icy blue carpet with **a** carpet in warm colors, such as dark red or warm beige. She also recommended replacing their classic-style furniture with more comfortable ⁵⁰ pieces. **The** Wangs report that, after they made **the** changes, **the** living room quickly became their favorite room for entertaining.

Clearly, **the** colors in an environment have **a** tremendous impact on **the** people who live or work there. Certain colors can ⁵⁵ improve moods dramatically, while others can actually bring on feelings of sadness or loneliness. It is crucial to carefully consider color choices when decorating **a** living space or office. ⁶⁰

B *Comprehension Check* Answer the questions.

1. Why is it important to choose colors carefully when decorating a room?
2. What advice did the decorator give to the Wangs?
3. What are some examples of color-feeling associations?

C *Notice* Find the words in the article. Then circle the meaning of each set of words within the context.

1. bright orange walls
   a. a group of walls in general   b. specific walls

2. the orange walls
   a. a group of walls in general   b. specific walls

3. a sensitive person
   a. one example from a category   b. something in particular that was previously
      or group   mentioned in the text

4. the problem
   a. one example from a category   b. something in particular that was previously
      or group   mentioned in the text

Can you make a generalization about the use of *a / an*, *the*, and no article?

2 Indefinite Article, Definite Article, and No Article

▶ Grammar Presentation

The indefinite articles *a* and *an* and the definite article *the* come before singular count nouns. The definite article *the* can come before plural count nouns and noncount nouns.	*The color blue in a bedroom may relax people.* *Choosing colors is an important part of decorating.* *The orange walls contributed to her insomnia.*

2.1 Indefinite Articles: *A / An*

a. Use *a/an* before a singular count noun when the noun is part of a category or if it is a profession.	*Blue is **a** color.* *The power of color is **an** issue that many researchers study.* *Her sister is **an** interior decorator.*
b. Use *a/an* to introduce a singular count noun when you first mention it.	***A** room with blue walls can seem formal.* ***An** orange bedroom can keep you awake.*
c. Use *a/an* before a singular count noun to give definitions or make generalizations.	***A** decorator is a person who chooses colors and furniture for a room.* ***A** yellow room is more cheerful than **a** blue room.*

2.2 Definite Article: *The*

a. You can use *the* before singular count nouns, plural count nouns, and noncount nouns.	*Where is **the** chair?* ***The** salespeople are very knowledgeable.* ***The** furniture in her house looks new.*
b. Use *the* before a noun when you mention it a second time.	FIRST MENTION SECOND MENTION *I took **an** interesting class. **The** class was about the effects of color on people's moods.*
c. Use *the* when a noun gives more information about a previously mentioned noun. The second noun is associated with the first noun.	*This is **a** good study on colors. **The** research makes* *some good points.* *That is **a** very interesting article. **The** information in it* *explains a lot about the power of color.*
d. Use *the* when the listener or reader can physically see or visualize the noun.	*Push **the** button in front of you.* *Your class is in **the** room just below this one.*
e. Use *the* when the noun is unique.	*The students are learning about **the** sun, **the** Earth, and **the** solar system.*
f. Use *the* before a singular noun used to represent a whole class or category. This is very formal.	***The** male robin is more colorful than the female.*

2.3 No Article

Use no article when a noncount noun or a plural count noun is used to make a generalization.	*Research has taught us many things about the ways that we are affected by colors.* *Colors can affect our moods.*

► Grammar Application

Exercise 2.1 *A/An* or *The*?

Complete the textbook excerpt about color theory. Circle the correct articles.
Sometimes more than one answer is possible.

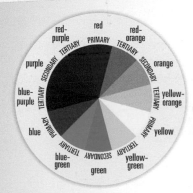

Color Theory

What is color theory? It is **a**/**the** tool and
(1)
a/**the** guide for understanding colors. There are
(2)
different versions of color theory, but in **a**/**the**
(3)
basic version, there are three primary colors.

A/**The** colors are blue, red, and yellow. As you
(4)
can see by looking at **a**/**the** color wheel, mixing equal parts of two primary
(5)
colors produces a secondary color. For example, if you mix blue and red,
you get purple. If you mix red and yellow, you get **a**/**the** color orange.
(6)

Tertiary colors are also created by mixing two primary colors. However,
to make **a**/**the** tertiary color, you use unequal amounts of two colors. By
(7)
doing that, you get colors like blue-green and yellow-orange.

Now, look at **a**/**the** color wheel again. **A**/**The** colors that lie opposite
(8)   (9)
each other on **a**/**the** color wheel are called complementary colors. For
(10)
example, **a**/**the** colors red and green are complementary colors. So are
(11)
a/**the** colors orange and blue. Look at **a**/**the** square below. It contains
(12)   (13)
a/**the** complementary colors red and green. Stare at it for 15 seconds,
(14)
then stare at **a**/**the** white wall or **a**/**the** piece of white paper.
(15)   (16)

Did you notice that the "ghost" image (the image
you see on the white wall or paper) has the opposite
colors? **A**/**The** green half of the square becomes red
(17)
and **a**/**the** red half becomes green. This is one
(18)
characteristic of complementary colors.

Exercise 2.2 A/An, The, or No Article?

A 🔊 Listen to the web article about color harmony. Write *a/an*, *the*, or Ø for no article.

Color Harmony

Some colors go together while some colors don't. Why? Is there a way to understand why some colors work better together than others? As many artists and designers know, __Ø__ color harmony is based on _____ color theory.

(1)   (2)

Let's think about _____ ways color harmony works in a room. One main rule

(3)

of color harmony is that one color must be stronger than _____ other colors in

(4)

the room. In other words, one color must be more intense than the others or cover a larger area than the others.

Another rule of color harmony is that you should not put two very intense colors next to each other. For example, you should not have _____ bright red sofa on

(5)

top of _____ bright green rug. _____ human eye cannot focus on both

(6)   (7)

colors at the same time, and _____ colors may seem to vibrate.

(8)

A third rule of color harmony is that the colors in a room should be related to each other in some way. You can determine colors' relationships to each other by looking at _____ color wheel. Colors that are next to each other on the color

(9)

wheel, such as red and red-orange, will usually look good together. You can also put _____ complementary colors together. These are colors that are on

(10)

opposite sides of the color wheel, such as yellow and purple. Color triads go well together, too. These are three colors that are the same distance from each other on the color wheel. For example, _____ primary colors, red, blue, and yellow, form

(11)

a color triad. The secondary colors, green, purple, and orange, also form a color triad.

B *Over to You* What is your favorite color combination? Write five sentences describing why you like this color combination and describing things that you own in these colors. Use nouns with *a/an*, *the*, and no article in your sentences. Then share your sentences with a partner.

My favorite color combination is pink and orange. I like it because both colors are bright. I have a T-shirt with the colors pink and orange. The shirt was a gift from my sister. I also have a pair of pink and orange shoes.

3 | Quantifiers

▶ Grammar Presentation

Quantifiers are words such as *all* (*of*), *some* (*of*), and *a lot of* that describe an amount or number.	**All of** the colors go well together. I have **some** information about colors.

3.1 Quantifiers with Count Nouns and Noncount Nouns

a. Quantifiers describe both large and small quantities or amounts. They are used with both count and noncount nouns.	**More** **Less**	*all* (*of*) *many / a lot of* *quite a few* (*of*) */ a great deal of* *some* (*of*) *a few* (*of*) */ a little* (*of*) *few* (*of*) */ little* (*of*) *not a lot of / not many* (*of*) */ not much* (*of*) *not any* (*of*) */ none of / no*
b. Use the following quantifiers only with count nouns: *quite a few* (*of*), *few, a few* (*of*), *not many* (*of*)		**Quite a few** <u>painters</u> have studied at that art school. **A few** <u>painters</u> shared the paint. **Few** <u>students</u> have time for art classes. **Not many** <u>students</u> have found a summer job.
c. Use the following quantifiers only with noncount nouns: *a great deal of, a little, little, not much* (*of*)		We have **a great deal of** <u>work</u> to do. I have **a little** <u>information</u>. She has **little** <u>patience</u>. There is **not much** <u>time</u> left to complete the work.
d. Use *a few* to say there are some but not many. Use *few* for a very small number.		There are always **a few** <u>students</u> who want to major in art. There are **few** <u>scholarships</u> for international students.
e. Use *a little* and *little* with noncount nouns. Use *a little* to say there is some but not much. Use *little* for a very small amount.		I have **a little** money, so I can pay for it. I have **little** money. I don't have enough money.

3.2 Quantifiers That Are Used with Count Nouns and Noncount Nouns

The following quantifiers can be used with both count and noncount nouns:

COUNT NOUNS	NONCOUNT NOUNS
All of the <u>students</u> in my class work hard.	I gave him **all of** the <u>money</u>.
She used **a lot of** <u>colors</u> in her painting.	I don't have **a lot of** <u>time</u> today to study.
Most of the <u>answers</u> are clear.	I knew how to use **most of** the <u>software</u>.
Some of the <u>students</u> don't know a lot about art.	I painted **some of** the <u>time</u> while I was on vacation.
I did**n't** take **a lot of** <u>notes</u> in class.	He did**n't** have **a lot of** <u>help</u> on the project.
We do**n't** have **any** <u>solutions</u>.	They did**n't** put **any** <u>effort</u> into the job.
None of the <u>students</u> is absent.	**None of** the <u>work</u> is good.
There are **no** <u>excuses</u> for poor work.	That room has **no** <u>sunshine</u>.

3.3 Quantifiers and *Of*

a. Use a quantifier without *of* when a noun is used in an indefinite or general sense.	**Some** students are late. I was interested in **a few** art classes.
b. Use a quantifier with *of* when the noun is specific and known to both the speaker and listener. Use *of* before a determiner such as *the, my, your, his, her, our, their, these,* or *those*.	**Some of** the <u>students</u> at my school are very smart. **A few of** the <u>activities</u> in class require artistic ability.
c. The quantifiers *a great deal of, a lot of,* and *none of* always include *of*.	**A lot of** people are interested in art. NOT A lot people are interested in art.

▶ Grammar Application

Exercise 3.1 Quantifiers

A Complete the article about color blindness. Circle the correct quantifiers.

Color Blindness

Color blindness is a condition in which a person cannot see the difference between certain colors. **All of /(Many)** people think that color-blind people see
(1)
no / none colors at all and only see black and white. However, complete color
(2)
blindness is very rare. **Not much / Not many** people are completely color blind.
(3)
However, **many / much** people do have some degree of color blindness. A large
(4)
number of the men in the world are color blind. Very **few / little** women, however,
(5)
are color blind.

A great deal of / Quite a few people who suffer from weak color vision have
(6)
red-green color blindness. They cannot tell the difference between red and green.
Think about the color purple. It is made up of two colors: red and blue. If you have
a little / a few red color blindness, and you look at a bright purple flower, you may
(7)
be able to see **a little / a few** red, but the flower will look almost blue. If you have
(8)
a more serious case of red color blindness, the flower may look completely blue to
you. You'll see **no / none of** the red at all.
(9)

So why are some people color blind? We have red, blue, and green cones in our
eyes. You need to have **all / little** of the types in order to see colors correctly. If you
(10)
don't have **all / much** of the types of
(11)
cones, or if **few / some** of them are not
(12)
working right, you may see a red flower as
green or a green vegetable as brown.

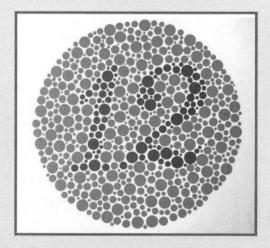

Look at this image. It is an Ishihara
plate. Ishihara plates are made up of
different-colored dots. Do you see a
number within the circle? If not, you may
have weak red-green color vision.

B *Pair Work* Work with a partner. Think about some activities (getting dressed, driving, watching TV, reading, using a computer) that people with color blindness might have trouble with. Write four sentences. Use different quantifiers in each sentence.

Many people with color blindness will have difficulty matching their socks.

Exercise 3.2 More Quantifiers

A Complete the report about car sales. Use the quantifiers in the box and the chart below. Use each quantifier only once. Sometimes more than one answer is possible.

a great deal of	few	little	many
many of	most	no	quite a few

Anderson Auto Sales
Percentage of Sales by Color 2010 & 2011

	White	Silver	Black	Grey	Red	Blue	Brown	Green	Yellow	Other
% of Total Sales 2011	23	19	14	15	3	7	9	5	1	3
% of Total Sales 2010	19	32	12	9	12	9	2	0	2	3

1. In 2011, there was _little_ demand for yellow cars.

2. In 2010, they had _____ success in selling green cars.

3. When Anderson Auto Sales created sales projections for 2012, they probably did not

   plan to sell _____ yellow cars.

4. _____ the cars sold in 2010 were white, silver, or black.

5. _____ of the cars sold in 2011 were white, silver, or black.

6. Compared to 2010, _____ the cars sold in 2011 were grey.

7. Compared to 2010, _____ customers favored red cars in 2011.

8. Compared to 2010, _____ customers bought brown cars in 2011.

B Rewrite five sentences from A using different quantifiers.

In 2011, there wasn't much demand for yellow cars.

1. _____

2. _____

3. _____

4. _____

5. _____

C *Over to You* Do Internet research to find out the most popular car colors this year or last year. Discuss your findings with a partner.

Exercise 3.3 ◄) Using Quantifiers with *Of*

Listen to the interview with the students about changes to their school. Complete the sentences with *of* or ✗ when *of* is not used.

Changes at Bay City University

Mark Recently, our university hired some __✗__ interior designers and color
(1)
experts to redesign the interior of the library at Bay City University. I asked
a group of students at the college what they thought about this. Here's what
they said:

Josh Some __of__ my friends don't like it. They think the colors are too bright.
(2)
Some ____ people don't like to study at the library because the bright
(3)
colors make them uncomfortable.

Amy All ____ my friends love the new colors, but we know that some ____
(4)   (5)
people don't like the color choices. You can never please all of the people
when you make a change, though.

Lynn A few ____ the people I know think it's great! They like being surrounded
(6)
by a lot ____ bright colors. I think a few ____ students would probably
(7)   (8)
prefer to have softer colors in the library, though.

Paulo None ____ my friends study in the library anymore. All ____ them study
(9)   (10)
in the dorms because they don't like the colors in the library. But I like the
new design. There were no ____ students studying on the first floor of the
(11)
library this morning, so I had the whole place to myself.

Exercise 3.4 More Quantifiers

A *Over to You* Interview some of your classmates. Have each student answer this question: *If you could make your room one color, which color would you choose and why?* Write the answers in the chart. Then write sentences about your classmates using quantifiers.

Name	Male (M) or Female (F)	Color
David	M	blue
Maria	F	beige (light brown)

Few of the male students chose blue. A lot of the female students chose beige.

B *Group Work* Share your sentences in a small group. What are the most popular colors for the women in your class? What are the most popular colors for the men in your class?

4 Avoid Common Mistakes ⚠

1. **Do not use *much* with plural nouns.**
   many
   We interviewed ~~much~~ interesting candidates, and we ended up hiring Ms. Stevens.

2. **Use an article before a singular occupation.**
   an
   I am ˄assistant researcher.

3. **Write *a lot* as two words.**
   a lot
   I have ~~alot~~ of friends.

Editing Task

Find and correct six more mistakes in this paragraph about color and memory.

Color and Memory

According to recent research, natural colors can help people remember things better.
a
Felix A. Wichmann, ˄research scientist, and two of his colleagues conducted experiments
on color and memory. In the first experiment, participants looked at 48 photographs
of nature scenes. None of the photographs were of people. Half of the photos were in

5 black and white, and half were in color. Afterward, they looked at the same 48 photos
mixed up with alot of new photos. They had to say which ones they had already seen.
They remembered the color scenes much better than the black-and-white ones. None of
the participants were sure about all of the photos. Another experiment involved much
artificially colored photos. When artificially colored photos were included in the set of

10 48 photos, participants forgot much of the photos. They did not remember the artificially
colored photos any better than they remembered the black-and-white photos. These
findings suggest that it is not just any colors that help to create alot of our memories. Only
natural colors have that power.

Why is this research important? For one thing, advertiser may find these results

15 interesting. If advertiser uses natural colors in ads, consumers may be able to remember
them better.

5 | Grammar for Writing ✎

Using Quantifiers and Pronouns to Hedge

Writers rarely use the absolute quantifiers *all*, *none of*, or *not any* or the pronouns *everybody*, *everyone*, *nobody*, or *no one* in academic writing. Instead, they use the quantifiers that fall between *all* and *none* in meaning, such as *little*, *many*, *not many*, and *quite a few*. They use these indefinite quantifiers to hedge, in other words, to indicate that the information is less certain because the writer knows that this information might not be true in all cases. Read these examples:

<u>All people</u> feel the effects of color without knowing it. (absolute quantifier)
<u>People</u> feel the effects of color without knowing it. (no quantifier)
<u>Many people</u> feel the effects of color without knowing it. (indefinite quantifier)

The first two sentences have the same meaning. The use of *many* rather than *all* or no quantifier in the third sentence makes the statement more likely to be true and more appropriate for academic writing.

Pre-writing Task

1 Read the paragraphs about color therapy. Do you believe that colors can heal?

Color Therapy

Many people agree that colors can affect the way we feel. But most of the time, we may not be aware of the effect. Colors can even cause physical reactions. For example, a person might feel cold in a room with blue walls. If that same room were painted red, the same person might feel warm. Because of these physical reactions, some people believe
5 that colors can heal. The use of colors to heal is called color therapy, or chromotherapy.

Only a few people believe in chromotherapy. Not many traditional scientists believe in it. In fact, quite a few of them call it a "pseudoscience," which means that it is not based on any real, proven science. These scientists also argue that colors have different meanings in different cultures, so the same colors are unlikely to have the same effect on
10 all patients. Furthermore, research has shown that the effects of a color are temporary. For example, people may feel happy while they are in a yellow room, but they will lose that feeling of happiness soon after they leave the room. The next time you feel warm or cold, happy or excited, look around you. Are colors affecting you?

2 Read the paragraphs again. Circle the use of *all*. Why does the writer use *all* here? Underline the quantifiers that describe a large or medium number. How does the meaning of each sentence change if you change these quantifiers to *all*? <u>Double underline</u> the quantifiers that describe a small amount.

Writing Task

1 *Write* Use the paragraphs in the Pre-writing Task to help you write about how colors affect people's lives. You can write about one of these topics or use your own ideas.

- color in advertising
- color in nature
- color in your home
- color in clothing
- color in video games
- color in your school

2 *Self-Edit* Use the editing tips to improve your paragraph. Make any necessary changes.

1. Did you use quantifiers to hedge?
2. Did you use quantifiers to avoid repeating yourself?
3. Did you avoid the mistakes in the Avoid Common Mistakes chart on page 147?

Pronouns

Unusual Work Environments

1 | Grammar in the Real World 🌐

A What are the characteristics of a good workplace? Read the article about a unique workplace. How is this workplace unique?

The Company You Keep

Imagine **yourself** living the good life[1] and working at the same time. Employees of SAS do that every day. The SAS Institute is a software development firm[2] in North Carolina. In 2010 and
5 2011, it was number one on *Fortune* magazine's list of "Best 100 Companies to Work for in America."

In the late 1980s, SAS started giving its employees free candy. The perks[3] grew from there. There is now a long list of on-site services at SAS.
10 These include a fitness center, massage therapy, dry cleaning, and a beauty salon. **Anyone** can walk on the nature trails outside the offices at SAS and enjoy gourmet food in the cafeteria. The perks reduce distractions so **everyone** can focus on work. These innovations[4] also encourage employees to interact with **each other**.

The company benefits[5] are impressive as well. One benefit is a company child-care
15 center. **Another** is a free health care facility. For employees and their families, there is also counseling and support for issues such as parenting, financial planning, and stress management.

With a voluntary turnover rate[6] of only 2 percent, most employees seem satisfied with their jobs and are not considering leaving. This appears to show that the perks
20 and benefits are a success. While not all companies go to such extremes to keep their employees happy, it is clear that this strategy works well for SAS.

---

[1]**the good life:** a happy and contented life without financial problems | [2]**firm:** a company | [3]**perk:** a special, extra service that companies offer their employees, such as free or low-cost health club memberships | [4]**innovation:** something new or different | [5]**benefit:** a helpful service given to employees in addition to pay | [6]**turnover rate:** the percent of workers who leave a company

B *Comprehension Check* Answer the questions.

1. What are some of the perks that SAS gives its employees?
2. What are some reasons SAS gives its employees these perks?
3. What does the voluntary turnover rate at SAS seem to show?

C *Notice* Find the sentences in the article. What nouns do the words in bold refer to?

1. Imagine **yourself** living the good life and working at the same time.
2. **Another** is a free health care facility.
3. These innovations also encourage employees to interact with **each other**.

2 | Reflexive Pronouns

▶ Grammar Presentation

Reflexive pronouns are used to talk about actions when the subject and object of a sentence are the same person or people. They are often used for emphasis to say that the action is performed by that person and nobody else.	*We should enjoy **ourselves** at work.* *Sue **herself** determines how she is evaluated.* (Sue determines this, not someone else.)

2.1 Forming Reflexive Pronouns

There is a reflexive pronoun for each subject pronoun.	*I* **myself**	*we* **ourselves**	
	you **yourself**	*you* (plural) **yourselves**	
	he **himself**	*they* **themselves**	
	she **herself**		
	it **itself**		

2.2 Using Reflexive Pronouns as Objects

a. Use a reflexive pronoun when the subject and object of a sentence are the same.

SUBJECT   OBJECT
*They can get **themselves** treats during the workday.*

SUBJECT   OBJECT
*We introduced **ourselves** to the new staff.*

b. Use a reflexive pronoun after an imperative in which you are directly addressing the reader or listener. The implied subject of the sentence is *you.*

*Imagine **yourself** living the good life and working at the same time.*
*Give **yourselves** a day off!*
*Ask **yourself** if this company is right for you.*

c. Reflexive pronouns are often used with the following verbs:

be hard on	*She was always hard on **herself**.*
be proud of	*He was very proud of **himself** and his grades.*
believe in	*You have to believe in **yourself**. You can do it.*
blame	*They blamed **themselves** for what happened.*
enjoy	*We really enjoyed **ourselves** at the conference.*
feel good about	*Eating well helps you feel good about **yourself**.*
help	*Please help **yourselves** to some food.*
hurt	*I hurt **myself** carrying those heavy boxes.*
look at	*Look at **yourself** in the mirror.*
push	*She should push **herself** to work harder.*
remind	*He reminded **himself** to get to work early.*
see	*The company saw **itself** as an innovator.*
take care of	*Take care of **yourself**. You're working too hard.*
tell	*I tell **myself** that I am good at what I do.*

d. Use an object pronoun, not a reflexive pronoun, after prepositions when the meaning is clear without a reflexive pronoun. If the meaning isn't clear, use a reflexive pronoun.

*They took the candy home with **them**. (They couldn't take the candy home with someone else.)*
*I'm very proud of **myself**. (I could be proud of someone else.)*

▸▸ Verbs That Can Be Used Reflexively: See page A6.

2.3 Other Uses of Reflexive Pronouns

a. You can put the reflexive pronoun directly after a noun or pronoun for greater emphasis or at the end of the clause for less emphasis.

*The manager **herself** gave us candy. (more emphatic)*
*I interviewed the candidates **myself**. (less emphatic)*

b. Use *by* + a reflexive pronoun to mean "alone" or without help.

*I can work by **myself**, or I can work on a team.*
*John completed the whole project by **himself**.*

▶ Grammar Application

Exercise 2.1 Reflexive Pronouns

A Complete the statements about conditions at different companies. Circle the correct reflexive pronouns.

1. When the CEO and the head of Human Resources saw **himself**/**themselves** in the "100 Best Companies" article, they were surprised.

2. A pet cannot take care of **itself**/**ourselves** while its owner is on a business trip, so JM Corporation offers free pet care to its employees.

3. My company lets us take special days off, so I gave **itself**/**myself** a day off from work on my birthday.

4. The president helped to make the company a good place to work, so he was very proud of **herself**/**himself** when JM Corporation got the "100 Best Companies" award.

5. Susan and I own our company, so we can give **themselves**/**ourselves** a vacation anytime.

6. Before you go to your interview, you should ask **myself**/**yourself** why you want to work at JM Corporation.

7. Our new CEO introduced **ourselves**/**himself** to us at a meeting this morning.

8. Our manager said, "You and your team should congratulate **yourself**/**yourselves**. You all did a great job on the last project!"

B *Over to You* Answer the questions with information that is true for you. Use reflexive pronouns.

- How do you take care of yourself?

- What should people tell themselves before a job interview?

- Think about a time when a friend or family member felt good about himself or herself. What happened?

Exercise 2.2 Reflexive Pronouns as Objects

Complete the excerpt from the Careers page of a company website. Write the correct reflexive or object pronoun.

Work at JM!

Imagine *yourself* working at JM Corporation! Read these comments from our
(1)
happy employees and their families:

Jane Recognition makes JM a great place to work. If we challenge

_____ and take on special projects, we get rewarded. Also,
(2)

I can give _____ a day off whenever I want.
(3)

Manuel We love the benefits, such as child care. My wife couldn't imagine

_____ leaving the twins all day while she worked. Now, she
(4)

takes the twins to work with _____ every day.
(5)

Lisa The work-life balance is great here. At JM Corporation, I never take my

work home with _____ . For example, I can get everything
(6)

done by Friday and enjoy _____ on the weekends. Just
(7)

ask _____ : If you could have all this and a great salary,
(8)

wouldn't you want to work here, too?

Exercise 2.3 Other Uses of Reflexive Pronouns

A Complete the sentences with reflexive pronouns. Use the information in parentheses to help you.

1. Bianca is a highly valued employee. She is able to handle difficult management crises

   by herself (alone).

2. Bianca _____ (emphasis) always takes responsibility for any problems on

   a project.

3. I _____ (emphasis) think she would be a good candidate for promotion.

4. Robert is on Bianca's team, but he prefers to work _____ (alone).

5. Only Robert _____ (emphasis) can learn to become a better team player.

6. Two other team members would also rather work _____ (alone).

7. Bianca recognized this issue and suggested team-building training

_____ (emphasis).

8. Only the employees _____ (emphasis) can fix this problem, in my

opinion.

B _Group Work_ Ask and answer the questions with your group members. Use reflexive pronouns. Then share your group's answers with the class.

- What kind of company do you imagine yourself working at someday?
- What kind of job do you see yourself doing someday?
- What kind of work tasks can you do by yourself?

Paulo imagines himself working at a big international company someday. He sees himself being the manager of a large group. He doesn't want to work by himself.

3 | Pronouns with _Other / Another_

▶ Grammar Presentation

Another, others, the other, and _the others_ are pronouns that refer back to a noun. _Each other_ and _one another_ are reciprocal pronouns. They are used when two or more people do the same thing.	_Some employees are happy, but_ **others** _are not._ _The fitness center is one benefit._ **Another** _is the dry-cleaning service._ _Employees help_ **each other**.

3.1 Pronouns: _The Other, the Others, Others, Another_

a. Use _the other_ to describe the remaining member of a pair. Use _another_ to describe an additional member of a group. It means "one more."	_I have two favorite sports. One is swimming._ **The other** _is tennis._ (There are only two sports.) _Swimming is one of my favorite sports._ **Another** _is tennis._ (There are more than two sports.)
Use third-person singular verb forms with _the other_ and _another_.	_One of my children goes to college and_ **the other** _works._
b. Use _the others_ for two or more remaining members of a specific group. Use plural verb forms with _the others_.	_One of my children is in high school._ **The others** _are in college._ (I have at least three children: the one in high school and at least two in college.)
c. Use _others_ (without _the_) for additional members of a group or to contrast these members with previous ones. Use plural verb forms with _others_.	_Some people without jobs look for work every day._ **Others** _look once a week._ (Two contrasting groups of people.)

3.2 Reciprocal Pronouns: *Each Other, One Another*

a. *Each other* and *one another* are reciprocal pronouns. Use them when two or more people or groups do the same thing. There is no difference in meaning.

Each other is more common and more informal than *one another*.

The teacher and the student respect **each other**.

The teacher and the student respect **one another**. (The teacher respects the student. The student respects the teacher.)

The five employees in my company help **each other**.

The five employees in my company help **one another**. (Each employee helps the other four employees.)

Data in the Real World

Each other is more common than *one another* in conversation and academic writing. *One another* is slightly more common in academic writing than in conversation.

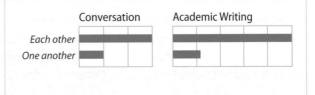

Reciprocal pronouns are less frequently used than personal pronouns (*I, you,* etc.).

▶ Grammar Application

Exercise 3.1 *The Other, the Others, Others,* or *Another?*

A Complete the article about the benefits at two companies. Circle the correct words.

Some Great Benefits

Vacation time is often a key benefit that attracts people to a company.

The others are / Another is child care. Although many companies today are cutting
(1)
these types of benefits, **others are / the other is** still providing them.
(2)
Two California companies offer great benefits for their workers. One is Amgen.

Others are / The other is Google. One of the benefits employees at Amgen enjoy is 17
(3)
paid days off and three weeks of paid vacation each year. **The others is / Another is** the
(4)
cafeteria. Many companies have on-site cafeterias, but **the others don't / the other doesn't**
(5)
tend to offer take-out breakfasts and lunches like Amgen does.

Free food is one of the perks that Google employees really love, and rightly so.

Another includes / Others include four gyms, free laundry machines, and on-site
(6)
doctors. Google also provides new parents with vouchers for take-out meals for three

months so they don't have to cook when they get home.

Some employees appreciate the free food and laundry services at companies like Google. **Others are / The other is** looking for long, paid vacations. When you are looking for a job, be sure to consider the benefits offered by the company, and not just the salary.

(7)

B *Over to You* What benefits do you look for in a job? On a separate sheet of paper, complete the sentences. Then share your sentences with a partner.

There are two major benefits that I look for in a job. One benefit is

_____ . The other is _____ . There are

other benefits that I think would be nice. One is _____ . Others are

_____ and _____ .

There are two major benefits that I look for in a job. One benefit is health insurance. The other is paid vacation days. There are other benefits that I think would be nice. One is help with child-care costs. Others are flexible hours and a gym.

Exercise 3.2 *The Other, Another, Each Other, or One Another?*

Complete the information from a company website. Use *the other*, *another*, *each other*, or *one another*. Sometimes more than one answer is possible.

Do you want your employees to respect _each other / one another_ ?
(1)
TeamBuilders has several programs to help you and your staff trust _____
(2)
more and work more productively together.

Read some of our reviews from our customers:

JM Corporation: My staff participated in five TeamBuilders activities, and we really

enjoyed them. One great activity was the Blindfold activity. _____ was
(3)
the "Say It Out Loud!" activity. With these activities, all 12 people on my team learned

how to communicate with _____ . Thanks, TeamBuilders, for giving us
(4)
the tools we need to help _____ get the job done!
(5)

Big Buy Stores: Our company did a couple of TeamBuilders activities. Even though we'd

only planned to do one activity called "Build-It," we had so much fun that we decided

to do _____ . We enjoyed both activities, but we preferred "Build-It" to
(6)
_____ activity.
(7)

4 Indefinite Pronouns

▶ Grammar Presentation

Indefinite pronouns (such as *everything*, *someone*, *anywhere*, *nobody*) are used when the noun is unknown or not important.	*The new boss wants to talk to **everybody**.* ***Someone** is moving into our office.*

4.1 Using Indefinite Pronouns

a. Use *everybody*, *everyone*, *everything*, and *everywhere* to describe all members or things in a group. Use *everybody* or *everyone* for people. Use *everything* for things. Use *everywhere* for places.

> ***Everybody** loves working here.*
> *Is **everyone** ready?*
> *He knows **everything** about this company.*
> *It seems you've looked **everywhere** for a job.*

b. Use *somebody*, *someone*, *something*, and *somewhere* to refer to an unnamed person, place, or thing.

Use indefinite pronouns with *some-* in questions to offer things or ask for things.

> ***Somebody** is going to review our work today.*
> *Can I ask you **something**?*
> *I'd like to work **somewhere** really interesting.*
>
> *Would you like **something** to drink?*

c. Use *anybody*, *anyone*, *anything*, and *anywhere* to refer to an unnamed person, place, or thing.

Use indefinite pronouns with *any-* to ask questions and in negative sentences.

> *"Can **anybody** receive financial help here?"*
> *"Sure. **Anyone** can ask for help."*
> *Do you need **anything** from the cafeteria?*
> *You can't take **anything** from this shelf.*
> *Have they advertised the product **anywhere**?*
> *I didn't go **anywhere** last night.*

d. Use *nobody*, *no one*, *nothing*, and *nowhere* to mean "none" or "not one" in affirmative statements.

> ***No one** likes this company.* (= not one person)
> *She said **nothing** important in the meeting.*
> (= not one thing)
> *There is **nowhere** I'd rather work.*
> (= not one other place)

▶ Grammar Application

Exercise 4.1 Indefinite Pronouns

Complete the interview between a career site and Ahn Nguyen, a corporate concierge for JM corporation. Circle the correct indefinite pronouns.

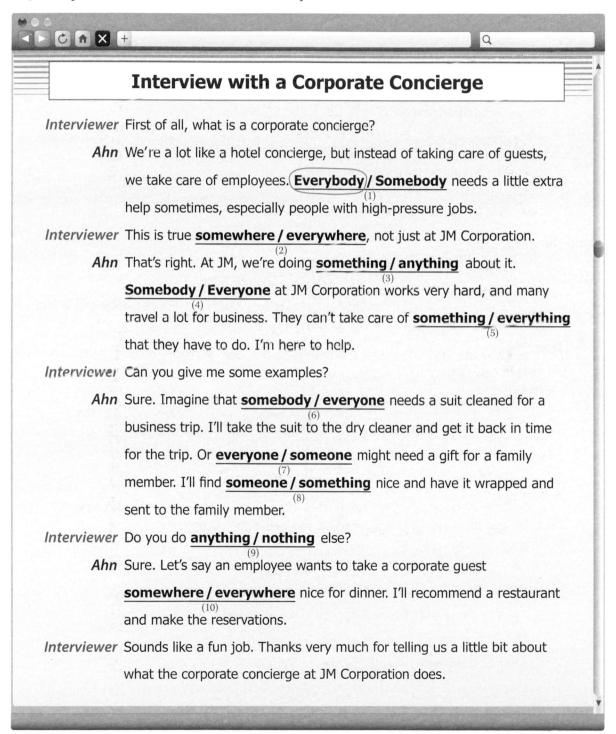

Interview with a Corporate Concierge

Interviewer First of all, what is a corporate concierge?

Ahn We're a lot like a hotel concierge, but instead of taking care of guests, we take care of employees. (**Everybody**)/ **Somebody** needs a little extra
(1)
help sometimes, especially people with high-pressure jobs.

Interviewer This is true **somewhere / everywhere**, not just at JM Corporation.
(2)

Ahn That's right. At JM, we're doing **something / anything** about it.
(3)
Somebody / Everyone at JM Corporation works very hard, and many
(4)
travel a lot for business. They can't take care of **something / everything**
(5)
that they have to do. I'm here to help.

Interviewer Can you give me some examples?

Ahn Sure. Imagine that **somebody / everyone** needs a suit cleaned for a
(6)
business trip. I'll take the suit to the dry cleaner and get it back in time
for the trip. Or **everyone / someone** might need a gift for a family
(7)
member. I'll find **someone / something** nice and have it wrapped and
(8)
sent to the family member.

Interviewer Do you do **anything / nothing** else?
(9)

Ahn Sure. Let's say an employee wants to take a corporate guest
somewhere / everywhere nice for dinner. I'll recommend a restaurant
(10)
and make the reservations.

Interviewer Sounds like a fun job. Thanks very much for telling us a little bit about
what the corporate concierge at JM Corporation does.

Exercise 4.2 More Indefinite Pronouns

A Complete the conversation about vacations. Use *anyone, anything, anywhere, no one, nothing,* or *nowhere.*

Jane   Are you going _anywhere_ for your vacation this summer?
(1)

Adam   No, we aren't doing _____ . We're too busy at this time of year.
(2)

_____ takes a vacation in the summer at my company.
(3)

Jane   Wow! Does _____ complain about that?
(4)

Adam   No. _____ complains because we get three weeks' paid vacation each
(5)

year. It's just that _____ can take it in the summer.
(6)

Jane   Well, I wouldn't say _____ negative about that, either!
(7)

Adam   What about you? Are you going _____ ?
(8)

Jane   Well, _____ important happens at my company in the summer, so my
(9)

family is planning a two-week trip to the mountains. We went there last summer, too.

It's very beautiful and peaceful. There's _____ I'd rather be this summer
(10)

than in those mountains with my family.

Adam   Sounds great!

B ◀))) Listen to a continuation of the conversation in A. Then answer the questions.

1. On average, how many paid vacation days do people in these places get?

European Union: _25–30 days_

Mexico: _____

The United States: _____

South Korea: _____

Japan: _____

2. Where do people get the most paid vacation time? _____

3. Where do people get the least paid time off? _____

C *Pair Work* Ask and answer the questions with a partner.

- Are you going anywhere for vacation this summer?

- Did you go anywhere last summer? If so, where did you go?

- Are you doing anything special during your time off this year?

- Does everyone in your family take off work at the same time for vacation?

5 | Avoid Common Mistakes ⚠

1. Use the plural pronoun *others* when talking about two or more people or things.

others
Some managers value discipline; ~~other~~ believe in praise for good work.

2. Use the object pronoun to form the reflexive pronouns *himself*, *itself*, and *themselves*.

themselves
Valuable employees can solve problems ~~theirselves~~.

3. Indefinite pronouns with *any-*, *every-*, and *no-* (such as *anyone*, *everyone*, and *no one*) take singular verb forms.

gets
Everyone in the company ~~get~~ a performance review once a year.

Editing Task

Find and correct six more mistakes in the paragraphs about management styles.

Management styles can vary widely. At one end of the extreme are the authoritarian managers who make all the decisions and are very strict. At the opposite end, there
others
are ~~other~~ who permit their employees to solve problems and suggest ideas theirselves. Permissive managers are most effective when innovation and problem solving are part of
5 the work process, for example, in technology. Stricter ones are effective when people are inexperienced or need a lot of guidance, or where there is high turnover of staff.

Mr. Jones is an example of an authoritarian manager. He relies only on hisself to make decisions at the restaurant where he works. Everyone are expected to follow his orders exactly. His style works because employees are constantly changing, so nobody
10 need to understand the rules and regulations.

Ms. Taylor is more democratic. The agents at her real estate agency manage their client accounts theirselves. Some of her agents focus on business while other work with private real estate accounts. It would be impossible for her to know what each agent is doing at any given time, so Ms. Taylor's style works well for her company.

15 There are different kinds of management styles ranging from very controlling to very open. Effective managers have a style of managing that is appropriate to the needs of their companies.

6 Grammar for Writing

Using Pronouns for Emphasis and to Avoid Repetition

Using reciprocal pronouns helps explain the relationship between two nouns, and using pronouns such as *one* and *another* is a useful way for writers to avoid repeating a noun too often. These two kinds of pronouns make your writing clearer and help it flow better. Read these examples:

The employees appreciate the company's generosity. They often talk with <u>one another</u> about the benefits of working there.

One important benefit for employees is health insurance. <u>Another</u> is a discount on lunch in the company cafeteria.

Notice that in the second sentence of each pair, there is no confusion about what nouns the pronouns refer to. If there is any confusion, it is better to repeat the noun.

Pre-writing Task

1 Read the paragraphs. What are the three different rules that good teams follow?

Job Satisfaction

Job satisfaction means different things to different people. However, for many people, the most important thing is having good co-workers. For some people, working with employees they like and respect is crucial. These people feel the workday is much more pleasant when they enjoy the people around them. For others, having co-workers

5 they like and respect isn't enough. They want to be able to actually work cooperatively with other people. These people generally like to work with people who are good team players. Teams that work well follow important rules. One is that members must be able to communicate easily with one another. Another is that team members should be able to listen to each other. Finally, team members should be flexible enough to

10 compromise when they don't agree with one another.

On the other hand, there are people who work better alone. They don't want to have to deal with others all the time. They say it slows them down to have to explain themselves. They like to work with others who enjoy working alone, but who are supportive and friendly and like to talk once in a while. Whatever their preferred work

15 style, most people prefer working with people they like.

2 Read the paragraphs again. Circle the reciprocal pronouns. Draw arrows to the nouns the pronouns refer to. <u>Double underline</u> the reflexive pronoun. Is the reflexive pronoun there for emphasis or because it is an object of a sentence with the same subject?

Writing Task

1 *Write* Use the paragraphs in the Pre-writing Task to help you write about working with other people. This could be at work or at school. You can write about one of these topics or use your own ideas.

- problems with working alone
- problems with working with people
- tasks that are good to do in teams

- tasks that are better to do alone
- types of people you like to work with

2 *Self-Edit* Use the editing tips to improve your paragraph. Make any necessary changes.

1. Did you use *other*, *another*, *others*, and *the others* to refer to people and things?
2. Did you use reciprocal pronouns (*one another*, *each other*) to show that two nouns have a mutual relationship?
3. Did you use a reflexive pronoun when the subject and object in a sentence are the same?
4. Did you avoid the mistakes in the Avoid Common Mistakes chart on page 161?

1 | Grammar in the Real World 🌐

A What can make attending college in the United States difficult? Read the web article about the cost of attending college. What are some ways to make college more affordable?

The Cost of U.S. Higher Education

In many countries, the cost of a college education is not very high. In France, for example, university students pay an affordable $220 a year. French students do
5 not have to **worry about paying** a lot for a college education because the government pays for it. In the United States, however, college tuition[1] is more expensive. Many students **have difficulty affording** it,
10 especially at private colleges.[2] In 2010, the average cost per year of a private college in the United States was $35,000.

Public colleges[3] generally cost less because they depend on the government to help pay some of the expenses of education. However, if budget cuts reduce that money, tuition can increase.
15 This can **prevent** students **from attending** even a public college.

The tuition at community colleges is the least expensive, costing about $2,500–$3,000 a year. Community colleges offer two-year programs with an associate's degree.[4] Other colleges and universities offer four-year programs and a bachelor's degree.[5] **Not attending** a four-year college right away is one option students use to save money. Many students attend
20 a community college for the first two years of college and then transfer to a more expensive school for the last two years.

[1]**tuition:** the money students pay for education | [2]**private college:** a school that does not receive its main financial support from the government | [3]**public college:** a school that depends on some financial support from the government | [4]**associate's degree:** a two-year degree at a community college | [5]**bachelor's degree:** a four-year degree at a college or university

To help pay for college, many students apply for financial aid. Financial aid consists of loans, grants,[6] scholarships, and work-study programs. Students can apply for a student loan at a low interest rate. They must, however, **plan on repaying** the loan plus interest after they graduate. Some students want to **avoid repaying** loans, so they apply for grants, which they do not have to repay. Scholarships are another form of financial aid that students do not have to repay. **Playing** a sport for a college team is one way to receive a scholarship. Finally, students can apply for work-study programs. In these programs, students work at jobs at their school and receive a small salary to help pay for expenses.

For students **interested in getting** a higher education in the United States, the cost can be high; however, there are ways to make it less expensive. Once students resolve the issue of money, they can **concentrate on having** the exciting experience of college life.

[6]**grant:** money that a university, government, or an organization gives to someone for a purpose, such as to do research or study

B Comprehension Check Answer the questions.

1. Why do public colleges cost less than private colleges? *because*
2. What is the difference between a grant and a loan? *the difference is what loan is*
3. What are two ways students can reduce or eliminate tuition costs?

C Notice Find the sentences in the article and complete them.

1. French students do not have to worry about _____*paying*_____ a lot for a college education because the government pays for it.

2. Some students want to avoid _____*repaying*_____ loans, so they apply for grants, which they do not have to repay.

3. _____*Playing*_____ a sport for a college team is one way to receive a scholarship.

What do the missing words have in common? In which sentence(s) does the missing word act as a subject? In which sentence(s) does the missing word act as an object?

2 Gerunds as Subjects and Objects

▶ Grammar Presentation

A gerund is the *-ing* form of a verb that functions as a noun. It can be the subject or object of a sentence.

subj   verb
Attending college is important these days.
I enjoy **learning**.
obj.

Noun = Sustantivo
as = como
Attending = asistir

2.1 Using Gerunds as Subjects and Objects

a. Use a singular verb form when the gerund is the subject of the sentence.	***Studying*** in the morning <u>is</u> difficult for me. ***Completing*** my application <u>has</u> taken hours.
b. Use a gerund as the object after the following verbs: Time: *delay, finish* Likes and dislikes: *appreciate, dislike, enjoy, mind* Effort and interest: *avoid, keep, practice* Communication: *defend, discuss, propose* Thinking: *consider, imagine, suggest*	I <u>finished</u> **working** on the project last night. My sister <u>dislikes</u> **working** in a bookstore. I <u>enjoy</u> **teaching**. <u>Practice</u> **interviewing** with a friend. <u>Discuss</u> **applying** for a loan with your parents. He <u>considered</u> **transferring** to another school.
c. Use *not* before a gerund to make it negative.	<u>**Not**</u> **attending** a four-year college is one option for students with little money.
d. Do not confuse a gerund with the present progressive form of the verb.	PRESENT PROGRESSIVE GERUND <u>I am considering</u> **working** at home.

▸▸ Verbs Followed by Gerunds Only: See page A7.
▸▸ Verbs followed by Gerunds or Infinitives: See page A7.

▶ Grammar Application

Exercise 2.1 Gerunds as Subjects and Objects

A Students are commenting on the process of applying for college in the United States. Use the words to write sentences with gerund subjects and objects. Use the simple present for the main verbs.

1. complete the college application / take / a long time

   Completing the college application takes a long time.

2. find the money for college / be / a problem for me

   Finding the money for College is a problem for me

3. my counselor / suggest / borrow money for college

   My counselor suggests borrowing money for college

4. not get into a good college / worry / me

   Not getting into a good college worries me

5. I / enjoy / discuss my future plans with my friends

   enjoy discussing my future plans with my friend

6. not have enough money for tuition / be / a concern

   Not having enough money for tuition is a concert

7. go to interviews at schools / make / me nervous

He goin to interviews at schools make me nervous

8. teachers / suggest / start the application process early

Teachers suggest starting the application process early

B *Pair Work* Discuss the gerunds in A with your partner. Which are subjects? Which are objects?

Exercise 2.2 Gerunds as Objects

A Complete the web article about tips for starting the college application process. Use the correct forms of the verbs in parentheses.

HW chapter hasta .13

Tips for Getting a College Education

Do you want a college education? First, _consider looking_ (consider / look) for the
(1)
right college as soon as possible. If you are in
high school or attending community college,
Keep studying (keep / study)
(2)
hard so you'll have good grades. Some schools
require an essay on their college application. Many students in this position
dislike writing (dislike / write) the essay, but it's important, so
(3)
don't _delay thinking about_ (not delay / think about) it. Some schools require
(4)
an on-site interview, so _practice interviewing_ (practice / interview) with
(5)
your friends or family.

Where will the money come from? Some students _conseder paying_
(6)
(consider / pay) for college themselves. Other students _don't mind borrowing_
(7)
(not mind / borrow) money from their families, but not all families can afford to
pay for a college education. Sit down with your family, and discuss all the options.
discuss working (discuss / work) at a part-time job while you go to
(8)
school, and _imagine working_ (imagine / work), studying, and adjusting
(9)
to a new lifestyle all at once. Is this really for you? If you think it is, then following
these tips will make the process easier.

thenselves = ellos mismos, sé
borrow = pedir prestado

B *Group Work* Answer the questions. Use gerunds in your sentences. Then share your ideas with the group.

- What should people in high school keep doing as soon as they decide to go to college?
- What should people consider doing when they need money for college?
- What should people try imagining before they make the final decision to go to college?

Exercise 2.3 More Gerunds as Objects

Use the words to write sentences about students and tuition costs. Use gerunds as objects and the <u>present progressive</u> form of the main verbs.

1. Jack / consider / go to a community college to save money

   <u>*Jack is considering going to a community college to save money.*</u>

2. Bo / think about / apply for financial aid instead of working

   working
   <u>Bo is thinking about applying for financial aid instead of</u>

3. Jane / avoid / borrow money by getting a part-time job at school

   <u>Jane is avoiding borrowin money by getting a part-time job at school</u>

4. My parents and I / not discuss / get a loan

   Prestamo
   <u>My parents and I aren't discussing getting a loan</u>

5. Tom / not enjoy / work while he goes to college

   <u>Tom isn't enjoying working while he goes to college</u>

6. My friend / delay / go back to school until he saves more money

   <u>My friend is delaying going to school until he saves more money</u>

7. Lisa and Henry / discuss / take part in a work-study program

   <u>Lisa and Henry are discussing taking in a work-study Program</u>

8. Mei-ling / not consider / start college without a part-time job

   <u>Meiling isn't considering starting college without a Part-time job.</u>

9. Naresh / avoid / apply to too many different institutions

   <u>Naresh is avoiding applying to too many diffent institutions</u>

3 | Gerunds After Prepositions and Fixed Expressions

▶ Grammar Presentation

The gerund is the only verb form used after prepositions and in certain fixed expressions.	*I **am interested in studying** art.* *I'm not **in favor of skipping** a year of college.*

3.1 Using Gerunds as Objects of Prepositions

Use a gerund as the object of prepositions after these common verb + preposition combinations:

Likes, dislikes, emotions: *be afraid of, care for, be excited about, be interested in, worry about* (or *be worried about*)

*Are you afraid of **failing**?*
*Bryn is excited about **applying** to college.*
*I worry about **not choosing** the right school.*

Interests and efforts: *be interested in, learn about, be responsible for, be successful at, take care of*

*Many students are responsible for **paying** their own tuition.*

Communication: *complain about, hear of, insist on, talk about, be warned of*

*Some parents complain about **having** more than one child in college at the same time.*
*My friend insisted on **visiting** the school with me.*
*Did anyone talk about **studying** together tonight?*

Thought: *be aware of, believe in, concentrate on, dream of, forget about*

*I believe in sometimes **staying** up all night to study for a test.*
*My sister dreams of **winning** a scholarship.*

Blame and responsibility: *admit to, apologize for, confess to, be guilty of*

*We apologize for **not contacting** you sooner.*

Other: *apply for, depend on, plan on, be used to*

*I'm used to **taking** care of myself. I've lived alone for years.*

▶◄ Verbs + Prepositions: See page A9.

3.2 Using Gerunds with Common Fixed Expressions

<table>
<tr>
<td>a. Use a gerund after certain common fixed verb + noun expressions: have a difficult time/have difficulty/have trouble, spend time/spend money, waste time/waste money</td>
<td>She had trouble finishing her degree.
I spent a lot of time helping in the library.
Don't waste time complaining.</td>
</tr>
<tr>
<td>b. Use a gerund after certain common fixed noun + preposition expressions: an excuse for, in favor of, an interest in, a reason for</td>
<td>There's no excuse for being late.
He has a reason for choosing this school.</td>
</tr>
</table>

handwritten annotations: gastar, basura, una razon para

▸▸| Expressions with Gerunds: See page A8.

▶ Grammar Application

Exercise 3.1 Gerunds as Objects of Prepositions

A student is talking about his plans for going to college. Match the sentence parts.

1. Many students worry __c__
2. To pay for their education, they depend __d__
3. I am very interested __a__
4. I hope I will be successful __f__ *(exito)*
5. I'm not used __g__
6. Fortunately, my parents want me to concentrate __e__
7. They are planning __b__

a. in getting a college education.
b. on applying for financial aid for me.
c. about being able to afford college tuition. *(becas)*
d. on receiving scholarships and loans.
e. on having an exciting college experience and not worrying about finances.
f. at getting into the school of my choice.
g. to studying and working at the same time.

Exercise 3.2 More Gerunds as Objects of Prepositions

A Complete the presentation on grants. Use the correct prepositions for the verbs in bold and the gerund form of the verbs in parentheses.

I know many of you are **excited** _about starting_ (start) college soon. Also,
many of you are **worried** _about paying_ (1) (pay) for school. I'm sure you have been
warned _of taking_ (2) (take) out a lot of big loans. You have heard some people
complain _about owing_ (3) (owe) money for the rest of their lives. Well, today, I'm
going to **talk** _about applying_ (4) (apply) for three grants. Grants aren't loans. You
aren't **responsible** _for paying_ (5) (pay) them back. (6)

The first type is the Pell Grant. The Pell Grant is for students who are going to college at least part-time and need financial aid. If you're **interested** _in asking_ (ask) for a Pell Grant, **insist** _on talking_ (talk) with a guidance counselor to find out more about this program.

Are any of you **planning** _on majoring_ (major) in the areas of science or mathematics? Then you might be **interested** _in trying_ (try) for the National Smart Grant. **Forget** _about getting_ (get) this grant unless you have maintained at least a 3.0 GPA in your first two years of college.

Finally, I know some of you are **dreaming** _of becoming_ (become) teachers. The TEACH Grant is for students who **plan** _on teaching_ (teach) at least four years in a low-income public or private school after graduation.

Now, are there any questions?

B Read about each person's situation and complete the advice. Use the words in parentheses with the correct preposition and the gerund form of the verbs.

1. Chelsea wants to be an engineer, but she doesn't have a 3.0 GPA. She should not _depend on getting_ (depend / get) a National Smart Grant.

2. Michael has completed two years of community college, but he doesn't have enough money to go to a four-year college. He should not _be afraid of applying for_ (be afraid / apply for) a Pell Grant.

3. Alison got a TEACH Grant, but she quit her teaching job after two years and got a high-paying job in computers instead. She must not _be worried about paying_ (be worried / pay) back her loan.

4. Brandon goes to the community college, but he spends time partying and has a low GPA. He must not _be interested in studying_ (be interested / study).

5. Jorge got a TEACH Grant, taught for several years, and now is the head teacher at a private school. He must _be successful at teaching_ (be successful / teach).

6. Sharon wants to major in computer science and get a National Smart Grant, but so far, her grades aren't that good. She should _concentrate on improving_ (concentrate / improve) her grades.

7. Rob's family can't help him pay for college, and he needs financial aid. He can probably _depend on receiving_ (depend / receive) a Pell Grant.

Exercise 3.3 Gerunds with Common Fixed Expressions

A Complete the conversations about college life. Use the correct forms of the fixed expressions in the box and the gerund forms of the verbs in parentheses.

(an) excuse for	have difficulty	in favor of	spend time
(an) interest in	have trouble	(a) reason for	waste time

Conversation 1

A I've heard some crazy _excuses for not handing in_ (not / hand in) papers.
(1)

B I don't think there's any good _a reason for not doing_ (not / do) your
(2)
work once you're in college.

Conversation 2

A You _spend_ a lot of _time studying_ (study). Does
(3)   (3)
it help?

B Yes, I would _have trouble keeping up_ (keep up) with my classes if I
(4)
didn't spend a lot of time studying.

Conversation 3

A A lot of people _waste time partying_ (party) in college. What do you
(5)
plan on doing after you leave this school?

B I have _interest in getting_ (get) a bachelor's degree, so I plan on
(6)
transferring to a four-year institution.

Conversation 4

A What type of student is the Joe Olinsky Foundation
in favor of giving (give) grants to?
(7)

B We have money from a government fund that we use
for students who would otherwise _have difficulty affording_ (afford) a
(8)
two-year college.

B 🔊 Listen and check your answers.

C *Group Work* Answer the questions. Use gerunds when appropriate. Then compare your sentences in your groups.

- What do you spend most of your time doing at school?

- What do you have the most trouble dealing with at school?

- What do you have an interest in doing after you leave this school?

Viet spends most of his time at school going to classes. I do, too. He has the most trouble dealing with parking. I have trouble dealing with the homework.

4 Gerunds After Nouns + *of*

▶ Grammar Presentation

Gerunds are often used after nouns + *of*.	**The cost of getting** an education is rising. I believe in the **importance of studying** hard.

4.1 Nouns + *of* + Gerunds

The following nouns are often used in noun + *of* + gerund combinations:

benefit of	A benefit of **going** to community college is cost savings.
cost of	The cost of **commuting** is rising because of gas prices.
danger of	There is a danger of **borrowing** too much money.
(dis)advantage of	What are some disadvantages of **taking** out loans for school?
effect of	The effects of **being** late are serious.
fear of	The fear of **being** jobless is what keeps me in school.
habit of	I'm in the habit of **not getting** up early.
idea of	The idea of **not going** to school is not an option.
importance of	It's impossible to underestimate the importance of **working** hard in school.
possibility of	The possibility of **not graduating** is worrisome.
problem of	The problem of **increasing** college costs affects a lot of students.
process of	He explained the process of **enrolling** in school.
risk of	She told me about the risks of **taking** out a loan.
way of	I'm thinking of a way of **paying** for school.

▶ Grammar Application

Exercise 4.1 Nouns + *of* + Gerunds

A Complete the conversations between Ms. Sparks, a community college counselor, and various families. Use the gerund form and the words in parentheses.

Conversation 1

Ms. Jones   We are concerned about _the cost of paying_ (the cost / pay) for our
(1)
son's education.

Ms. Sparks   I understand _the fear of_ _____
(2)
(the fear / not be able to) afford college.

Ms. Jones   Of course, I want my son to have _the possibility of getting_
(3)
(the possibility / get) the best education there is, but it's expensive.

Conversation 2

Mr. Allen   What are _the advantages of going_ (the advantages / go)
(4)
to a community college?

Ms. Sparks   _the benefits of attending_ (the benefits / attend) a
(5)
community college are numerous. It's especially helpful for students
who aren't sure of their major.

Mr. Allen   Is there _a possibility of getting_ (a possibility / get) in
(6)
this semester?

Ms. Sparks   Yes, you can register today, if you like.

Conversation 3

Luisa   _the process of applying_ (the process / apply) to college is long!
(7)
Ms. Sparks   I know it takes time, but you can reduce _the risk of leaving_
(8)
(the risk / leave) something out by being organized. Here's a checklist to use.

B *Over to You*   Write four sentences on a separate piece of paper about your family's and your thoughts about going to school. Use some of the noun + *of* expressions in the box with gerunds. Then share your sentences with a partner.

| benefit of | effect of | habit of | idea of | possibility of | risk of | way of |

One benefit of going to school when you are older is that you know what you want to do.

5 | Avoid Common Mistakes ⚠

1. Remember to use a gerund after a preposition.

getting

Students often worry (about) ~~get~~ into college.

2. As a general rule, when you use a verb as a subject, use a gerund.

Paying

~~Pay~~ for a private college can be very expensive.

3. Always use a singular verb with a gerund subject.

is

Interviewing at several colleges ~~are~~ time-consuming.

Editing Task

Find and correct <u>seven</u> more mistakes in the paragraphs about study habits.

       All students start the semester with the intention of ~~study~~ *studying* hard; however, find time to study can be challenging. Finding good places to study ~~are~~ *is* one challenge. Another is finding enough hours in the day and creating a schedule. Successful students face these problems realistically.

5   Different people have different purposes and needs when it comes to doing college work. Study*ing* in a quiet library works well for some people. At the same time, a coffee shop or cafeteria can also be a good place to work for those who get energy from be in a stimulating environment.

       Then there is the question of time. Most students today are working, paying bills, *is*

10 and taking classes at the same time, so they do not have the luxury of spend many hours with their books. However, research offers hope. Studying for a few minutes several times a day are a good way to learn new material.

       Learn what works for you is the key to academic success.

ing

6 | Grammar for Writing ✎

Using Noun + *of* + Gerund Constructions

Noun + *of* +gerund constructions are common in academic writing. These constructions can make your writing sound clearer and more precise. Read these examples:

A lot of learning can take place in the <u>process of making</u> mistakes.
The teachers tried to teach the <u>importance of getting</u> enough sleep before taking a test.

Pre-writing Task

1 Read the paragraphs. What type of student are the paragraphs about? How many advantages and disadvantages are listed?

Completing a College Degree

Many students at community colleges do not go to school full-time because the cost of getting a degree requires them to work while they are in school. There are both advantages and disadvantages of getting a degree while working. The disadvantages may be more obvious. First, students have to balance work, class, and homework. This can be

5 particularly difficult to do sometimes. Also, students can face the danger of losing interest. It can be hard to maintain interest in something that takes a very long time to complete. Another potential problem is that some classes are only offered at specific times. Students may not be able to change their work schedules to fit these classes into their schedules.

However, there are some advantages, too. Working students can usually finish their

10 studies without having any loans to pay back. Some employers might also help their employees with their educational fees. In addition, working students sometimes have the possibility of using what they learn in class at work. The experience of working and going to school at the same time can be difficult, but there are some important advantages of being a part-time working student, too.

2 Read the paragraphs again. Underline the noun + *of* + gerund constructions. Notice which of these gerund constructions are subjects and which are objects.

Writing Task

1 *Write* Use the paragraphs in the Pre-writing Task to help you write about the advantages and disadvantages of one aspect of being a student. You can write about one of these topics or use your own ideas.

- returning to school as an adult
- taking morning/afternoon/evening classes
- being in a big class or small class
- working on or off campus
- doing your homework in the evening or in the morning

2 *Self-Edit* Use the editing tips to improve your paragraph. Make any necessary changes.

1. Did you use gerunds as both subjects and objects?
2. Did you use any noun + *of* + gerund constructions?
3. Did you use any verb + preposition + gerund constructions?
4. Did you avoid the mistakes in the Avoid Common Mistakes chart on page 175?

1 | Grammar in the Real World

A What are some unusual types of advertising that you have noticed recently? Read the article on "guerrilla marketing." How do advertisers measure the success of a guerrilla marketing campaign?

Advertising, Guerrilla Style

Would you tattoo a website address on your body? One woman from Utah did just that. A company **got her to tattoo** its website address on her forehead for $10,000. She **wanted to do** it to raise money for her son's education. The company **wanted her to do** it for cheap advertising space. They also got free publicity[1] because the story was
5 on the news. This kind of extreme advertising – known as guerrilla marketing – uses surprising ways to advertise a product and get people's attention.

A **way to advertise** with guerrilla marketing is **to use** the environment in an unexpected way. For example, a few years ago, a popular candy company painted park benches so that they looked like giant chocolate bars. This creative ad[2] strategy got
10 consumers' attention in a positive way.

For guerrilla marketing to be successful, people must talk about the ads. In the 1990s, the company Half.com **persuaded** the town of Halfway, Oregon, **to change** its name to Half.com. People all over the United States heard about Half.com, and soon thousands of consumers went to the website.

15 Not all guerrilla marketing works. In 2007, an ad company **decided to place** signs with flashing lights around different cities to advertise a television show. However, in Boston, the police thought the signs were bombs. The police **tried to find** and **destroy** all of the signs.

Unlike those who use traditional advertising strategies, guerrilla marketers are not
20 **afraid to shock** people. The idea is to **convince people to talk** about the products. However, it is **important** for companies **to consider** how people will react. Not all publicity is always good publicity.

[1]**publicity:** the attention received as a result of an activity meant to attract interest | [2]**ad:** advertisement; advertising

B *Comprehension Check* Answer the questions.

1. What is guerrilla marketing? What is the purpose of guerrilla marketing?
2. How does guerrilla marketing get people's attention?
3. How is it different from traditional advertising?

C *Notice* Find the sentences in the article and complete them.

1. She wanted ___to do___ it to raise money for her son's education.
2. The police tried ___to find___ and destroy all of the signs.
3. A way to advertise with guerrilla marketing is ___to use___ the environment in an unexpected way.

What do all the verbs you wrote have in common? Look at the words that come before these verbs. What kinds of words are they?

2 | Infinitives with Verbs

▶ Grammar Presentation

An infinitive is *to* + the base form of a verb. Some main verbs in a sentence are followed by an infinitive, not a gerund.	I decided **to learn** about advertising. The company planned **not to use** traditional advertising.

2.1 Verbs + Infinitives

Use an infinitive after the following verbs:

Time: *hesitate, wait*
Likes or dislikes: *care = el cuidado*
Plans or desires: *decide, hope, need, plan*
Efforts: *attempt, help, learn, manage*

Communication: *agree, offer, promise*
Possibility: *appear, seem, tend*

Use *not* before the infinitive to show the infinitive is negative.

We hesitated **to use** guerrilla marketing.
I don't care **to see** *aburrido* boring ads on TV.
The company is hoping **to buy** advertising space. *anunciar*
Guerrilla marketers attempt **to get** your attention.
Our company promised **not to waste** money.
Guerrilla ads tend **to shock** consumers. *impactar*

▶▶ Verbs Followed by Infinitives Only: See page A7.

2.2 Verbs + Objects + Infinitives

a. After some verbs, an object comes before the infinitive. The object performs the action of the infinitive. The following verbs are followed by an object + infinitive: *advise, allow, convince, encourage, get, persuade, prepare, teach, tell, urge,* and *warn.*

> VERB + OBJ + INF
>
> He <u>got us</u> **to try** a new advertising technique.
>
> The company didn't <u>tell the salespeople</u> **to educate** consumers.
>
> They <u>urged the advertisers</u> **not to surprise** people.

b. Some verbs can be followed by either an object + infinitive or an infinitive only. These verbs include *ask, choose, expect, help, need, promise, want,* and *would like.*

> VERB + OBJ + INF
>
> My department <u>chose Sally</u> **to create** the new ads. (Sally will create the ads.)
>
> VERB + INF
>
> My department <u>chose</u> **to create** the new ads. (My department will create the ads.)

▶▶ Verbs + Objects + Infinitives: See page A8.

Data from the Real World

Research shows that these are the most common verbs + infinitives in academic writing:

appear, begin, continue, fail, seem, tend, try, want	Sales of the new product **continued to rise** last month. The boss **failed to recognize** the company's problems.

▶ # Grammar Application

Exercise 2.1 Verbs + Infinitives

Complete the online homework assignment about guerrilla marketing with the correct forms of the words in parentheses. Use the simple present form of the main verbs.

Guerrilla Marketing 101

Guerrilla marketing <u>*attempts to reach*</u> (attempt / reach) consumers
(1)
in unexpected or unusual contexts, such as public places. Guerrilla marketers
<u>*hopes to shock*</u> (hope / shock) or surprise potential consumers.
(2)
Why is guerrilla marketing so popular? One reason for this is that it
<u>*tends to cost*</u> (tend / cost) less than traditional marketing. Guerrilla
(3)
marketing usually <u>*manages to generate*</u> (manage / generate)
(4)

a lot of publicity for little money. It _**Seems to be**_ (seem/be)
(5)

effective for most products; however, several experts think that people are getting

tired of it. I _**hosetate to admit**_ (hesitate/admit) this, but I agree.
(6)

Exercise 2.2 Verbs + Objects + Infinitives

A Complete the conversation about a nontraditional type of advertising called reverse graffiti. Use the words in parentheses. Use the correct form of the main verbs according to the context.

Dae Ho Our advertising consultants _are advising us to try_ (advise / us / try) a type of
(1)

guerrilla marketing called reverse graffiti.

Erin What's reverse graffiti?

Luis It's a way to write an image on a dirty public surface by removing the dirt. It

_____ (get / consumers / notice) a product.
(2)

Do you think the managers will like the idea?

Erin Actually, I think the managers will _____ _____ _____
(3)

(tell / us / not do) it.

Dae Ho Why? I think we can probably _____
(4)

(convince / them / try) it because it's cheap.

Luis I bet we can _____ (persuade / them / do) it.
(5)

Dae Ho OK. We'll need help though.

Luis I'll _____ (tell / Mike / create) a presentation.
(6)

Erin OK, Luis, but you should _____
(7)

(warn / him / prepare) for a lot of questions. Some people think it destroys property,

so it's vandalism. It might not be legal.

B *Over to You* Answer the questions with information that is true for you. Include the verbs from A in your answers. Then share your sentences with a partner.

- What is your opinion of guerrilla marketing?
- Does it work for you and your demographic (that is, people who are your age and have similar likes and dislikes)? Why or why not?

Guerrilla marketing tends to work well with people my age because my generation likes innovative ideas.

Exercise 2.3 Verbs + Infinitives and Verbs + Objects + Infinitives

Complete the report on quick response (QR) codes.[1] Use the words in parentheses with the simple present or simple past form.

Last week, Steve Green *asked me to look into* (ask/me/look into) QR
(1)
codes, so I decided to interview people who use QR codes for marketing. One

way companies use QR codes is through smartphones. Consumers point their

smartphones at QRs, and the code takes them immediately to a company or product website.

I _____ (choose/interview) two different people. Steve
(2)

_____ (urge/me/interview) the manager from Dan's Gourmet
(3)

Food for this report because his company uses QR codes. Dan said the QR codes

_____ (help/inform) consumers about the nutritional content of
(4)

the product and _____ (help/them/use) the product correctly.
(5)

Dan also _____ (want/consumers/find out) about
(6)

new products, so the QR code contains a link to Dan's company's website. The QR code

_____ (promise/become) an important marketing tool.
(7)

After I interviewed the manager from Dan's, I _____
(8)

(prepare/visit) Liz Kurikova, the owner of a small flower shop. She was unable to meet

with me this week, but she _____ (encourage/me/contact)
(9)

a friend of hers who runs a small ice cream shop. I spoke with Ned Searby at Astoria

Ice Cream. Currently, they _____ (not need/offer) this
(10)

option to their customers. Once they start selling other products, however, they

_____ (expect/include) QR codes for products on the shelves.
(11)

They _____ (would like/use) this technology to expand their
(12)

business and promote their new products.

[1]**QR code:** an image like a bar code on products that contains links to text, web addresses, and other types of information

3 | Infinitives vs. Gerunds

▶ Grammar Presentation

Some verbs can be followed by an infinitive or a gerund. Much of the time, the meaning is the same or very close, but sometimes there is a difference in meaning.	The woman **stopped to read** the ad. (The woman saw the ad as she was walking and stopped. She read the ad.) The woman **stopped reading** the ad. (The woman was reading the ad. Then she stopped.)

3.1 Similar Meanings of Infinitives vs. Gerunds

After some verbs, you can use either a gerund or an infinitive without any change in meaning. Verbs that can be followed by either an infinitive or a gerund include *begin*, *can't stand*, *continue*, *hate*, *like*, *love*, *prefer*, and *start*.	Broadcasters <u>love</u> **to get** free publicity. Broadcasters <u>love</u> **getting** free publicity.
When *begin*, *continue*, or *start* are in a progressive form, use an infinitive.	I'm <u>beginning</u> **to work** on the assignment now. NOT *I'm beginning ~~working~~ on the assignment now.*

3.2 Different Meanings of Infinitives vs. Gerunds

a. The following verbs can be followed by either an infinitive or a gerund, but the meaning is different:

INFINITIVES	GERUNDS
Did you <u>forget</u> **to tell** your secretary you'd be late today? (You never told your secretary.)	Did you <u>forget</u> **telling** your secretary you'd be late today? (You told your secretary, but you do not remember it.)
I <u>regret</u> **to tell** you that our sales have dropped. (I'm sorry that our sales have dropped, but I'm telling you about it.)	I <u>regret</u> **telling** you that our sales have dropped. (I told you our sales had dropped, but I wish I hadn't.)
They <u>remembered</u> **to e-mail** the sales figures. (They almost forgot, but then they sent the e-mail.)	They <u>remembered</u> **e-mailing** the sales figures. (They sent the e-mail. Later, they thought about it again.)
People <u>stopped</u> **to look** at the colorful signs. (People stopped and looked at them.)	People <u>stopped</u> **looking** at the colorful signs. (People were looking at them but then stopped.)
The mayor <u>tried</u> **to change** the town's name, but the citizens didn't want to. (This was an experiment to see if he could do it. The mayor didn't succeed. He couldn't change the name.)	The mayor <u>tried</u> **changing** the town's name, but it didn't help tourism. (The mayor made an effort to do this, and he succeeded. He changed the name.)

3.2 Different Meanings of Infinitives vs. Gerunds *(continued)*

b. Note that the meaning of *tried* is only different in the past.

I tried **to pay** with a credit card, but the store only accepted cash. (I wanted to pay with a credit card, but they wouldn't let me.)	I will <u>try</u> **to call** you tomorrow. *infinitive*
	= I will <u>try</u> **calling** you tomorrow. *Gerund*
≠ I tried **paying** with a credit card, but I didn't like it. (I did pay with a credit card.)	(= Tomorrow I plan to call you, but it may not work.)

▸▸ Verbs Followed by Gerunds or Infinitives: See page A7.

▶ Grammar Application

Exercise 3.1 Meanings of Infinitives vs. Gerunds

A Rewrite the sentences about paying people to promote products through social media. Replace the infinitives in bold with gerunds. Replace the gerunds in bold with infinitives. Then label the sentence *S* (if the meaning is the same) or *D* (if the meaning is different).

1. Companies have begun **to pay** people to blog about their products.

   Companies have begun paying people to blog about their products.   S

2. LP Social Friends regrets **to tell** the media that they pay people to be "friends."

   LP Socia Friend regret telling the media that they pay people   D

3. I stopped **to read** the article about social media marketing.

   I stopped reading the article about social media marketing   D

4. Alison forgot **mentioning** GamerWorld in her blog yesterday.

   Alison forgot to mention Gamer World in her blog yesterday   D

5. Upside Energy Drinks continues **to pay** fans on social networking sites.

   Upsid Energy Drinks cont Paying fans on social networking   S

6. People have started **questioning** Upside Energy Drinks' marketing strategy.

   People have started to question upside Energy Drinks marketing   S

7. A lot of people can't stand **reading** blogs that are full of ads.

   A lot of people cant stand to read blogs that are full of ads   S

8. GamerWorld tried **to pay** me to write about them in my blog.

   Gamer world tried Paying me to write about them in my blog   D

9. I tried **changing** the privacy settings since I don't want messages from advertisers.

   I tried to chang the privacy settings since I don't want   D

B *Pair Work* In which sentences in A does the meaning change? Explain the difference in meaning to a partner.

Exercise 3.2 Infinitive or Gerund?

A 🔊 Listen to a discussion of the results of a focus group.[1] The focus group watched a reality TV show called *Jake's Life* and tried to remember a product that they saw in the show. Match the sentence parts.

1. Bo regrets *e*
2. Bo tried *g*
3. Jocelyn doesn't regret *h*
4. Participant 1 stopped *f*
5. Participant 2 stopped *b*
6. Participant 3 didn't remember *d*
7. Nobody forgot *a*
8. Jocelyn told Bo *c*

a. to push the button when Jake drank soda.
b. to get a snack.
c. to stop reading.
d. seeing Jake drink anything.
e. to say that the product placement isn't working.
f. watching after the third episode.
g. doing things differently this time.
h. hiring Bo.

[1] **focus group:** a group of people whose opinions help marketers

B 🔊 Listen again and check your answers.

4 | Infinitives After Adjectives and Nouns

▶ Grammar Presentation

| Infinitives can also follow some adjectives and nouns. | The consumers were **happy to see** some interesting advertising.
The advertisers needed more **time to educate** the community. |

were ready to destroy
are afraid to use

4.1 *Be* + Adjectives + Infinitives

| Use infinitives after the following adjectives: *afraid, amazed, difficult, easy, embarrassed, fun, interesting, lucky, necessary, ready, sad, shocked, sorry, surprised, (un)likely, upset.* | Some companies are <u>afraid</u> **to use** new marketing techniques.
The police were <u>ready</u> **to destroy** the ads.
The advertisers were <u>sorry</u> **to cause** a problem. |
| *It + be* is frequently used with many of these words. | <u>It would be fun</u> **to surprise** people with guerrilla advertising. |

▸▸ *Be* + Adjectives + Infinitives: See page A9.

ability to excite

4.2 Nouns + Infinitives

| Use infinitives after the following nouns: *ability, chance, decision, time, way.* | Some ads have the <u>ability</u> **to excite** the public.
It was a great <u>chance</u> **to learn** something new.
It's <u>time</u> **to be** more creative in advertising. |

▶ Grammar Application

Exercise 4.1 *It* + *Be* + Adjective + Infinitive

Complete the article about tracking technology. Use the adjective + infinitive combinations in the box.

difficult / avoid	fun / go	necessary / use	~~surprising / know~~
easy / acquire	interesting / read	shocked / find out	unlikely / change

Who is watching you as you visit Internet pages? It may be _surprising to know_ (1) that advertisers are following you as you surf the Web. Many Internet users would be _shocked to find out_ (2) how much companies know about them through tracking technology such as cookies, which allow websites to identify visitors and their web page preferences. Today, because of tracking technology, it is _easy to acquire_ (3) data on people's habits and tastes. Most websites have this technology, so it is _difficult to avoid_ (4). Companies believe that it is _necessary to use_ (5) tracking because it helps consumers find out about products that they like.

Here is an example of what companies can learn through tracking.

Maria thinks it is _fun to go_ (6) to websites and comment on movies she has seen. She also thinks it is _interesting to read_ (7) about health issues on several sites. She notices that ads pop up on topics that she has done searches on, but she is _unlikely to change_ (8) her search habits because of this.

Exercise 4.2 Nouns + Infinitives

Complete the conversations about using nontraditional marketing. Use the words in parentheses to write sentences.

1. *A* We're going to do a survey on how well guerrilla marketing really works.
   B (that / be / a good way / get / information)
   That's a good way to get information.

2. *A* Our survey shows that product placement isn't working.
   B (it / be / time / do / something different now)
   It's time to do something different now

3. *A* Are you going to use QR codes or reverse graffiti?
   B (we / make / the decision / use / QR codes / yesterday)
   We made the decision to use QR codes yesterday

4. *A* Why should I hire your advertising agency?
   B (we / have / the ability / attract / the 18- to 24-year-old demographic)
   We have the ability to attract the 18 to 24 year old demographic

5. *A* Why are you considering paying sports bloggers to write about your product?
   B (it / be / a chance / introduce / our product to athletes)
   It is a chance to induduce our product to athletes

6. *A* Why doesn't guerrilla marketing work, in your opinion?
   B (it / not / be / the best way / get / messages across / to older demographics)
   It isn't the best way to get messages across to older demographics

7. *A* Why is the character holding the soda can so we can see the brand?
   B (it / be / a chance / sell / the product to viewers)
   It's a chance to sell the product to viewers

Exercise 4.3 Using Infinitives After Adjectives and Nouns

Group Work Think about the different types of marketing below. Evaluate each strategy in terms of how it works with children, teens, adults, and seniors (people over age 65). Compare and discuss your ideas with your group members. Use an infinitive + adjective and noun in each statement.

Guerrilla marketing may not be an effective way to attract seniors because it may be too shocking for some of them.

- Traditional advertising (TV commercials, magazine ads)
- Guerrilla marketing
- Product placement (placement of products in movies and TV shows)
- Viral marketing (paying bloggers and people with social networking sites)

5 | Avoid Common Mistakes ⚠️

1. With the verb *want*, use verb + object + infinitive, not verb + *that* clause.

The advertisers want ~~that~~ you ∧ to buy their products.

2. Use the correct word order when using the negative form of an infinitive.

The company decided ∧ to ~~not~~ pay bloggers to write about their products. *(not)*

3. Do not confuse the preposition *to* with an infinitive *to*.

PREP + GERUND

I look forward to ~~see~~ the new dragon movie. *(seeing)*

VERB + INFINITIVE

Many people like to ~~seeing~~ familiar places and objects in a movie. *(see)*

4. Use an infinitive (*to* + the base form of verb), not *for* + base form of verb, where appropriate.

It is important ~~for~~ make sure the advertisement targets the right audience. *(to)*

Editing Task

Find and correct the mistakes in the paragraphs about advertising in movies.

Product placement in movies is a type of advertising that is popular today. Advertisers want ~~that~~ consumers ∧ see their products in movies so that their products will seem more appealing. That's why advertisers pay filmmakers ~~for~~ place their products in movies. For example, in one movie, a director arranged to ~~using~~ a pair of famous

5 brand-name sunglasses ~~for~~ make his characters appear fashionable. In another movie, the plot required a certain type of luxury car. The filmmakers used the car in their film, but in this case they did not receive any money from the auto's manufacturers. For the automaker, it was an easy way to not pay for advertising. Filmmakers seem to not mind the advertising because they can earn extra money. Moviegoers do not seem to mind it, either.

10 In my opinion, product placement in movies is acceptable, but I want ~~that~~ advertisers use product placement carefully. If directors expect to making a film that is believable, then everything in the film must fit the story. Otherwise, the movie will seem more like an advertisement. This would be terrible. I hope that filmmakers continue to making wise decisions and use products that look natural on screen.

6 Grammar for Writing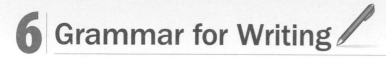

Using Verb + Infinitive and Adjective + Infinitive Constructions

Writers often use verb + infinitive and adjective + infinitive constructions in academic writing. Read these examples:

All advertising agencies <u>attempt to find</u> new ideas that will get the attention of consumers. At one time, it was <u>inappropriate to say</u> the name of your competitor in an ad.

Pre-writing Task

1 Read the paragraph. Are the advertising techniques discussed in the paragraph creative or not creative? Why do advertising companies continue to use them?

Tried and True Advertising Techniques

There are many new kinds of advertising techniques, such as guerrilla advertising and reverse graffiti, but it is wrong to think that the old techniques are gone. Advertising companies continue to use many of them. For example, ads have appeared inside buses and subways for a long time. They are effective because they give people on buses and subways something to look at, and the ads are inexpensive. Creativity with these ads is not necessary to grab the audience's attention. These techniques appear to be effective for certain products and in certain environments. However, if a company wants its ads to be very creative, these techniques are unlikely to be the answer.

2 Read the paragraph again. Underline the verb + infinitive constructions. Can any of these infinitives be changed to gerunds? If so, does the meaning change? Circle the adjective + infinitive and noun + infinitive constructions.

Writing Task

1 *Write* Use the paragraph in the Pre-writing Task to help you write about advertising techniques. You can write about one of these topics or use your own ideas.

- advertising techniques that appeal to you
- new advertising trends that you've seen
- advertising techniques that don't appeal to you
- T-shirt advertising and other free strategies

2 *Self-Edit* Use the editing tips to improve your paragraph. Make any necessary changes.

1. Did you use verb + infinitive constructions and adjective + infinitive constructions?
2. Did you include objects before infinitives when necessary?
3. Did you avoid the mistakes in the Avoid Common Mistakes chart on page 188?

Negative Questions and Tag Questions

Geographic Mobility

1 | Grammar in the Real World

A Have you moved very often in your life? If so, why did you move? Read the interview about geographic mobility. What are some of the reasons why people move?

Geographic Mobility Across Cultures

Interviewer Today we're speaking with two specialists in geographic mobility. They will discuss some reasons why people move from one place to another. Professor O'Neill is from
5 Carlow University in the United States, and Professor Tabenkin is from Zala University in Russia. Let's start with Professor O'Neill. Professor, you have
10 been interested in geographic mobility for a long time, **haven't you**?

O'Neill Well, yes. When I was a boy, my best friend moved away, and that affected me deeply. As I grew older, I saw more people move away. I noticed that the population decrease affected local businesses. As a
15 result, I got interested in the choices people make about moving.

Interviewer People are very mobile and are moving a lot. But most people aren't moving long distances, **are they**? **Isn't** that curious?

O'Neill Yes. That's interesting. In fact, I've been studying the connection between moving and distance recently. Every year, about 11.6 percent
20 of people in the United States move, and of these, about 14.8 percent move to a different state.

Interviewer **Doesn't** that surprise you?

O'Neill No, not really. Often, people who change jobs have to move long distances. On the other hand, people looking for better housing usually
25 stay near their original home. And people who relocate[1] for family reasons may move far away or stay nearby.

¹**relocate**: move to a new place

Interviewer So, I guess it depends on the situation, **doesn't it**?

30 **O'Neill** That's right. It's more complicated than you may think. For example, my wife was living in California when we met. When we got married, she moved a long distance to live with me in Chicago. Now her sister, who lives near Chicago, is expecting a baby. She and her husband plan to move a short distance to be closer to us.

Interviewer Professor Tabenkin, people in Russia have the same issues, **don't they**?

35 **Tabenkin** To a certain extent, yes. It's harder to find housing in Russia, so people tend to move less frequently. In fact, the mobility rate in Russia is less than 2 percent. In my research, I found that young people often decide not to move because available, affordable housing would take them further from family.

Interviewer OK. But **don't** people sometimes have to move long distances for 40 economic reasons?

Tabenkin Yes, that's true. Personally, I had to move a very long distance ten years ago because there were no jobs nearby. However, my experience doesn't seem to be the norm.[2]

Interviewer Mobility isn't easy to explain, **is it**? Thank you both for your thoughts on 45 this issue.

[2]**norm**: an expected situation or a situation considered to be typical

B *Comprehension Check* Answer the questions.

1. What are some reasons why people move long distances?
2. What are some reasons why people stay nearby when they move?
3. Why is the mobility rate in Russia lower than in the United States?

C *Notice* Find the sentences in the article and complete them.

1. Professor, you **have been** interested in geographic mobility for a long time,

   _____ you?

2. Mobility **isn't** easy to explain, _____ it?

Look at the verbs you wrote and the verbs in bold. What do you notice about the use of *not*?

2 | Negative Questions

▶ Grammar Presentation

| Negative questions are similar to *Yes/No* questions in that they begin with an auxiliary verb, a modal, or a form of *be*. | *Haven't you moved recently?*
Aren't there many reasons why people move? |

2.1 Forming Negative Questions

a. Negative questions usually begin with a contraction.	***Don't*** *you live around here?* ***Can't*** *you help me move?* ***Wasn't*** *he living in Chicago?*
b. The full form of *not* in negative questions is very formal. The word *not* comes between the subject and the main verb.	*Were they* **not** *living in Chicago?* *Have you* **not** *moved recently?*
c. With a contraction, use *are* instead of *am* with *I*. Use *am* when you use the full form.	***Aren't I*** *correct?* ***Am I not*** *correct?*

2.2 Using Negative Questions

a. Use negative questions when you think the information is true and you expect people to agree.	*Don't people often move when they change jobs?* (My experience tells me people often move when they change jobs.) *Isn't it unusual for people to move in Russia?* (I've read that it's unusual to move in Russia.)
b. Use negative questions to show surprise or disbelief.	*"Tom has changed his major to English."* *"Really?* **Isn't he still planning to work at a bank?**"
c. Use negative questions to show annoyance or anger.	*Didn't you say you would call me?* (I'm angry that you didn't call me.) *Shouldn't Bob have finished that report by now?* (I'm annoyed because Bob hasn't finished the report.)

2.3 Answering Negative Questions

| Respond to a negative question just as you would a regular *Yes/No* question. Typically, we answer negative questions with *yes* or *no* and an explanation. | *"Don't you want to move?"* (Do you want to move?)
*"***Yes***, I do. I'd like to live somewhere else."*
*"***No***, I don't. I really want to stay here."* |

▶ Grammar Application

Exercise 2.1 Negative Questions

A family is packing for a big move. Complete the negative questions with the correct form of the words in parentheses.

1. _____ *Didn't I tell* _____ (I told) you to be careful with that lamp?
2. *Haven't you been listening* (you have been listening) to what I've been saying?
3. *Can't you stop* (you can stop) texting and help me?
4. *Shouldn't you have bought* (you should have bought) bigger boxes?
5. *Am I not* _____ (I am) correct that you promised to help?
6. *Weren't you going to take* (you were going to take) the baby to the neighbor's?

Exercise 2.2 More Negative Questions

Read the sentences about moving and migration. Then write negative questions with the information in parentheses. Use contractions when possible.

1. A lot of people left Ireland in the 1800s.
   Didn't a lot of people leave because of a famine?
   (You heard that a lot of people left because of a famine.)

2. Hope of employment brings a lot of immigrants to rich countries.
   Didn't hope of employment bring good schools have made rich more ^attractive to
   (You heard that good schools have made rich countries more attractive, too.)

3. Some people move great distances.
   Didn't some people move great distance to reunite with family members
   (You heard that some people move great distances to reunite with family members.)

4. Some corporations require their employees to move to another country.
   Aren't some corporations
   (You think that this is happening more because of globalization.)

5. People are able to move around more freely because of globalization.
   _____
   (You heard that the laws are changing to allow even more movement.)

Exercise 2.3 Responding to Negative Questions

Pair Work Read the chart on migration in the United States. Study it for 30 seconds. Then cover it. What details can you remember? Ask your partner negative questions. Then switch roles, and answer your partner's negative questions.

A *Haven't 60 percent of men moved?*

B *Yes, that's right.*

A *And haven't 50 percent of college graduates moved?*

B *Actually, no. Seventy-seven percent of college graduates have moved.*

People Who Move: Percentages of people who have moved at least once in their lifetimes		
	% of People Who Have Moved	**% of People Who Have Never Moved**
Total	63	37
By Gender		
Men	60	40
Women	65	35
By Education		
College graduates	77	23
High school graduates	56	44

www.pewsocialtrends.org/2008/12/17/who-moves-who-stays-put-wheres-home

3 | Tag Questions

▶ Grammar Presentation

Use tag questions to confirm information or ask for agreement.	*You're a professor, **aren't you**?* *He hasn't been studying, **has he**?*

3.1 Forming Tag Questions

a. The verb in a tag question is an auxiliary verb, a modal, or a form of *be*.	*Your parents have never moved, **have** they?* *She got the job, **did**n't she?* *You can't stay, **can** you?*

3.1 Forming Tag Questions *(continued)*

b. The pronoun in a tag question agrees with the subject.	*The students will be on time, won't* **they**? *Your sister lives close by, doesn't* **she**?
Use *it* when the subject is *that* or *something*.	*That's amazing information, isn't* **it**?
Use *they* when the subject is *someone* or *everyone*.	*Someone recorded the interview, didn't* **they**? *Everyone respects the professor, don't* **they**?

c. Use an affirmative tag with a negative statement.	NEGATIVE STATEMENT *They* <u>don't live</u> *in Chicago,* *You're not from Russia,*	AFFIRMATIVE TAG **do they**? **are you**?
Use a negative tag with an affirmative statement.	AFFIRMATIVE STATEMENT *Geography* <u>is</u> *interesting,* *Her sister* <u>moved</u> *to Chicago,*	NEGATIVE TAG **isn't it**? **didn't she**?

3.2 Answering Tag Questions

a. In negative tags, we expect the listener to answer *yes*, but it is possible to answer *no*.	*"They moved from Miami to Chicago, <u>didn't they</u>?"*
	   *"**Yes**, they got jobs in Illinois."* (That's right, they moved.)
	   *"Actually, **no**."* (That's not right. They didn't move.)

b. In affirmative tags, we expect the listener to answer *no*, but it is possible to answer *yes*.	*"They didn't move from Miami to Chicago, <u>did they</u>?"*
	   *"**No**, they decided to stay."* (You're right, they didn't move.)
	   *"**Yes**, they had to move for work."* (Actually, they did move.)

c. You cannot answer *Yes . . . not*.	*"They didn't move from Miami to Chicago, <u>did they</u>?"*
	   "Yes, they did."
	   OR **"No, they didn't."**
	   NOT ~~"Yes, they didn't."~~

▶ Grammar Application

Exercise 3.1 Tag Questions

Match the statements and tags about a friend who is moving.

1. Erica and her family are moving overseas, _d_
2. You knew about their move, _e_
3. Erica's company is relocating to London, _f_
4. Erica's husband won't get a new job, _g_
5. They don't have a place to live yet, _a_
6. Erica will get an international driving permit, _h_
7. I have a lot of information about their move, _b_
8. You're giving them a going-away party, _c_

a. do they?
b. didn't you?
c. aren't you?
d. aren't they?
e. don't I?
f. isn't it?
g. will he?
h. won't she?

Exercise 3.2 Tags

Complete the questions about the stresses of moving. First underline the subject and circle the auxiliary verb in each sentence. Then write the correct tag.

1. Moving (can) be stressful as well as expensive, _can't it_ ?
2. People can sometimes deduct moving costs from their income taxes, _can't they_ ?
3. Things have sometimes disappeared from a moving truck, _don't it_ ?
4. Your friends will give you boxes, _won't they_ ?
5. Everyone should read reviews of a moving company before hiring one, _didn't they_ ?
6. Marta has been disorganized since the move, _hasn't she_ ?
7. Vinh and Ahn weren't moving today, _were they_ ?
8. It's been a stressful time for you, _isn't it_ ?

Exercise 3.3 Statements in Tag Questions

Complete the questions about people who are moving. Use the words in parentheses with the correct verb forms.

1. _Mary is retiring to Florida_ , isn't she?
   (Mary / retire / Florida)
2. _Raul has relocate London_ , hasn't he?
   (Raul / relocate / London)
3. _Annette did attend school France_ , didn't she?
   (Annette / attend school / France)
4. _Mariam and Amir will turn down the promotion N.Y_ , won't they?
   (Miriam and Amir / turn down the promotion / New York)

5. _You like the air quality Hong Kong_ , did you?
   (You / like / the air quality / Hong Kong)
6. _Bernard will take the children with him Texas_ , will he?
   (Bernard / take the children / with him / Texas)

Exercise 3.4 Answering Tag Questions

Complete the conversations with the expected answers.

Conversation 1

Paolo I'm interviewing for a job in New York. You grew up

there, didn't you?

Luis _Yes, I did_ . What do you want to know?
       (1)

Paolo Well, I'm worried about housing. Apartments aren't

cheap there, are they?

Luis _Yes we are_ . They're also hard to find.
      (2)

Conversation 2

Phoebe You've read the article on migration patterns for class today, haven't you?

Alex _Yes, I have_ . It was interesting.
      (3)

Phoebe Oh, good. You don't have time to tell me about it before class, do you?

Alex _Yes, I don't_ . But you can borrow my copy of the article.
      (4)

Conversation 3

Claudia I heard the company is moving to Dallas, Texas. Some of us will have to move,

won't we?

Jun _Yes, you will_ . I'll know exactly who next week.
     (5)

Claudia You have family there, so you won't mind moving, will you?

Jun _Yes, I won_ . My family's excited.
     (6)

Conversation 4

Fen There are a lot of new families moving into the neighborhood, aren't there?

Bin _Yes there are_ . I'm glad to see new faces.
     (7)

Fen It's nice to see a lot of young children around again, isn't it?

Bin _No, it isn't_ . It's wonderful!
     (8)

Exercise 3.5 🔊 Pronunciation Focus: Intonation and Meaning in Tag Questions

Use rising intonation in the tag when you are not certain your statement is true.	"Moving wasn't difficult, **was it**?" ↗ "Yes, it was!" "There won't be a quiz tomorrow, **will there**?" ↗ "No, there won't."
Use falling intonation when you expect the listener to agree with you.	"His research is really boring, **isn't it**?" ↘ "Yes, it is." "You didn't go to class, **did you**?" ↘ "No, I didn't."

A 🔊 Listen and repeat the questions in the chart above.

B 🔊 Listen to the conversations about a student moving far away to attend college. Draw the intonation pattern above the tag. Then write *U* if the speaker is <u>uncertain</u> of the information or *E* if the speaker is <u>expecting</u> agreement.

Conversation 1

1. You're not still thinking about going to college in Pennsylvania, are you? ↗ __U__

2. But that college doesn't offer the major you want, does it? _____

Conversation 2

3. Your son is thinking of going to college far from home, isn't he? _____

4. Duquesne University is in Pittsburgh, isn't it? _____

Conversation 3

5. You're excited about moving to Pennsylvania for college, aren't you? _____

6. You're not worried about moving so far from home, are you? _____

Conversation 4

7. Your son is worried about moving so far from home, isn't he? _____

8. But you and your wife feel OK about him moving so far away, don't you? _____

C *Pair Work* Find out information about your partner by asking tag questions. Use both intonation patterns. Use rising intonation when you are uncertain and falling intonation when you expect agreement.

   A *You're from Egypt, aren't you?*
   B *Yes, I am. You're studying culinary arts, aren't you?*
   A *Actually, no. My major is geography.*

4 | Avoid Common Mistakes

1. In negative questions, use the auxiliary verb + *not*.

Didn't she
~~She no~~ call you?

2. Answer negative questions the same way as regular *Yes/No* questions.

"Aren't you coming with us?"

No, I'm not.   *Yes, I am.*
"~~Yes.~~" (I'm not coming.)   "~~No.~~" (I'm coming.)

3. In tag questions, remember to use an auxiliary verb + a pronoun in the tag.

wasn't it
The research was old, ~~no~~?

4. In the tag, use an auxiliary verb that agrees with the main verb + the correct pronoun for the subject.

aren't they
They are still living in their hometown, ~~isn't it~~?

Editing Task

Find and correct six more mistakes in the conversation about economic mobility.

A That article on economic mobility in America was really interesting, ~~no~~? *wasn't it*

B It sure was. Some of the facts were surprising, ~~isn't it~~? *weren't* I was especially surprised that there is more economic mobility in countries like France and Germany. *aren't having*

A I was, too. I thought there was more mobility here. By the way, don't you have a class right now?

5 B Yes. I'm finished for today. I'm free for the evening.

A But you're working tonight, ~~no~~? *aren't you?*

B No, I quit my job. *aren't* *don't you like it?*

A Really? Why? ~~You no like it~~?

B The job was fine. The truth is I'm moving to Florida with my family at the end of the semester,

10 so I'm really busy. *doesn't your family like it here?*

A You're kidding! Why? ~~Your family no like it here~~?

B They like it here, but there aren't many good jobs. We're moving where the jobs are.

A But you only have one semester left, ~~isn't it~~? *don't*

B That's right, but I have to go with them.

Yes, it does

5 Grammar for Writing ✎

Using Negative Questions and Tag Questions in Blogs

Students are often asked to post comments on online message boards about topics they discussed in class. Negative questions and tag questions are useful to confirm understanding or check information. Read this example blog:

Miguel   More journalists should be writing about the impact of the new immigration laws.

Stephanie   Miguel, _aren't a lot of reporters already writing about immigration?_ I've seen a lot of articles about that.

Theresa   _Didn't our teacher say that there has been a lot of news on this issue?_

Miguel   Yes, Theresa, I think you're right. However, there haven't been many articles on the impact of these new laws on people's lives, _have there?_

Note that negative questions and tag questions are not used in academic writing.

Pre-writing Task

1   A group of students is working on a class project. Read the entries from their online message board. What are "boomerang kids"? What are some reasons students move back home?

Thread: Moving Back Home Project

Damien: So, we've all agreed to focus the project on students moving back in with their parents after college, haven't we? The textbook said that there are more of these "boomerang kids" than before. Jo said she thought it was because of the bad job market. I agree that is one reason, but shouldn't
5   there be other reasons, too? I think young people might be closer to their parents than they used to be. Wouldn't you guys agree?

Moving Back Home Project, Feb. 3, 3:30

Jo: I agree that many young people seem closer to their parents, but I don't know if that is a reason to move back home with them. Gabriel, you said that you
10   think family is generally more important to people these days, didn't you?

Moving Back Home Project, Feb. 3, 7:45

Gabriel: Yes, I did. I'll try to find some articles. Don't you think that the economy has something to do with it? Young people feel insecure about their future. We could write about positive and negative reasons why young people live
15   at home after college, couldn't we? What do you think?

2 Read the online message board again. Circle the tags in tag questions. How are they used? Underline the negative questions. How are they used?

Writing Task

1 *Write* Use the online message board entry in the Pre-writing Task to help you write comments for an online message board. You can write about one of these topics or use your own ideas.

- geographic mobility

- issues that people have when they move away from family and friends

2 *Self-Edit* Use the editing tips to improve your online message board comments. Make any necessary changes.

1. Did you use negative questions? What is the purpose of each of your negative questions?
2. Did you use tag questions? What is the purpose of each of your tag questions?
3. Did you avoid the mistakes in the Avoid Common Mistakes chart on page 199?

That Clauses

Cultural Values

1 | Grammar in the Real World

A Is it possible to identify "typical" American values? Theories exist about the values Americans hold today – and why. Read the article about one view of American values. Do you agree with the writer's point of view?

U.S. Cultural Values

Values are beliefs held in common by members of a group. They often come from shared experiences. For example, some historians assert[1] **that the settlement of the American West in**
5 **the nineteenth century shaped many American values**. These include the importance of hard work, optimism, and individualism.

Countless U.S. children have learned in school **that hard work is essential**. In fact, many
10 Americans believe **that they must work hard in order to be happy**. How did this belief develop? According to some researchers, as Americans moved deeper into the continent, they discovered **that the West was mostly wilderness**.[2] Their lives were
15 difficult, and they had to work hard to survive. Some historians are convinced **that their success helped form a general belief in the value of hard work**.

Furthermore, many Americans believe **that they should have a positive view of the future**. A few historians suggest **that this perspective helped**
20 **put men on the moon**. What is the origin of this optimism? Some research suggests **that struggles on the frontier[3] encouraged this attitude**. People found **that they could survive, even in difficult situations**.

Another common belief about Americans is **that they are individualistic**. Traditionally, American children have learned **that they are responsible for**
25 **their own lives**. This way of thinking supports the idea **that every person**

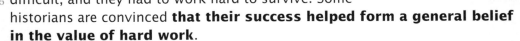

[1]**assert:** to state an opinion | [2]**wilderness:** an area of land that has not been farmed or had towns and roads built on it
[3]**frontier:** the western area of the United States that did not have many white settlers from the eastern part of the United States

can succeed through hard work. In addition, Americans tend to believe **that they can start over when they make mistakes**. Why do they feel this way? It is the belief of some historians **that this idea developed as a result of frontier life**. Because there were few towns and traditions, settlers created
30 their own rules. Each new settlement developed its own ways of getting things done. When settlements faced problems, they had no choice but to try new and different approaches.

Not all historians agree **that frontier life influenced modern American values**. Furthermore, the United States is becoming more and more culturally
35 diverse all the time. Undoubtedly, this is already affecting the values held by its citizens. In what way might American values change?

B *Comprehension Check* Match the two parts of the sentences.

1. According to some historians, the difficulty of living on the frontier led to _____

2. Survival under difficult circumstances may have led to _____

3. The lack of towns and traditions may have led to _____

a. optimism.

b. the value of hard work.

c. individualism.

C *Notice* Find the sentences in the article and complete them.

1. Many Americans _____ they must work hard in order to be happy.

2. Traditionally, American children _ _____ they are responsible for their own lives.

3. Not all historians _____ frontier life influenced modern American values.

How many subjects are in each of these sentences? What word connects the two clauses?

2 *That* Clauses

▶ Grammar Presentation

Noun clauses function like nouns in sentences. They often begin with the word *that*.	*Many people believe **that they must work hard in order to be happy**.*

2.1 Forming *That* Clauses

a. *That* clauses have their own subject and verb.

MAIN CLAUSE		*THAT* CLAUSE	
SUBJECT	VERB	SUBJECT	VERB

*Many Americans think **that anyone can succeed**.*

b. In conversation and informal writing, *that* is often omitted. In academic writing, *that* is usually not omitted.

*Most people recognize **cooperation is important**.* (informal)

*Most people recognize **that cooperation is important**.* (formal)

2.2 Using *That* Clauses

Use *that* clauses after the following verbs that express mental activity:

assume, believe, decide, discover, expect, feel, find (out), guess, hear, hope, imagine, know, learn, notice, read, realize, recognize, say, see, show, suppose, think, understand

*Can we <u>assume</u> **that the core values have remained basically the same**?*

*Some people <u>believe</u> **that hard work brings happiness**.*

*I've <u>discovered</u> **that some cultures don't have a positive view of the future**.*

*I <u>read</u> **that American values developed during the colonial period**.*

▶ Grammar Application

Exercise 2.1 Forming *That* Clauses

Combine the sentences about employees in the United States. Use *that* clauses.

1. Many Americans notice something. They are working harder but have less money.

   Many Americans notice that they are working harder but have less money.

2. In fact, recent research has found something. Hard work doesn't always lead to wealth.

3. Many older Americans are realizing something. They are unable to retire after working hard all their lives.

4. Many employees assumed something. Their companies would reward them for their hard work.

5. Researchers recently reported something. Job satisfaction has declined in recent years.

6. Employers are beginning to understand something. It is important to give people some freedom at work.

Exercise 2.2 Using *That* Clauses Without *That*

Over to You Do you believe that money makes people happy? Why or why not? Write five sentences. Use *that* clauses but do not use *that* in your sentences. Then share your sentences with a partner.

A *I don't think money makes people happy because having money causes many problems.*

B *I disagree. I believe you need a certain amount of money to feel secure, and this makes people happy.*

Exercise 2.3 Using *That* Clauses

A Write statements with *that* clauses using the words in parentheses.

1. Europeans work fewer hours than Americans. (I / understand)

   I understand that Europeans work fewer hours than Americans.

2. The average European gets about two months' vacation every year. (Michael / read)

   Michael read that

3. The average American works 46 weeks per year. (international labor statistics / show)

   International labor statistics show that

4. Culture may be one reason for the difference in attitudes toward work.
   (some experts / believe)

   Some experts believe that

5. Europeans tend to value leisure more highly than Americans.
   (a group of scholars / found)

   A group of scholars found that

6. Americans tend to value earning money more highly than Europeans.
   (some scholars / believe)

   Some scholars believe that

7. Many Americans seem to use possessions as a measure of success.
   (a professor at Gradina University / wrote)

   A professor at Gradina University wrote that

B *Group Work* As a group, talk about differences between Americans and Europeans. You may also include another culture that you know about. Discuss the following questions, or use your own ideas.

- How much vacation time do Americans usually get?

- How much vacation time do Europeans usually get?

- How much vacation time do people from other cultures usually get?

- Who tends to relax on vacation?

- Who tends to bring work to do on vacation?

Use the following verbs in your discussion:

believe	hear	imagine	read	see	suppose	think

A *I've heard that Americans get less vacation time than Canadians.*
B *I think that's true. My brother lives in Canada, and he told me the same thing.*

3 | Agreement Between *That* Clauses and Main Clauses

▶ Grammar Presentation

<table>
<tr>
<td>Use a past form in a that clause when the verb refers to a past event. When it refers to a present event or state, use a present form.</td>
<td>Some historians believe that American values developed a long time ago. (present belief about a past action)

Some historians believe that early American history explains certain American values. (present belief about a present state)</td>
</tr>
</table>

3.1 *That* Clauses in Sentences with Present Verbs in the Main Clause

<table>
<tr>
<td>a. When the main clause is in the present, use a present form in the that clause to express a fact or general truth.</td>
<td>Many Americans feel that nothing is impossible.

Some cultures think that cooperation is very important.</td>
</tr>
<tr>
<td>b. When the main clause is in the present, use a past form in the that clause to describe a past event.</td>
<td>Some historians don't think that early American history influenced American culture.</td>
</tr>
<tr>
<td>c. When the main clause is in the present, use a future form in the that clause to describe a future event.</td>
<td>I assume that you are going to do more research.</td>
</tr>
</table>

3.2 *That* Clauses in Sentences with Past Verbs in the Main Clause

<table>
<tr>
<td>a. When the main clause is in the past, use a past form in the that clause to describe an event or idea that happened at the same time as the event in the main clause.</td>
<td>Nineteenth-century Americans knew that hard work was necessary.

My professor noticed that many students were writing about the nineteenth century.</td>
</tr>
<tr>
<td>b. When the main clause is in the past, use a present form in the that clause to express a universal truth or a fact that applies to the present.</td>
<td>Who discovered that the Earth is round and not flat?

Scientists discovered that DNA holds the code for life.
When I started living on my own, I found out that life is sometimes very hard.</td>
</tr>
</table>

| **c.** Use the past perfect or past perfect progressive when the event in the *that* clause happened before the event in the main clause. | *I discovered* **that she had been copying my history research for years**!
 I heard **that she had failed the test**. |
| **d.** Use *would* or *was / were going to* when the event of the *that* clause happened after the event of the main clause. | *I heard* **that a famous historian would be speaking at the conference**.
 We discovered **that we were going to study twentieth-century history**. |

▶ Grammar Application

Exercise 3.1 *That* Clauses in Sentences with Present Verbs in the Main Clause

Complete the sentences about the influence of Latin American cultures on mainstream U.S. culture. Use a *that* clause with the correct verb form. Sometimes more than one answer is possible.

1. Anthropologists agree / there be / links between Latin American cultures and U.S. culture (present for general truth)

   Anthropologists agree that there are links between Latin American cultures and U.S. culture.

2. Research / shows / contemporary Latin American cultures / have / roots in African, European, and indigenous cultures (present for general truth)

   _____

3. Sociologists / believe / Latin American cultures / influence / world culture as well as U.S. culture (past event)

   _____

4. Many musicologists / agree / modern U.S. music / be / derived in part from Latin American cultures (present for general truth)

   _____

5. Many language experts / assert / Spanish speakers / contribute / a great many words to the English language (past event)

   _____

6. Most sociologists / agree / Latin American cultures / continue / to influence U.S. culture (future for future action)

   _____

Exercise 3.2 ◀)) *That* Clauses in Sentences with Past Verbs in the Main Clause

Listen to part of a lecture on westward movement in nineteenth-century North America. Complete the sentences with the words you hear.

In the nineteenth century, many people <u>believed that</u> Americans <u>had</u> the right
(1)   (2)
to expand across the continent. John Quincy Adams, the sixth president of the United

States, _____ one large country
(3)
_____ good for all Americans.
(4)
However, some people _____
(5)
the westward expansion _____
(6)
some negative consequences. For example, some people _____
(7)
westward expansion _____ a negative impact on Native American
(8)
culture. In fact, some Americans at the time _____ the U.S. government
(9)
_____ Native American land unfairly. They also
(10)
_____ westward expansion ____ _____
(11)   (12)
many wars, such as the Mexican-American War of 1836. Most people

_____ Americans _____ native plants and
(13)   (14)
wildlife as well.

Exercise 3.3 Agreement Between *That* Clauses and Main Clauses

Group Work Do Internet research on how a culture, such as Irish-American or Latin American culture, has influenced culture in the United States or Canada. Write statements with *that* clauses. Use simple present for general truths, simple past for past events, and future for future action. Share your sentences with your group members. Use the following phrases in your sentences:

- I learned / discovered / found that . . .
- For example, . . .
- Another area that . . .
- A recent study showed / found that . . .

I learned that Indian culture has influenced American culture. One area that Indian culture has influenced is entertainment. Many film specialists agree that Bollywood movies are influencing American movies.

4 *That* Clauses After Adjectives and Nouns

▶ Grammar Presentation

<table>
<tr>
<td>

That clauses can follow some adjectives and nouns.

</td>
<td>

I'm sure **that a cultural group shares at least some values**.
I have the feeling **that our values are quite different**.

</td>
</tr>
</table>

4.1 *That* Clauses After Adjectives

<table>
<tr>
<td>

a. You can use a *that* clause after adjectives that express certainty or emotion.

</td>
<td>

I'm <u>certain</u> **that I haven't read enough about American culture**.

The conference organizers were <u>pleased</u> **that he accepted the invitation**.

</td>
</tr>
<tr>
<td>

b. You can use *that* clauses after *It + be +* certain adjectives. These adjectives often express emotions or degrees of certainty. They include:

certain, clear, evident, (un)fortunate, interesting, (un)likely, surprising, understandable

</td>
<td>

It is <u>evident</u> **that many other cultures have influenced U.S. culture**.

It is <u>unfortunate</u> **that many students don't know more about their country's history**.

It is <u>unlikely</u> **that we'll finish the unit by the next class**.

It is <u>understandable</u> **that historians disagree about the development of cultural values**.

</td>
</tr>
</table>

4.2 *That* Clauses After Nouns

<table>
<tr>
<td>

a. You can use *that* clauses after nouns that express thoughts and ideas, such as *belief, feeling, impression,* and *possibility*.

</td>
<td>

It was our <u>impression</u> **that the historian was wrong**.

There was no <u>possibility</u> **that he was going to convince us**.

</td>
</tr>
<tr>
<td>

b. You can use noun *+ be + that* clauses with these commonly used nouns: *concern, difference, hope, idea, impression, point, problem, saying,* and *views*.

</td>
<td>

The <u>concern was</u> **that we would never find out the truth**.

The <u>point is</u> **that the United States is a very large country**.

The <u>problem is</u> **that very individualistic people can find it hard to work in a group**.

</td>
</tr>
</table>

Data from the Real World 🌐

Research shows that the following nouns frequently occur with *that* clauses:

assumption, belief, claim, conclusion, doubt, fact, hope, idea, impression, possibility, report, suggestion, view	Is it your **assumption** that we cannot find jobs in other companies? We came to the **conclusion** that he would never understand our point of view.

▶ Grammar Application

Exercise 4.1 *That* Clauses After Adjectives

Complete the magazine interview with a cultural studies expert. For each item, use the words in parentheses with the correct form of *be* and a *that* clause.

U.S. Culture and the World

Interviewer Some experts are studying culture, and they have expressed some concerns. What are they concerned about?

Dr. Green *They are concerned that U.S. culture may have a negative impact on global culture.*
(1. they / concerned / U.S. culture may have a negative impact on global culture)

Interviewer Why are they worried?

Dr. Green _____
_____
(2. some people / worried / Americanization is making everything the same)

Interviewer Why do they think this?

Dr. Green _____
_____
(3. they / aware / Hollywood and fast-food chains are influencing culture)

Interviewer What's your opinion?

Dr. Green _____
(4. I / convinced / culture is a two-way street)

Interviewer Why do you think that?

Dr. Green _____
_____
_____
(5. I / positive / other cultures influence U.S. culture as much as U.S. culture influences them)

Interviewer	Can you give some examples?
Dr. Green	_____
	(6. a lot of people / surprised / the French invented movies)
Interviewer	What else?
Dr. Green	_____
	_____
	(7. they / surprised / the British invented one of the original fast foods, fish and chips)
Interviewer	So what can we conclude?
Dr. Green	_____
	(8. I / sure / we all benefit from global cultural exchange)

~◼~

Exercise 4.2 *That* Clauses After Nouns and Adjectives

A *Group Work* Complete the answers to these questions about the spread of U.S. culture worldwide. Explain your answers.

1. Is the exportation of U.S. culture to the rest of the world a good thing?

   It is my belief that _the exportation of U.S. culture is in some ways a good_
   _thing and in some ways a bad thing_____.

2. Survey your group members: Do you think that most people outside of the United States have a favorable opinion of U.S. popular culture?

   It is our feeling that _____.

3. Does your group think that most people outside of the United States have good feelings about American fast-food restaurants opening up in cities around the world?

   It is our group's impression that _____.

B *Over to You* Read the results of a survey about the exportation of U.S. culture. Write three sentences about the survey results. Use the following adjectives: *amazed, disappointed, glad, pleased, relieved, surprised.* Discuss your reactions with a partner.

What is your opinion of U.S. popular culture, such as music, TV shows, and movies?

Very favorable	21%	Somewhat unfavorable	25%	No Answer	1%
Somewhat favorable	39%	Very unfavorable	14%		

I'm not surprised that most people have mixed feelings about U.S. culture.

5 | Avoid Common Mistakes ⚠️

1. Do not use a comma before a *that* clause.

Their parents are pleased~~,~~ that they are getting married.

2. Remember that *that* clauses need a complete verb.

I noticed that she _{was} leaving.

3. *That* clauses must have a subject.

Records show that _{many settlers} hoped to return east later.

4. In academic writing, do not omit *that*.

Some cultures believe _{that} individuals should put other people first.

Editing Task

Find and correct six more mistakes in the paragraphs about a famous American of the mid-nineteenth century.

Settlers from the east who traveled across the American West in the mid-nineteenth century understood _{that} they faced a difficult journey across deserts and mountains. They knew, that the trip would take years and that some people lose their lives. However, they were optimistic.

5   Michael T. Simmons was one of those determined travelers. Someone told him to go to the Pacific Northwest for new opportunities. He sold his business to pay for the supplies that he and his family needed. He knew that the area was largely unknown. He also knew that was dangerous. This did not stop him.

When Simmons and his group reached Oregon, he announced that was going

10   to continue north. The Hudson's Bay Trading Company heard the news, and they discouraged him. However, Simmons was certain, that the trip going to be successful, and he did not listen. Instead, he continued north as planned. After he arrived, he helped to establish the first settlement in the territory that is now known as Washington State. Documents show that Simmons built the first mill using water from the

15   Tumwater waterfall for power. For this, he is sometimes called the father of Washington industry.

6 Grammar for Writing

Using *That* Clauses to State Reasons, Conclusions, Research Results, Opinions, and Feelings

That clauses are very common in academic writing. They are particularly useful for stating:

- reasons and conclusions
- research results or information from other sources
- opinions and feelings

Sociologists agree that it can be very difficult to adapt to a different culture.

One reason for this may be that people arrive in new cultures with unrealistic expectations.

The teachers were frustrated that they couldn't communicate well with the international students.

For expressing opinions and feelings, the following expressions are common before *that* clauses in academic writing: *It is (not) clear, It is (not) possible, It is likely / unlikely,* and *It is obvious.* Read these examples:

It is unlikely that people from different cultures will change many of their beliefs and values to match the values of a new culture.

It is possible that some cultures have become stronger because of globalization.

Pre-writing Task

1 Read the paragraph below. What problems did the students have? Where did the writer's information come from?

Cultural Differences in the Classroom

The first semester at college can be very difficult for international students. A recent study investigated the main difficulties international students had in their first semester in colleges in the United States and Canada. Ten students participated. The first difficulty that students had was speaking in class. There were a few reasons for
5 this. One reason was that the students were embarrassed about their English. They felt that it was not good enough. However, it was unlikely that their English was not good. After all, each student had to receive a high score on an entrance exam in English. It is possible that the students did not have enough confidence at first. Many of the students were not used to speaking in class because they did not speak in class in their
10 home countries. Another problem many students had was that they did not know what to call their teachers. The reason for this is that the students call their teachers

"Teacher" as a sign of respect when they are in their home countries. However, they
discovered that *Teacher* sounded rude to some U.S. teachers. The teachers asked the
students to call them by their first names, although they realized that some students
15 would be uncomfortable with this at first. It was interesting that many of the students
reported having these problems in the beginning. However, most found that they were
able to adjust fairly quickly.

2 Read the paragraph again. Underline the *that* clauses. Find and label one noun clause
for each of these purposes: (1) reasons and conclusions, (2) research results and
information, and (3) opinions and feelings. Circle the expressions *It is (not) possible that*
and *It was likely / unlikely that.* Do these expressions introduce the writer's opinions and
feelings or the international students' opinions and feelings?

Writing Task

1 *Write* Use the paragraph from the Pre-writing Task to write about cultural differences.
You can write about one of these topics or use your own ideas.

- classroom practices
- dealing with teachers
- family life
- studying
- dating
- eating
- making friends
- taking tests

2 *Self-Edit* Use the editing tips to improve your paragraph. Make any necessary changes.

1. Did you use the correct verb forms in your noun clauses with *that*?
2. Did you use any of the common expressions that come before noun clauses with *that*?
3. Did you avoid the mistakes in the Avoid Common Mistakes chart on page 213?

Noun Clauses with *Wh-* Words and *If/Whether*

Inventions They Said Would Never Work

1 Grammar in the Real World

A Have you ever thought of inventing something? If so, what was it? Read the article about inventors. What obstacles did Edison and the Wright brothers face?

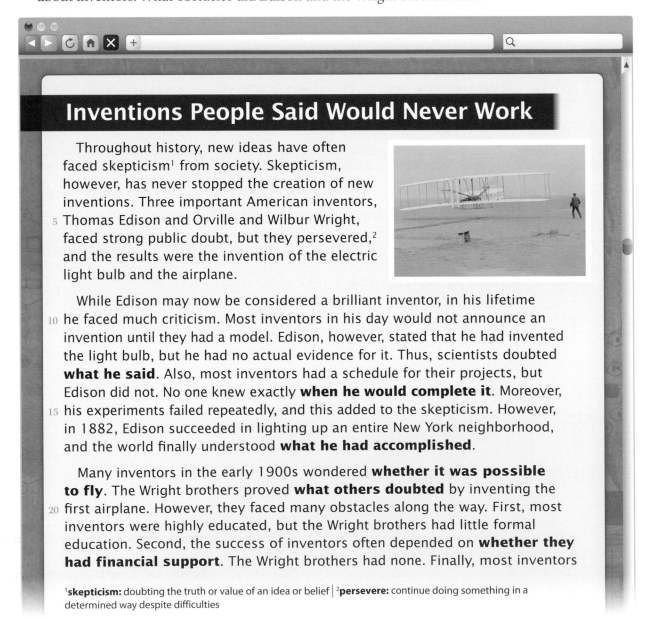

Inventions People Said Would Never Work

Throughout history, new ideas have often faced skepticism[1] from society. Skepticism, however, has never stopped the creation of new inventions. Three important American inventors,
5 Thomas Edison and Orville and Wilbur Wright, faced strong public doubt, but they persevered,[2] and the results were the invention of the electric light bulb and the airplane.

While Edison may now be considered a brilliant inventor, in his lifetime
10 he faced much criticism. Most inventors in his day would not announce an invention until they had a model. Edison, however, stated that he had invented the light bulb, but he had no actual evidence for it. Thus, scientists doubted **what he said**. Also, most inventors had a schedule for their projects, but Edison did not. No one knew exactly **when he would complete it**. Moreover,
15 his experiments failed repeatedly, and this added to the skepticism. However, in 1882, Edison succeeded in lighting up an entire New York neighborhood, and the world finally understood **what he had accomplished**.

Many inventors in the early 1900s wondered **whether it was possible to fly**. The Wright brothers proved **what others doubted** by inventing the
20 first airplane. However, they faced many obstacles along the way. First, most inventors were highly educated, but the Wright brothers had little formal education. Second, the success of inventors often depended on **whether they had financial support**. The Wright brothers had none. Finally, most inventors

[1]**skepticism:** doubting the truth or value of an idea or belief | [2]**persevere:** continue doing something in a determined way despite difficulties

publicized their research, but the Wright brothers did not. No one knew
25 exactly **what they were doing**. Consequently, the public did not believe
that the Wright brothers would succeed. Wilbur himself was not sure **what
would happen**. He could not predict **if their airplane would fly or not**.
Then, in 1903, the Wright brothers flew their airplane for 12 seconds in
Kitty Hawk, North Carolina. No one could believe **what they were seeing**.
30 Five years later in France, they flew another plane higher and longer.

   Inventors almost always face public disbelief. Some people have trouble
believing that new ideas are possible, but they certainly are. No one can be
sure about **what the future holds**.

B *Comprehension Check* Answer the questions.

1. Why did people doubt Thomas Edison?
2. How did Edison convince the world of his accomplishment?
3. What were the obstacles the Wright brothers faced?

C *Notice* Find the sentences in the article and complete them.

1. No one knew exactly _____ .

2. Second, the success of inventors often depended on

   _____ .

3. He could not predict _____ .

Look at the sentences again. Answer the questions.

1. In sentence 1, what type of question is the missing clause similar to?
   a. an information question   b. a *Yes / No* question

2. In sentences 2 and 3, what type of question is the missing clause similar to?
   a. an information question   b. a *Yes / No* question

2 | Noun Clauses with *Wh-* Words

▶ Grammar Presentation

Noun clauses with *wh-* words can act as subjects, direct objects, or objects of prepositions.	***What they wanted*** *was financial support.* *The inventor understood* ***how we should build the machine***. *I learned about* ***how many inventions are made every year***.

2.1 Forming Noun Clauses with *Wh-* Words

a. Noun clauses with *wh-* words use statement word order (subject + verb).	*I've just realized* **what he did**! *I don't know* **when Edison invented the light bulb**.
b. When noun clauses with *wh-* words *who*, *what*, and *which* act as subjects, they take a singular verb.	**What happened next** <u>is</u> *going to surprise you*.

2.2 Using Noun Clauses with *Wh-* Words

a. Noun clauses with *wh-* words often appear after the following verbs: Thoughts and opinions: *consider, know, remember* Learning and perception: *figure out, find out, see, understand, wonder* Emotions: *care, doubt, hate, like, love*	*I don't* <u>remember</u> **who invented the airplane**. *We need to* <u>figure out</u> **why our invention failed**. *Our professor* <u>cares</u> **how we do our work**.
b. Noun clauses with *wh-* words often follow verbs + prepositions, including *care about, decide on, find out about, forget about, know about, learn about, read about*, and *see about*.	*We shouldn't* <u>forget about</u> **which inventions succeeded and which didn't**. *I* <u>read about</u> **where Edison grew up**.

2.3 Reduced Noun Clauses with Infinitives

Noun clauses with *wh-* words can often be reduced to *wh-* word + infinitive. Common infinitives used this way include *to ask, to consider, to decide, to figure (out), to find (out), to forget, to know, to learn, to remember, to say, to see, to show, to understand*, and *to wonder*.	*We're not sure* **who / whom**[1] **to ask for information**. = *We're not sure* **who / whom**[1] **we should ask for information**. *I don't know* **what to say about your invention**. = *I don't know* **what I can say about your invention**.

[1]The use of *whom* is infrequent, except in very formal writing.

▶ # Grammar Application

Exercise 2.1 Noun Clauses with *Wh-* Words

A ◀)) Listen to the conversation among a group of students doing Internet research on recent inventions and inventors. Complete the sentences with the noun clauses you hear.

Peter   OK, let's start with Randi Altschul.

Larry   I don't know <u>who Randi Altschul is</u>.

                              (1)

Paula Neither do I. I don't know _____ .
                                              (2)

Peter I know _____ . She invented the disposable
                        (3)

cell phone.

Paula I'm impressed! I wonder _____ .
                                          (4)

Larry I don't know.

Peter Got it! It says here her cell phone wasn't working well, and she felt like throwing it away.

Larry Let's find out _____ .
                              (5)

Peter It says here she got a patent for it in 1999.

Larry I just found out _____ at the time.
                                (6)

It was Florida.

Paula I wonder _____ .
                          (7)

Peter It says here that it was only 2 inches by 3 inches – kind of like a

credit card.

Larry I wonder _____ .
                          (8)

Peter It was made of recycled paper.

B *Pair Work* With a partner, talk about what you know or don't know about other
inventions. Use the verbs in A with *wh-* noun clauses.

*I know when the smartphone was invented. It was in 2007. I remember what company
first made it, but I don't know who invented it.*

Exercise 2.2 Reduced Noun Clauses with *Wh-* Words + Infinitives

Some college students are talking to a business adviser about their new product. Rewrite the
sentences with *wh-* words + infinitives.

1. We don't know where we should start.

   We don't know where to start. _____

2. Amy wonders where she could find a good patent lawyer.

   _____

3. I don't know how I can find a manufacturer for our product.

   _____

4. Binh is wondering who he can ask for money for our invention.

   _____

5. I'll figure out who we can contact for financial advice.

_____

6. I wonder what we should charge for our product.

_____

3 | Noun Clauses with *If / Whether*

▶ Grammar Presentation

Noun clauses can begin with *if* or *whether*. These noun clauses are similar in some ways to *Yes / No* questions, but they follow statement (subject + verb) word order.	I'm not sure **if the Wright brothers invented the airplane**. He doesn't know **whether we will get money for our experiment**.

3.1 Forming Noun Clauses with *If / Whether*

a. Use statement word order (subject + verb) for noun clauses with *if / whether*.	I don't know **if the public will accept our idea**. I don't know **whether Edison really invented the light bulb**.
b. You can use the words *or not* at the end of both *if* and *whether* clauses.	The scientist didn't know **if / whether you would understand her invention <u>or not</u>**.
Or not can immediately follow *whether*, but not *if*.	The scientist didn't know **whether <u>or not</u> you would understand her invention**. NOT *The scientist didn't know if ~~or not~~ you would understand her invention*.
c. You can use *if / whether* to introduce two options.	We don't know **whether the new phone <u>or the</u> new tablet will come out first**.

3.2 Using Noun Clauses with *If / Whether*

a. You can use noun clauses with *if / whether* after the following verbs: Thoughts and opinions: *decide, know, remember* Learning and perception: *figure out, find out* Emotions: *care, doubt, matter, mind*	I <u>haven't decided</u> **if I'm going to write a report about the Wright brothers**. He can't <u>find out</u> **if Edison first tried the light bulb in New York**. They <u>doubted</u> **whether anyone would steal their idea**.

3.2 Using Noun Clauses with *If / Whether* (continued)

b. You can also use noun clauses with *whether* after verbs + prepositions, including *care about, decide on, find out about, forget about, know about,* and *read about*. You cannot use *if* after prepositions.	You should <u>forget about</u> **whether you'll make a lot of money with that invention**. NOT *You should forget about ~~if you'll make a lot of money with that invention.~~*
c. You can use an infinitive with *whether*. You cannot use an infinitive with *if*.	He didn't know **whether <u>to share</u> his discovery**. (= He didn't know whether he should share his discovery.) NOT *He didn't know ~~if to share his discovery.~~*

Data from the Real World

Noun clauses with *if* are much more frequent than noun clauses with *whether*. *Whether* is more frequent in writing than in speaking.

▶ Grammar Application

Exercise 3.1 Forming Noun Clauses with *If / Whether*

Combine the sentences. Use a noun clause with *if* or *whether*. Sometimes more than one answer is possible.

1. Scientists have not decided something. Is time travel possible?

   Scientists have not decided whether time travel is possible.

2. Many people don't know something. Do some robots think like humans?

   _____

3. Many people don't know this. Can we invent a nonpolluting fuel?

   _____

4. We can't remember this. Has anyone invented a self-cleaning house?

   _____

5. Many people don't know about this. Are hybrid cars good for the environment?

   _____

6. Scientists haven't figured this out. Are there other planets humans can live on?

   _____

Exercise 3.2 Using Clauses with *If / Whether*

A Read the inventor's list of questions about her invention. Rewrite the questions as sentences. Use noun clauses with *if* or *whether*.

> **Notes on My Invention – Key Questions**
>
> 1. Can I really invent a solar-powered car?
>   *I don't know if I can really invent a solar-powered car.*
>
> 2. Will it take a long time to invent it?
>   _____
>
> 3. Am I smart enough to do it by myself?
>   _____
>
> 4. Do people really want solar-powered cars?
>   _____
>
> 5. Will a solar-powered car work on cloudy days?
>   _____
>
> 6. Is my car going to be too expensive?
>   _____

B Read more questions from the inventor in A. Rewrite the questions as sentences. Use *whether or not* with an infinitive.

1. Should I get some help?
   I can't decide whether or not to get some help.

2. Should I take out a loan from the bank?
   _____

3. Should I patent my idea first?
   _____

4. Should I see a lawyer?
   _____

4 Noun Clauses in Direct and Indirect Questions

▶ Grammar Presentation

Wh- noun clauses and noun clauses with *if* and *whether* can be used in direct and indirect questions.	Do you know **when New York got electricity**? (direct question) I was wondering **when New York got electricity**. (indirect question)

4.1 Forming Direct and Indirect Questions

a. Direct questions with noun clauses have question word order and end with a question mark. Common phrases include: *Do you know . . . ? Can you tell me . . . ? Would you know . . . ?*	Do you know **who invented the first calculator?** Are you trying to find out **if Edison was born in this country?** Can anyone tell me **if Edison was born in Scotland?**
b. Indirect questions with noun clauses have statement word order and end with a period. Common phrases include: *I want to find out . . . I'd like to know . . .* *I don't know why . . .*	I have been wondering **what a patent is**. My group really needs to find out **if the Wright brothers had financial support for their invention**. I'd like to know **if people need to get patents for their inventions**.

▸▸ Verbs and Fixed Expressions that Introduce Indirect Questions: See page A10.

▶ Grammar Application

Exercise 4.1 Direct and Indirect Questions

Complete the interview with artist and inventor Crispiano Columna. Rewrite the questions in parentheses as noun clauses in direct and indirect questions. Sometimes more than one answer is possible.

ArtOnline I'm wondering _if you are both an artist and an inventor_ .
(1. Are you both an artist and an inventor?)

Crispiano Columna Yes, I'm both.

ArtOnline I'd like to know _____ .
(2. What is your most famous invention?)

Crispiano Columna I make sculptures that you can wear as gloves.

ArtOnline I was wondering _____ .
(3. Can you show us an example?)

Crispiano Columna Yes, I'm wearing a pair right now.

ArtOnline I'm interested in knowing _____ .
(4. Do you market your gloves?)

Crispiano Columna Not yet. I'm still trying to get funding to manufacture my gloves.

ArtOnline Can you tell us _____ ?
(5. Where were you born?)

Crispiano Columna I was born in San Pedro Sula, Honduras.

ArtOnline I was wondering _____ .
(6. Did you study art in college?)

Crispiano Columna No. In fact, I studied literature.

ArtOnline I'd like to know _____ .
(7. How did you become an artist?)

Crispiano Columna I taught myself. I learned about color and drawing from books.

ArtOnline Please tell us _____ .
(8. What is your self-regenerating car?)

Crispiano Columna It's an electric car that you never have to stop and recharge.

ArtOnline Please let us know _____ .
(9. How does it work?)

Crispiano Columna It uses solar power. The solar power charges the batteries.

ArtOnline I'd like to know _____ .
(10. What was your first invention?)

Crispiano Columna I invented a toy airplane for my nephew when I was a teenager.

Exercise 4.2 More Indirect Questions

A Look at the pictures of inventions. Write one indirect question about each picture. Use the following phrases:

I wonder / I'm wondering . . .   I'd like to know . . .   I'm interested in knowing . . .

The hair protector	**The food cooler**	**The baby mop**	**The butter stick**

I wonder who invented the hair protector.

1. _____
2. _____
3. _____
4. _____

B *Pair Work* Take turns reading your questions.

5 | Avoid Common Mistakes ⚠️

1. Remember that a noun clause with a *wh-* word follows statement word order.

No one knows what ~~will~~ the next great invention ^will be.

2. Be careful to spell *whether* correctly.

The success of the invention depended on ~~wether~~ *whether* people would buy it.

3. Do not confuse *whether* and *either*.

The newest electronic devices will always tempt us, ~~either~~ *whether* we like them or not.

Editing Task

Find and correct the mistakes in the paragraphs about the importance of the Internet in daily life.

   Many inventions make life more convenient, but the Internet is the most essential one today. The Internet is a part of daily life. Although some people worry about *whether* ~~wheather~~ this fact is harmful or not, many agree that they do not know what would they do if they could not go online.

5   First of all, the Internet helps people communicate instantly with family and friends who are far away. In the past, people had to write a letter or pay for a long-distance call to find out how were they doing. While they waited, they worried about whether their loved ones were all right. Now there are many ways to contact people and find out if they are well.

10   In addition, the Internet helps people find information. If we want to know what is the temperature in Seoul today, we only have to type the question. Also, it is very easy to look for employment, research solutions to a problem, and even find out wether a movie is playing nearby.

   It is too early to tell either the Internet causes serious problems for society or not.

15 To me, it seems extremely valuable because it connects me to people I care about and to information I need.

6 | Grammar for Writing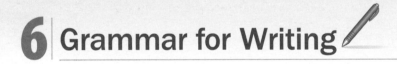

Using Noun Clauses with *Wh-* Words and *If / Whether*

   Noun clauses that begin with *wh-* words, *if*, or *whether* are useful when describing how events happened. They are particularly useful for explaining what people think, feel, or know. Read these examples:

   Some inventors don't care <u>if their inventions change the world</u>.
   Many doctors wonder <u>when scientists will discover cures for all kinds of cancer</u>.
   The Facebook creators had no idea <u>how fast the site would grow</u>.

Pre-writing Task

1 Read the paragraph below. What discovery is the story about? What things did the discoverer not realize during the discovery process?

An Accidental Discovery

Penicillin is effective against many serious bacterial infections. Alexander Fleming, a Scottish scientist, discovered penicillin in 1928. However, he did not immediately understand what he had discovered. At the time, he was observing substances that could destroy bacteria. However, Fleming was not a very neat scientist. He often left
5 trays of bacteria around his lab. In August 1928, he went away for a vacation. When he returned, he found that something strange had happened to one of the trays. A fungus had grown on the bacteria and killed them. At first, Fleming did not understand why this had happened, but he later realized what he had discovered. He realized that the fungus was powerful and could be useful in curing bacterial infections, but he still
10 had not understood how important it was. He doubted whether the fungus could be effective long enough to kill bacteria inside a human body. The penicillin he grew in the first few years was too slow in taking effect, so he stopped working on it. After a few years, he returned to it. Fleming and other scientists discovered ways to make the substance work more rapidly, and it soon became the most effective antibiotic in
15 existence. This discovery has saved millions of lives.

2 Read the paragraph again. Underline the noun clauses with *whether* and *wh-* words. Notice how they help to tell the story of the discovery.

Writing Task

1 *Write* Use the paragraph in the Pre-writing Task to help you write the story of a discovery or an invention. You may need to do some research. Include discoveries that the inventor or discoverer made along the way. You can write about inventions or discoveries that were:

- accidental
- controversial
- extremely popular
- never popular
- unnecessary
- life-saving

2 *Self-Edit* Use the editing tips to improve your story. Make any necessary changes.

1. Did you use noun clauses to help to tell the story?
2. Did you begin indirect questions with a *wh-* word, *whether*, or *if* ?
3. Did you avoid the mistakes in the Avoid Common Mistakes chart on page 225?

UNIT 17

Direct Speech and Indirect Speech

Human Motivation

---

1 | Grammar in the Real World

A What makes people work hard at their jobs? Read the article about employee motivation. What type of reward is particularly effective in motivating workers?

Workplace Motivation

Motivation is the desire to do something. Billionare Donald Trump **said**, "Money was never a big motivation for me. . . . The real excitement is playing
5 the game." Trump meant that he enjoys doing the work more than making millions of dollars. Can that be true? What other factors are important in motivating employees?

10   Many psychologists believe that there are two types of rewards that affect motivation: external rewards and internal rewards. External rewards are rewards that someone gives you. A pay raise is a common external reward. A good grade at school is also an example of an external reward. Internal rewards are connected to the feelings people have about the work they do. The satisfaction
15 you get when you do something well is an internal reward. Researcher Frederick Herzberg (1923–2000) studied motivation in the workplace for many years. Herzberg **said that** employers must think about factors that affect employees' feelings of satisfaction. Herzberg **explained that** working conditions and relationships among co-workers affect workers' motivation. Therefore,
20 employers need to create an environment that makes employees feel safe, valued, and accepted.

    Some studies on workplace motivation have focused on autonomy, which is the freedom to work independently. This is an important internal reward. Daniel Pink, the author of a book on motivation, **told** an audience once **that** Google
25 was a good example of a company that supported autonomy. One day each week, Google engineers focus on their own ideas. Pink **informed** the audience **that** Google News and Gmail had been created during this free time.

Research also shows that appreciation is a powerful reward. In his book *The 1001 Rewards and Recognition[1] Fieldbook*, Bob Nelson described a study on the
30 effects of appreciation on motivation. The study **asked**, "What motivates you?" Workers ranked the importance of 65 motivating factors. Nelson **indicated that** appreciation for their work ranked first for the workers.

The subject of worker motivation is complex. People expect fair pay for their work. However, research **shows that** people find internal rewards more
35 meaningful than a high salary.

[1]**recognition:** special positive attention

B *Comprehension Check* Complete the chart. Check (✓) whether each reward is external or internal.

	External Reward	Internal Reward
1. Pay raise		
2. Feeling successful		
3. Freedom to work independently		
4. Good salary		
5. Good grades		

C *Notice* Find similar sentences in the article and complete the sentences below.

1. Donald Trump _____ , "Money was never a big motivation for me.... The real excitement is playing the game."

2. Daniel Pink, the author of a book on motivation, _____ an audience once that Google was a great example of a company that supported autonomy.

3. Pink _____ the audience that Google News and Gmail had been created during this free time.

Each sentence tells what someone says. Which sentence gives the actual words of the speaker? How do you know?

2 | Direct Speech

▶ ## Grammar Presentation

Direct speech repeats people's exact words.	*Donald Trump said, "Money was never a big motivation for me. . . . The real excitement is playing the game."*

2.1 Forming Sentences with Direct Speech

a. Direct speech consists of a reporting clause and a person's exact words.	REPORTING CLAUSE *Donald Trump said, "Money was never a big motivation for me."*
The most common reporting verb is *said.* Use a comma after the verb.	*Our manager **said,** "Treat the customers like family, and they will come back."*
To quote speech, use quotation marks and a capital letter to begin the direct speech. End the direct speech with punctuation inside the quotation marks.	*My colleague said, **"W**e are going to lead the company in sales next year**!"***
b. The reporting clause can also come at the end or in the middle of direct speech. Notice that the verb can also come before the subject in the reporting clause when the reporting clause comes at the end or in the middle.	*"The company pays its workers fairly," **the president said**.* *"We didn't do well this year," **said Liz,** "so we won't get a sales bonus."*
c. Use the verb *asked* to quote a question.	*Mr. Smith **asked,** "What do you hope to accomplish in this job**?"***

▶ ## Grammar Application

Exercise 2.1 Statements in Direct Speech

A Rewrite the quotations about motivation as direct speech. Sometimes more than one answer is possible.

1. in my experience, there is only one motivation, and that is desire –Jane Smiley

   Jane Smiley said, "In my experience, there is only one motivation,
   and that is desire."

2. the ones who want to achieve and win championships motivate themselves. –Mike Ditka

_____

_____

3. the ultimate inspiration is the deadline –Nolan Bushnell

_____

_____

4. motivation is the art of getting people to do what you want them to do because they want to do it –Dwight D. Eisenhower

_____

_____

5. I'm a great believer in luck, and I find the harder I work, the more I have of it –Thomas Jefferson

_____

_____

6. great work is done by people who are not afraid to be great –Fernando Flores

_____

_____

7. nothing great was ever achieved without enthusiasm –Ralph Waldo Emerson

_____

_____

8. you miss 100 percent of the shots you don't take –Wayne Gretzky

_____

_____

9. the journey of a thousand miles begins with a single step –Lao Tzu

_____

_____

B *Over to You* Choose two of the quotations, and write a sentence that explains what each one means.

When Jane Smiley said, "In my experience there is only one motivation, and that is desire," she meant that the only real motivation is wanting to do something.

C *Pair Work* Share your sentences with a partner. Discuss whether you agree or disagree with your partner's interpretation.

Exercise 2.2 Questions in Direct Speech

A Read the transcript of an online discussion about motivating employees. Then rewrite each question as a direct speech question. The information in parentheses tells you where to put the reporting clauses – at the beginning or end of the sentences.

Working Today

Today, motivational expert Camila Valdez is here to answer your questions.

Claire **Is money the best way to get employees to work harder?**
(1)
Camila No. Studies show that appreciation and recognition are the best ways.

Pedro **Do you have guidelines for rewarding employees?**
(2)
Camila Try to match the size of the reward to the size of the accomplishment.

Roxana **When should you give the rewards?**
(3)
Camila It's really best to give them as soon as possible after employees have accomplished something.

Hong **What are some ways to motivate employees?**
(4)
Camila Give rewards that fit your employees' working style.

Chelsea **Can you give an example of what you mean?**
(5)
Camila Certainly. For example, give a more flexible schedule to working parents. They will feel more focused at work because they will be able to take care of their home-related responsibilities.

1. (beginning) _Claire asked, "Is money the best way to get employees to_
   work harder?"

2. (end) _____

3. (beginning) _____

4. (end) _____

5. (beginning) _____

B *Over to You*   Ask two classmates these questions: Would money motivate you to work harder? Why or why not? Then write a short report on your interviews with direct speech statements and questions.

   I talked to Anne and Mike. I asked, "Would money motivate you to work harder?" Anne said, "No, it wouldn't." I asked, "Why not?" Anne said, "I work to please myself. That's my reward." Then I asked Mike, "Would money motivate you to work harder?" Mike said, "Yes, it would."

3 | Indirect Speech

▶ Grammar Presentation

Indirect speech tells what someone says in another person's words. Indirect speech is also called reported speech.	Donald Trump said, "Money was never a big motivation for me." (direct speech) Donald Trump said that money had never been a big motivation for him. (indirect speech)

3.1 Forming Indirect Speech

An indirect speech statement consists of a reporting verb such as *say* in the main clause, followed by a *that* clause. The word *that* is optional and is often omitted when speaking.	She said, "The boss is angry." (direct speech) She **said (that)** the boss was angry. (indirect speech)

3.2 Tense Shifting in Indirect Speech

a. After a past verb in the reporting clause, the verb form in indirect speech usually changes. The verb shifts to express a past time.

DIRECT SPEECH	INDIRECT SPEECH
She said, "The boss **is** angry."	She said that the boss **was** angry.
He said, "She **is enjoying** the work."	He said that she **was enjoying** the work.
They said, "The store **closed** last year."	They said that the store **had closed** last year.
The manager said, "The group **has done** good work."	The manager said that the group **had done** good work.

b. The following forms usually change in indirect speech.

DIRECT SPEECH	INDIRECT SPEECH
He said, "The department **will add** three new managers."	He said that the department **would add** three new managers.
She said, "They **are going to hire** more people soon."	She said that they **were going to hire** more people soon.
The teacher said, "The students **can work** harder."	The teacher said that the students **could work** harder.
Their manager said, "Money **may not be** very important to them."	Their manager said that money **might not be** very important to them.

c. The forms of *should, might, ought to,* and *could* are the same in direct and indirect speech.

DIRECT SPEECH	INDIRECT SPEECH
The boss said, "He **should go** home."	The boss said that he **should go** home.

3.2 Tense Shifting in Indirect Speech *(continued)*

d. Do not change the form of verbs in general truths or facts.	She said, "Martin Luther King, Jr. **was** a great man."
	She said (that) Martin Luther King, Jr. **was** a great man.
	NOT *She said that Martin Luther King Jr. ~~had been~~ a great man.*

▸▸ Tense Shifting in Indirect Speech: See page A11.

▶ Grammar Application

Exercise 3.1 Tense Shifts in Indirect Speech

Read the quotes about a psychology course. Then rewrite each quote as indirect speech. Sometimes more than one answer is possible.

1. The professor said, "Psychology 101 includes a unit on motivation."

   The professor said that Psychology 101 included
   a unit on motivation.

2. A student said, "The class is discussing motivation and personality this week."

   _____

   _____

3. The professor said, "The class is reading about Abraham H. Maslow's theories on motivation."

   _____

   _____

4. One student said, "I'm learning a lot in the class."

   _____

   _____

5. Another student said, "I don't understand the lectures."

   _____

   _____

6. The teaching assistant said, "The readings have great practical value."

   _____

   _____

Exercise 3.2 Modals and Future Forms in Indirect Speech

Read the excerpt from a lecture on how to motivate adult learners. Then complete the e-mail. Rewrite each sentence from the lecture as indirect speech. Sometimes more than one answer is possible.

Welcome to Motivating Adult Learners. This class is for people who teach adults. Participants in the course are going to learn all about motivating adult learners. The course will rely heavily on participants' own experiences. Students should come to class prepared to discuss their own experiences. We may occasionally have guest speakers. The course will include presentations, homework, and weekly quizzes. There will be three papers and two oral presentations. Participants can substitute an oral presentation for one of the papers.

Send   Attach   Save Draft   Spelling ▾   Cancel

To: jake15@cambridge.org
From: marta34@cambridge.org
Subject: First Class Meeting

Hi Jake,

Here's what happened in class today. The instructor welcomed us, and then she said Motivating Adult Learners was for people who teach adult learners.

1. *She said that participants in the course were going to learn all about motivating adult learners.*

2. _____

3. _____

4. _____

5. _____

6. _____

4 | Indirect Speech Without Tense Shift

▶ Grammar Presentation

Indirect speech usually includes a shift in verb tense. However, in some cases the form of the verb does not change.	*The president announced that she **was going** to start an employee program next year.* *The president announced that she **is going** to start an employee program next year.*

4.1 Keeping the Original Tense in Indirect Speech

You may use the tense in the original direct speech clause when you report statements that are still true now, such as:	
Facts or general truths	*He said, "A pay raise **is** a common reward."* *He <u>said</u> that a pay raise **is** a common reward.*
Habits and routines	*Leo said, "Our meetings always **begin** on time."* *Leo <u>said</u> that their meetings always **begin** on time.*
Actions in progress	*Eve said, "I**'m studying** hard for the exam.* *Eve <u>said</u> that she **is studying** hard for the exam.*

▸▸ Tense Shifting in Indirect Speech: See page A11.

4.2 Using Present Tense Reporting Verbs

Use a present tense verb in the reporting clause when what was said relates to the present and is still important at the moment of speaking. Keep the same tense as in the quote.	*Everybody always **says**, "Employees **need** to be motivated."* *Everybody always **says** that employees **need** to be motivated.*

▶ Grammar Application

Exercise 4.1 Keeping the Original Tense in Indirect Speech

Read the quotes from a business meeting. Then rewrite the quotes as indirect speech. Use the same tense as the direct speech. Sometimes more than one answer is possible.

1. "We are trying to improve our new marketing plan." –the marketing manager

   <u>*The marketing manager said that we are trying*</u>
   <u>*to improve our new marketing plan.*</u>

2. "The client loves it." –the manager

_____

3. "We have always solved these problems in the past." –Janet

_____

4. "Staff satisfaction has been very important." –Janet

_____

5. "Tomorrow, we are going to have a half-day training session on giving constructive feedback." –Rodrigo

_____

_____

6. "We will all work together, as a team." –Rodrigo

_____

_____

Exercise 4.2 Using Present Tense Reporting Verbs

A Complete the sentences. Use the correct form of the verbs in parentheses.

1. My father always says that money _makes_ (make) the world go round.

2. My friend Amanda insists that a good night's sleep _____ (be) more important than studying.

3. Donald Trump says that he _____ (enjoy) doing the work more than making money.

4. My friend says that he _____ (enjoy) having autonomy at work.

5. My colleague says that it _____ (not / be) always easy to stay motivated.

6. My manager says that you _____ always _____ (should / ask) questions if something is not clear.

B *Pair Work* Discuss the sentences in A. Do you agree with the statements?

5 Other Reporting Verbs

▶ Grammar Presentation

<table>
<tr><td>Although say is the most common reporting verb, many other verbs can introduce indirect speech.</td><td>The president explained that our company's workers deserved higher pay.
The president told us that our company's workers deserved higher pay.</td></tr>
</table>

5.1 Other Reporting Verbs

<table>
<tr><td>a. Tell is a common reporting verb. Always use a noun or object pronoun after tell.</td><td>The president said that he was doing a great job.
The president told him that he was doing a great job.</td></tr>
<tr><td>b. You can use these verbs in place of say: admit, announce, complain, confess, exclaim, explain, mention, remark, reply, report, state, and swear.</td><td>"The workers need recognition," said the manager.
The manager admitted that the workers needed recognition.</td></tr>
<tr><td>When used with an object, the object comes after to.</td><td>He swore <u>to us</u> that he'd be on time in the future.</td></tr>
<tr><td>c. You can use these verbs in place of tell: assure, convince, inform, notify, and remind. Always use a noun or object pronoun with these verbs.</td><td>The president told the managers, "All workers need to be creative."
The president reminded them that all workers need to be creative.</td></tr>
</table>

▸▸ Reporting Verbs: See page A11.

Data from the Real World

<table>
<tr><td>Commonly used reporting verbs in formal writing include claim, explain, find, show, state, and suggest.</td><td>The author claimed that internal motivation was more effective than external motivation.
The results of the study showed that money was not always an effective way to motivate employees.</td></tr>
</table>

▶ Grammar Application

Exercise 5.1 Other Reporting Verbs

Complete the excerpt from an e-mail about a presentation on cultural differences in motivation. Circle the correct verbs.

> **Send** **Attach** **Save Draft** **Spelling ▾** **Cancel**
>
>   Wei **said** /**told** me that he had attended a presentation on the cultural differences that
> (1)
> affect motivation. He **said** / **told** that an expert on motivation gave the presentation. He
> (2)
> **said** / **told** me that the expert was Dr. Ghosh. He **reminded** / **mentioned** me that we had
> (3)   (4)
> read one of her articles in class.
>
>   Anyway, Dr. Ghosh **said** / **informed** the group that the typical workplace included
> (5)
> people with various cultural backgrounds. She **explained** / **reminded** that these workers
> (6)
> had different expectations. She **informed** / **explained** the group that these workers often
> (7)
> had different motivations.
>
>   At the same time, Dr. Ghosh **reminded** / **remarked** that there was no one way to
> (8)
> motivate all workers. She **admitted** / **reminded** that in multicultural settings, it was even
> (9)
> more complicated.
>
>   She **stated** / **reminded** the group that managers shouldn't make generalizations about
> (10)
> cultures. She **assured** / **remarked** that the "human touch," getting to know employees as
> (11)
> individuals, was the best way to motivate them.

Exercise 5.2 More Reporting Verbs

A ◀)) Listen to the conversation about a presentation on cultural differences in classrooms. Complete the sentences with the words you hear.

David What happened in class today?

 Mira We had a guest speaker. He _told us_ about the importance of motivation in
                       (1)
      the language classroom. He _____ there are two kinds
                                 (2)
      of motivation: intrinsic and extrinsic.

David Right. Last week, the professor _____ there were two
                                      (3)
      different types, and she gave examples.

Mira Yes. So anyway, the speaker _____ he had done (4) a study of students in Japan and students in the United States. He

_____ both groups had native-speaking English (5)

teachers. He _____ the purpose of the study was to see (6)

whether the teachers' remarks had a negative effect on the motivation of the

Japanese students.

David What did he find out?

Mira He _____ the study found four ways in which the teachers' (7)

behavior had a negative effect on Japanese students' motivation.

David Did he give any examples?

Mira He _____ classroom discussion is one area where there (8)

are key differences. He _____ in the Japanese classroom, (9)

students generally listen more and talk less.

David And as we know from our reading, Porter and Samovar

_____ in the U.S. classroom, some students speak up (10)

spontaneously, and that a lot of teachers encourage discussion.

Mira Right. So, he _____ when a teacher criticizes a Japanese (11)

group for not participating, it has a bad effect on motivation.

B 🔊)) Listen again and check your answers.

C *Over to You* Compare the behavior of American and Japanese students to students from another culture that you are familiar with. Use sentences with indirect speech.

The speaker said that in the Japanese classroom, students listen more and talk less.
That is true in my culture, too. Students show respect that way.

6 | Avoid Common Mistakes ⚠

1. **For verbs such as *admit*, *announce*, *complain*, *explain*, and *mention*, the object pronoun comes after the preposition *to*.**

   He explained ~~us~~ the objective. _{to us}

2. **Change the form of the verb in indirect speech in most cases.**

   He claimed that they followed the directions. _{had}

3. **Use beginning and ending quotation marks with direct speech.**

   The director said, "All designers may work from home on Fridays."

Editing Task

Find and correct the mistakes in the paragraphs about a memorable event.

One of the highlights of my life happened through an experience at work. It started when my manager announced ~~us~~ some interesting news. He said, I am starting a company band. Then he asked, "Who wants to join?" I mentioned him that I had played guitar for many years. He said, You should definitely try out.

5   On the day of tryouts, I was a little nervous because everyone played extremely well. After I auditioned, the manager thanked me and explained me that he will let me know soon.

I forgot about it, so I was very surprised when I got a phone call from my manager a few days later. He said, You can play lead guitar. I said, Wow! That's great! After that, the

10 band practiced a few times a week. A few months later, we played at the company party. We were nervous, but we played well. The president of the company spoke to me later and said I have a lot of talent. I was embarrassed by his compliment, but I said I am proud to play for the company. I will never forget that experience.

7 | Grammar for Writing ✎

Using Descriptive Reporting Verbs

There are a number of verbs that writers can use in indirect speech. Some of these verbs add additional meaning; others are more neutral. Read these examples:

The teacher <u>argued</u> that he could motivate students from any culture with special rewards.
Many of his <u>students</u> <u>claimed</u> that the rewards did not motivate them, however.
A few students <u>pointed out</u> that many of their teachers offer rewards for good work.

Notice that *argued* and *claimed* show that the speaker is sharing an opinion or feels strongly about the statement, whereas *pointed out* is more neutral.

The following reporting verbs are especially useful in academic writing.

These are more neutral:	*announce, ask, explain, inform, mention, note, notify, observe, point out, remark, remind, reply, report, say, state, tell*
These add more precise meaning:	*admit, advise, argue, assure, claim, complain, confess, convince, exclaim, suggest, swear*

Pre-writing Task

1 Read the paragraphs below. Where did the survey take place? What was the purpose of the survey? What did the writer decide to do?

A Motivation Survey

I find it hard to motivate myself to exercise, so I went to a gym to get some advice. I asked people what motivated them. A few of the people said that they made exercise a routine or habit. They explained that they didn't think about whether or not to go to the gym on any particular day. They just went on the same days every week. One of the trainers

5 there swore that money was one of the most important motivators. She argued that people who paid for something tended to use it more.

Two other people told me that they promised themselves a reward each week that they went to the gym three times. They claimed that they wouldn't reward themselves if they missed a day. I asked them what their rewards usually were, and they explained that

10 they often went out to dinner with friends as a reward. I pointed out that having dinner in a restaurant might ruin the benefits of going to the gym, but they assured me that they always ate healthy meals at restaurants. I decided I could use all of these ideas for motivation, so I joined the gym.

2 Read the paragraphs again. Circle the reporting verbs. Underline the reporting verbs that add meaning to the writer's statements.

Writing Task

1 *Write* Use the paragraphs in the Pre-writing Task to help you write about what motivates people to do something. Survey four people. Then write a paragraph reporting your results. You can write about how they motivate themselves to:

- do laundry
- lose weight
- get enough sleep
- eat well
- not procrastinate
- study hard

2 *Self-Edit* Use the editing tips to improve your paragraph. Make any necessary changes.

1. Did you choose neutral reporting verbs where appropriate?
2. Did you use reporting verbs that add meaning to your statements?
3. Did you use the correct verb form after each reporting verb?
4. Did you avoid the mistakes in the Avoid Common Mistakes chart on page 241?

UNIT 18

Indirect Questions; Indirect Imperatives, Requests, and Advice

Creative Problem Solving

1 Grammar in the Real World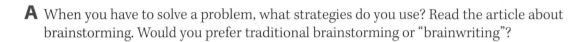

A When you have to solve a problem, what strategies do you use? Read the article about brainstorming. Would you prefer traditional brainstorming or "brainwriting"?

Brainstorming as a Problem-Solving Tool

There is more than one way to solve a problem. One method many people use is brainstorming. Brainstorming is an activity designed to produce a number of ideas in a
5 short time. Alex Osborn invented the word in 1939. In his book *Unlocking Your Creative Power*, Osborn said that the word *brainstorm* means using the brain to solve a problem creatively. Although he **said that groups should**
10 **brainstorm** in a particular way, variations on his technique have also become popular.

Osborn's original brainstorming method had four rules. First, he **told participants not to judge** other people's ideas. Second, he welcomed all ideas, even wild ideas. Osborn said that crazy ideas could get people thinking along new lines and could
15 lead to effective solutions. Therefore, he **asked participants to shout out** even unusual ideas. Third, Osborn **asked group members to produce** a large number of ideas. He thought that the group would find a few really good ideas if many different ones were available. Finally, Osborn **asked the brainstorming group if they could improve** the ideas that had been suggested.

20 One alternative to brainstorming is brainwriting. Brainwriting is a silent version of brainstorming. With brainwriting, participants write down their ideas instead of shouting them out. In his book *Thinkertoys*, creativity expert Michael Michalko suggests that brainwriting may be more productive than traditional brainstorming. This is because people often think of additional ideas as they write. He also asserts
25 that this method is better for quieter individuals because they do not have to express their ideas out loud.

Brainstorming and brainwriting are flexible methods. Anyone can use them because they do not require a lot of training or expensive materials. These processes are all effective tools for creative problem solving in professional, academic, and
30 personal situations.

B *Comprehension Check* Answer the questions.

1. What are the four rules of brainstorming?
2. Why does Michalko believe that brainwriting may be more productive than brainstorming?
3. According to the writer, who can use brainstorming?

C *Notice* Find the sentences in the article and complete them.

1. First, he told participants _____ other people's ideas.

2. Therefore, he asked participants _____ even unusual ideas.

What are the forms of the missing verbs?

2 | Indirect Questions

▶ Grammar Presentation

Indirect questions tell what other people have asked. There are two kinds of indirect questions: *Yes/No* questions and information questions.	*He asked, "Are your jobs satisfying?"* *He asked if our jobs were satisfying.* *The director asked, "Which technique do you prefer?"* *The director asked us which technique we preferred.*

2.1 Forming Indirect Questions

a. Use *asked* in the reporting clause and *if* to introduce an indirect *Yes/No* question.	*"Will we start attending brainstorming sessions?"* Mia **asked**. Mia **asked if** we will/would start attending brainstorming sessions.
Use *asked* in the reporting clause and the same *wh-* word to introduce an indirect information question.	*"**When** will the training begin?"* our manager **asked**. Our manager **asked when** the training will/would begin.

2.1 Forming Indirect Questions (continued)

b. Use statement word order in the indirect question.	*He asked if Rita was one of our most productive employees.*
c. After *ask*, you can use a direct object. The direct object can be a noun or pronoun.	*She **asked the students** if they understood.* *She **asked me** when I wanted to leave the company.*

▶ Grammar Application

Exercise 2.1 Forming Indirect Questions

Read the interview between Joanna and Dr. Martin, a critical thinking expert. Then rewrite each of Joanna's questions as an indirect question.

Joanna Dr. Martin, why is creative thinking in the business world so important?

Dr. Martin Companies need very creative people to help design and market new products.

5 **Joanna** Why will creative thinking be even more important in the future?

Dr. Martin Competition is getting stronger. You have to be creative to stay competitive.

Joanna What techniques have worked to get people to think creatively?

10 **Dr. Martin** One technique that really works is to move the body. I tell people who are sitting at a desk to move into the conference room or take a walk outside.

Joanna How does moving promote creativity?

15 **Dr. Martin** Moving stimulates the brain.

Joanna Are there any other ideas like this?

Dr. Martin Of course. Try putting colorful pictures on the wall. Never try to be creative in an empty room.

Joanna Do objects and colors stimulate creative thinking?

20 **Dr. Martin** They definitely do.

1. What did Joanna ask Dr. Martin about creative thinking in the business world?

   Joanna asked Dr. Martin why creative thinking in the business world was important.

2. What did Joanna ask Dr. Martin about the future?

   _____

3. What did Joanna ask about creative techniques?

   _____

4. What did Joanna ask about moving?

_____

5. What did Joanna ask about other ideas?

_____

6. What did Joanna ask about stimulating creative thinking?

_____

Exercise 2.2 More Forming Indirect Questions

Read the conversation about a company's creativity exercises. Then rewrite each of Ahmet's questions as an indirect question.

Ahmet How was your creativity session yesterday?

Irina It was fun, and we had some really good ideas, too.

Ahmet Was the session here?

Irina Yes, it was here.

5 **Ahmet** Who was your leader?

Irina It was Dr. Martin, a creativity expert. She gave us a problem to solve. Then she gave us large pieces of white paper and markers in a lot of different colors.

10 **Ahmet** What did you do with the paper and the markers?

Irina We drew pictures of things that we wanted to say, that is, the solutions we had for the problem.

Ahmet Interesting. How long were you drawing pictures?

Irina We did that for about an hour. Then we had a thing called "incubation." We stopped
15 working, had lunch, and then watched a TV show!

Ahmet Why did you watch TV in the office?

Irina The idea was to forget about everything and then come back to the problem. When we went back to work, we then found the best solution.

Ahmet Are you going to continue tomorrow?

20 **Irina** Yes.

1. What did Ahmet ask Irina about yesterday?

   He asked her how her creativity session was.

2. What did Ahmet ask Irina about the location?

   _____

   _____

3. What did Ahmet ask Irina about the leader?

   _____

   _____

4. What did Ahmet ask Irina about the paper and the markers?

   _____

5. What else did Ahmet ask Irina about the activity with the paper and markers?

_____

_____

6. What did Ahmet ask Irina about watching TV in the office?

_____

7. What did Ahmet ask Irina about tomorrow?

_____

Exercise 2.3 Using Indirect Questions

Group Work Ask and answer the questions about creativity with two students. Then share your answers with the whole class.

- What are some situations in which people have to be creative?
- Why is creativity difficult for some people?
- When you have to be creative, do you have any techniques to stimulate your thinking? What are they?

3 | Indirect Imperatives, Requests, and Advice

▶ Grammar Presentation

Imperatives, requests, and advice are usually made indirect with an infinitive.	*"Please sit down."* He asked us **to sit down**. *"Would you please turn off your phones?"* He asked us **to turn off** our phones.

3.1 Indirect Imperatives, Requests, and Advice

a. Use an infinitive in indirect imperatives. Use *not* + infinitive in negative indirect imperatives. You can use *tell* or *say*.	*"Don't make a lot of noise,"* said Mr. Jung. Mr. Jung <u>said</u> **not to make** a lot of noise.
Use an infinitive in indirect requests. You can use *ask*, *tell*, or *say*.	*"Please turn off your cell phones,"* said Mr. Cho. Mr. Cho <u>told</u> us **to turn off** our cell phones.
Use an infinitive to report advice given with modals such as *should*. Use *not* + infinitive to report advice with *should not*. You can use *tell* or *say*.	*"You shouldn't reject any ideas,"* Carl said. Carl <u>told</u> us **not to reject** any ideas.

3.1 Indirect Imperatives, Requests, and Advice *(continued)*

b. Always use an object after *tell*.	Ms. Ali **told** <u>us</u> to work quietly. NOT ~~Ms. Ali told to work quietly~~.
Use a pronoun or noun after *ask* to show the person who is the object of the request.	Sam **asked** <u>her</u> to share her ideas with the group.

▶ Grammar Application

Exercise 3.1 Indirect Imperatives and Requests

Read the directions that a trainer gave to a group of employees. Then rewrite the steps with infinitives and the words in parentheses.

1. "Get into groups of three or four."
2. "Don't get into a group with someone you usually work with."
3. "Cut out pictures from magazines that show your ideal working environment."
4. "Don't criticize your group members' choices."
5. "Present your picture to the other groups."
6. "Comment on the other groups' pictures, but don't criticize people's choices."
7. "Discuss the emotions that the pictures suggest."

I attended a problem-solving session with Dr. Martin yesterday. The goal was to help us get along better with each other. She helped us a great deal. Here's what she did:

1. (First / she / tell) *First, she told us to get into groups of three or four.*
2. (Then / she / say) _____
3. (She / tell) _____
4. (Dr. Martin / say) _____
5. (Then / she / tell) _____
6. (After that / she / say) _____
7. (Finally / Dr. Martin / say) _____

Exercise 3.2 🔊 Indirect Requests and Advice

Listen to the marriage counseling session. Then answer the questions. Use the words in parentheses and *ask*, *say*, or *tell*.

1. What did the therapist tell the husband and wife to do?

   The therapist told them to take a pad

   of paper and a pencil.
   (take a pad of paper and a pencil)

2. What did the husband ask?

   _____

   _____
   (take a different pencil)

3. What did the wife ask?

   _____
   (use her own pen)

4. What did the therapist say?

   _____
   (write for 15 minutes without stopping)

5. What did the therapist tell the clients?

   _____
   (not look at each other's writing during the activity)

6. What did the therapist say?

   _____
   (not talk to each other)

7. What did the therapist tell the clients?

   _____
   (be prepared to read their descriptions to each other)

8. What did the husband ask?

   _____
   (have a little more time to write)

Exercise 3.3 Indirect Advice

A *Over to You* Think of some good and bad advice you or people you know have received. What was the advice? Write six sentences.

Good Advice

My father's doctor told him not to eat meat and to exercise more.

1. _____

2. _____

3. _____

Bad Advice

Economists told Americans in 2005 to buy real estate because prices would increase.

4. _____

5. _____

6. _____

B *Group Work* Compare your answers with your group members. Discuss why the advice was good or bad. Take notes on your group members' answers.

    A *My father's doctor told him not to eat meat and to exercise more. This was good advice because it helped him to get into better shape.*

    B *Many economists told their clients to buy real estate because prices would increase. This was bad advice because real estate prices went down.*

4 Avoid Common Mistakes ⚠

1. Use infinitives in indirect imperatives.

                   to

    The leader asked us ~~that we~~ write for 5 minutes about the topic.

2. In indirect *Yes/No* questions, remember to use an *if* clause.

              if wanted

    He asked me ~~did I want~~ to be the group leader.

3. Remember to use an object pronoun or noun after *tell*.

      them

    I told∧my ideas, and we ended up using two of them in the project.

Editing Task

Find and correct the mistakes in the paragraph about a brainstorming session.

                                                 if   wanted

       When my psychology professor asked our class ~~did we want~~ to try brainstorming as part of our next group project, I had no idea that the experience would be so challenging or successful. First, when we started, one of our members asked many unimportant questions. When the team leader asked her that she asks the questions later, that person

5 began complaining. Then the team leader asked the person did she want to be the group leader. The rest of us told this was a bad idea, and there was an argument. A different problem arose when we met the second time. The leader asked one student that he takes electronic notes, but he forgot. As a result, when we met the third time, the leader had to tell the information again. She asked me that I write the notes this time, and I did. Aside

10 from these minor problems, the group generated a lot of ideas and finally came up with a successful proposal for a project. So, if someone asked me do I want to work as a group again, I would say yes because even though it is hard to work as a group, the outcome can be better.

5 | Grammar for Writing ✎

Using Indirect Questions, Imperatives, Requests, and Advice

Students often communicate with other students through online message boards and chat rooms, especially when they are working together on an assignment. In these situations, it is often necessary to report what other people have asked, commanded, requested, or advised. Read these examples:

Marielle asked when the first draft is due. Does anyone know? (question)
Professor Harper told us to make a list of creative problem-solving strategies. (command)
Jorge asked us not to have our meetings on Friday because he works on Fridays. (request)
He also said to use a different strategy for each problem we have to solve. (advice)

Pre-writing Task

1 A group of students is working on a project. They are using an online message board to talk to each other. Read their entries. What is the focus of their project, and how many students are in the group?

> ### Thread: Study skills project
>
> Clara: Professor Moss asked us to write outlines for our reports on good problem-solving strategies. He said to identify our own creative problem-solving processes before we try to find new ones. I'll start.
> 5   When I have a problem I can't solve, I think about my older sister, Susannah. She's really good at solving difficult problems. I ask myself how Susannah would solve the problem. That helps me to think about things in a different way.
>
> ### Study skills project, May 9, 7:30
>
> Carmen: That's interesting, Clara. I never thought of doing that. I have a different technique. A few years ago, I had a teacher who always told
> 10   us to try to solve problems by thinking of the end result we wanted and working backward. I try to do that sometimes. Why don't we try everyone else's creative thinking processes and see how they work? Also, could everyone say when they can meet next?

Study skills project, May 9, 8:41

Jun: I don't think I use any special creative problem-solving strategies.

15 Hao: Jun, Carmen asked if we could try each other's strategies. If you don't have one, why don't you just try everyone else's and let us know how they work for you?

Study skills project, May 12, 10:07

Carmen: I just realized it's already Thursday and no one has written here for a while. We have to get working. Does anyone remember when we have
20 to turn in our outline?

Study skills project, May 12, 10:14

Jun: Yes, I asked Prof. Moss when our outline was due. Prof. Moss asked if we could turn it in by Friday. He said he could get us some feedback by Monday. He told us not to spend too much time on the outline, though, because he wants to approve our ideas before we
25 write our report.

---

2 Read the online message board again. Underline the examples of indirect speech. Label each example as *I* (for an imperative), *Q* (for a question), or *A* (for advice). Which verbs show you that the sentence reports advice?

Writing Task

1 *Write* Use the online message board in the Pre-writing Task to help you write a paragraph. Get into pairs and interview each other about one of the following problem-solving strategies. Get instructions and advice from your partner. Then write a paragraph reporting what you asked your partner and what your partner said. You can write about one of these topics or use your own idea.

- backward problem solving
- journaling
- talking about problems with others
- thinking about possible outcomes

2 *Self-Edit* Use the editing tips to improve your paragraph. Make any necessary changes.

1. Did you use the correct tenses after the reporting verbs?
2. Did you use the correct form for indirect questions?
3. Did you avoid the mistakes in the Avoid Common Mistakes chart on page 251?

The Passive (1)

English as a Global Language

1 Grammar in the Real World

A Should everyone speak English? Why or why not? Read the web article on the use of English around the world. Why is English important to learn?

English Is Spoken Here

An Italian businesswoman in Russia speaks English in meetings. Teenagers from Argentina, Turkey, and Japan chat online – in English. Learning English is clearly important in today's
5 world. David Crystal, a linguist[1] who studies the English language, believes that English has become a global language, although it is not an official language in many countries. According to Crystal, no other language **has been spoken** in
10 so many countries and by so many speakers. Currently, over 275 million people speak English as a first language around the world, and approximately one billion speak it as a second language. This means that there are more nonnative speakers of English than native speakers. How **is** English **used** by nonnative speakers? Employees of international companies **are** often **asked** to learn
15 English for their jobs. In addition, the Internet **is dominated**[2] by English. Some experts say that more than half of the information on the Internet is in English. Also, English **has** long **been viewed** as a common language among travelers from different countries. The use of English worldwide appears to have clear benefits for everyone.

20 Does this increase in the use of English worldwide have any disadvantages? Some say that cultures may lose some of their identity if people use English instead of their native languages. For example, much of a culture's identity

---

[1]**linguist:** someone who studies languages and their structures │ [2]**dominate:** control a place or person, want to be in charge, or be the most important person or thing

is reflected in its music and literature. Would these songs and stories be as effective in English? Others say that the English language itself could change.

25 In fact, this is happening now. When English **is spoken** by a group of people whose native language is not English, words from the native language **are** sometimes **mixed in**, and the pronunciation of words is different from British or American English. This means that dialects[3] and different forms of English **are being spoken** in various areas around the world. Sociologists

30 **are** currently **studying** this phenomenon. The loss of cultural identity and the creation of varieties of English are two areas of interest for sociologists and linguists.

English **is being used** worldwide more and more, and for many people, learning it is necessary for their personal and professional lives. There are

35 obvious advantages to learning English. The disadvantages remain unclear. It is clear that varieties of English will continue to evolve. How will this affect how English **is taught**? In the future, will greater numbers of people have to decide which variety of English they learn?

[3]**dialect:** a local variety of language that differs in its pronunciation and word usage

B *Comprehension Check* Answer the questions.

1. Where is English being spoken?
2. When do people around the world speak English? *internet, traveling*
3. What might be some disadvantages of English being a global language?

C *Notice* Match the sentences in A with the sentences in B that mean the same thing.

A *simple present*

b 1. International companies **ask** their employees to learn English for their jobs.

c 2. In addition, English **dominates** the Internet.

a 3. How do nonnative speakers **use** English?

B *simple past*

a. How **is** English **used** by nonnative speakers?

b. Employees of international companies **are** often **asked** to learn English for their jobs.

c. In addition, the Internet **is dominated** by English.

Look at the forms of the verbs in bold in each of the matched sentences. How are the verbs in column B different from the verbs in column A?

2 | Active vs. Passive Sentences

▶ Grammar Presentation

A passive sentence and an active sentence have similar meanings, but the focus of the sentences is different. In the passive sentence, the focus is on the action or on the person or thing receiving the action.

The president **asked** the employees to speak English. (active)

The employees **were asked** to speak English. (passive)

2.1 Passive Sentences with *By* + Agent

a. In active sentences, the agent (or doer of the action) is in subject position. In passive sentences, the object of the active sentence becomes the subject. The word *by* comes before the agent.

      AGENT   OBJECT
People **spoke** English at the meeting. (active)

English **was spoken** by people at the meeting. (passive)

b. The agent is not always necessary.

English **was spoken** at the meeting. (We assume *people* were doing the speaking.)

c. Use the *by* + agent phrase if the agent is important or if the meaning of the sentence would be unclear without it.

The Internet **is dominated** by English.
NOT ~~The Internet is dominated.~~ (By who or what?)

2.2 Present and Past Forms of the Passive

a. For the simple present form of the passive, use the present form of *be* + the past participle of the main verb.

Some international companies **ask** their employees to learn English. (active)
Employees **are asked** to learn English by some international companies. (passive)

b. For the present perfect form of the passive, use *has / have* + *been* + the past participle of the main verb.

The company **has told** the employees to speak English. (active)
The employees **have been told** to speak English. (passive)

c. For the present progressive form of the passive, use the present form of *be* + *being* + the past participle of the main verb.

These days, people around the world **are speaking** many dialects of English. (active)
These days, many dialects of English **are being spoken** by people around the world. (passive)

2.2 Present and Past Forms of the Passive *(continued)*

d. For the simple past form of the passive, use the past form of *be* + the past participle of the main verb.

This form is the most common.

*Years ago, people **did** not **consider** English a global language.* (active)

*Years ago, English **was** not **considered** a global language.* (passive)

e. For the past progressive form of the passive, use the past form of *be* + *being* + the past participle of the main verb.

This form is rare.

*Ten years ago, fewer people **were using** English online.* (active)

*Ten years ago, English **was being used** by fewer people online.* (passive)

f. In passive sentences, do not use a form of *do* in questions and negative statements in the simple present and simple past.

***Do** most travelers **speak** English?* (active)

***Is** English **spoken** by most travelers?* (passive)

*Turkish teenagers **didn't use** English to chat online a decade ago.* (active)

*English **wasn't used** by Turkish teenagers to chat online a decade ago.* (passive)

 Research shows that the simple present, present perfect, and simple past forms of the passive are much more frequent than the present progressive, past progressive, and past perfect forms of the passive.

▸▸ Irregular Verbs: See page A1.
▸▸ Passive Forms: See page A12.

Data from the Real World

Research shows that in academic writing, these are the most common verbs used in the passive:

analyze, calculate, carry out, collect, determine, expect, find, measure, observe, obtain, prepare, see, set, show, test, and *use.*

► Grammar Application

Exercise 2.1 Active and Passive Sentences

A Complete the online interview with a reporter from BusinessTimes Online and the CEO of an international company. Circle the correct verb forms.

Reporter I would like to ask some questions about your use of English here at BR Corporation. **Do people speak English / (Is English spoken)** by
(1)
most executives?

CEO Yes, most executives **speak / are spoken** English at this branch.
(2)

Reporter Do only executives speak English? I mean, do lower level employees
use / are used English here, too?
(3)

CEO No, English **isn't used / doesn't use** by them much.
(4)

Reporter Why is English necessary for some employees?

CEO English **is needed / needs** by executives who travel. Also, we
(5)
are expected / expect them to read technical documents in English.
(6)

Reporter **Does BR Corporation support / Is BR Corporation supported** English
(7)
language learning?

CEO Yes, BR Corporation **is offered / offers** onsite English courses.
(8)

Reporter **Are the courses taught / Do the courses teach** by native English speakers?
(9)

CEO Yes, native speakers **are conducted / conduct** all of our English classes.
(10)

Reporter Thank you for speaking with me today.

B *Pair Work* Which sentences in A are in the passive? Rewrite them as active sentences.

Do most executives speak English?

C *Group Work* Rewrite the active sentences in A as passive sentences. In which sentences is the *by* + agent phrase necessary? Share your answers with the group.

4- they don't use English much
5. Executives who travel need English
9. Do Native English speakers team courses?

(Hw)
19

Exercise 2.2 Present Forms of the Passive

Complete the article about foreign-language teaching. Use the simple present or present perfect form of the passive with the verbs in parentheses. Sometimes more than one answer is possible.

English _has been taught_ (teach) in
(1)
many countries all over the world for years.

It __15__ currently _Spoken_
(2)   (2)
(speak), at least to some degree, by

one–quarter of the world's population.

Schools in the United States also recognize

the importance of learning other languages.

For some time, languages other than English _have been included_(include) in
(3)

these schools' programs. Recently, a growing number of languages has become

available. Which languages _are offered_ (offered) by U.S. high schools
(4)

nowadays? The results may surprise you.

French is one of the most popular foreign languages for high school students.

It _has been taught_(teach) in most U.S. high schools for many years. Arabic
(5)

is becoming more and more popular. In fact, Arabic _15 offered_ (offer)
(6)

at many Massachusetts public schools these days. Chinese is also beginning

to gain popularity. An increase in the number of students learning Chinese

has been reported (report) for several years in various states across the
(7)

country. It _has been estimat_(estimate) that more than 50,000 U.S. high
15 estimated
(8)

school students <u>are</u> now enrolled in Chinese classes.

Exercise 2.3 Past Forms of the Passive

A Read the active sentences about language. First underline the object in each sentence. Then rewrite the sentences as passive sentences. Sometimes more than one answer is possible.

1. At one time, many people used <u>Latin</u> as a global language.

   At one time, Latin was used as a global language by many people.

2. The ancient Romans <u>spoke</u> Latin.

   Latin was spoken by ancient Romans

3. Ancient Roman authors wrote many important manuscripts.

   Many important manuscripts were written by ancient Roman authors

4. For many centuries, the Romans <u>conquered</u> neighboring nations.

   Neighboring nations were conquered by the Romans for many centuries

5. These conquered groups spoke versions of Latin.

   Versions of latin were spoken by these conquered groups

6. Conquered people from Britain to Africa used <u>Latin</u>.

   Latin was used by conquered people from Britain to Africa

7. People were still speaking Latin after the Roman Empire fell.

   Latin was still being spoken by people after the Roman empire fell.

8. Scholars and scientists were using <u>Latin</u> until the eighteenth century.

   Latin was being used by scholars and scientist until the eighteenth century

B Read the sentences in A again. In which sentences are the agents not important? Discuss the reasons for your answers with a partner. Then rewrite these sentences in the passive without the agent.

A In the first sentence, many people isn't important because we know that only people use language.

B You're right. The sentence could be At one time, Latin was used as a global language.

3 | Verbs and Objects with the Passive

▶ Grammar Presentation

Was seen = Past participle

Transitive verbs (verbs that take an object) can occur in the passive.	*Someone **saw** her at the conference.* (transitive) *She **was seen** at the conference.*
Intransitive verbs (verbs that do not take an object) cannot occur in the passive.	*I **fell** asleep.* (intransitive)

3.1 Transitive and Intransitive Verbs

a. Some common transitive verbs that occur in the passive are *call, concern, do, expect, find, give, know, left, lose, make, put, see, take,* and *use.*	*Improvement of your language skills **is expected**.* *I **was given** a new English textbook.* *The reasons for his success **were not known**.*
b. *Born* is the past participle of *bear. Born* is used almost exclusively in the passive.	*I **was born** in a small town.* *Where **were** you **born**?*
c. Some common intransitive verbs, which have no passive form, include *appear, arrive, come, die, fall, go, happen, live, look, occur, sit, smile, stay, wait,* and *walk.*	*When **did** your symptoms first **appear**?* NOT *When were your symptoms first appeared?* *Globalization of some languages **happens** over time.* NOT *Globalization of some languages is happened over time.*

3.2 Passive Forms with Direct and Indirect Objects

Some verbs, such as *give, offer, show,* and *tell,* can have two objects: a direct and an indirect object. In passive sentences, either the direct object or the indirect object can become the subject. Use *to* before an indirect object that is not in subject position.	INDIRECT OBJ DIRECT OBJ *The team gave the manager the report.* *The manager **was given** the report by the team.* *The report **was given** to the manager by the team.*

▶ Grammar Application

Exercise 3.1 Transitive or Intransitive?

Read the sentences about "dead" languages. Underline the verb in each sentence. If the sentence can occur in the passive, write the passive sentence on the line. Do not use an agent. Write ✗ if a passive form is not possible.

1. People in Ancient Rome spoke Latin.
   Latin was spoken in Ancient Rome.

2. People don't use Latin for everyday communication today.
   Latin isn't used for everyday communication today

3. Some languages die.
   ✗

4. This occurred with Dalmatian.
   ✗

5. People spoke Dalmatian in Croatia. Dalmatian was spoken in Croatia

6. Dalmatian speakers lived in coastal towns of Croatia. ✗

7. Groups in different regions developed dialects of Dalmatian. *Groups*

Dialects of Dalmatian were developed ~~by groups~~ in different regions

8. Native speakers didn't record the grammar of Dalmatian.

The grammar of Dalmatian wasn't recorded by Native speakers

Exercise 3.2 Using Transitive and Intransitive Verbs

A *Over to You* Answer the questions about a language you know. Use the underlined verbs in your answers. Use passive sentences when possible. Use the indirect object as the subject of the passive sentence when possible. Write sentences that are true for you.

1. What is a computer <u>called</u> in this language?

   A computer is called "bilgisayar" in Turkish.

2. What English words are <u>used</u> in this language?

   Whiteboard and mobile are Spanish used in D.R

3. Do any other foreign words <u>occur</u> in this language? If so, what are they?

   _____

4. Is this language <u>spoken</u> by more people or fewer people than it was 50 years ago?

   Spanish is spoken by more people than it was 50 years ago

5. What advice is frequently <u>given</u> by teachers to people learning this language? *study grammar.*

   People learning Spanish are frequently advice by teachers to

6. Do speakers of this language <u>tell</u> their children traditional stories?

   Arabic speaking children are told traditional stories

B *Group Work* Share your sentences with your group members.

Exercise 3.3 Direct Objects in Passive Sentences

A Read the sentences about Esperanto, a language that was created as a global language. Underline the agents.

1. The first book about Esperanto was published by a <u>company</u> in 1887.
2. Esperanto was invented by <u>L. L. Zamenhof</u>.
3. Esperanto was created by <u>its inventors</u> to be a very easy language to learn.
4. The grammar was designed by <u>Zamenhof</u> to be simple and clear.
5. It is spoken by <u>about 10,000</u> people.
6. It is being used by <u>people in</u> about 115 countries.
7. It has not been recognized as an official language by <u>any country</u>.
8. The language is used by <u>some international travelers</u>.

B *Pair Work* Read the sentences in A again. Circle the direct objects. Compare your answers with a partner.

4 | Reasons for Using the Passive

▶ Grammar Presentation

The passive is used to describe processes and to report news events. The agent is not important. The focus is on the action or on the person or thing receiving the action.	First, the students **were shown** a video in English. A "dead" language **has been brought** back to life in one community.

4.1 Reasons for Using the Passive

a. Use the passive to describe a process or a result. Common verbs to describe a process or a result are *compare*, *develop*, *examine*, *make*, *measure*, *study*, and *test*.	First, the information **was studied**. Then recommendations **were made**. (process) Therefore, English **was made** the official language of the company in 2010. (result)
b. Use the passive when you don't know who performed the action. You can also use the passive to avoid directly blaming or criticizing someone.	The report **was poorly written**. (We don't know, or we don't want to say, who wrote the report.)
c. Use the passive to report news events.	Recommendations for the teaching of languages **were published** today.

▶ Grammar Application

Exercise 4.1 Describing Processes and Results

A ◀)) Listen to a report on a language study of English as a Second Language (ESL) students. Then complete the answers to the questions. Use the passive and the words in parentheses.

1. How many groups of students were there? (put into)

   The students *were put into two groups* .

2. What was the assignment at the beginning of the semester? (give)

   Students in each group _____ .

3. What did group 1 study? (teach)

   Group 1 _____ .

4. What did group 2 study? (teach)

   Students in group 2 _____ .

5. Who read the essays? (read)

The first and final essays _____ .

6. What did the judges do with all of the final essays? (put)

All of the final essays from group 1 and group 2 _____

_____ .

7. How did the judges rate all the final essays? (rate)

The essays _____ .

8. What rating did the essays produced by group 1 receive? (give)

Most of the final essays produced by group 1 _____ .

9. What did the results seem to indicate? (include)

ESL students' writing improves when grammar and writing instruction

_____ .

B 🔊 Listen again and check your answers.

Exercise 4.2 Reporting News Events

Read the sentences about preserving two Native American languages. Then rewrite each
sentence in the passive. Do not use an agent. Sometimes more than one answer is possible.

1. In 2009 in Minnesota, the legislature established a volunteer group
to preserve Native American languages.

   In 2009 in Minnesota, a volunteer group was
   established to preserve Native American languages.

2. The legislature recognized the importance of preserving the Native
American languages.

   _____

   _____

3. The volunteer group collected data on the use of the Ojibwe and
Dakota languages.

   _____

4. In Minnesota, many Native American people no longer spoke the Ojibwe and
Dakota languages.

   _____

5. The volunteer group developed a strategy to teach the Ojibwe and Dakota languages
in schools.

   _____

6. The group is developing teacher-training programs.

   _____

7. In 2011, a nonprofit business released software for teaching the Ojibwe language.

   _____

8. The preservation of the languages will strengthen the Native Americans' cultural identities.

   _____

Exercise 4.3 Avoiding Blame and Criticism

Read each classroom scenario and pretend you are the teacher. Then write passive statements to avoid directly blaming or criticizing someone. Use the underlined sentences in your answers. Sometimes more than one answer is possible.

1. Someone stole some valuable equipment from the classroom. You think that someone in the class is responsible, but you aren't sure. You tell the class:

   Some valuable equipment was stolen from the classroom.

2. One student's essay contained plagiarized material. The student copied some material in his essay from the Internet. You tell the student:

   _____

3. A hacker broke into the school's e-mail system last night. No one knows who is responsible, but you must inform the students. You tell the class:

   _____

4. A student hands in the second draft of an essay. You see a lot of grammar mistakes. The student did not edit the paper carefully. You tell the student:

   _____

5 | Avoid Common Mistakes ⚠

1. Remember to use a form of *be* in passive sentences.

        is

English ∧ spoken at most airports.

2. Always use the past participle form of the verb in passive sentences.

             translated

The words have been ~~translating~~ into Spanish, Arabic, Chinese, and Urdu.

3. Do not use the passive form when the subject is the doer of the action.

      studying

I have been ~~studied~~ English for 5 years.

Most students have ~~been~~ used an English dictionary.

4. With questions, remember to put *be* before the subject.

  was

Why ∧ he ~~was~~ given an award?

Editing Task

Find and correct the mistakes in the paragraphs about English spelling.

Even good writers will tell you that English spelling has ~~been~~ confused them at one
time or another. The same sound spelled many different ways. For example, the words *lazy*
and *busy* are pronouncing with a /z/ sound, but they are not consistent in their spelling
because of strange rules that are being related to the vowels. Why English is written this

5 way? English is an ancient language that contains old spelling rules. Also, other languages
have been contributed many words to English.

Some experts who have been studied the English language for years would like to see
English spelling simplified. They ask important questions: Why so much time is wasted on
spelling lessons? Why is literacy lower in English-speaking countries than in countries

10 with simplified spelling? They point to the fact that many other languages simplified
successfully. They suggest that in places such as Sweden, France, and Indonesia, changes
to the written form have helped make learning to read easier.

6 Grammar for Writing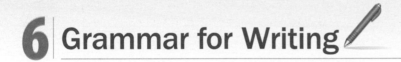

Using the Passive to Write About the Object of an Action

Writers often use passive sentences when the main topic of their writing is a noun that
does not usually perform an action. For example, the nouns *English*, *idea*, and *information*
usually receive an action rather than perform an action. Read these examples:

English *is spoken* very differently in different parts of the world.
Maxwell's ideas *are* always *expressed* in a way that makes people angry.
The information *was provided* in both English and Spanish.

Pre-writing Task

1 Read the paragraph below. What forms of English are being compared?

Jamaican English

English is spoken in many countries around the world, but in most places, it is
more similar to British English than it is to American English. However, Jamaican English
is different. The English that is spoken in Jamaica has similarities to both British and
American English. Because Jamaica was once a British colony, Jamaican English used

5 to be similar to British English. However, because Jamaican people get more exposure to American media than to British media these days, and because Jamaica is so close to North America, many changes have occurred. For example, in Jamaica, people say *do you have* instead of the British *have you got.* In addition, *you don't need to do that* is used instead of the British expression *you needn't do that.* Also, many American English words are used

10 in Jamaica in place of their British equivalents. For example, baby beds are *cribs* rather than the British *cots,* and people live in *apartments* rather than the British *flats.* Despite the changes in expressions and vocabulary, the words are pronounced in a more British way than in an American way. As English becomes more of a global language, it will be interesting to see what other changes occur.

2 Read the paragraph again. Underline the passive verbs. Draw arrows to the nouns that receive the action. What is the agent in each clause with a passive verb? In each case, is it unknown, unimportant, or obvious?

Writing Task

1 *Write* Use the paragraph in the Pre-writing Task to help you write about language use or language change. You can write about one of these topics or use your own ideas.

- the languages that are spoken in your home
- the use of English or another language in a country you know well
- the use of foreign words in a language you know

2 *Self-Edit* Use the editing tips to improve your paragraph. Make any necessary changes.

1. Did you use the passive to place the focus on the action or on the person or thing receiving the action?
2. Did you use active sentences to place the focus on the doer of the action?
3. Did you avoid the mistakes in the Avoid Common Mistakes chart on page 265?

The Passive (2)
Food Safety

1 | Grammar in the Real World

A What do you know about genetically modified food? Read the article about genetically modified food. What are some genetically modified foods?

 <u>Genetically Modified Food</u>

Genetically modified¹ (GM) foods come from plants that **have been changed** in a laboratory. This technology alters the genes² of the plants. It was developed so that food could have specific, desirable traits. For example, the first GM crop in the United States consisted
5 of tomatoes that were genetically changed to stay firmer longer.

Many people have strong opinions about the potential³ benefits and risks of GM agriculture. For example, those in favor of GM foods believe that crops **should be designed** to resist insects. They point to the example of sweet corn. They say that sweet corn **used to be destroyed** by pests. This created serious problems. Farmers lost
10 money. Crops **got damaged** and **could not be eaten**. Therefore, they say that a great benefit **can be found** in GM sweet corn, which has been modified to resist insects that cause damage. People who oppose GM foods see the issue differently. They cite⁴ a study that links GM corn to organ⁵ damage in rats. They claim that the safety of these crops has not been tested adequately.⁶

15 GM supporters see GM soybeans as another beneficial crop. These crops are not harmed by a powerful weed-killing chemical. This chemical kills weeds the first time it is applied, so farmers use less of it. Supporters say that this improves air and water quality since fewer pollutants enter the environment. Critics argue that the weeds are no longer affected by the weed killer, and new "superweeds" are growing. Therefore, farmers have
20 to use more chemicals to save their crops.

---

¹**modify:** change something in order to improve it | ²**gene:** a code that controls the development of particular characteristics in a plant or animal | ³**potential:** possible but not yet achieved | ⁴**cite:** mention something as an example or proof of something else | ⁵**organ:** a vital part of the body, like the heart, lungs, and kidneys | ⁶**adequately:** good enough but not very good

Finally, those in favor of GM foods say that better control of pests and weeds has made it possible for GM crops to produce more food in a shorter time. They believe this increased production will help feed a world population which is expected to grow to 9 billion by 2050. Opponents insist that the problem of world hunger **will**
25 **not be solved** by producing more food. They argue that farmers grow enough food now and that global hunger is a result of unequal food distribution, not the result of a food shortage.[7]

Clearly, there are pros and cons to this debate. GM foods seem to have the potential to benefit the world. However, **should** extra care **be taken** until the
30 long-term risks are known?

[7]**shortage:** a lack of something needed

B *Comprehension Check* Answer the questions.

1. What are genetically modified foods?
2. What are some advantages of genetically modified foods?
3. What are some concerns about genetically modified foods?

C *Notice* Find the sentences in the article and complete them.

1. For example, those in favor of GM foods believe that crops _____ to resist insects.

2. Opponents insist that the problem of world hunger _____ by producing more food.

3. However, _____ extra care _____ until the long-term risks are known?

What verb comes after modals in passive verb forms?

2 | The Passive with *Be Going To* and Modals

▶ Grammar Presentation

You can use the passive with *be going to* and modals.	GM foods **will replace** natural foods. (active) *Natural foods* **will be replaced** *by GM foods.* (passive)

2.1 Forming the Passive with *Be Going To* and Modals

a. For the passive with *be going to,* use *be going to* + *be* + the past participle of the main verb. *Not* comes before *be going to* in the negative form.	Only natural foods **are going to be served** in our house. The food **is not going to be eaten** immediately. **Is** more GM food **going to be grown** in the future?
b. For the passive with modals, use a modal + *be* + the past participle of the main verb. *Not* follows the modal in the negative form.	People **could be harmed** by GM food. People **must be informed**. Food **should not be eaten** if it isn't fresh. **Will** questions about GM food **be answered** by scientists?

▸▸◂ Passive Forms: See page A12.

▶ Grammar Application

Exercise 2.1 The Passive with *Will* and *Be Going To*

Complete the interview about plans for a food conference. Circle the passive form of the verbs.

> **Reporter** A conference called *The Future of Food* **will hold /(will be held)** at
> (1)
> Bay City Tech next week. Issues concerning the food industry
> **will be discussed / will discuss** by experts from a variety of fields. We
> (2)
> interviewed two participants, Dr. Fred Bell, a biologist, and Deniz Martin,
> the president of the *Traditional Food Society*. First, what major issues
> **are going to address / are going to be addressed** at next week's
> (3)
> conference?
>
> **Dr. Bell** Policies on food aid **are going to debate / are going to be debated** in
> (4)
> one session.
>
> **Reporter** What are the issues there?
>
> **Dr. Bell** Well, GM plants **are going to be promoted / are going to promote**
> (5)
> as the main solution to hunger in poor nations.
>
> **Reporter** World hunger is a serious problem. What's your opinion as a biologist?
> Will the situation **improve / be improved** by GM plants?
> (6)
>
> **Dr. Bell** No, the problem of world hunger **will not solve / will not be solved** by
> (7)
> GM crops, in my opinion.

Reporter Don't some experts believe that GM food will help increase crop

production?

Dr. Bell In my opinion, crop production **will not be increased / will not increase**
(8)
by GM plants. In fact, there is no proof of this so far.

Reporter Ms. Martin, what *Traditional Food Society* issues

will be presented / will present at the conference?
(9)

Ms. Martin The issue of sustainable food production – growing food without

harming people or the environment – **will address / will be addressed**.
(10)
For example, ways to improve organic farming methods

will be demonstrated / will demonstrate.
(11)

Reporter Thank you both for your time.

Exercise 2.2 The Passive with Modals

A Read the facts that a student collected for a report on pesticides.[1] Rewrite the facts as
passive sentences. Sometimes more than one answer is possible.

1. Pesticides can harm humans, animals, and the environment

Humans, animals, and the environment can be harmed by pesticides.

2. Pesticides can cause air pollution.

_____

3. In the United States, scientists can find pesticides in many streams.

_____

4. Pesticides may have harmed some farm animals.

_____

5. Pesticides may have affected meat from farm animals.

_____

6. Pesticides in water could affect fish.

_____

7. In some cases, pesticides can affect humans.

_____

[1]**pesticide:** a weed-killing chemical

B *Pair Work* Compare your sentences with a partner.

Exercise 2.3 More Passive with Modals

Complete the web article about a government recall. Rewrite the steps as passive
sentences with modals. Use the indirect object as the subject of the passive sentence
when possible. Sometimes more than one answer is possible.

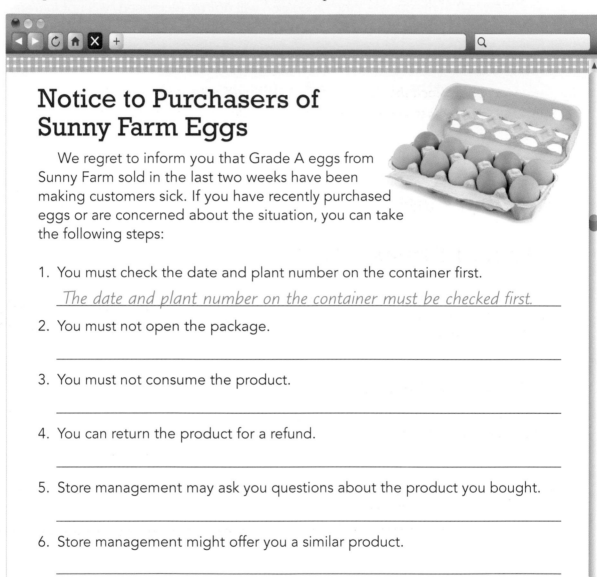

Notice to Purchasers of Sunny Farm Eggs

We regret to inform you that Grade A eggs from
Sunny Farm sold in the last two weeks have been
making customers sick. If you have recently purchased
eggs or are concerned about the situation, you can take
the following steps:

1. You must check the date and plant number on the container first.

   The date and plant number on the container must be checked first.

2. You must not open the package.

   _____

3. You must not consume the product.

   _____

4. You can return the product for a refund.

   _____

5. Store management may ask you questions about the product you bought.

   _____

6. Store management might offer you a similar product.

   _____

Exercise 2.4 Using Passive Forms of Modals

Group Work Discuss the questions about GM food. Use passive sentences with modals.

- Should food be genetically modified? Why or why not?
- In your opinion, can people be harmed by eating genetically modified food? If yes, in what ways?
- Should genetically modified food be labeled in the United States? Why or why not?

A *In my opinion, food should not be genetically modified because we don't know the dangers.*

B *I disagree. I think food should be genetically modified because it's the best way to end world hunger.*

3 | *Get* Passives

▶ Grammar Presentation

Passive sentences with *get* instead of *be* are more informal and are often used to express stronger emotions.	*The storm **destroyed** the crops.* (active) *The crops **got destroyed** by the storm.* (passive)

3.1 Forming *Get* Passives

a. For the *get* passive, use a form of *get* + the past participle of the main verb.	*He **is getting transferred** to the research department.* *Our orange trees **got damaged** last night.*
b. For negative statements and questions in the simple present and simple past, use a form of *do* + *get* + the past participle of the main verb.	*In my opinion, food **doesn't get inspected** carefully enough.* ***Did** your crops **get damaged** in the hurricane?*

3.2 Using *Get* Passives

We often use *get* passives to talk about negative situations or situations we think are beyond our control.	*Some food companies **are getting fined** for using unsafe equipment.*

Data from the Real World 🌐

The *get* passive is more common in speaking than in general writing. In formal academic writing, the *get* passive is very infrequent.

speaking
general writing
formal academic writing

Say: "She **got arrested and charged** with murder."
Write: She **was arrested and charged** with murder.

▶ Grammar Application

Exercise 3.1 *Get* Passives

Complete the interview about food contamination. Write *get* passives with the words in parentheses. If there is a line through the agent, do not use it in the passive.

Alternative Review

Interviewer There's been another case of contaminated[1]

lettuce. How does this happen? An anonymous

lettuce grower agreed to be interviewed if we

did not mention his name. So, I hear

you're getting investigated by the FDA
(1. the FDA[2] is investigating you)

for problems with food safety. What happened?

Grower _____ .
(2. ~~Something~~ contaminated our lettuce)

Interviewer _____ ?
(3. Did the FDA recall the lettuce)

Grower Yes, _____ .
(4. ~~The FDA~~ recalled it)

Interviewer What happened, exactly?

Grower I'm not sure. As you know, _____
(5. ~~workers~~ pick our produce)

right here on the farm. _____ here.
(6. ~~Workers~~ also pack it)

_____ . This can cause contamination.
(7. ~~Workers~~ sometimes mishandle it)

[1]**contaminated:** less pure and potentially harmful | [2]**FDA:** Food and Drug Administration, a U.S. government agency

Interviewer Don't you have strict procedures?

Grower Yes, but it's been very hot lately. Working conditions have been difficult. Perhaps

_____ .
(8. ~~something~~ distracted the workers)

Interviewer _____ before it goes to the stores?
(9. Doesn't ~~someone~~ check your produce)

Grower No, _____ . That's our responsibility, and
(10. ~~people~~ don't inspect it)

my company is very sorry that we didn't catch it.

Interviewer I see. Well, thank you very much for agreeing to be interviewed.

Exercise 3.2 More *Get* Passives

A *Over to You* Look at the following statements about food safety. Check (✔) the statements you agree with.

☐ 1. When a restaurant gets inspected, the results should be posted on the restaurant's front door.

☐ 2. Food recalls get publicized too much. This hurts farmers, and a lot of perfectly good food gets thrown away.

☐ 3. If a supermarket sells spoiled food, the manager should get fired.

☐ 4. If a restaurant gets temporarily shut down for food safety problems, no one should ever eat there again.

☐ 5. All foreign fruit and vegetables should get inspected before entering the country.

B *Group Work* Compare your answers with your group members. Discuss your reasons. Use *get* passives.

A *I think that when a restaurant gets inspected, the results should be posted on the restaurant's front door.*

B *I disagree. If a restaurant gets inspected and receives a low rating, it's bad for business.*

4 | Passive Gerunds and Infinitives

▶ Grammar Presentation

Gerunds and infinitives can occur in the passive.	*Some people worry about genetically modified food **harming** them.* (active)
	*Some people worry about **being harmed** by genetically modified food.* (passive)
	*Consumers should expect food companies **to give** them accurate information about their food.* (active)
	*Consumers should expect **to be given** accurate information about their food.* (passive)

4.1 Forming Passive Gerunds

a. To form passive gerunds, use *being* + the past participle of the main verb.	*Consumers are afraid of food companies **harming** them.* (active) *Consumers are afraid of **being harmed** by food companies.* (passive)
b. Common verbs that are followed by passive gerunds include *avoid, consider, dislike, enjoy, like, miss, quit,* and *remember.*	*I remember **being given** information about GM foods in the supermarket.*
c. Common verbs + prepositions that are followed by passive gerunds include *complain about, keep on, succeed in,* and *worry about.*	*The restaurant worried about **being closed** by the food inspectors.*
d. Common adjectives + prepositions that are followed by passive gerunds include *afraid of, aware of, concerned about, content with, interested in, tired of,* and *worried about.*	*The company was interested in **being seen** as a socially responsible company.*

▶▶ Verbs Followed by Gerunds Only: See page A7.
▶▶ Verbs Followed by Gerunds or Infinitives: See page A7.
▶▶ Verbs + Prepositions: See page A9.
▶▶ Adjectives + Prepositions: See page A10.

4.2 Forming Passive Infinitives

| **a.** To form passive infinitives, use *to be* + the past participle of the main verb. | *Food companies are not likely **to solve** the problem of world hunger.* (active)
*The problem of world hunger is not likely **to be solved** by food companies.* (passive) |

4.2 Forming Passive Infinitives *(continued)*

b. Common verbs followed by passive infinitives include *ask, expect, hope, manage, refuse, seem,* and *want*.

*The manager of the restaurant expected **to be told** that the restaurant passed the inspection.*

▶▸ Verbs Followed by Infinitives Only: See page A7.
▶▸ Verbs Followed by Gerunds or Infinitives: See page A7.

▶ Grammar Application

Exercise 4.1 Passive Gerunds and Infinitives

Complete the sentences about restaurant food safety. Circle the correct passive forms of the verbs.

1. Customers at Corner Café recently complained about (being)/ to be served undercooked food.

2. The manager of the café was concerned about **to be / being** inspected.

3. The owners were afraid of **to be / being** told they must close the cafe if the problems were not corrected.

4. The owners expected **being / to be** cited by the county food safety bureau.

5. The staff hoped **to be / being** paid for the time that the restaurant was closed.

6. The manager was not happy about **being / to be** told to close the restaurant.

Exercise 4.2 More Passive Gerunds and Infinitives

A ◀)) Listen to an interview with consumers about food labeling. Write the passive gerund or infinitive forms you hear.

Reporter	Hello to everyone. Today I'll be asking people their thoughts on food labeling. First, let's talk to Andrew. Andrew, do you read food labels?
Andrew	I refuse _to be forced_ to do so much (1) work when I go shopping! I just want _____ decent, healthy food. (2) No, I don't read them.
Reporter	I can understand that. Al and Mei?

Nutrition Facts
Serving Size 3 oz. (85g)

Amount Per Serving	As Served
Calories 38	Calories from Fat 0

	% Daily Value
Total Fat 0g	0%
Saturated Fat 0g	0%
Cholesterol 0g	0%
Sodium 0g	2%
Total Carbohydrate 0g	3%
Dietary Fiber 0g	8%
Sugars 0g	
Protein 0g	

Vitamin A 270%	•	Vitamin C 10%
Calcium 2%	•	Iron 0%

Percent Daily Values are based on a 2,000 calorie diet. Your daily values may be higher or lower depending on your calorie needs:

	Calories	2,000	2,500
Total Fat	Less than	65g	80g
Sat Fat	Less than	20g	80g
Cholesterol	Less than	300mg	300mg
Sodium	Less than	2,400mg	2,400mg
Total Carbohydrate		300g	375g
Dietary Fiber		25g	30g

Al We expect _____ the truth by food companies,
(3)
but we know labels aren't always accurate.

Mei You have to inform yourself. All consumers have to start
_____ better _____ , so we always read them.
(4)   (4)

Reporter OK. And you, Roxana, do you read food labels?

Roxana Yes, because I'm a pretty informed consumer. I'm not too
concerned about _____ by food companies, but
(5)
I'm not interested in _____ , either!
(6)

Reporter Thank you, Roxana. And finally, Jessica. What do you think?

Jessica It's sometimes easy _____ by product labeling, so
(7)
I don't read them much because they don't matter. Take the
word *natural*, for example. You expect it _____ for
(8)
food that has few or no artificial ingredients. However, the word
natural can be used for genetically modified food products.

Reporter Thanks to you all. It appears that consumers are tired of
_____ by food companies.
(9)

B *Over to You* Complete the sentences about food labeling with passive gerunds or
infinitives and the verbs in the box. Write sentences that are true for you.

~~confuse~~	give	lie to	tell
do	inform	sell	use

1. I'm tired of _being confused by food labels_____ .

2. I expect _to be_ı_____ .

3. I'm (not) concerned about _____ .

4. I hope _____ .

5. It's (not) easy _____ .

C *Pair Work* Compare your answers with a partner.

A *I'm tired of being confused by food labels. I don't want to be told something is "organic"*
when it really isn't.

B *Well, I know what you mean, but actually, I'm tired of being told to eat organic and*
healthy food all the time. Why can't I enjoy a candy bar once in a while?

5 | Avoid Common Mistakes ⚠️

1. In passive sentences, use a past participle after *be*, not the base form of the verb.

produced
Unintended side effects can be ~~produce~~ by new technologies.

2. Don't forget to use *be* + the past participle to express a passive meaning.

be caused
An allergic reaction can ~~cause~~ by many different kinds of foods.

Editing Task

Find and correct seven more mistakes in the paragraph about some GM food concerns.

made
It is certain that many advances in technology will be ~~make~~ in the twenty-first century. Although many of these advances will improve our future, others may do as much harm as good. GM foods are one example. Currently, many new foods are creating by scientists. For instance, many people suffer from food allergies. Certain GM
5 foods may help avoid this problem; the food's DNA has been change so that the food no longer causes allergic reactions. Also, one day, the world's growing population may be feed with GM foods that grow quickly. This will make it possible for more food to be produce. These new foods can be use to feed more people. However, GM foods have another side. Because these foods have not existed very long, scientists do not know all
10 their effects. For example, some people fear that cancer can cause by GM foods. This is especially troubling because GM foods might not mark as such, so consumers may not know what they are buying. When they develop new foods, scientists should be aware of the concerns that consumers have. In my view, we should be careful with any new technology.

6 | Grammar for Writing ✏

Using the Passive with Modals, Gerunds, and Infinitives

Writers use the passive to focus on actions, results, or processes rather than on the agents of action. Read these examples:

The origin of grocery products <u>has to be included</u> on labels.
Local farmers are happy about their food <u>being purchased</u> by the restaurants in town.
Organic food is likely <u>to be priced</u> higher than nonorganic food.

Pre-writing Task

1 Read the paragraph below. What two reasons does the writer give for not buying certain organic products all the time?

Are Organic Foods Always the Best Choice?

Buying organic foods has been popular for a long time, but it can be expensive. Some organic foods may not be worth the extra expense. For example, consumers do not necessarily have to buy organic bananas. The reason for this is that the banana itself seems to be protected from the pesticides by the thick banana peel. Other

5 nonorganic foods that have thick peels or skins and that can be eaten safely are avocados and watermelons. There are also some nonorganic foods that are safe for other reasons. For example, some foods are simply not attractive to bugs, so it is a waste of farmers' time and money to spray pesticides on these foods. No one is sure why, but the reason for this might be that insects don't like the taste of these foods.

10 Broccoli, cabbage, and onions fall into this category. However, these nonorganic foods can still be priced higher because no chemical residue can be found in them. Should the public be informed of this? Consumers should be worried about not being made aware of this information since they could be spending more than they need to.

2 Read the paragraph again. Underline the passive forms of modals. Circle the passive gerund. <u>Double underline</u> the passive infinitive.

Writing Task

1 *Write* Use the paragraph in the Pre-writing Task to help you write about some aspect of food. You can write about one of these topics or use your own ideas.

- children and food choices
- eating vegetarian or vegan
- the lack of healthy fast-food options
- pros and cons of GM foods

2 *Self-Edit* Use the editing tips to improve your paragraph. Make any necessary changes.

1. Did you use the passive to place the focus on the action or process?
2. Did you use different forms of the passive?
3. Did you use passive gerunds and infinitives correctly?
4. Did you avoid the mistakes in the Avoid Common Mistakes chart on page 279?

UNIT

21

Subject Relative Clauses (Adjective Clauses with Subject Relative Pronouns)

Alternative Energy Sources

1 Grammar in the Real World

A What are some alternative sources of energy (other than oil or coal)? Read the article about one type of alternative energy. Is "people power" an efficient energy source? Why or why not?

Exercising for Electricity

Much of the world's energy comes from sources like oil and coal, **which cannot be replaced when used up**. Renewable sources – water, wind, and
5 the sun – are better for the environment. However, these alternative sources of energy have not always been sufficiently explored for political and economic reasons. People **who care**
10 **about the environment** are looking for more alternative sources that might appeal to people **who make decisions about these things**. One source **that is becoming popular** uses energy
15 **that is generated by humans**, sometimes called "people power."

With people power, people create electricity through exercise. People exercise in green gyms, **which**
20 **contain special treadmills**. These machines convert human energy into electricity **that helps run the lights and air-conditioning**. People power also helps prevent air pollution.
25 Someone **who exercises for one**

hour can feel good about the fact that he or she is helping prevent carbon dioxide from going into the air. Professional athletes, **whose exercise routines can last for several hours**, 30 could help power a house!

Exercise is not the only way people can make energy. One company has created surfaces **which are powered by humans**. People dance or walk on 35 special dance floors and sidewalks. This movement generates electricity, **which can light up the dance floor or power street lamps**. Body heat is used for power, too. One system in 40 Sweden gathers the body heat from

adjctive clause come with (who, that, wich) + verb

commuters in a train station. This heat, **which is sent to a nearby building**, cuts the energy bill by 25 percent.

45   People power is not perfect, though. Large gyms need a lot of energy to run. People power, **which only generates a part of the total electricity needed**, does not lower the gym's electric bill

50 much. Also, the use of this technology is moving slowly. Business leaders, **who must focus on making a profit**, do not always want to be the first to create new products. They are afraid to spend

money on technology **which might not** 55 **be successful**. However, people **who support green energy** are confident that this technology will catch on in the near future.

People power is not a major 60 energy source yet, but it could be soon. Meanwhile, this "green energy" encourages people to exercise, and it makes people more aware of the environment. It is one kind of 65 technology **that helps people and the planet** at the same time.

B *Comprehension Check* Answer the questions.

which is use for things
who + verb
that + n-erb
which + verb

1. What are some ways that people can make energy?
2. How can "people power" help the environment?
3. What are some problems with people power?

C *Notice* Find the sentences in the article and complete them. Then draw an arrow from each missing word to the word that it refers to.

1. Professional athletes, _____ *whose* _____ **exercise routines** can last for several hours, could help power a house!

2. This heat, _____ *which* _____ **is sent** to a nearby building, cuts the energy bill by 25 percent.

3. However, people _____ *who* _____ **support** green energy are confident that this technology will catch on in the near future.

Look at the words in bold that follow the words you wrote. What parts of speech are the words in bold?

2 | Identifying Subject Relative Clauses

▶ Grammar Presentation

Relative clauses modify – define, describe, identify, or give more information about – nouns. In a subject relative clause, the relative pronoun is the subject of the clause. An identifying relative clause gives essential information about the noun it modifies.

SUBJECT
I go to a gym. The gym creates its own electricity.

RELATIVE
PRONOUN
*I go to a gym **that creates its own electricity**.*

2.1 Forming Identifying Subject Relative Clauses

a. The subject of an identifying subject relative clause is the relative pronoun. The relative pronoun refers to the noun before it. Use *who* or *that* for people, and *which* or *that* for things.	NOUN RELATIVE PRONOUN *Nowadays, people often drive cars **that don't use a lot of gas.***
Do not add a second subject to the clauses.	*People **that exercise** can use special machines to create electricity.* NOT *People that ~~they~~ exercise can use special machines to create electricity.*
b. The information in an identifying subject relative clause is essential. Do not add a comma before this type of clause.	*People **who care about the environment** often recycle their garbage.* (The relative clause tells which people.) *The school uses the electricity **that comes from the exercise machines in the gym**.* (The relative clause tells which electricity.)
c. The verb in the relative clause agrees with the noun that the relative pronoun modifies.	SINGULAR NOUN SINGULAR VERB *Someone **that supports** the environment recycles.* PLURAL NOUN PLURAL VERB *Many people **that support** the environment recycle.*

▶▶ Relative Clauses: See page A13.

2.2 Using Identifying Subject Relative Clauses

a. Use an identifying relative clause to give essential information about a noun. These clauses are also called restrictive subject clauses.	*People power is a kind of energy.* (What kind of energy? What is important about it?) *People power is a kind of energy **that creates electricity**.* (The relative clause gives essential information.)
b. Use an identifying relative clause in definitions, especially with words such as *anyone, people, someone,* or *something*.	*Green energy is something **which doesn't hurt the environment**.* *Environmentalists are people **who care about the environment**.*

▶ Grammar Application

Exercise 2.1 Subject Relative Pronouns

A Complete the article about people power. Use *who* or *which* and the simple present form of the verbs in parentheses.

> Silvia is a student at Bay City University (BCU) _who works out_ (work out) at the campus gym every day. Today, she is exercising on a bike ___that connects___ (2) (connect) to a power grid. Silvia is possibly producing the energy ___that keeps___ (3) (keep) the gym lights on or _____ (power) a professor's laptop in (4) another part of the campus. BCU and Bay City Tech are just two educational institutions _____ (use) human energy as power. (5)
>
> We interviewed Mark Sandoval, a BCU employee _____ (run) (6) campus operations. He said, "This is not a program ___which saves___ (save) (7) the university money. It's more of an experiment ___that illustrates___ (8) (illustrate) to the students how they affect their environment." GreenGo is a Bay City human energy company _____ (provide) BCU with the exercise (9) equipment. Rita Crane, a GreenGo spokesperson, said, "We enjoy working with students and faculty_____ (take) their impact on the environment (10) very seriously."

B 🔊 Listen to the article and check your answers.

Exercise 2.2 Definitions with Identifying Relative Clauses

A Complete the energy definitions with *who* or *that* and the correct form of the verbs in parentheses. Sometimes more than one answer is possible.

1. Geothermal energy is heat _that comes_ (come) from inside the earth.

2. Renewable energy is something _____ (not / disappear).

3. Ecologists are people _____ (study) the relationship between organisms and the environment.

4. A green politician is someone _____ (put) environmental issues ahead of other issues.

5. A sustainable engineer is anyone _____ (design) objects to protect the environment.

B Complete the energy definitions with subject relative pronouns and the words in the box.

chemicals / trap / heat in the atmosphere
~~fuel / come / from vegetable oil or animal fat~~
people / be / part of a political group focused on good environmental policy
someone / work / to protect the environment
structures / not have / a large negative impact on the environment

a type of energy / come / from human exercise
a type of energy / use / the sun as its source
a vehicle / use / two sources of power to run

1. Biodiesel is a kind of _fuel that/which comes from vegetable oil or animal fat_ .
2. A conservationist is _____ .
3. "Greens" are _____ .
4. Greenhouse gases are _____ .
5. A hybrid car is _____ .
6. Solar energy is _____ .
7. People power is _____ .
8. Green buildings are _____ .

Exercise 2.3 Sentence Combining

A Combine the sentences from an alternative energy company's advertisement. Use *who*, *that*, or *which* in subject relative clauses. Sometimes more than one answer is possible.

1. GreenGo is a company. It develops renewable energy systems.
   GreenGo is a company that/which develops
   renewable energy systems.

2. GreenGo developed a technology. The technology turns exercise machines into power generators.
   _____
   _____

3. GreenGo builds machines like exercise bikes. These exercise bikes let exercisers generate electricity from their workouts.
   _____
   _____

4. The electricity connects to a power grid. The power grid covers a large geographic area.
   _____
   _____

5. Sachiko Hanley is the woman. The woman invented this technology.

   _____

6. Many GreenGo clients are colleges and other institutions. The institutions have on-site gyms.

   _____

   _____

7. GreenGo provides an energy source. The energy source is good for the environment.

   _____

8. "We are proud to work with institutions. They have the same environmental goals that we do."

   _____

   _____

B In each of the sentences you wrote in A, underline the subject relative clause and draw an arrow from the relative pronoun to the noun in the main clause it refers to.

   GreenGo is a company that develops renewable energy systems.

3 | Nonidentifying Subject Relative Clauses

▶ Grammar Presentation

Nonidentifying subject relative clauses have the same form as identifying clauses. Unlike identifying clauses, nonidentifying clauses provide additional, not essential, information about the nouns they modify.	*Biodiesel fuel,* **which often comes from plants**, *is an economical source of energy.* (Where the fuel comes from is extra information. It is not essential information about *Biodiesel fuel*.)

3.1 Forming Nonidentifying Subject Relative Clauses

a. Like identifying subject relative clauses, the subject of a nonidentifying subject relative clause is the relative pronoun. The relative pronoun refers to the noun before it.

Use *who* for people and *which* for things. Do not use *that* in a nonidentifying clause.

People power, **which** *is a way to create energy, is popular.*
NOT *People power,* ~~that~~ *is a way to create energy, is popular.*

3.1 Forming Nonidentifying Subject Relative Clauses (continued)

b. Use commas before and after the nonidentifying subject relative clause. The commas indicate that the information is not essential to the meaning of the noun. It is extra information.	*Hybrid cars, **which are better for the environment**, use less gas.*

3.2 Using Nonidentifying Subject Relative Clauses

a. Use a nonidentifying subject relative clause to give nonessential information about a noun. These clauses are also called nonrestrictive clauses.	*People power, **which is a way to create energy**, is popular with environmentalists.*

b. Nonidentifying relative clauses are more common in writing and formal speaking than in informal speaking.

3.3 Identifying vs. Nonidentifying Subject Relative Clauses

a. Identifying relative clauses provide essential information about the noun. The information in the clause identifies or distinguishes the noun.	*Renewable energy **that comes directly from the sun** is called solar energy.* (The information identifies a particular type of renewable energy – not all types of renewable energy.) *My sister **who lives in Maine** loves being outside.* (The information distinguishes this sister from the other or others; it implies there is more than one sister.)
b. Nonidentifying clauses give extra information about a noun. The information is not essential. In speaking, use a short pause before and after the clause. In writing, separate the clause between commas.	*Renewable energy, **which releases fewer greenhouse gases**, is becoming more popular.* (The information does not identify the type of renewable energy; it gives more information about it.) *My sister, **who lives in Maine**, loves being outside.* (The information is extra, not essential; it also implies the speaker has only one sister.)

▶ Grammar Application

Exercise 3.1 Identifying or Nonidentifying?

A Read the news report on building affordable green homes in New Orleans. Underline the relative clauses. Label each of the relative clauses *I* (for identifying) or *NI* (for nonidentifying).

As the environment changes, hurricanes and other severe storms have become a

serious problem in the United States and Latin America. Hurricanes, which primarily attack

southern and southeastern parts of the United States, have been increasing in severity.
The hurricane that did the most damage in recent history was Hurricane Katrina. Since then,
5 a great number of Americans, including many celebrities, have helped the people of New
Orleans rebuild their homes.

The celebrity who is best known for building homes in New Orleans is Brad Pitt.
Pitt, who created a foundation called Make It Right, helps build new "green" homes in
New Orleans. The goals of this foundation are admirable. Make It Right volunteers, who
10 work for free, want to build 150 new green homes in the Lower 9th Ward.

The foundation is not simply providing new homes. Make It Right homes have
many features which are environmentally sound. For example, Make It Right homes
have metal roofs which absorb heat and keep them cool. It is possible that Make It
Right homes will inspire new home builders not only in New Orleans but around the
15 world as well.

B *Pair Work* Compare your answers with a partner. Discuss the reason for each of
your answers.

The relative clause which primarily attack southern and southeastern parts of
the United States *is nonidentifying, because it is not essential to understanding the
sentence. You can say* Hurricanes have been increasing in severity, *and the idea is
complete.*

Exercise 3.2 Nonidentifying Subject Relative Clauses

Combine the facts and the additional information about green architecture. Use
nonidentifying relative clauses.

1. **Fact:** Green architecture is becoming more common.
   Additional Information: Green architecture considers
   both design and the environment.

   Green architecture, which considers both design
   and the environment, is becoming more common.

2. **Fact:** The Turning Torso building uses only renewable energy.
   Additional Information: The Turning Torso building is
   located in Malmö, Sweden.

   _____

   _____

   _____

   _____

3. **Fact:** The Turning Torso building was inspired by a sculpture of a twisting human being.
   Additional Information: The Turning Torso building is the tallest building in Sweden.

   _____

   _____

4. **Fact:** The Burj al-Taqa will be a wind- and solar-powered green skyscraper.
   Additional Information: The Burj al-Taqa will be in Dubai.

   _____

   _____

5. **Fact:** Eckhard Gerber has also designed a green building in Riyadh.
   Additional Information: Eckhard Gerber designed the Burj al-Taqa.

   _____

   _____

6. **Fact:** Architect Eric Corey Freed believes that people will pay more for green buildings.
   Additional Information: Eric Corey Freed has written several books on building green structures.

   _____

   _____

4 | Subject Relative Clauses with *Whose*

▶ Grammar Presentation

| Subject relative clauses that begin with the pronoun *whose* show possession. | In Sweden, there are train commuters. <u>The commuters'</u> body heat supplies energy for a building.

In Sweden, there are train commuters **whose body heat supplies energy for a building**. |

4.1 Forming Relative Clauses with *Whose*

a. The pronoun *whose* shows a possessive relationship between the noun before and after it.	They are the scientists **whose research has won awards**. (The research belongs to the scientists.) That is the product **whose inventor attended this college**. (The product is related to the inventor.)
b. The verb in the relative clause agrees with the noun following *whose*.	WHOSE + SINGULAR NOUN + SINGULAR VERB He's the scientist **whose newest idea is often quoted.** WHOSE + PLURAL NOUN + PLURAL VERB He's the scientist **whose ideas are often quoted**.

4.2 Using Relative Clauses with *Whose*

Relative clauses with *whose* can be identifying or nonidentifying subject relative clauses.

IDENTIFYING RELATIVE CLAUSE

*They are the journalists **whose articles have explained green energy**.* (The information in the clause identifies which journalists.)

NONIDENTIFYING RELATIVE CLAUSE

*Brad Pitt, **whose movies are well known**, gives a lot of money to environmental causes.* (The information about his movies is not essential to identifying Brad Pitt.)

▶ Grammar Application

Exercise 4.1 Subject Relative Clauses with *Whose*: Identifying or Nonidentifying?

A Read the article about a human-powered vehicle. Underline the subject relative clauses. Add commas when necessary.

Meet Charles Greenwood, the inventor of a new type of car. Greenwood, <u>whose human-powered car can go up to 60 miles per hour</u>, is an engineer. This inventor whose dream is to sell the cars to the public has also started a business to manufacture it. A car whose power source is human energy is obviously good for the environment. How does

5 it work? The car whose main power source is human-operated hand cranks[1] also runs with a battery. It's not expensive, either. The car – the HumanCar Imagine PS – will sell for about $15,000. A hybrid car whose selling price will only be about $15,000 should be very popular with energy-conscious consumers.

There are other benefits to a human-powered car. A car whose

10 power source is human energy might also help drivers stay fit. In addition, owners expect to save money operating the HumanCar. The HumanCar whose main source of power is human-operated hand cranks gets the equivalent of 100 miles to the gallon of gas in a regular car.

[1]**crank:** a handle or bar on a machine that you can turn to make another part turn

B *Pair Work* Compare your answers with a partner. Discuss whether each subject relative clause is identifying or nonidentifying.

The relative clause whose human-power car can go up to 60 miles per hour *is nonidentifying because it is not necessary for identifying* Greenwood.

Exercise 4.2 *That*, *Who*, or *Whose*?

Complete the article about green awards. Use *that*, *who*, or *whose*. Sometimes more than one answer is possible.

Awards for Being Green

There are many organizations _that_ offer awards to companies _____
(1)   (2)
practices help the environment and society. Some organizations recognize the work of

companies _____ focus on environmentally responsible practices. The Evergreen
(3)
Award program honors companies _____ create environmentally friendly products.
(4)
An award in 2010 went to Play Mart Inc., a maker of plastic playground equipment

_____ products were made from jugs and bottles from landfills.
(5)

The One Show is another awards organization, _____ Green Pencil award
(6)
celebrates environmentally conscious advertising. In 2009, Häagen-Dazs received the

award for their advertisements _____ raised awareness about the disappearance
(7)
of honeybees. Häagen-Dazs, _____ ice-cream is well known, also donates
(8)
money to research _____ studies honeybees. People _____ buy certain
(9)   (10)
flavors of Häagen-Dazs ice-cream help support this research.

Exercise 4.3 Subject Relative Clauses with *Whose*

Pair Work Answer the questions. Use subject relative clauses with *whose* in your sentences. Then compare your answers with a partner.

- What are the benefits of human-powered vehicles and flying machines?
- What are the disadvantages to these inventions?

A *I said, "A vehicle whose power source is human energy is good for the environment."*

B *I said, "A vehicle whose power source is human energy probably won't go very far or very fast."*

5 | Avoid Common Mistakes ⚠

1. Use *which* or *that* for things, not *who*.

which/that

Scientists are looking for new energy sources ~~who~~ don't harm the environment.

2. Use *who* or *that* for people, not *which*.

who/that

Governments support researchers ~~which~~ are trying to develop alternative approaches to energy.

3. Don't use *who's* when you mean *whose*.

whose

An inventor ~~who's~~ innovative technology solves the energy crisis will help all of us.

4. Don't include a second subject in the relative clause.

A fuel that ~~it~~ is renewable will help solve the world's pollution problems.

Editing Task

Find and correct eight more mistakes in the paragraph about an alternative renewable energy source.

People think renewable energy only comes from water, wind, or the sun, but there is

which/that

another renewable energy source: biofuels. Biofuels are fuels ~~who~~ are derived from oils in

plants. Farmers who's fields were once planted with food crops can now grow energy on

their land. The most commonly used example of this is ethanol, a biofuel who is usually

5 made from corn and added to gasoline. However, ethanol has been criticized. Some critics

say that the world, who's population continues to grow, needs all of its corn for food

production. Others have argued that it takes too much energy to produce corn ethanol.

Recently, scientists which do biofuels research have been working to overcome these

problems. For example, some scientists have produced a genetically modified tobacco

10 that it contains more oil than usual. Other scientists have produced genetically modified

tobacco plants that they produce a lot of oil. This oil can be made into ethanol. In fact,

some scientists have produced ethanol from inedible grass that it grows in the wild. The

scientists which made these inventions hope that biofuels will become an important part

of our renewable energy future.

6 Grammar for Writing ✎

Using Subject Relative Clauses to Avoid Repetition

Writers use subject relative clauses to avoid repeating information and to condense – or package – the information into fewer sentences. This can improve the clarity and flow of a reading passage. Read these examples:

Hybrids have been getting more efficient every year. However, they are not getting any less expensive.

Hybrids, which have been getting more efficient every year, are not getting any less expensive.

The environmentalist's work was featured on a recent television program. That environmentalist is speaking today at the university.

The environmentalist whose work was featured on a recent television program is speaking today at the university.

Pre-writing Task

1 Read the paragraph below. What change does the writer promote and why?

Small but Effective Changes

People everywhere are concerned with the future of our planet, whose environment is rapidly deteriorating. Environmentalists who want to help protect the planet are working hard to find environmentally sound alternatives that are also economical. However, there are many changes that are relatively easy to make. One change that
5 could make a significant impact is using reusable bags instead of plastic or paper bags when shopping. Plastic bags, which might take up to 1,000 years to degrade, are very destructive for the environment. Between 500 billion to 1 trillion plastic bags are used each year around the world. In various parts of the world, laws which would stop the use of plastic bags entirely are being discussed or implemented. Paper bags are not as harmful
10 for the environment as plastic, but they still cause a significant amount of damage. Approximately 14 million trees are cut down each year just to supply Americans with paper bags. In some stores in the United States, shoppers who use their own bags are given five cents back for each bag. However, even though using reusable shopping bags instead of plastic or paper is a very easy change to make, only a small minority of people in
15 the United States have begun to do it voluntarily. In years to come, there will likely be laws that regulate the use of shopping bags to protect the environment.

2 Read the paragraph again. Underline the subject relative clauses. Circle the relative pronoun in each relative clause and draw an arrow to the noun it refers to.

Writing Task

1 *Write* Use the paragraph in the Pre-writing Task to help you write about small or big changes people can make to help the environment or about ways people can be green. You can write about one of these topics or use your own ideas.

- alternative energy
- daily life
- entertainment
- housing
- transportation
- work

2 *Self-Edit* Use the editing tips to improve your paragraph. Make any necessary changes.

1. Did you use identifying subject relative clauses to help define or clarify the noun that is being discussed?
2. Did you use nonidentifying subject relative clauses to add additional information?
3. Did you avoid the mistakes in the Avoid Common Mistakes chart on page 293?

Object Relative Clauses (Adjective Clauses with Object Relative Pronouns)

Biometrics

1 Grammar in the Real World

A What are some techniques that the police use to solve crimes? Read the article about how the police analyze evidence. What are some modern techniques for analyzing evidence?

Forensics: An Imperfect Science

Someone steals a painting from a private home. The victim shows the police the room **in which the theft occurred**. Police collect clothing fibers and dirt left on the carpet. Experts then use the fibers
5 and dirt to identify the thief. The thief is caught, and the art is returned. The use of scientific tests to investigate crimes like this one is called forensics. Traditional forensic techniques include collecting and analyzing evidence **that police find at the**
10 **crime scene**. This evidence includes dust, hair, or fibers **that thieves leave behind**. Police sometimes use dogs to investigate a crime. Scents **that dogs are trained to recognize** include the scents of people, drugs, and explosives. Police also look for fingerprints, **which they often find on hard surfaces**. Unfortunately, fingerprints are often incomplete. However, new techniques use computer programs to help police
15 identify suspects or missing people. Computer programs can produce a list of matches for partial fingerprints. This kind of list, **which police use to narrow a large field of suspects**, helps investigators work efficiently.

In addition, new technology is being used to analyze other evidence. New video cameras can automatically identify a face **whose image police have on film**. Police
20 can compare the faces of suspects to the image of the criminal and find the actual person more quickly. There is also a new way **in which police can identify someone who may be a "missing person."**[1] This new technology compares a digital image of the person's iris[2] with the irises of people who are listed as missing in a database.

[1]**missing person:** someone who has disappeared | [2]**iris:** the colored part of the eye

Forensic evidence **that police collect** is not always accurate. For example, fiber
25 matching is inconclusive.[3] Currently, fibers **that investigators analyze** can only be
matched to a type of cloth. The fibers may not be from clothes **that the suspect owns**.
Another concern is that there are no strict training standards for forensic dogs. Therefore,
agencies like the FBI have only a few dog teams **whose work they trust**.

Combining technology with traditional methods is changing the way **that criminal**
30 **investigations are done**. Forensic science is not perfect, but it is still an important
tool in investigations.

[3]**inconclusive:** not leading to a definite result or decision; uncertain

B *Comprehension Check* Answer the questions.

1. What are some types of forensic evidence?
2. What is one way that police can identify someone?
3. Why can forensic evidence sometimes be inaccurate?

C *Notice* Match the first part of the sentence from the article on the left with the
second part on the right.

A	B
1. The victim shows the police the room _____	a. **that** thieves leave behind.
2. Traditional forensic techniques include collecting and analyzing evidence _____	b. in **which** the theft occurred.
3. This evidence includes dust, hair, or fibers _____	c. **that** police find at the crime scene.

Do the words in B in bold act as the subjects or objects of the clauses they are in?

2 | Identifying Object Relative Clauses

▶ Grammar Presentation

In an object relative clause, the relative pronoun is the object of the clause. An identifying object relative clause gives essential information about the noun it modifies.	OBJECT *Evidence is sometimes inaccurate. Police collect this evidence.* RELATIVE PRONOUN *Evidence **that police collect** is sometimes inaccurate.*

always put a (,) with (which). Never put (,) with (that)

2.1 Forming Identifying Object Relative Clauses

a. The object relative pronoun follows the noun it replaces and comes at the beginning of the relative clause. In an object relative clause, the relative pronoun is the object of the clause.	Humans aren't aware of <u>smells</u>. A dog can recognize <u>smells</u>. RELATIVE NOUN PRONOUN Humans aren't aware of smells **that a dog can recognize.**
b. Use the relative pronouns *who*, *that*, or *whom* with people. Use *which* or *that* for things.	Detectives are <u>people</u> **who**/**that**/**whom** I respect tremendously.
These pronouns are frequently omitted in speaking, but not in formal writing.	Forensic evidence is something **which**/**that police count on.** (in writing) Forensic evidence is something **police count on.** (in speaking)
When referring to people, *that* is more common than *who*. The pronoun *whom* is very formal and is much less common than *that* or *who* in conversation.	least formal ↕ most formal Detective Paula Cho is a person **that** I admire very much. Detective Paula Cho is a person **who** I admire very much. Detective Paula Cho is a person **whom** I admire very much.
c. Use *whose* + a noun to show possession. *Whose* cannot be omitted.	The person **whose car the thieves stole** was a friend of mine.

▸▸ Relative Clauses: See page A13.

2.2 Using Identifying Object Relative Clauses

Use an identifying relative clause to give essential information that defines or identifies the noun it modifies.	Evidence **that criminals leave at the crime scene** is called forensic evidence. (*That criminals leave at the crime scene* identifies the evidence.)

▶ Grammar Application

Exercise 2.1 Forming Identifying Object Relative Clauses

Complete the sentences about forensic technology. Use *who* or *which* and the verbs in parentheses.

1. *Biometrics* refers to the techniques <u>*which*</u> people <u>*use*</u> (use) to identify individuals by their physical or behavioral characteristics.

2. Biometric information _____ experts _____ (analyze) includes DNA, fingerprints, eyes, and voice patterns.

3. People _____ the police _____
   (suspect) of a crime can be excluded with the use of
   biometrics.

4. Biometric technology can match fingerprints with ones
   _____ the police _____ (have) on file.

5. One type of biometric technology _____ people
   _____ (utilize) for security is the
   fingerprint scanner.

Fingerprint scanner

6. For example, people _____ Disney World _____ (admit) to the park must
   have their fingerprints scanned.

7. The fingerprint scanners _____ Disney World _____ (use) help to stop
   people from entering the park without a proper ticket.

Exercise 2.2 Using Identifying Object Relative Clauses

Complete the web interview about forensic technology. Rewrite the sentence pairs in
parentheses as single sentences with object relative clauses. Sometimes more than one
answer is possible.

Reporter I understand that our police department has some new forensic technology.

Mayor Yes, it has a new system that it uses to analyze DNA.
(1. Yes, it has a new system. It uses the system to analyze DNA.)

Reporter What does it look like?

Mayor _____
(2. It's a hand-held device. Officers bring it to the crime scene.)

_____
(3. It helps the police to analyze data. They find the data at the scene.)

Reporter I understand that not everyone is happy about this device.

Mayor _____
(4. The device has privacy issues. Some people are concerned about these privacy issues.)

Reporter Why is this a concern?

Mayor _____
(5. Well, the DNA might get the person in trouble. The device collected this DNA.)

_____
(6. For example, many people have health issues. They want to keep these issues private.)

Reporter Oh, I see. This is certainly a lot to think about. Thank you for the interview.

Exercise 2.3 Sentence Combining

A Rewrite the reporter's notes on local crimes. Use identifying object relative clauses with the relative pronouns in parentheses.

Recent Crime Reports

1. A man was arrested for theft. Police raided his house last night. (whose)

   A man *whose house police raided last night was arrested* *for theft* .

2. The detectives made their report. The police sent the detectives to the crime scene. (whom)

   The detectives _____ .

3. Several valuable items had been stolen. The police recovered the items. (that)

   Several valuable items _____ .

4. The man has not been identified. Burglars invaded the man's home. (whose)

   The man _____ .

5. Detectives have visited the house. The thief broke into the house yesterday. (which)

   Detectives _____ .

6. The man is in good condition. A car hit him last night. (that)

   The man _____ .

B *Pair Work* In which sentences in A can you omit the pronoun? Discuss the answer with a partner. Then rewrite the sentences with the pronoun omitted.

3 | Nonidentifying Object Relative Clauses

▶ Grammar Presentation

Nonidentifying object relative clauses have the same form as identifying clauses. Unlike identifying clauses, nonidentifying clauses provide additional, not essential, information about the nouns they modify.	*Evidence from crimes, **which we call forensic evidence**, can help police solve cases.* (*Which we call forensic evidence* is extra information. It is not essential to understanding *Evidence from crimes*.)

3.1 Forming Nonidentifying Object Relative Clauses

a. Use *who* or *whom* for people. Use *which* for things. Use *whose* for possessive people and things.	*The Sherlock Holmes stories were written by the Scottish author Arthur Conan Doyle, **who / whom many people think was English**.*
Do not use *that* in nonidentifying relative clauses.	*Forensic science, **which Sherlock Holmes used**, has been recognized as science since the 1800s.* NOT *Forensic science, ~~that~~ Sherlock Holmes used, has been recognized as science since the 1800s.*
Do not omit the relative pronoun in nonidentifying object clauses.	*The character Sherlock Holmes, **who Arthur Conan Doyle created**, was a fictional detective.* NOT *The character Sherlock Holmes, ~~Arthur Conan Doyle created~~, was a fictional detective.*
b. Use commas before and after the nonidentifying object relative clause.	*Arthur Conan Doyle, **whose medical clinic not many patients attended,** had time to write his stories.*

▶ Grammar Application

Exercise 3.1 Nonidentifying Object Relative Clauses

Read part of a presentation on a forensic science program. Underline the nonidentifying clauses. Add commas.

Forensic science, <u>which many of you know about from popular TV shows,</u> has become a popular career. Forensic science courses which many colleges are offering today prepare students for careers in crime scene investigation. The University of Central Florida (UCF) which I attended has a forensic science program. Your area of specialization

5 which you choose during your time here depends on your interests and skills. The area that I chose was forensic biochemistry because I wanted to study odontology. Forensic odontology which the police use to analyze teeth is challenging and fascinating. Forensic analysis which focuses on chemistry and analysis of different kinds of evidence is also available. Introduction to Forensic Science which you take after other preliminary courses

10 will help you decide on the area of specialty. I wish you all the best of luck!

Exercise 3.2 Using Nonidentifying Object Relative Clauses

Read the sentences about a TV show that popularizes forensics. Combine the sentences with nonidentifying object relative clauses. Add commas when necessary.

1. *CSI: Crime Scene Investigation* is an American TV series. Anthony E. Zuiker created it.

   CSI: Crime Scene Investigation <u>, which Anthony E. Zuiker created, is an</u>
   <u>American TV series</u> .

2. The program was an immediate hit. CBS first aired it in 2000.

   The program _____ .

3. *CSI* has been on the air for over 10 years. The entertainment industry has awarded it six Emmys.

   CSI _____

   _____ .

4. The program is shown around the world. Over 70 million people have watched it.

   The program _____ .

5. "Who Are You?" is the *CSI* theme song. Pete Townsend wrote it in the 1970s.

   "Who Are You?" _____ .

6. *CSI: Miami* and *CSI: NY* also had high ratings. CBS created the shows on the same model as the original *CSI*.

   CSI: Miami and *CSI: NY* _____

   _____ .

4 | Object Relative Clauses as Objects of Prepositions

▶ Grammar Presentation

The relative pronouns in object relative clauses can be the object of prepositions.	OBJ. OF PREP. *There's the police officer. I spoke to her.* RELATIVE PRONOUN *There's the police officer **to whom I spoke**.* *There's the police officer **who I spoke to**.*

4.1 Object Relative Clauses as Objects of Prepositions

a. The prepositions in object relative clauses can come at the end of the clause in informal speaking and writing.	*The police examined the chair **that / which I was sitting on**.* *The witness, **who / whom I spoke to** yesterday*, will appear in court.
In identifying relative clauses, use the relative pronouns *who, that,* or *whom* for people and *that* or *which* for things. You can also omit the relative pronoun.	IDENTIFYING RELATIVE CLAUSE *The police examined the chair (**that / which**) I was sitting on*. *The police officer (**who / that / whom**) I met with was robbed.*
In nonidentifying relative clauses, use the relative pronouns *who* or *whom* for people and *which* for things. You cannot omit the relative pronoun.	NONIDENTIFYING RELATIVE CLAUSE *The door, **which I entered through**, was broken during the crime.* *The witness, **who / whom I spoke to yesterday**, will appear in court.* NOT *The witness, ~~I spoke to yesterday~~, will appear in court.*
b. In more formal spoken and especially in written English, the preposition comes before the relative pronouns *whom* or *which*. Do not use *that* or *who*.	*The police examined the chair **on which I was sitting**.* NOT *The police examined the chair on ~~that~~ I was sitting.* *The witness, **with whom I spoke yesterday**, will appear in court.* NOT *The witness, with ~~who / that~~ I spoke yesterday, will appear in court.*
You cannot omit the relative pronoun.	NOT *The police examined the chair ~~on I was sitting~~.* NOT *The witness, ~~with I spoke yesterday~~, will appear in court.*

▶ Grammar Application

Exercise 4.1 Prepositions and Object Relative Clauses

A 🔊 Listen to a detective describe a crime scene. Complete the sentences with the words you hear.

I arrived at the crime scene at 11:00 a.m. The crime had taken place in a restaurant.
The room __*that*__ the crime occurred __*in*__ was the kitchen. The back door was open.
(1) (1)
The back wall was covered in graffiti. I found a spray can under a table. The spray can,

_____ I found fingerprints _____ , matched the color of the graffiti. I asked the
(2) (2)
kitchen staff to talk to me as a group. The group, _____ the chef was the only
(3)
one missing, was very nervous. I learned that the chef had a lot of enemies. I spoke to a

cleaning person _____ the chef had argued _____ last week. I also interviewed
                    (4)   (4)
several waitresses _____ the chef had gone out _____ . One waitress showed me
                      (5)   (5)
the chef's locker, _____ I found more spray cans _____ .
                      (6)   (6)

B 🔊 Listen again and check your answers.

Exercise 4.2 Using Prepositions and Object Relative Clauses

A Combine the sentences from a crime scene investigator. Use identifying object relative clauses with a preposition at the end of the clause. Sometimes more than one answer is possible.

1. The room was the office. I found broken furniture in it.

   The room _which/that I found broken furniture in_ was the office.

2. I found fibers on the floor. The broken furniture was lying on the floor.

   I found fibers on the floor _____ .

3. The neighbors said they heard nothing. I spoke to them.

   The neighbors _____ said they heard nothing.

4. The house was unlocked. The crime took place in it.

   The house _____ was unlocked.

5. There were fingerprints on the door. The criminal entered through it.

   There were fingerprints on the door _____ .

6. The lab matched the fingerprints immediately. I sent the evidence to it.

   The lab _____ matched the fingerprints immediately.

B Rewrite your answers in A as formal sentences.

1. _The room in which I found broken furniture was the office._

2. _____

3. _____

4. _____

5. _____

6. _____

5 | Avoid Common Mistakes ⚠

1. Use *who/whom/that*, not *which*, for people and *which/that* for things.

The investigator is someone ~~which~~ he respects. *(who/whom/that)*

CSI *is a crime show* ~~who~~ *I watch.* *(that/which)*

2. Remember to omit the object pronoun after the verb in object relative clauses.

The evidence that the police found ~~it~~ was used to find the suspect.

3. Do not use a comma before an identifying object relative clause.

The TV crime program,that people thought was the most popular,worked closely with the police to develop its stories.

4. Do not use *what* in relative clauses.

The crime ~~what~~ I am talking about happened yesterday.

Editing Task

Find and correct six more mistakes in the paragraphs about eyewitness testimony.

A victim who police have taken ~~her~~ to the police station gives testimony. She looks at a man in a police lineup and says, "That's the person which I saw in my car." During the trial, the woman gives her testimony in front of the jury, and the jury makes a decision. Soon, the man goes to jail. However, it is possible the woman whose testimony
5 was used is wrong. Researchers now claim that the eyewitness stories what courts often rely on are not always reliable.

Psychologists have conducted experiments who revealed some surprising results. They played a crime-scene video for participants and then asked the participants to remember details. Results showed that participants often described events, which
10 they knew nothing about and had not seen in the video. Similarly, the suspect what participants chose out of a police lineup was rarely the actual criminal.

Psychologists who courts have hired them have testified that eyewitness testimony is not as accurate as was once assumed. As such, psychologists have developed new rules to guide the use of eyewitness testimony.

6 | Grammar for Writing

Using Object Relative Clauses to Provide Background Information

Writers often use object relative clauses to condense information, just as they do with subject relative clauses. Read these examples:

Joaquin's brother helped solve the crime. The detective had met him years ago.
Joaquin's brother, <u>whom the detective had met years ago</u>, helped solve the crime.

Writers also use object relative clauses to provide background information. Read these examples:

The detectives talked to the woman <u>whose husband they had arrested</u>.
The thief stole the money <u>which the shop owner had left in the store</u>.

Pre-writing Task

1 Read the paragraph below. Who does the Innocence Project help, and how many people has it helped?

Innocent or Guilty?

The Innocence Project is a legal organization whose purpose is to free innocent people from prison. These people have been imprisoned for crimes that they did not commit. The Innocence Project was created in 1992 by two lawyers who knew about a famous study about how unreliable eyewitness reports could be. This study showed
5   that it was important to find another way of proving a person's guilt or innocence, especially in the case of serious crimes. At that time, DNA testing was a relatively new process. The first time that DNA testing helped prove someone's innocence was in the 1980s in England. In this case, police arrested a man who had been accused of committing two serious crimes. However, the police were not convinced that they
10 had the right man, so they hired a doctor whose specialty was working with DNA. The DNA testing that the doctor performed proved that the suspect was not guilty. The founders of the Innocence Project thought that DNA testing might help prove that some prisoners were innocent of the crimes for which they had been convicted. Since the Innocence Project was established, it has been very successful. DNA testing, with
15 which most people are now very familiar, has been responsible for freeing almost 300 prisoners since 1989.

2 Read the paragraph again. Underline the object relative clauses. <u>Double underline</u> the subject relative clauses. Circle the relative pronouns and draw arrows to the nouns they modify. Find the one nonidentifying clause, and notice that the information is interesting but not essential. Then look at the identifying relative clauses, and notice that the information in the clauses is essential.

Writing Task

1 *Write* Use the paragraph in the Pre-writing Task to help you write about forensics or crime in general. You can write about one of these topics or use your own ideas.

- the case of a person who was convicted, then found to be innocent
- the difficulty of apprehending criminals
- the advantages and disadvantages of using DNA evidence

2 *Self-Edit* Use the editing tips to improve your paragraph. Make any necessary changes.

1. Did you use both subject and object relative clauses to condense information?
2. Did you use relative clauses to provide background information?
3. Did you avoid the mistakes in the Avoid Common Mistakes chart on page 305?

UNIT 23

Relative Clauses with *Where* and *When*; Reduced Relative Clauses

Millennials

1 | Grammar in the Real World

A Do you know anyone born in the 1980s or 1990s? Some studies suggest that individuals born during these years have similar traits, such as high self-confidence. Read the article about Millennials, a term for these individuals. How might these people be different from other, older people in the workplace?

Millennials in the Workforce

Millennials, **also known as Generation Y**, are people born in the 1980s and 1990s. There are over 70 million of them in the United States alone, **where they are now the fastest**
5 **growing group in the workplace**. It is hard to generalize about such a large group, but these young workers often share certain positive and negative traits.

This group has high opinions and expectations
10 of themselves. Bruce Tulgan, a **Generation Y expert**, believes this is the result of the way they were raised. They were raised at a time **when parents and teachers believed in a lot of praising and rewarding**. For example,
15 **everyone playing** a game was often given a trophy, not just members of the winning team.

In the workplace, this self-confidence shows up in several ways. Millennials expect a lot of positive feedback. For example, if they do something well, they want to be praised for it. They also want their opinions to be heard and valued.
20 In fact, they often speak out when they disagree with a boss's decision. Some employers call them challenging and demanding.

Millennials, **raised in the era of computers, cell phones, and the Internet**, understand technology very well. They are also multitasking 25 experts. They can text, listen to music, and chat online at the same time. Their experience with technology usually makes them good at technology-based jobs.

However, their technology habits can sometimes 30 serve as distractions.[1] Working while e-mailing friends can cause moments of inattentiveness,[2] **during which serious errors can occur**. Some members of Generation Y are known for being distracted on the job. Older colleagues may find 35 this trait annoying.

This generation of employees is sometimes known for being demanding and outspoken. Tulgan says that Generation Y is "the most high maintenance[3] workforce in the history of the world." However, Millennials are also smart, driven, and tech savvy.[4] These are the traits **helping them** succeed in workplaces around the 40 country.

[1]**distraction:** something that takes your attention away from what you are doing or should be doing |
[2]**inattentiveness:** not listening to what is being said; not giving complete attention to what is happening |
[3]**high maintenance:** requiring a large amount of attention to remain happy and efficient | [4]**tech savvy:** having good skills with technology and electronics

B *Comprehension Check* Answer the questions.

1. When were Millennials born?
2. Why do Millennials have such high self-confidence and expectations?
3. What kind of jobs are they good at? Why?

C *Notice* Read the sentences. What words could you add to the words in bold to make them relative clauses? Are the new clauses subject or object relative clauses?

1. Bruce Tulgan, **a Generation Y expert**, believes this is the result of the way they were raised.

2. For example, everyone **playing a game** was often given a trophy, not just members of the winning team.

2 | Relative Clauses with *Where* and *When*

▶ Grammar Presentation

The adverbs *where* and *when* can be used in relative clauses. *Where* is used to modify nouns of place, and *when* is used to modify nouns of time. In these cases, we call these words relative adverbs.

*The computer lab is a place **where many young students feel comfortable**.*

*Night is a time **when many students study for exams**.*

2.1 Relative Clauses with *Where*

a. Use *where* in relative clauses to modify a noun referring to a place. Common nouns include *area*, *country*, *house*, *place*, and *room*.	*This is the only <u>area</u> **where you can find Wi-Fi outside of the office**.* *The United States is a <u>country</u> **where a lot of research on young people is done**.* *The office is a <u>place</u> **where workers often compete**.*
b. Do not use a preposition before *where*. Use *which* instead. The use of preposition + *which* is common in academic writing.	*It's a city **<u>in which</u> you can find Wi-Fi almost everywhere**.* NOT *It's a city ~~in where~~ you can find Wi-Fi almost everywhere.*

▸▸ Relative Clauses: See page A13.

2.2 Relative Clauses with *When*

a. Use *when* in relative clauses to modify a noun referring to a time. Common nouns include *day*, *moment*, *period*, *season*, *time*, and *year*.	*The <u>day</u> **when you graduate** is the <u>day</u> **when you will need to find a job**.* *Spring is the <u>time</u> **when most students graduate**.* *The 1980s and 1990s are the <u>years</u> **when many young people in the workforce were born**.*
b. Do not use a preposition before *when*. Use *which* instead. The use of preposition + *which* is very formal.	*Summer is the time **<u>during which</u> many jobs become available**.* NOT *Summer is the time ~~during when~~ many jobs become available.* *The day **<u>on which</u> you start your new job** will be very busy.* NOT *The day ~~on when~~ you start your new job will be very busy.*
c. You can omit the relative adverb *when* in identifying relative clauses.	*Ricardo remembered the moment **he met his boss**.* = *Ricardo remembered the moment **<u>when</u> he met his boss**.*

Data from the Real World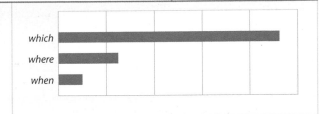

Research shows that in writing, nonidentifying relative clauses with *where* and *when* are much less common than nonidentifying relative clauses with *which*. Clauses with *when* are the least common and are used in rather formal writing.

▶ # Grammar Application

Exercise 2.1 Object Relative Clauses with *Where* and *When*

Complete the sentences about Millennials. Circle the correct words. Note Ø means no relative adverb.

1. Millennials believe America is a place (where)/ **when** anyone can be successful.
2. They were born at a time **in which / where** technology was part of everyday life.
3. They came into the workplace during a period **when / which** the economy was bad.
4. They came from families **when / in which** they were the center of attention.
5. They expect a work environment **Ø / where** people collaborate and work together.
6. They grew up during a period **when / where** national security was an issue.
7. The day **Ø / where** they graduate from school is a time of both joy and anxiety.

Exercise 2.2 More Object Relative Clauses with *Where* and *When*

A ◀)) Listen to an interview with a Millennial who is helping to change the world in a positive way. Circle the answers to the questions.

1. Where did Sean go?
   (a. To Haiti)   b. To Florida

2. When did Sean go?
   a. After a rainstorm   b. After an earthquake

3. Why did Sean go?
   a. To help people   b. To take a break from school

4. What did he do there?
   a. Work in a large city to give basic medical care   b. Work in small towns to give basic medical care

B ◀)) Listen again. Complete the interview with the words you hear.

Interviewer Some people think that members of the Millennial generation only think about themselves, but there are a lot of young people who are making a difference. They are helping others and trying to make the world a better place. One of these young people is Sean Green. Sean is a medical student in Florida. He went to Haiti at a time *in which* they needed him the most. Sean, tell us your story.
(1)

Sean Sure, I'd be happy to. I went to Haiti at a time _____ many people
(2)
were suffering – right after the 2010 earthquake.

Interviewer Why did you go?

Sean Haiti is a place _____ there aren't enough doctors. I'm in medical
(3)
school now. So it seemed like a good opportunity for me to get experience and to help people as well.

Interviewer What did you do there?

Sean I worked in small towns _____ the earthquake destroyed the homes
(4)
of many people. I lived in a town _____ a lot of people were hurt, and
(5)
helped give basic medical care. It was the season _____ there is a lot
(6)
of rain. There was mud everywhere. It was a challenge to keep things clean.

Interviewer Tell us a little about the people you worked with.

Sean The people in the town _____ I worked gave us a lot of help. They
(7)
were very friendly and welcoming. It was an amazing experience.

Interviewer Thank you for your time, Sean.

C ◀)) Listen again and check your answers.

Exercise 2.3 Relative Clauses with *When*

Look at the information in the chart. It shows three important generations in the United States and the major events or influences in their lifetimes. Then write sentences about the years in parentheses. Use relative clauses with *when*, *in which*, and *during which*. Sometimes more than one answer is possible.

	Name of Generation	Years Born	Important Lifetime Events or Influences
	Baby Boomers	1946–1964	President Kennedy dies, 1963 Vietnam War ends, 1975
	Generation X (Gen Xers)	1965–1981	The Berlin Wall falls, 1989
	Millennials	1980–2000	The Great Recession occurs, 2007–2009

1. (1946–1964)

   The years 1946–1964 are the years when the Baby Boomers were born.

2. (1963)

   _____

3. (1975)

   _____

4. (1965–1981)

   _____

5. (1989)

   _____

6. (1980–2000)

   _____

7. (2007)

   _____

3 | Reduced Relative Clauses

▶ Grammar Presentation

Relative clauses with *be* can often be reduced to phrases. There are three types of reduced relative clauses: participle phrases, prepositional phrases, and appositives.	RELATIVE CLAUSE The expert **who is giving tomorrow's talk on Millennials** is very well known. REDUCED RELATIVE CLAUSE The expert **giving tomorrow's talk on Millennials** is very well known.

3.1 Forming Reduced Relative Clauses

a. Reduce a subject relative clause by omitting the relative pronoun (*that*, *which*, *who*) and *be*.	*My brother, **a Millennial**, likes a fast-paced environment.* = *My brother, **who is a Millennial**, likes a fast-paced environment.*
b. Do not shorten a subject relative clause with *be* + a single adjective. Instead, move the adjective before the modified noun.	*I know a lot of people **who are self-confident**.* *I know a lot of **self-confident people**.* NOT *I know a lot of ~~people self-confident~~.*
c. Do not reduce object relative clauses.	*Our new assistant, **who I am meeting tomorrow**, is a Millennial.* NOT *Our new assistant, ~~meeting tomorrow~~, is a Millennial.*

3.2 Reduced Relative Clauses with Participle Phrases

Participle phrases are a reduced form of relative clauses with a verb that includes a form of *be*.	*Students **concerned with the environment** should get involved in environmental groups on campus.* = *Students who **are concerned with the environment** should get involved in environmental groups on campus.*
This verb can be in the form of verb + -*ing* (present participle) or the past participle form. This includes progressive verbs and passive verbs.	VERB + -*ING* *He is the person **using the Internet too much at work**.* PAST PARTICIPLE *She did the things **not expected of her**.* *This is the intern **known to be the hardest working**.*

3.3 Reduced Relative Clauses with Prepositional Phrases

You can omit the relative pronoun and the verb *be* when they are followed by a prepositional phrase in identifying relative clauses.	PREP. PHRASE *The computers **in our classroom** are fast.* *= The computers **that are** **in our classroom** are fast.*
An adjective can also come before the prepositional phrase.	ADJ. + PREP. PHRASE *Young workers **low in self-esteem** are unusual.*

3.4 Reduced Relative Clauses with Appositives

a. You can omit the relative pronoun and the verb *be* when they are followed by a noun phrase in nonidentifying relative clauses. This is called an appositive.	*Jan Smith, **an expert on Millennials**, will be speaking at noon today.* *= Jan Smith, **who is** **an expert on Millennials**, will be speaking at noon today.*
Often the position of the modified noun and the appositive is interchangeable.	***An expert on Millennials**, Jan Smith, will be speaking at noon today.*
b. Appositives begin and end with commas.	*Résumés, **brief documents that summarize an applicant's work background,** are necessary for all job applications.*
In academic writing, appositives often occur in parentheses, instead of commas.	*Résumés (**brief documents that summarize an applicant's work background**) are necessary for all job applications.*

▶ Grammar Application

Exercise 3.1 Reducing Relative Clauses

A Read the sentences about different generations. Check (✓) the sentences that can be reduced.

☑ 1. Young people who are entering the workforce are different from other generations.

☐ 2. In general, Millennials, who attentive parents raised, are confident workers.

☐ 3. Millennials who are in the workforce tend to have a "can-do" attitude.

☐ 4. Generation X, which is another large group in the workforce, does not tend to equate age with respect.

☐ 5. Baby Boomers who work with Millennials often think they do not show enough respect.

☐ 6. Baby Boomers, who are loyal employees, have started to retire from their jobs.

☐ 7. Millennials, who the recession has hurt, still tend to be optimistic.

☐ 8. Baby Boomers who were graduating from college in the 1960s lived in prosperous times.

☐ 9. Most Millennials who are not attending school say they intend to go back.

☐ 10. Many Millennials who are in school also have jobs.

☐ 11. Millennials that dress casually at work sometimes upset Baby Boomers.

B Rewrite the sentences in A with reduced relative clauses. If a sentence cannot be reduced, write ✗.

1. *Young people entering the workforce are different from other generations.*
2. ✗ _____
3. _____
4. _____
5. _____
6. _____
7. _____
8. _____
9. _____
10. _____
11. _____

C *Pair Work* Compare your answers with a partner. Discuss what kind of reduced relative clause each sentence is. If a sentence couldn't be reduced, say why not.

A *The reduced relative clause in number 1 is a participle phrase, so it can be reduced.*

B *That's right, but the relative clause in 2 can't be reduced because it is an object relative clause.*

Exercise 3.2 Relative Clauses with *Be* + Prepositional Phrases and *Be* + Adjectives + Prepositional Phrases

Combine the sentences from a company website about the type of employees it seeks. Use relative clauses. Then rewrite the sentences using reduced relative clauses.

1. People are at JP Corporation. They represent every generation.

   People *who are at JP Corporation* represent every generation.

   People at JP Corporation represent every generation.

2. People are good with technology. They have an advantage here.

   People _____ _____ have an advantage here.

   _____

3. Workers are familiar with social networking. They will be able to use these skills here.

   Workers _____ will be able to use these skills here.

   _____

4. Employees are good at multitasking. They will enjoy our fast-paced environment.

   Employees _____ _____ _____ will enjoy our fast-paced environment.

   _____

5. Employees are high in self-esteem. They do well here.

   Employees _____ do well here.

   _____

6. People are interested in advancement. They will find it here.

   People _____ will find it here.

   _____

7. Employees are in our training programs. They appreciate learning new skills.

   Employees _____ appreciate learning new skills.

   _____

8. People are accustomed to a dynamic environment. They will be happy here.

   People _____ will be happy here.

   _____

Exercise 3.3 Relative Clauses with Adjectives

Read the advice for managers who work with Millennials. Rewrite the sentences that you can shorten. If you can't shorten the sentence, write ✗.

1. Managers should encourage Millennials who are self-assured.
   Managers should encourage self-assured Millennials.

2. Workers who are Millennials seek approval from their managers.

   _____

3. Even Millennials who are confident appreciate feedback.

   _____

4. Millennials appreciate work environments that are structured.

   _____

5. Employees who are Millennials want their managers to listen to them.

   _____

6. It's important to provide challenges for Millennials who are bored.

   _____

7. Managers must not overwork Millennials who are family oriented.

   _____

8. Managers who are Baby Boomers might expect Millennials to work longer hours.

   _____

9. Employees who are Millennials sometimes need more direction than older workers.

   _____

10. Millennials who are unemployed don't always have a lot of experience in job interviews.

    _____

Exercise 3.4 Using Adjective Phrases

Pair Work With a partner, discuss the work styles of people at your school, such as students, teachers, and administrators. Write five sentences with relative clauses. Then write shortened versions without relative clauses. Use the words in the box or your own ideas.

appreciate feedback	are family oriented	enjoy team work
appreciate work-life balance	are self-assured	have a "can-do" attitude

Students who are at this school tend to have a "can-do" attitude.
Students at this school tend to have a "can-do" attitude.

4 Avoid Common Mistakes ⚠

1. Do not use a preposition before *when*.

There was a period ~~in~~ when people did not change jobs often.

2. In clauses with *where*, remember to use a subject.

The place where ^he^ works is very busy.

3. When shortening relative clauses to appositives, be sure to omit both the pronoun and *be*.

My mother, ~~is~~ an office manager, often works late.

Editing Task

Find and correct eight more mistakes in the paragraphs about the separation between younger and older technology users.

Digital Natives vs. Digital Immigrants

There was a time ~~in~~ when my mother always complained about my use of

technology. She did not understand why I had to constantly text friends and go online.

My mother, is a digital immigrant, grew up without a lot of tech gadgets. As a result, she

is uncomfortable using technology at the office where works. On the other hand, my

5   brothers and I, are all digital natives, are happy to use technology all the time.

Digital natives, are lifelong technology users, use electronic devices instinctively.

These people do not remember a time in when they were not connected to the Internet.

In fact, they find it annoying when they go to places where cannot connect to the Internet.

Digital immigrants, in contrast, remember a time in when there was no Internet. As

10   a result, some of them see the Internet as useful but not essential. In addition, digital

immigrants sometimes find it difficult to figure out how to use technology. For example,

when my mother first began uploading information, she had to call someone for help.

Lately, however, my mother has found a social networking site where often goes in her

free time to stay in touch with friends and family members.

5 | Grammar for Writing ✏

Using Reduced Subject Relative Clauses to Make Ideas Clearer

Writers often reduce subject relative clauses with *be* to condense information. Reducing relative clauses makes sentences more compact and the author's ideas clearer. Read these examples:

Preteens who were raised after cell phones became common can't imagine life without them.

Preteens <u>raised after cell phones became common</u> can't imagine life without them.

Facebook and other social networking sites, which are tools that Millennials commonly use, offer new ways to communicate.

Facebook and other social networking sites, <u>tools that Millennials commonly use</u>, offer new ways to communicate.

Pre-writing Task

1 Read the paragraph below. What skills does the writer say Millennials are known for?

Technology and Millennials

Millennials, experts at multitasking, are the first generation to grow up in a digital age. Some people believe that in addition to making Millennials good at multitasking, this has also made them good at teamwork, a much valued skill in American workplaces. Because many U.S. Millennials had access to cell phones,

5 computers, and social networks from their early teens, they grew up accustomed to having conversations with more than one person at a time, a common feature of texting and social networking. This ability to talk to more than one person at a time seems to have prepared Millennials for communicating successfully with several team members at once. Multitasking is a skill that they have mastered easily. In addition,

10 the idea of waiting to talk to someone is a strange idea to this generation. Millennials, used to talking to people whenever they need to, don't wait to find a landline phone or to see someone in person in order to communicate. They tend to deal with things as they come up, rather than waiting until later. This can be a valuable quality because team members who get things done quickly help create a more efficient team. Perhaps

15 because of these factors, smart employers are recruiting Millennials to build strong teams in their companies.

2 Read the paragraph again. Underline the reduced relative clauses. Rewrite each one, making it a full relative clause by adding the correct relative pronoun and the correct form of *be*.

Writing Task

1 *Write* Use the paragraph in the Pre-writing Task to help you write about Millennials or any other generation you are familiar with. You can write about one of these topics or use your own ideas.

- another characteristic of Millennials that makes them good at something
- characteristics of a different generation that make them good at something
- characteristics of a particular generation that makes something challenging for them

2 *Self-Edit* Use the editing tips to improve your paragraph. Make any necessary changes.

1. Did you form reduced relative clauses correctly?
2. Did you use these reduced relative clauses to condense information where appropriate?
3. Did you avoid the mistakes in the Avoid Common Mistakes chart on page 319?

Real Conditionals: Present and Future

Media in the United States

1 | Grammar in the Real World

A Do all the news sources you read (websites, magazines, newspapers, etc.) have similar viewpoints about current topics and issues? Read the article about the news media in the United States. What is the writer's view of the media?

The Influence of Media on Public Opinion

The media[1] provide news from a wide range of sources with a variety of viewpoints. Some sources provide a more balanced look at the issues than others. These more balanced news sources offer a deeper

5 understanding of the issues without the influence of the views of political parties. This unbiased[2] view of the news may appear to align[3] with the values of Americans, but is it, in fact, what Americans really want?

1 Some political analysts claim that many Americans tend
10 to read, watch, and listen to the news media that reflect their own views. **If people surround themselves with media that reflect only their beliefs,** they may not be exposed to opposing ideas. The media, in this case, are not informing people, but reinforcing that their view of the world is right.

2 One example of this occurs during an economic crisis. **If people watch certain TV news**
15 **stations,** they will hear mostly positive things about the president's solutions. **If they support the president's policies,** they may also choose to read online news pages with a similar view. These websites likely explain how the crisis was caused by politicians from the opposing party. **If those people read only these websites,** they might be convinced that the crisis was the fault of the opposing party. They might conclude that the president was doing a wonderful
20 job. On the other hand, **if people mostly disagree with the president's policies,** they often

President Proposes Solution to Economic Troubles

NATIONAL NEWS

Presidential Policies Cause Economic Troubles

[1]**media:** newspapers, magazines, television, and radio, considered as a group | [2]**unbiased:** not influenced by personal opinion | [3]**align:** agree with and support something or someone

choose to watch news shows that criticize the president. They might also visit websites and read blogs that do not support the president's policies. **When they rely only on these news sources,** they come to a different conclusion. They are convinced that the president is failing.

If predictions of increased Internet use are correct, people will likely become even more
25 isolated in their beliefs. This is because links in blogs and web pages will connect people with information that supports only their views. How might this affect politics in the future? **If we don't address this issue today,** could the isolation of beliefs become problematic in our political future?

B *Comprehension Check* Answer the questions.

1. How do some political analysts describe the behavior of Americans toward media?
2. What is an example of how media sources reinforce someone's political views?
3. Why might people become even more isolated in their beliefs in the future?

C *Notice* Read the sentences from the article. Which sentence describes a present situation? Which sentence describes a future situation?

1. On the other hand, if people mostly disagree with the president's policies, they often choose to watch news shows that criticize the president.
2. If predictions of increased Internet use are correct, people will likely become even more isolated in their beliefs.

2 | Present Real Conditionals

▶ Grammar Presentation

| Present real conditionals describe situations that are possible now and their results. They describe general truths, facts, and habits. | *If people share beliefs*, they often get along better. I usually believe something *when I read it in a good newspaper*. |

2.1 Forming Present Real Conditionals

| **a.** Use an *if* clause to describe a possible situation. The *if* clause is the condition. The main clause describes the result. It expresses what happens when the condition exists. | IF CLAUSE (CONDITION) MAIN CLAUSE (RESULT) *If I like a reporter*, I read her articles. |
| Use the simple present in the *if* clause and in the main clause. | *If I have time in the morning*, I read the newspaper. |

2.1 Forming Present Real Conditionals *(continued)*

b. You can use *when* or *whenever* in the *if* clause. The meaning does not change.

When you trust people, *you tend to believe them.* = **If you trust people,** *you tend to believe them.*

c. You can put the *if* clause or the main clause first, but the punctuation is different. If the *if* clause is first, a comma follows it. If the main clause is first, do not use a comma. Usually the *if* clause comes first.

IF CLAUSE   MAIN CLAUSE
If you control the media, *you control public opinion.*

MAIN CLAUSE   IF CLAUSE
You control public opinion **if you control the media.**

d. You can use conditionals in questions. Use question word order only in the main clause.

IF CLAUSE   MAIN CLAUSE
If you see something on the news, <u>do you</u> *always* <u>believe</u> *it?*

▸▸Conditionals: See page A15.

2.2 Using Present Real Conditionals

a. Use present real conditionals to describe:
     Facts and general truths
     Habits and routines

If a website is popular, *people talk about it.*
I always read the news online **if I wake up early**.

b. You can emphasize the result by putting the *if* clause first and using *then* to introduce the main clause. Using *then* is more common in speaking.

If you only read one news website, <u>then</u> *you never get the full story.*

▶ Grammar Application

Exercise 2.1 Present Real Conditionals for Habits and Routines

Complete the article about news habits. Use present real conditionals with the verbs in parentheses. Add commas when necessary.

City Voices: The News and You

City Voices talked to several area residents. Here's what they had to say.

"When I __am__ (be) in the car, I __listen__ (listen) to the radio. My husband
   (1)   (2)

__watches__ (watch) the comedy news shows if he __stays__ (stay) up
   (3)   (4)
late." – Alexa, 28, office manager.

"If a friend __texts__ (text) me about something interesting, I generally
          (5)

__check__ (check) out other websites to find out more information." – Su Ho, 32, engineer.
   (6)

Exercise 2.2 Present Real Conditionals for Facts, General Truths, Habits, and Routines

Complete the interview with a foreign correspondent. Use the conditions and results in the chart.

Condition	Result
1. I hear about a story	I get on the phone
2. I hear about a good story	I try to go beyond the basic facts
3. I feel like I'm getting emotionally involved in a story	I drop it
4. A story is important	Many people talk about it
5. My editor calls and tells me to investigate a story	I move quickly

Careers Magazine

Careers Today, we are talking to our foreign correspondent, Mercedes Rivera. Ms. Rivera, how do you get a story?

Mercedes If _I hear about a story, I get on the phone_ (1). I make appointments to interview people connected with the story.

Careers What makes your reporting special?

Mercedes If _I hear about a good story, I try to go..._ (2). I look at all the details to give both sides of the story.

Careers How do you avoid bias?

Mercedes If _I feel like, I'm getting..., I drop it_ (3). I give it to another reporter.

Careers What is difficult about your job?

Mercedes There's a certain amount of pressure. _Many people talk about it_ (4) when _A story is important_ (4). I have to work fast in the digital age. _I move quickly_ (5) if _My editor calls and tells_ (5) _me to investigate a story_.

Careers Well, thank you for talking to us today, Ms. Rivera.

Exercise 2.3 Emphasizing the Result in Present Real Conditionals

A Read the tips on how to detect bias in the media. Then rewrite the tips as present real conditionals with the words in parentheses and *probably (not) be*. Emphasize the result by using *then*.

How to Detect Bias in the Media

To detect bias in the media, be aware of the following conditions. These conditions often indicate bias.

(1) A newspaper, website, or TV station ignores important stories.
(2) A newspaper prints sensational headlines.
(3) A newspaper prints an important story in the back of the newspaper.
(4) A magazine prints an unflattering[1] photo of a politician.
(5) A reporter uses words with negative connotations[2] instead of neutral terms.

[1]**unflattering:** making someone look less attractive or seem worse than they usually do | [2]**connotation:** a feeling or idea that is suggested by a word in addition to its basic meaning

1. (impartial) _If a newspaper, website, or TV station ignores important stories, then it probably isn't impartial._

2. (accurate) ~~exact~~ _If a newspaper prints sensational headlines, then it probably isn't accurate_

3. (balanced) ~~balanced~~ _If a newspaper prints an important story in the back of the newspaper, then it probably isn't balanced_

4. (biased) ~~Parcial~~ _if a magazine prints unflattering photo of a politician, then it probably is biased_

5. (fair) ~~50%~~ _if a reporter uses words with negative connotations instead of neutral terms, then her probably isn't fair._

B *Pair Work* Discuss other ways that the media show that they are biased or fair. Write two sentences using *if* clauses and the expressions with *probably (not) be* in A.

If a reporter reads a history negatwe about President, then he probably isn't fair.

If a producers make boring progams, they are probably aren't successful.

Exercise 2.4 Present Real Conditionals

A *Over to You* Answer the questions with information that is true for you. Write present real conditionals on a separate piece of paper. Use the phrases in the box or your own ideas.

get the news online	pay attention to the news
know a story is accurate	read a newspaper
listen to news on the radio	watch TV news

- Do you pay attention to the news?
- How do you get the news?
- How do you know a news story is accurate?

If there's a big story in the news, I watch one of the TV news channels, but I don't pay attention to the news much in general.

B *Pair Work* Interview your partner. Ask and answer the questions in A. Do not look at your sentences when you answer. Look at your partner.

3 | Future Real Conditionals

▶ Grammar Presentation

Future real conditionals describe possible situations in the future and the likely results.	*If you don't like a politician, you won't like his or her policies.*

3.1 Forming Future Real Conditionals

a. Use the simple present in the *if* clause and a future verb form in the main clause.	*If you arrive early tomorrow at the debate, you will get a good seat.*
b. Use a comma after the *if* clause only when it begins the sentence.	*We will have a more balanced view if we read a variety of news websites.* *If Sandra doesn't agree with a politician's ideas, she will not vote for him.*

3.2 Using Future Real Conditionals

a. Use future real conditionals to describe:

Plans

If traditional media don't cover the debate tonight, I'll read a blog about it.

Predictions

If you read this article, you won't be disappointed.

b. Use *even if* when you believe the result will not change. *Even if* means "whether or not." ~~Puede que sea~~

al menos
Use ~~unless~~ to state a negative condition more strongly. It often has the same meaning as *if . . . not.*

*Some people will believe the news **even if it isn't true**.* (The news may or may not be true. Some people will believe it either way.)

Unless a reporter interviews many people, she won't find out the truth.

= ***If a reporter does not interview many people***, she won't find out the truth.

c. When an *if* clause has many results, use the *if* clause only once.

If people believe everything they hear, they won't know the truth. They will be easily fooled.

NOT *If people believe everything they hear*, they won't know the truth. ~~If people believe everything they hear, they will be easily fooled.~~

< *Whether or not it is true*
  Whether it isn't true

▶ Grammar Application

Exercise 3.1 Future Real Conditionals for Predictions

Complete the sentences about being well informed about political viewpoints. Circle the correct verb forms. Add commas when necessary.

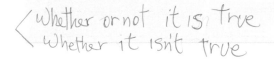

1. If a person (**studies**) / **will study** history, she **understands** / (**will understand**) political issues better.

2. You **are** / (**will be**) a better critical thinker if you (**listen**) / **will listen** to opposing viewpoints.

3. You **become** / (**will become**) a more informed voter if you (**understand**) / **will understand** the issues.

4. You **make** / (**will make**) better choices in future elections if you (**learn**) / **will learn** about the candidates' voting records.

5. If a person (**learns**) / **will learn** about economics he (**makes**) / **will make** wiser financial decisions.

6. If people (**get**) / **will get** the news from several sources they **have** / (**will have**) a more complete picture of an issue.

Exercise 3.2 Future Real Conditionals for Predictions and Plans

A A newspaper is having financial difficulties. Write future real conditionals with the information in the chart.

Proposals	Predictions and Plans
1. fire 10 reporters	be able to stay in business
2. stop home deliveries	lose money
3. charge for online access	increase revenue
4. not find new advertisers	not make more money
5. put more articles online	attract new readers

1. _If we fire 10 reporters, we'll be able to stay in business._
2. _If we stop home deliveries, we'll lose money_
3. _If we charge for online access, we'll increase revenue_
4. _If we don't find new advertisers, we won't make more money_
5. _We'll attract new readers if we put more articles online_

B Read what members of the staff have to say about the proposals in A. Circle the correct meaning for each opinion.

1. Even if we fire 10 reporters, we won't be able to stay in business.
   a. Firing reporters will help.   **b. Firing reporters won't help.**

2. Unless we fire 20 reporters, we'll go out of business.
   a. Firing reporters will help.   b. Firing reporters won't help.

3. Unless we charge for online access, we won't increase revenue.
   a. Charging will help.   b. Charging won't help.

4. Even if we stop home deliveries, we'll lose money.
   a. Stopping home deliveries will help.   **b.** Stopping home deliveries won't help.

5. Even if we find new advertisers, we won't make more money.
   a. Finding new advertisers will help.   **b. Finding new advertisers won't help.**

6. Unless we put more articles online, we won't attract new readers.
   a. Putting more articles online will help.   b. Putting more articles online won't help.

Exercise 3.3 Future Real Conditionals with More than One Result

Over to You Complete the sentences about being informed. Write two or more results for the conditions. Don't repeat the *if* clauses for the second or third results. Write sentences that are true for you.

1. If people stop reading newspapers, *newspapers will go out of business. Many reporters will be unemployed.*

2. If people get only one source of news, *they will stop hearing different sind of stories, they may also be less.*

3. If you only listen to people you agree with, *you won't be able to learn about different opinions*

4. If you are not an informed voter, *you will make wrong choises*

4 | Real Conditionals with Modals, Modal-like Expressions, and Imperatives

▶ Grammar Presentation

Modals, modal-like expressions, and imperatives can be used in the main clause of real conditionals.	***If I watch a lot of TV***, I may become more aware of political issues. ***If you have finished reading the paper***, put it in the recycling container.

4.1 Forming Real Conditionals with Modals, Modal-like Expressions, and Imperatives

a. In present and future real conditionals with modals and modal-like expressions, use a present form of the verb in the *if* clause. Use a present or future modal or modal-like expression in the main clause.	***If you haven't heard the news yet***, you <u>should read</u> the newspaper. ***If you <u>are planning</u> to vote***, you <u>have to register</u>. She <u>might learn</u> more about politics ***if she <u>subscribes</u> to that political magazine***.
b. In present and future real conditionals, you can use the imperative in the main clause.	***If you are at home tonight at 7:00 p.m.***, <u>watch the</u> president's speech.

imperative
(una orden)

▸▸◂ Modals and Modal-like Expressions: See page A3.

She (should throw) the ball

Exercise 4.1 Real Conditionals with Modals and Modal-like Expressions

Complete the sentences about being an involved citizen. Use the words in parentheses.

1. If people don't vote, *they must not be interested in politics* .
   (be interested in politics / not / must)
2. If you haven't registered to vote yet, you should do it today .
   (do it today / should)
3. People Ough to Vulunteer if they want to become involved in
   (volunteer / ought to)
   their community.
4. People can tutor children if they enjoy teaching.
   (tutor children / can)
5. If you want to become informed, you have to watch the news .
   (watch the news / have to)
6. If people participate in elections, they might influence the outcome.
   (influence the outcome / might)
7. If you aren't happy, you could change things .
   (change things / could)
8. People shouldn't complain if they have not already tried to
   (complain / not / should)
   find solutions to community problems.

Exercise 4.2 Real Conditionals with Imperatives

Pair Work Answer the questions about how you think people can be better citizens. Write real conditionals and share them with a partner. Use *you* in the *if* clause and an imperative in the main clause. Use the phrases in the box or your own ideas.

be aware of bias in the media	study both sides of an issue
research alternative news sources	2 volunteer

deberia

1 • What should people do if they want to become better informed?

2 • What should people do if they want to become better citizens?

If you want to become better informed, research alternative news sources.

1- If you want to become better
informed, research alternative news
sources.

2- If people want to become
better citizens, become
a volunteer.

Exercise 4.3 Real Conditionals with Modals, Modal-like Expressions, and Imperatives

A 🔊 Listen to an interview about how to be an informed voter. As you listen, complete the chart. Check (✔) *Do* if this is something an informed voter should do. Check (✔) *Don't* if this is something an informed voter should not do.

Action	Do	Don't
1. register early	✔	
2. visit campaign headquarters	✔	
3. visit candidates' websites	✔	
4. rely on campaign ads		✔
5. pay attention to what media sources say		✔
6. be influenced by other people's opinions		✔

B 🔊 Listen to the interview again. As you listen, complete the sentences with the words you hear.

1. If you _aren't registered_ to vote, _register_ early so you don't miss the deadline.

2. If you _want_ to be an informed voter, _visit_ the local campaign headquarters for the candidates of both parties.

3. If you _want_ to make the right choice, you _must_ also _visit_ the websites of all the candidates.

4. _Don't rely on_ campaign ads for information about the candidates or the issues if you _want_ to be an informed voter.

5. _Don't pay_ attention to what media sources say about a candidate, either, if you _want_ the truth.

6. Finally, _don't let_ other people's opinions influence your vote if you _want_ to make good choices.

5 | Avoid Common Mistakes ⚠

1. In future real conditionals, use the simple present in the *if* clause.

has
If my son ~~will have~~ time, he will buy tickets for the show.

2. Remember that *if* clauses are followed by a comma when they start a sentence.

If I get the time off work and the weather looks good‸ I will join you.

3. Remember to use *if*, not *when*, to describe possible future conditions.

if
We will cancel the speech ~~when~~ it rains tomorrow.

4. In questions with *if* clauses, remember to use question word order in the main clause.

should
If I don't have a signal, what I ~~should~~ do?

Editing Task

Find and correct the mistakes in the paragraphs about the advantages of a campus blog.

should
If incoming students want to learn what this college is like, where they ~~should~~ look?

will
If they visit the college website, they ~~can~~ learn about sports and campus events. However,

incoming freshmen might want a more personal perspective. They may not have the time

to attend lectures and other events, or they may want some anonymity. I have decided to

5 start a blog that provides an alternative source of information and help.

If
~~When~~ I want the blog to be successful at helping students, I will need to provide

practical suggestions. For example, one concern may be, "If I want to meet people with

can I
similar interests, what ~~I can~~ do?" I will tell that person places where he or she can post

requests on the school website and how to write his or her requests. I will also include

10 ways to safely respond to queries.

In addition, if a student w~~i~~ll have a problem with a teacher, I will write about it in my

can they do
blog and provide possible ways to solve it. If people want to add advice, how ~~they can do~~

so? They can share advice by commenting. If professors want to comment, they can, too.

won't
I ~~will not~~ try to write like a journalist and give a lot of facts. If students w~~i~~ll want

15 facts, they can go to the college website. In contrast, I will give them personal advice that

will help them with everyday problems. If students want real answers to their problems‸

they should try my blog.

6 | Grammar for Writing ✎

Using a Single *If* Clause with Multiple Main Clauses

> When writing about present or future real conditions, writers often use one *if* clause with more than one main clause. Additional main clauses can be separate sentences. Read these example paragraphs:
>
> *If people stop getting their news from different sources, they will stop hearing different sides of the stories. If they only get their news from one source, they are likely to grow overly confident of their own opinions. If they never hear any other opinions, they may also be less knowledgeable.*
>
> *If people stop getting their news from different sources, they will stop hearing different sides of the stories. They are likely to grow overly confident of their own opinions. They may also be less knowledgeable.*

Pre-writing Task

1 Read the paragraph below. What problem is the writer concerned about? What is the writer's suggestion?

Choosing Movies

It is the weekend and you want to see a movie. How do you choose which movie to see? If you are like some people, you choose movies based on the actors that are in them. However, if that is how you choose, you probably are not always happy with your movie choice. You probably end up wasting your money sometimes on forgettable movies or
5 even on movies that put you to sleep. Many moviegoers choose movies based on their previews and TV advertisements. However, trusting these sources is another ineffective way to choose movies because previews and ads are expertly created to make even the worst movie look like an award-winning film. You are more likely to be happy with your choices if you read movie reviews before choosing movies. However, even reading
10 movie reviews can cause problems. You might not agree with the reviewer. If you want to minimize your chances of being disappointed with your movie choice, read more than one movie critic's review. Choose your reviewers carefully. Find reviewers with whom you almost always agree. If you use the Internet for finding movie times and locations, use it to read reviews of movies you loved, too. When you find reviewers that like the same movies
15 you like, return to those reviewers' websites when choosing a movie to see. This technique will not guarantee that you will love every movie that you choose from now on, but you probably will not fall asleep at the next movie you see.

2 Read the paragraph again. Underline the *if* clauses that have more than one main clause. <u>Double underline</u> all of the main clauses that relate to the *if* clauses. Circle the *if* clauses that have only one main clause. Choose one *if* clause and rewrite it with another main clause.

Writing Task

1 *Write* Use the paragraph in the Pre-writing Task to help you write about how you use a particular type of media, and recommend this type of media to others. You can write about one of these topics or use your own ideas.

- how you find out about sales
- how you follow politics
- how you learn about new music
- websites that you find useful
- where you get the news

2 *Self-Edit* Use the editing tips to improve your paragraph. Make any necessary changes.

1. Did you use present or future real conditional sentences and questions correctly?
2. Did you use real conditionals with one *if* clause and more than one main clause?
3. Did you avoid the mistakes in the Avoid Common Mistakes chart on page 333?

Unreal Conditionals: Present, Future, and Past

Natural Disasters

1 Grammar in the Real World 🌐

A Think of some natural disasters in recent history. Were there any positive effects or changes that resulted from the disasters? Read the article about Hurricane Katrina. What is one positive effect of Hurricane Katrina?

Hurricane Katrina

1   In 2005, Hurricane Katrina devastated New Orleans, Louisiana. The storm killed over 1,800 people and caused over $75 billion in damages. Certainly, Katrina was a catastrophe.[1] **People wish it had**
5   **never happened.** Nonetheless, some say Katrina saved the city's schools from failure. In fact, U.S. Education Secretary, Arne Duncan, said, "I think the best thing that happened to the education system in New Orleans was Hurricane Katrina." Although some
10 people thought Duncan's comment was inappropriate, is it possible that the storm did the city a favor and helped its school system?

   If you had been a public school student in New Orleans prior to 2005, you would have had little hope for the future of your education. With low test scores and high dropout rates, the New Orleans School District was already in trouble when the hurricane
2 15 struck. The storm destroyed almost every school in the city. State legislators realized the hurricane was tragic. They also knew it provided a fresh start to rebuild the city's schools. **If they found a strong school superintendent**, they could hope for real change.

   In 2007, Paul Vallas was hired to rescue the poverty stricken and low-performing district. He knew that in order to succeed, he would have to make drastic changes. He
20 hired top teachers and modernized classrooms. Vallas also started several charter schools.
3 Charter schools are independently run public schools. They control their own academics and policies but must show the state how their students have improved. Vallas knew that **if state exam scores improved**, the charter schools would be considered a success.

[1]**catastrophe:** a sudden event that causes great suffering or destruction

25 Vallas received national praise for his experiment with charter schools. Student scores on state tests went up every year that he worked for the district. The Sophie B. Wright Charter School is a good example. It was a failing traditional school before the hurricane. **If Katrina hadn't happened**, the school might have been closed down. Instead, it became a successful charter school.

30 As for Duncan's comment about Katrina, **some wish he had used a better choice of words.** A number of educational experts disagree. They say that in the end, New Orleans schools are only successful because of the work that Vallas did to rebuild the school system.

B *Comprehension Check* Answer the questions.

1. Why is Hurricane Katrina considered a catastrophe?
2. What did Paul Vallas do to improve New Orleans's schools?
3. What are charter schools? charter schools are independly run public school

C *Notice* Read the sentences from the article. Underline the main clause in each sentence.

1. If they found a strong school superintendent, they could hope for real change.
2. If you had been a public school student in New Orleans prior to 2005, you would have had little hope for the future of your education.
3. Vallas knew that if state exam scores improved, the charter schools would be considered a success.
4. If Katrina hadn't happened, the school might have been closed down.

Is the situation in each main clause real or imaginary?

2 | Present and Future Unreal Conditionals

▶ Grammar Presentation

Present and future unreal conditionals describe imagined situations (situations that are not true).	***If children got better grades on their exams,*** *parents wouldn't be so worried.* Imagined

2.1 Forming Present and Future Unreal Conditionals

a. Use the simple past or the past progressive in the *if* clause. Use the modals *could*, *might*, or *would* in the main clause.	*If I **studied every day**, I could pass all my tests.* (But I don't study every day, so I can't pass all my tests.)
	*Parents **wouldn't worry** so much about their children's future **if their children's grades were improving**.* (But the children's grades aren't improving, so their parents are worried.)
b. In formal language, use *were* for the verb *be* for all subjects, including *I*. In informal language, native speakers often use *was* for the subject pronouns *I*, *he*, *she*, and *it*.	*If I **were better at math**, I would become an engineer.* (formal)
	*If I **was better at math**, I would become an engineer.* (informal)

▶▶ Conditionals: See page A15.

2.2 Using Present and Future Unreal Conditionals

a. The *if* clause describes an imagined condition (something that is not true at the time of speaking or writing). The main clause describes the predicted result or possible outcome.	*If all public schools **worked well**, parents wouldn't choose private schools.* (But some public schools don't work well, so parents choose private schools.)
b. Use *would* in the main clause to express the predicted result.	*If teachers gave students study guides, more students **would pass** their exams.* (Passing is a predicted result.)
Use *could* or *might* in the main clause to express something that is possible or doable.	*If students studied more for exams, more of them **could / might pass**.* (Passing exams is doable.)
c. Use *could* or the past progressive in the *if* clause to describe an imagined possible situation.	*If the city **could hire** more teachers, we would have smaller classes.* (But they can't hire more teachers, so we have large classes.)
	*We wouldn't feel hopeful **if schools weren't improving**.* (But schools are improving, so we do feel hopeful.)
d. Use time words to show present or future time.	*We wouldn't have a place to learn **if our school closed next year**.*
	*If classes were smaller **today**, students might be more motivated.*
e. Use unreal conditionals with *If I were you* to give advice. Use *I would* in the main clause.	*If I **were you**, I'd study harder.* (My advice is to study harder.)
	*I wouldn't drop out of school **if I were you**.* (My advice is to stay in school.)

▶ Grammar Application

Exercise 2.1 Present and Future Unreal Conditionals

Complete the sentences about natural disasters. Use present and future unreal conditionals. If you are writing a main clause, use the modals in parentheses.

1. Their house is damaged, so they have to build a new one.

   If their house weren't damaged, _they wouldn't have to build a new one_ (wouldn't).

2. We don't have flood insurance, so we have to pay for water damage.

   If we had flood insurance , we wouldn't have to pay for water damage.

3. There aren't earthquakes here, so we don't need earthquake insurance.

   If there were earthquakes here, _We might need earthquake insurance_ (might).

4. There's a tsunami[1] warning, so they have to leave the beach.

   If there weren't a tsunami warning, they wouldn't have to leave the beach.

5. We don't have a first-aid kit, so we aren't prepared for an earthquake.

   If we had a first-aid kit, _We would be prepared for an earthquake_ (would).

6. There's a tornado warning, so José is going into the basement.

   If there weren't a tornado warning, José wouldn't go into the basement.

7. The fire alarm is ringing, so we have to leave the building.

   If the fire alarm weren't ringing, _We might not have to leave the building_ (might not).

8. Everyone is worrying about the storm, so we are leaving.

   If Everyone weren't worrying about the storm, we wouldn't be leaving.

[1]**tsunami:** an extremely high wave of water that is caused by an earthquake

Exercise 2.2 Present and Future Unreal Conditionals: Imagined Possibilities

Complete the statements made by earthquake experts. Use present and future unreal conditionals with _could_ (_not_) in the _if_ clause and _would_ (_not_) in the main clause.

Dr. Sarah Green:

1. The government can't repair old bridges. Therefore, people don't feel safe.

   If the government _could repair_ old bridges, people _would feel_ safe.

2. They can't build quake-proof bridges very quickly, so we aren't optimistic.

   If the government _could build_ quake-proof bridges quickly, we _would be_ optimistic.

Dr. Joe Wu:

3. Certain regions can build quake-proof buildings. Therefore, they don't suffer a lot of damage.

   If certain regions _Couldn't build_

   quake-proof buildings, they _would suffer_

   a lot of damage.

Dr. Rafael Rodriguez:

4. Some countries often can't avoid contaminated water after an earthquake. Therefore, people get sick.

   If some countries _could avoid_ contaminated water after an

   earthquake, people _wouldn't get_ sick.

5. Engineers aren't able to improve the water systems in all places, so people are not healthy.

   If engineers _could improve_ the water systems in all places, people

   would be healthy.

Exercise 2.3 Present and Future Unreal Conditionals: Predicted Results

A *Over to You* Answer the questions with information that is true for you. Write your answers on a separate piece of paper. Use the ideas in the box or your own ideas. Write present and future unreal conditionals.

basement	escape	exit	higher ground
emergency services	evacuate	find shelter	take cover

What would you do if:

- you knew a hurricane were coming?
- an earthquake struck?
- you were driving and heard a tornado warning on the radio?
- you were within a half mile of a wildfire?
- you were at the beach and got a tsunami warning?
- you were in a heat wave?

If I knew a hurricane were coming, I would evacuate the area immediately.

B *Group Work* Brainstorm other answers to the questions in A. Share them with another group.

Exercise 2.4 *If I Were You . . . for Advice*

A Complete the conversations. Write sentences that give advice. Use *If I were you* and the ideas in the box. Sometimes more than one answer is possible.

~~build a new one~~   leave immediately   not go to work
get earthquake insurance   leave the building   stay indoors

1. *A* The house was damaged in the hurricane. What should we do?

   B If I were you, I'd build a new one.

2. *A* I live in an earthquake zone. What should I do?

   B If I were you, I'd get earthquake insurance.
          tormenta de nieve
3. *A* There's a blizzard warning for tomorrow. What should I do?

   B If I were you, I wouldn't go to work
                                      ola de calor
4. *A* Forecasters are predicting a terrible heat wave for tomorrow. What should we do?

   B If I were you, I'd stay indoors

5. *A* There's a wildfire three blocks from our house. What should we do?

   B If I were you, I'd leave immediately

6. *A* The fire alarm is ringing. What should we do?

   B If I were you, I'd leave the building

B *Pair Work* Take turns asking and answering the questions in A. Use your own ideas in your answers.

3 | Past Unreal Conditionals

▶ Grammar Presentation

Past unreal conditionals express situations that were not true in the past. They describe something that was possible but did not happen.	***If I had stayed home from school**, I would have missed the exam.* (But I went to school, so I didn't miss the exam.)

3.1 Forming Past Unreal Conditionals

a. Use the past perfect in the *if* clause. Use *could have*, *may have*, *might have*, or *would have* and the past participle of the verb in the main clause.	***If the city had hired more teachers***, *the schools might have improved.* (But the city didn't hire more teachers, and the schools didn't improve.)
b. The *if* clause typically comes before the main clause, but it may also follow the main clause.	*The schools might have improved **if the city had hired more teachers**.*

3.2 Using Past Unreal Conditionals

a. The *if* clause expresses the past unreal condition (a situation that was untrue in the past). The main clause describes an imagined result.	***If the hurricane had missed our city***, *the schools wouldn't have received money from the government.* (But it didn't miss our city, so the schools have received money.)
b. Use *would have* in the main clause to express a predicted result.	***If you had applied***, *you would have gotten the job.* (Getting the job was a predicted result.)
c. Use *could have* or *might have* in the main clause to express something possible or doable.	*I could have / might have passed the test **if I had studied harder**.* (Passing the test was doable.)
d. You can use past unreal conditionals to express regrets or sadness.	***If I hadn't quit school***, *I would have become an engineer.* (But I quit school, and I regret it.)
e. Use *If I had been you* to give advice indirectly. Use *I would (not)* in the main clause. *Had* is often contracted (*'d*).	***If I'd been you***, *I wouldn't have quit school.*

▶ Grammar Application

hadn't used, hadn't been
(use Past Perfect)

Exercise 3.1 Past Unreal Conditionals

Complete the interview with a scientist who studied Mount Vesuvius, a volcano that erupted[1] in 79 CE near Pompeii, Italy. Use past unreal conditionals with the verbs in parentheses.

Reporter Today, I'm talking to Dr. Adam Gannon. Dr. Gannon, we are all fascinated

by Vesuvius, I think, because it practically erased an ancient city.

Dr. Gannon That's correct. If Vesuvius _hadn't erupted_ (not / erupt), Pompeii
(1)

would not have disappeared (not / would / disappear).
(2)

[1]**erupt:** throw out smoke, fire, and melted rocks

Would not have = Wouldn't of

Reporter   So, Pompeii __would have survived__
(3)
(would / survived) if Vesuvius
__hadn't exploded__ (not / explode)?
(4)

Dr. Gannon   Yes, that's correct. On the other hand, if ash
__hadn't covered__ (not / cover) the
(5)
city, it __wouldn't have been preserved__ (not / would / be preserved).
(6)

Reporter   The volcano caused other great changes, too, didn't it?

Dr. Gannon   Yes. In fact, it completely changed the direction of a nearby river. The Sarno
__would've stayed__ (would / stay) in the same place if Vesuvius
(7)
__hadn't changed__ (not / change) the course of the river.
(8)
It was a very powerful eruption.

Reporter   How do we know so much about the eruption of Vesuvius?

Dr. Gannon   We have the writer Pliny the Younger to thank for that. If he and his
uncle __hadn't been__ (not / be) near Pompeii that day,
(9)
we __wouldn't have known__ (not / would / know) much about the
(10)
eruption of Vesuvius. But we still don't know everything.

Reporter   Fascinating. Thank you, Dr. Gannon.

Exercise 3.2 Past Unreal Conditionals: Regret

A *Group Work* Look at the pictures and discuss these questions in groups: What does
a volcanic eruption look like? What are some of the effects of a volcanic eruption?

Mount St. Helens,
Washington State

landslide
derrumbe

ash cloud
nube de ceniza

B ◀)) Listen to a man talk about his experience surviving the 1980 Mount St. Helens volcano eruption. Circle *T* if the statement is true. Circle *F* if the statement is false.

1. The speaker and his family were hiking on the mountain the day the volcano erupted.   T   (F)
2. Falling trees hit the speaker and his friends.   T   (F)
3. The speaker thinks it's possible that many people on the mountain survived.   (T)   (F)
4. The speaker's wife wasn't affected by the eruption.   (T)   F
5. The sideways eruption of Mount St. Helens caused a lot of damage.   (T)   F
6. Ten years after the eruption, the speaker returned to his campsite.   (T)   F
7. Scientists didn't learn anything from the eruption.   (T)   F

C ◀)) Listen again and check your answers.

D Complete the statements about the story. Use the words in parentheses to write past unreal conditionals with possible or predicted results.

1. If we hadn't gone camping that day, we _might have avoided the disaster_ (**possible:** avoid / the disaster).
2. If we hadn't been in a hole, falling trees _migh have hit us_ (**possible:** hit) us.
3. If people hadn't been on the mountain, they _Would have survived_ (**predicted:** survive).
4. If his wife had been with him, the eruption _Could have effected_ (**possible:** affect) her.
5. If Mount St. Helens hadn't been a sideways explosion, it _Wouldn't have done_ (**predicted:** not / do) so much damage.
6. If the speaker and his friends hadn't returned to the mountain, they _Wouldn't have seen_ (**predicted:** not / see) the site of the destruction.
7. If the eruption hadn't happened, scientists _Wouldn't have learned_ (**predicted:** not / learn) how quickly plant and animal life can return.

4 | Wishes About the Present, Future, and Past

▶ Grammar Presentation

Sentences with *wish* express a desire for something to be different, or feelings of sadness or regret.	*I **wish (that)** every child could have a better education.* (Unfortunately, not every child can have a better education.)

desear

4.1 *Wish* in the Present, Future, and Past

a. *Wish* is followed by a *that* clause. Use a past form of the verb in the *that* clause, similar to conditional sentences. The word *that* is often omitted in informal speaking.	*There aren't enough teachers. We **wish that** we could hire more teachers.* *sub verb* *auxiliary verb* *main verb*
b. Wishes about the present are followed by *that* clauses with verbs in the simple past or past progressive, or the modal *could*.	*I **wish (that)** we had more classrooms.* (We don't have a lot of classrooms.) *I **wish (that)** my son were doing well in school.* (My son is not doing well in school.) *Some people **wish (that)** they could afford to go to college.* (They can't afford to go to college.)
c. Wishes about the future are followed by *that* clauses with *was / were going to* or the modals *could* or *would*.	*I **wish (that)** I were going to have time to meet you tonight.* (I'm not going to have time to meet you.) *She **wishes (that)** she could go to class tonight, but she has to work.* (She can't go to class tonight.) *We **wish (that)** the school would build a parking lot, but it's too costly.* (The school will not build a parking lot.)
d. Wishes about the past are followed by *that* clauses with the verb in the past perfect.	*We **wish (that)** we had had more time to study for the test.* (We didn't have enough time to study.)

Data from the Real World

In academic writing, *wish* followed by a singular subject is more commonly followed by *were* than *was*.	Wish + singular subject + *were* ▐▐▐▐▐▐▐▐▐▐ Wish + singular subject + *was* ▐▐▐

*The president wishes the solution to the problem **were** simpler.* (more common in academic writing)

*The president wishes the solution to the problem **was** simpler.* (less common in academic writing)

▶ Grammar Application

Exercise 4.1 Present and Future Wishes

Complete the sentences about a family's disaster. Write wishes in the present and future. Sometimes more than one answer is possible.

Could = Past

1. There isn't a lot of light. Ben _wishes (that) there was/were more light_.
2. We don't have enough bottled water. We _wish (that) we had enough bottled water_
3. The roof is leaking. Mom _wishes the roof weren't leaking_.
4. We are running out of batteries. Paul _wishes we weren't running out of batteries_
5. The electricity doesn't work. Dad _wishes that the electricity had worked_
6. The Internet isn't working. Sue _wishes that the internet were working_
7. The furniture is going to be ruined. Grandma and Grandpa _wish that the furniture weren't going to be ruined_.
8. We can't go to a hotel. We _wishes we could go to a hotel_.

Exercise 4.2 Past Wishes

Read the sentences about some past disasters. Then write sentences about the speakers' wishes. Use past wish forms. Sometimes more than one answer is possible.

1. An architect: The 1906 earthquake destroyed a historic building. There wasn't enough money to rebuild it.

   I wish the earthquake hadn't destroyed the building./I wish there had
   been enough money to rebuild it.

2. A surfer: They closed my favorite beach after the storm. They didn't let people in to clean it up.

   I wish they hadn't closed my favorite beach / I wish they had let people into

3. A historian: A flood destroyed the ancient city. There were no records of what life was like there.

   I wish the flood hadn't destroyed the ancient city / I wish there had been

4. A student: A hurricane destroyed my high school. We weren't able to attend graduation.

   I wish the hurricane hadn't destroyed my high school / I wish we had been able
   attend graduation

5 | Avoid Common Mistakes ⚠

1. **When forming the present unreal conditional, use the past (not present) form of the verb after *if*.**

   understood
   If I ~~understand~~ my teacher, I would enjoy my class more.

2. **Remember to include a subject when forming an *if* clause.**

   she
   She would feel safer if ∧ could stay with us during the storm.

3. **When forming the past unreal conditional, use the past perfect form in the *if* clause.**

   had not ruined
   If the flood ~~did not ruin~~ his car, he would have arrived home safely.

4. **When making past unreal wishes, use the past perfect (not the simple past).**

   had not moved
   I wish I ~~did not move~~ to such a dangerous place.

Editing Task

Find and correct eight more mistakes in the story about Hurricane Ike.

       had   *hadn't*
If Hurricane Ike did not come, we would have had an easier time. If the storm missed

                                             n't
us, we would not have lived without electricity for two weeks. We would have been able to

                                             they
go to work and school. Our trees would look a lot better if had not been destroyed by the

                                                     had
strong winds. For these reasons, some people wish that Hurricane Ike never happened.

                   did   *had*
5 However, I do not. If the storm did not come to Houston, we would not have learned many

valuable lessons.

       First, we learned about our neighbors. We all came together to help each other

                            had *d*
before and after the storm. If I live in a different place, maybe I would not have gotten to

                                      'd
know my neighbors in this way. Second, we learned good emergency survival skills. If we

                                      they
10 had not learned to board our houses, might have been damaged. If another storm comes

                 n't
today, my house would be safe.

                                         had   *d*
       Sometimes I wish that my family did not move to this city. However, I do not feel this

way because of the hurricanes. The hurricanes have made our community stronger.

6 | Grammar for Writing ✎

Using *If* Clauses to Support Ideas

Unreal conditionals are useful to explain and illustrate a writer's ideas using hypothetical situations. Read these examples:

It is still very difficult to predict many earthquakes and volcanic eruptions. If more money had been spent on research before the Northridge earthquake, scientists might have been able to warn people.

Last year's fire moved very slowly. If it had moved faster, firefighters wouldn't have stopped it so quickly.

Pre-writing Task

1 Read the paragraph below. What should the writer's family have done earlier?

A Family Plan

Every family should have an escape plan in case of a house fire, but California families need escape plans for wildfires as well. My family discovered this last year. A wildfire began several miles away from our house on a Sunday afternoon. By Tuesday, it was very close. We didn't have an escape plan because we were new to California. At

5 the time, we did not know about the dangers of wildfires. If we had lived in California longer, we would have thought about wildfire preparation more carefully. At 7:00 that evening, the police called to tell us that our area was in a warning zone. They told us that we should start getting prepared to leave. My children and I started packing up our belongings. We also thought about where to go. We decided that we would go to a friend's

10 house. We could not have brought our pets if we had gone to the emergency shelter. By 8:30, the wildfire had started moving faster, and we got the call that we had to evacuate. We had not finished packing, but we put the animals in the car and left. Two days later, we were able to return to our home. We were lucky because our house was fine. When we looked around, we realized we had taken silly things and left important things. If our

15 house had burned down, we could have lost many important papers. We decided that we had to make a list of important things immediately in case of another fire. We would not have panicked as much, and we might have packed better, if we had made that list before the fire. Next time, we will be prepared.

2 Read the paragraph again. Underline the past unreal conditional sentences. <u>Double underline</u> the conditional sentences that have the main clause first and the *if* clause last. What other modals besides *would* are used in the main clauses?

Writing Task

1 *Write* Use the paragraph in the Pre-writing Task to help you write about a surprising situation that happened to you or to people you know. You can write about one of these topics or use your own ideas.

- a natural disaster
- a power outage
- a time you or someone you know got caught in bad weather

2 *Self-Edit* Use the editing tips to improve your paragraph. Make any necessary changes.

1. Did you use unreal conditional sentences to support important ideas or to give reasons for why things happened the way they did?
2. Did you use the correct verb forms in the main and *if* clauses?
3. Did you include any conditional sentences that have the main clause first and the *if* clause last?
4. Did you avoid the mistakes in the Avoid Common Mistakes chart on page 347?

UNIT 26

Conjunctions
Globalization of Food

1 | Grammar in the Real World

A Have you ever had fast food in a foreign country? Do you think the food looks and tastes the same everywhere that it is sold? Read the web article about the globalization of fast-food chains. What do fast-food businesses do to their products to make customers happy?

The Globalization of Fast Food

Mochi Ring Donut

Do you want a glazed[1] donut for breakfast? Go to your favorite Dunkin' Donuts in Arizona, New York, **or** almost anywhere in the United States **and** you will find it. That is not surprising since sweet foods are popular with
5 Americans, **but** you might not be able to find that donut in other countries. Instead, in parts of Asia you might find green tea or mango mochi ring donuts. In Korea, they offer kimchi[2] croquettes, donuts filled with pickled[3] vegetables. In Singapore, you would find donuts filled with wasabi[4]

10 cheese **and** seaweed cheese. The wasabi creates a very hot-tasting donut that appeals to people in Singapore. In Thailand, Dunkin' Donuts makes delicious Kai-yong donuts, a combination of glazed donut and shredded chicken that is topped with a
15 spicy Thai chili paste. In Indonesia, they sell donuts filled **not only** with red bean paste **but also** with lychee[5] **and** orange. Thinking globally **but** acting locally has been one of the reasons for Dunkin' Donuts' success in over 32 countries **and** over 10,000 restaurants worldwide.

Kai-yong Donuts

20   American fast-food chains, like Dunkin' Donuts, seem to be everywhere, **but** these days they are serving **both** food from their U.S. menus **and** food adapted to the tastes **and** customs of other cultures in other countries. McDonald's is another example. In India, there are many people who do not eat meat, **so** McDonald's

---

[1]**glazed:** covered with a sweet, shiny coating made of sugar | [2]**kimchi:** a Korean dish of pickled vegetables | [3]**pickled:** preserved in a liquid containing salt or vinegar | [4]**wasabi:** a strong-tasting condiment | [5]**lychee:** a sweet, juicy fruit often found in Southeast Asia and other parts of Asia

in India serves only vegetarian burgers **and** prepares non-vegetarian (chicken and
25 fish) meals in a separate area. McDonald's is one of the largest fast-food restaurants
worldwide. More than one third of its 33,000 restaurants are located outside the
United States. Adapting to local cultures is very important.

The globalization of the fast-food industry is happening with restaurants from
all over the world. Pollo Campero, a fast-food restaurant that began in Guatemala
30 in 1971, started adding stores in **both** Europe **and** Asia after expanding in Central
America. In 2002, it opened its first restaurant in the United States **and** has been
growing ever since. In order to appeal to health-conscious consumers in the United
States, Pollo Campero decided to offer customers a choice: **either** a healthier grilled
chicken **or** a lightly fried chicken. Grilled **or** fried, the uniquely seasoned chicken has
35 become popular with **both** immigrants from Latin American countries **and** Americans
from other cultural backgrounds.

These days, more and more chain restaurants are selling their food in different
countries. Adapting their products to local preferences is a way to keep customers
happy **and** to keep business booming.[6] It appears to be a strategy for success.

....

[6]**boom:** grow rapidly, especially economically

B Comprehension Check Answer the questions.

1. What has Dunkin' Donuts done to succeed globally?
2. How has McDonald's changed its menu to attract vegetarians in India?
3. How is the United States affected by the globalization of fast food?

C Notice Find the sentences in the article and complete them. What is the function of the missing words? Circle *a* or *b*.

1. That is not surprising since sweet foods are popular with Americans,

   _____ you might not be able to find that donut in other countries.
   a. to add information
   b. to show a contrast

2. In Indonesia, they sell donuts filled _____ with red bean paste

   _____ with lychee and orange.
   a. to emphasize additional negative information
   b. to emphasize surprising information

3. Adapting their products to local preferences is a way to keep customers happy

   _____ to keep business booming.
   a. to add information
   b. to show a contrast

2 Connecting Words and Phrases with Conjunctions

▶ Grammar Presentation

Conjunctions connect words and phrases. Coordinating conjunctions include *and*, *but*, and *or*.
Correlative conjunctions include *both . . . and*, *neither . . . nor*, *either . . . or*, and *not only . . . but also*.

*I love pizza, hamburgers, **and** hot dogs.*
*I eat **not only** fast food **but also** healthy food.*

2.1 Coordinating Conjunctions

a. Use coordinating conjunctions to link two or more nouns, gerunds, verbs, or adverbs. Use the same part of speech in linked words or phrases to create parallel structure. This makes speech and writing clearer.	*Have you ever eaten pizza with <u>shrimp</u> **or** <u>olives</u>?* (nouns) *I've been to fast-food restaurants in <u>Asia</u>, <u>Europe</u>, <u>Africa</u>, **and** <u>North America</u>.* (proper nouns) *I don't like <u>cooking</u> **or** <u>baking</u>.* (gerunds) *The meal is <u>unhealthy</u> **but** <u>delicious</u>.* (adjectives)
b. Use *and* to add information.	*There are many vegetarians in India **and** the U.K.*
Use *but* to show a contrast.	*This food is cheap **but** very good.* (*But* contrasts the price of the food and the quality.)
Use *or* to connect related ideas or items in a negative statement or to show alternatives.	*I <u>don't like</u> hamburgers **or** pizza.* *Do you want to eat at a restaurant **or** at home?*
c. When you connect three or more words or phrases, use a comma between each one. Put the conjunction before the last word or phrase.	*I select my food based on taste, nutritional value, **and** price.* *Would you like to have juice, milk, **or** water with your meal?*

2.2 Correlative Conjunctions

a. Correlative conjunctions have two parts. They often emphasize equality between the words or phrases they connect.	***Both** fried foods **and** grilled foods are served here.* *Fast food is **neither** delicious **nor** healthy.*

2.2 Correlative Conjunctions (continued)

b. Use *both . . . and* to add information. When connecting two subjects, use a plural verb.	**Both** the food **and** the atmosphere <u>are</u> wonderful.
Use *either . . . or* to emphasize alternatives. The verb agrees in number with the noun that is closest to it.	**Either** potatoes **or** rice <u>is</u> fine with me. (Use a singular verb with *rice*.) **Either** rice **or** potatoes <u>are</u> fine with me. (Use a plural verb with *potatoes*.)
Use *not only . . . but also* to emphasize surprising information. The verb agrees in number with the noun that is closest to it.	**Not only** two drinks **but also** dessert <u>comes</u> with this entree. (Use a singular verb with *dessert*.) **Not only** dessert **but also** two drinks <u>come</u> with this entree. (Use a plural verb with *drinks*.)
Use *neither . . . nor* to emphasize additional information in negative statements. The verb agrees in number with the noun that is closest to it.	**Neither** my parents **nor** my brother <u>wants</u> to try eel. (Use a singular verb with *brother*.) **Neither** my brother **nor** my parents <u>want</u> to try eel. (Use a plural verb with *parents*.)

▶ Grammar Application

Exercise 2.1 Coordinating Conjunctions

Combine the sentences about global food. Use the coordinating conjunctions in parentheses. Sometimes more than one answer is possible.

1. There's a Taco Bell in Iceland. There's a Taco Bell in India. (and)

   There's a Taco Bell in Iceland and in India.

2. Starbucks operates in Asia. It operates in Europe. It operates in Latin America. (and)

   _____

3. The U.S. branch doesn't have vegetarian burgers. It doesn't have lamb burgers. (or)

   _____

4. Would you prefer to try something unusual? Would you prefer to try something familiar? (or)

   _____

5. Vegans don't eat eggs. Vegans don't eat cheese. Vegans don't eat yogurt. (or)

   _____

6. The food is cheap. The food is very healthy. (but)

   _____

7. The coffee is expensive. The coffee is very popular. (but)

   _____

Exercise 2.2 Correlative Conjunctions

A Read the monthly sales report from Branch #345. Then complete the report to headquarters. Circle the correct correlative conjunctions.

Branch #345 – Shanghai, China – June		
Products		
Frozen Yogurt and Smoothies	**Drinks**	**Snacks**
frozen yogurt: 55% smoothies: 45%	coffee: 50% tea: 43% mineral water: 5% milkshakes: 2%	chips: 59% cookies: 41%

Flavors of Frozen Yogurt and Smoothies		
Western Flavors	chocolate: 3%	
	vanilla: 2%	
Asian Flavors	dragon fruit: 55%	
	lychee: 40%	

Report to Headquarters on Branch #345

This branch offers **both** / neither Western **and** / or Asian flavors. Asian flavors seem to be
  (1)   (1)
more popular. For example, dragon fruit and lychee are the most popular flavors this month.

Most customers tend to choose **neither / either** dragon fruit **nor / or** lychee yogurt. Therefore,
                                        (2)   (2)
please note that **both / neither** chocolate **and / nor** vanilla is selling well at this branch.
                         (3)   (3)

   Neither / Not only frozen yogurt **nor / but also** smoothies are popular at this branch.
              (4)   (4)

Either / Neither mineral water **or / nor** milkshakes sold well this month. The reason is that
       (5)   (5)
most customers prefer **neither / either** coffee **nor / or** tea. **Both / Neither** coffee **and / nor**
                              (6)   (6)   (7)   (7)
tea are selling well. It is interesting to note that customers are buying snacks. Surprisingly,

neither / not only chips **nor / but also** cookies are selling well.
         (8)   (8)

   I recommend that we create more locally flavored products to offer at this location.

B *Group Work* In groups, choose a country that you know well. Discuss possible frozen yogurt flavors and types of drinks and snacks that you think would or would not sell well in this country. Then write five sentences about your choices with correlative conjunctions.

Both chocolate and vanilla would sell well in Mexico.

Exercise 2.3 More Correlative Conjunctions

Combine the sentences about the availability of items in a Latin American coffee chain's global locations. Use the correlative conjunctions in parentheses.

1. Milk is available in the United States. Juice is available in the United States. (both . . . and)

    Both milk and juice are available in the United States.

2. Tea is inexpensive in Egypt. Tea is very popular in Egypt. (both . . . and)

3. You can use your own mug at coffee shops in the U.K. You can use a store cup at coffee shops in the U.K. (either . . . or)

4. Donuts are available in the United States. Muffins are available in the United States. (not only . . . but also)

5. Recycling is encouraged in China. Reusing cups is encouraged in China. (not only . . . but also)

6. Generally, forks are not available in Chinese restaurants. Generally, knives are not available in Chinese restaurants. (neither . . . nor)

7. Hot dogs are not typically eaten for lunch in the Dominican Republic. Pizza is not typically eaten for lunch in the Dominican Republic. (neither . . . nor)

3 Connecting Sentences with Coordinating Conjunctions

▶ Grammar Presentation

The coordinating conjunctions *and*, *but*, *or*, *so*, and *yet* can connect independent clauses.	*Kevin doesn't eat meat, **but** he eats fish.* *Jennifer is a vegetarian, **so** we shouldn't put meat in the lasagna.*

3.1 Connecting Sentences with *And*, *But*, and *Or*

a. Use a comma before the coordinating conjunction when you connect two complete sentences. The comma implies a pause.	*Starbucks opened in 1971**, and** it has become an international success.* *The café sold muffins**, but** it did not sell sandwiches.* *Consumers liked the food**, so** sales were good.*
b. When you connect sentences with the same subject with *and* or *or*, you do not need to repeat the subject. The result is a compound verb. Do not use a comma with compound verbs. If the modals or the auxiliary verbs are the same, you do not have to repeat the modals or auxiliaries.	CLAUSE, + *AND* + CLAUSE *We ate at that restaurant last week**, and** we really liked it.* VERB + *AND* + VERB *We ate at that restaurant last week **and** really liked it.* *Karen can ride with us**, or** she can meet us at the restaurant.* *Karen can ride with us **or** meet us at the restaurant.* *My brother has visited India**, and** he has eaten fast food there.* *My brother has visited India **and** eaten fast food there.*
c. In some writing, such as in newspapers and magazines, sentences begin with conjunctions like *and* and *but* to emphasize information. Do not do this in academic writing.	*The changes to the menu attracted many new customers.* ***And** the company's profits rose significantly.*

3.1 Connecting Sentences with *And*, *But*, and *Or* (continued)

d. Use *and* to connect an independent clause that adds information. You can also use *and* to show a sequence of events.	*He is an excellent cook,* **and** *I love his recipes.* *This restaurant changed its chef,* **and** *now it is very popular.*
Use *but* to introduce contrasting or surprising information.	*This is supposed to be a good Mexican restaurant,* **but** *my Mexican friends don't like it.*
Use *or* to introduce a choice or alternative. It is often used in questions or statements with modals of possibility.	*We could have seafood,* **or** *we could make pasta.* *Could you prepare the meal,* **or** *should I ask Sam to prepare it?*

3.2 Connecting Sentences with *So* and *Yet*

a. Use *so* to connect a cause and its result.	CAUSE	RESULT
	Henry doesn't like pizza, **so** *we ordered pasta.* *That spice is rare in my country,* **so** *I substitute a different one.*	
Use *yet* to connect contrasting ideas or surprising information. *Yet* sometimes expresses a stronger contrast than *but*.	*Cathy doesn't eat clams,* **yet** *she eats oysters.* *The restaurant serves wonderful food,* **yet** *it is known more for its music.*	
b. Use a comma to combine sentences with *so* and *yet*. Do not use a compound verb.	*Mary is a vegetarian,* **so** *she eats tofu.* NOT ~~Mary is a vegetarian so eats tofu.~~	

▶ Grammar Application

Exercise 3.1 Connecting Sentences with *And*, *But*, *Or*

Complete the sentences about a European supermarket chain that opened stores in the United States. Circle the correct conjunctions. Add commas when necessary.

1. FoodCo opened 100 stores in the United States in 2008, **and** / **but** the managers expected to have great success in certain areas.

2. First, they studied the new market **but** / **and** they even sent anthropologists to study U.S. eating and shopping habits.

3. They opened stores in wealthy neighborhoods **or** / **and** they also opened some in low-income neighborhoods.

4. The trend in the United States is toward "big box" stores[1] **and** / **but** FoodCo decided to open small, convenience-type stores.

[1] **"big box" store:** a very large store that sells almost everything, including food

5. Convenience stores in the United States usually do not sell fresh produce **but / or** FoodCo has changed the definition of *convenience store* with its new stores.

6. FoodCo has positioned itself as a healthy convenience store **and / or** it provides high-quality groceries and produce at reasonable prices.

7. Customers can use FoodCo's shops to pick up last-minute items **but / or** they can do their weekly shopping there.

8. Now shoppers in low-income neighborhoods have a choice. They can buy junk food at a convenience store **but / or** they can buy healthy products at a FoodCo shop.

Exercise 3.2 Connecting Sentences with *So* and *Yet*

Complete the article about Chinese-American dishes. Use *so* or *yet*. Add commas when necessary.

Many Chinese restaurants serve dishes that are not authentic. Chinese restaurant owners wanted to be successful in foreign countries , *so* they adapted
(1)
dishes to local tastes. Here are some examples: Fortune cookies are popular desserts in many Chinese restaurants _____ they were never popular in China. In fact, the
(2)
cookies were actually invented in Japan and then introduced to the United States by an immigrant in the early 1900s (although some people dispute this and say that a Chinese immigrant invented them first). General Tso's Chicken is another example. No one is absolutely certain of its origin _____ it appears on many U.S. Chinese
(3)
restaurant menus. It's fried chicken with a sweet sauce. Fried chicken is a traditional American dish _____ a clever Chinese restaurant owner probably invented it to
(4)
appeal to American tastes for sweet sauces. Chop suey is another Chinese-American invention. There are many legends about its creation _____ no one really knows
(5)
for sure how it came about. In one story, a Chinese-American dishwasher created the dish from leftover bits of meat and vegetables. The man received part of his pay in food _____ he took what he could find at
(6)
the end of the day. Customers asked about the delicious-smelling creation _____ the restaurant manager put it on the menu.
(7)
Some of these dishes may seem inauthentic _____ they have
(8)
been extremely popular in the United States since the 1900s.

Exercise 3.3 Combining Sentences

Combine the sentences about the localization of food. Use the conjunctions in parentheses. Omit the subject and use a compound verb when possible. Add commas when necessary.

1. You can travel to many countries. You can still find dishes from home. (and)

   You can travel to many countries and still find dishes from home.

2. I have eaten tacos in China. I have ordered kimchi in France. (and)

   _____

3. You might get an authentic dish abroad. You might find a local version of it. (or)

   _____

4. I often find international dishes abroad. They are usually adapted to local tastes. (but)

   _____

5. Beef isn't eaten in some countries. A fast-food chain might sell lamb burgers. (so)

   _____

6. I travel constantly. I never miss food from home. (yet)

   _____

Exercise 3.4 Using So and Yet

Over to You On a separate piece of paper, complete the answers about local food tastes. Write sentences that are true for you. Discuss your ideas with a partner.

1. How do supermarkets in your neighborhood address local tastes?

   Supermarkets in my neighborhood want to address local tastes, so

   they have an imported-food section .

2. How might an international food company adapt a product to local tastes?

   People in _____ like _____ , so _____ .
             (name a country)   (food or taste)

3. What inauthentic ethnic dishes are sometimes very popular?

   _____ is inauthentic, yet _____ .
     (name of dish)

4 Reducing Sentences with Similar Clauses

▶ Grammar Presentation

When you connect sentences that have similar clauses, you can often reduce the words in the second clause.

Shrimp is one of my favorite foods. Chicken is one of my favorite foods.
*Shrimp is one of my favorite foods, **and** chicken is, **too**.*

4.1 Reducing Sentences

a. In sentences with *be* as the main verb, use the *be* verb in the reduced clause.	*Their Chinese food <u>isn't</u> very good, **but** their Thai food <u>is</u>.*
b. For other verb forms with auxiliaries, you can reduce the verb form in the reduced clause.	*My brother <u>didn't eat</u> fast food in college, **and** I <u>didn't</u>, **either**.*
For the present or past progressive, keep the form of *be* and omit verb + *-ing*.	*The price of beef <u>was rising</u> last month, **but** the price of chicken <u>wasn't</u>.*
For simple verb forms, use *do/does* (*not*) or *did* (*not*).	*I <u>don't like</u> this restaurant, **and** Lisa <u>doesn't</u>, **either**.* *We <u>went</u> out to eat, **and so** <u>did</u> Victor.*
For the present or past perfect, use *have/has* or *had* and omit the past participle.	*The cost of eating out <u>has risen</u>, **and** the cost of cooking at home <u>has</u>, **too**.*
For modals or future forms, use the modal or future form by itself.	*Jason <u>can join</u> us for lunch, **and** Liz <u>can</u>, **too**.* *I <u>won't eat</u> fried food, **and** Greg <u>won't</u>, **either**.*
c. Use *and . . . too* or *and so* to combine two affirmative sentences. Use: • *and* + subject + auxiliary + *too* • *and so* + auxiliary + subject Note that the order of the auxiliary and subject are reversed in *and so* reduced clauses. We usually use a comma before *too*.	AFFIRM. SENT. + AFFIRM. SENT. *I ate there yesterday. She ate there yesterday.* AND + SUBJ. + AUX. + TOO *I ate there yesterday, **and** <u>she did</u>, **too**.* AND SO + AUX. + SUBJ. *I ate there yesterday, **and so** <u>did she</u>.*

4.1 Reducing Sentences (continued)

d. Use *and . . . not, either* or *and neither* to combine two negative sentences. Use:

- *and* + subject + auxiliary + *not, either*

- *and neither* + auxiliary + subject

NEG. SENT. + NEG. SENT.
I don't have any coffee. Kim doesn't have any coffee.

AND + SUBJ. + AUX. + *NOT, EITHER*
*I don't have any coffee, **and** Kim doesn't, **either**.*

AND NEITHER + AUX. + SUBJ.
*I don't have any coffee, **and neither** does Kim.*

e. Use *but* to combine an affirmative and a negative sentence.

AFFIRM. SENT. + NEG. SENT.
The beef is dry. The chicken isn't dry.

AFFIRM. CLAUSE + *BUT* + NEG. CLAUSE
*The beef is dry, **but** the chicken isn't.*

NEG. CLAUSE + *BUT* + AFFIRM. CLAUSE
*The chicken isn't dry, **but** the beef is.*

f. You can also use *too, so, either,* and *neither* in separate sentences in speaking and less formal writing.

Use *too* and *so* for two affirmative sentences. Use *either* and *neither* for two negative sentences.

*Japanese food is delicious. Korean food is, **too**.*
*Japanese food is delicious. **So** is Korean food.*
*The coffee isn't warm. The tea isn't, **either**.*
*The coffee isn't warm. **Neither** is the tea.*

Exercise 4.1 Reducing Sentences with Similar Clauses

Combine the sentences about food localization in India. Use coordinating conjunctions. If there are two lines, write the sentence in two different ways.

1. Americans like fast food. Indians like fast food.

   Americans like fast food, and Indians do, too.
   Americans like fast food, and so do Indians.

2. Some U.S. food companies are successful in India. Some U.S. food companies aren't successful in India.

   _____

3. Beef isn't popular in India. Pork isn't popular in India.

   _____

   _____

4. McDonald's adapts its menu to local tastes. Pizza Hut adapts its menu to local tastes.

   _____

   _____

5. Pizza Hut doesn't serve meat in some regions. McDonald's doesn't serve meat in some regions.

   _____

   _____

Exercise 4.2 Reducing Verb Forms

A *Group Work* Match the words with pictures of food. Tell the group which foods you have eaten raw.

_b_ 1. eel

____ 2. jellyfish

____ 3. sea urchin

____ 4. seaweed

____ 5. tuna

a

b

c

d

e

B 🔊 Listen to the interview with the chef of a restaurant. Circle *T* if the statement is true. Circle *F* if the statement is false.

1. The chef is talking about Asian dishes that he serves at his restaurant. (T) F

2. All the dishes he offers are popular with his customers. T F

3. The chef has adapted some dishes to local tastes. T F

4. The chef does not plan to make any changes to his menu. T F

C 🔊 Listen again. Rewrite the statements to match what the chef says. Use reduced forms.

1. Raw fish is getting more popular. Seaweed salad is getting more popular.

   Raw fish is getting more popular_, and so is seaweed salad_ .

2. Tuna has been selling well. Eel hasn't been selling well.

   Tuna has been selling well, _____ .

3. Jellyfish didn't sell well last month. Sea urchin didn't sell well last month.

   Jellyfish didn't sell well last month, _____ .

4. Spicy noodles have sold well. Cold noodles have sold well.

   Spicy noodles have sold well, _____ .

5. This restaurant can't get customers interested in Thai dishes. Our other restaurants can't get customers interested.

   This restaurant can't get customers interested in Thai dishes,

   _____ .

6. We'll probably stop offering Thai dishes. The other branches will probably stop offering Thai dishes.

   We'll probably stop offering Thai dishes, _____ .

7. We won't serve that. Most other Asian restaurants won't serve that.

   We won't serve that, _____ .

8. The ice cream has been selling well. The cake has been selling well, too.

   The ice cream has been selling well, _____ .

5 | Avoid Common Mistakes ⚠

1. Use *or* to connect ideas in a negative sentence.

   There were no nuts in the vegetarian ~~and~~ the meat dishes. (or)

2. Use *both*, not *either*, when joining ideas with *and*.

   They use ~~either~~ butter and oil for cooking. (both)

3. Use *either*, not *too*, after a negative verb.

   They do not eat pork, and we don't, ~~too~~. (either)

4. Do not use a comma when a conjunction joins two phrases.

   Most local people love durian fruit, but dislike the smell.

Editing Task

Find and correct eight more mistakes in the paragraphs about food.

Intercultural Dinners

My roommate and I come from different cultures, so ~~either~~ (both) our eating habits and food preferences differ. Fortunately, we have some food preferences in common. I do not eat junk food, and he does not, too. There are no cookies and other desserts in our house. Instead, we have either fresh fruits and nuts for snacks.

5   However, we have some differences. I eat either rice and pasta every day. My roommate, however, thinks meals with rice, and dishes with pasta will make him gain weight, so he does not want to eat them often. Likewise, I do not like to eat a lot of meat and dairy products because I believe they are not healthy. Fortunately, I do not complain about his tastes, and he does not complain about mine, too. When we cook, we try to

10 make food that represents either his culture and mine.

6 Grammar for Writing

Using Coordinating and Correlative Conjunctions to Join Words and Clauses

The coordinating conjunctions *and*, *but*, and *or* and the correlative conjunctions *both . . . and, neither . . . nor, either . . . or,* and *not only . . . but also* are used in writing to add information or to show a sequence of events, a contrast, or alternatives.

When you connect words or phrases with these conjunctions, be sure to use the same part of speech for the words that you connect. This is called parallel structure. Read these examples:

NOUN   NOUN
My neighborhood has <u>several Japanese restaurants</u> but <u>no Chinese restaurants</u>.

GERUND   GERUND
I enjoy not only <u>eating</u> Mexican food but also <u>cooking</u> it.

Pre-writing Task

1 Read the paragraph below. What is one difference between Mexican and Tex-Mex food?

Tex-Mex or Mexican?

Mexican food can be found in most parts of the United States, but Americans will probably be very surprised on their first trip to Mexico. U.S. visitors to Mexico are unlikely to find many of the foods they usually order in their favorite Mexican restaurants. For example, they will find neither nachos nor chimichangas, which are foods commonly

5 found in typical Mexican restaurants in the United States. That's because these dishes are either American foods that were influenced by Mexican foods or Mexican dishes that were combined with American dishes. A common U.S. variation of Mexican food is the addition of sour cream and cheese to many dishes. Mexicans sometimes use a little bit of something similar to sour cream or sprinkle some cheese on their dishes, but they do not

10 use much. Many of these Mexican-influenced American dishes originated in Texas near the Mexican border and then spread throughout the United States. This is where the term "Tex-Mex" came from.

2 Read the paragraph again. Underline the uses of *but*. <u>Double underline</u> the correlative conjunctions. Circle the remaining uses of *and* and *or*.

Writing Task

1 *Write* Use the paragraph in the Pre-writing Task to help you write a paragraph about variations of ethnic foods. You can write about one of these topics or use your own ideas.

- the influence of foreign foods in your culture
- popular ethnic foods in your country

2 *Self-Edit* Use the editing tips to improve your paragraph. Make any necessary changes.

1. Did you use coordinating conjunctions and correlative conjunctions to add information, show a contrast, show a sequence of events, or show alternatives?
2. Did you use the conjunctions to link parallel structures?
3. Did you avoid the mistakes in the Avoid Common Mistakes chart on page 363?

27

Adverb Clauses and Phrases
Consumerism

1 | Grammar in the Real World

A What are some normal behaviors that can become problems under certain circumstances? Read the web article about shopping addiction. When is shopping an addiction?

Shopping Addiction:
When Spending Hurts

Some people have closets filled with new clothes that they do not wear. Others have desks covered with electronics that they never use. **Even though these people**
5 **do not need more clothes or electronics,** they keep buying them. They cannot help themselves. **Although many people like to shop,** some people shop too much. If someone is unable to control spending, he or she may be a shopping addict, or "shopaholic." **Because shopping may be seen as an amusing addiction,** society does
10 not always consider it a serious problem. As a result, many people do not recognize they have a problem that needs treatment. However, if this addiction is not treated, it can ruin a person's life.

Shopping can activate[1] chemicals in the brain associated with pleasure, so some people get a natural "high"[2] while shopping. Also,
15 some people shop **because it makes them feel in control.** This often happens **when they face difficulties in their personal or professional lives.** These feelings could be signs of shopping addiction. **While it may appear to some that many more women than men are affected by this addiction,** current statistics show that this is not true. The percentage of
20 men addicted to shopping is about the same as the percentage of women (around 5 percent).

[1]**activate:** cause something to start | [2]**high:** a feeling of being excited or full of energy

Like most addictions, a shopping addiction can cause serious problems. First of all, it is difficult for addicts. **Even though shopaholics enjoy the excitement**, they often feel depressed or guilty after a shopping trip. 25 **Spending more money than they have**, many shopaholics have financial problems. **As they spend**, they may lie to their families about their spending habits. These lies are almost always hurtful and can even destroy the family.

Fortunately, shopping addiction can be treated. **In order to change** 30 **their behavior**, shopping addicts must admit that they have a problem and then seek help. In addition, shopping addicts should always take a friend along **when they need to** buy something. Most shopping addicts only overspend **when they shop alone**.

While shopping is usually a harmless activity, an addiction 35 to shopping can cause financial and personal problems. Therefore, people should understand the signs of a shopping addiction **so that they can get help**. Shopping should be a constructive activity, not a destructive one.

B *Comprehension Check* Answer the questions.

1. Why aren't shopping addictions considered a serious problem by most people?
2. What problems can a shopping addiction lead to?
3. What are two ways in which shopaholics can treat their problem?

C *Notice* Find the sentences in the article and complete them. Then circle the meaning of the words.

1. _____ these people do not need more clothes or electronics, they keep buying them.
   a. The words introduce contrasting ideas.   b. The words give a reason.

2. _____ shopping may be seen as an amusing addiction, society does not always consider it a serious problem.
   a. The word introduces contrasting ideas.   b. The word gives a reason.

3. _____ shopaholics enjoy the excitement, they often feel depressed or guilty after a shopping trip.
   a. The words introduce contrasting ideas.   b. The words give a reason.

2 | Subordinators and Adverb Clauses

▶ Grammar Presentation

Adverb clauses show a relationship between ideas in two clauses. They begin with subordinators, such as *although* and *because*.

Although she enjoys wearing new clothes, *she doesn't enjoy shopping.*

Eric doesn't go shopping often ***because he doesn't like to spend money***.

2.1 Forming Adverb Clauses

a. An adverb clause has a subject and a verb, but it is a dependent clause. It is not a complete sentence.	MAIN CLAUSE DEPENDENT CLAUSE *She shops* ***because it makes her feel good***.
b. In general, use a comma when an adverb clause begins the sentence.	***Although I sometimes buy things I don't need,*** *I'm not a shopping addict.*

2.2 Using Adverb Clauses

a. Use *because* and *since* to give reasons. *Because* is more common.	***Because shopping is necessary***, *shopping addicts aren't easily recognized.* *Treatment is important for shopping addicts* ***since it is very difficult to overcome this problem on one's own***.
b. Use *although*, *even though*, and *though* to show a contrasting idea or something unexpected. *Although* is a little more formal. Use a comma with adverb clauses that include these subordinators, whether they begin or end the sentence.	***Even though shopping addicts enjoy shopping***, *they feel depressed afterward.* *She spends a lot on clothing,* ***though she doesn't make much money***.
c. Use *while* to show contrasting ideas. Use a comma whether the adverb clause begins or ends the sentence.	*Shopping addicts buy things they don't need,* ***while nonaddicts tend to buy mostly things they need***.
d. You can use *as*, *since*, *when*, and *while* in adverb clauses to express time relationships.	*It has been six weeks* ***since he went shopping***. ***While she was at the mall***, *she bought many useless things.*

▶ Grammar Application

Exercise 2.1 Adverb Clauses

Combine the sentences about shopping addiction. Use the subordinators in parentheses. Add commas when necessary. Sometimes more than one answer is possible.

1. We are surrounded by advertising messages. It is often difficult to avoid shopping. (since)

   Since we are surrounded by advertising messages, it is often difficult to avoid shopping.

2. Many people feel that it is patriotic to shop. Some politicians say that it is good for the economy. (because)

   _____

   _____

3. We may not need items. We sometimes want what others have. (even though)

   _____

   _____

4. Shopping addiction seems to be a recent problem. It has almost certainly existed for centuries. (although)

   _____

   _____

5. Addicts may shop to escape negative feelings. Normal people shop to buy things they need. (while)

   _____

   _____

6. Normal shoppers use the items they buy. Compulsive shoppers often do not use them. (while)

   _____

   _____

Exercise 2.2 More Adverb Clauses

A Complete the interview with a shopping addict. Rewrite each pair of sentences as one sentence. Use one of the subordinators in parentheses.

Jane   So, Claire, how did you know you were a shopping addict?

Claire   I saw a show on TV. I realized I was an addict. (when / since)

     1.   *When I saw a show on TV, I realized I was an addict.*

Jane   I understand that you're getting help.

Claire   Yes. My insurance pays for it. I was able to sign up for therapy. (because / although)

     2.   _____

Jane   Is your therapy helping?

Claire   Definitely. I've only been in therapy a short time. I'm feeling better already. (although / when)

     3.   _____

Jane   How are things different now?

Claire   I only buy what I really need. I'm spending much less money. (since / although)

     4.   _____

Jane   Describe a recent shopping trip.

Claire   I was at the mall yesterday. I only went to one store. (even though / since)

     5.   _____

     I had a list. I only bought things I truly needed. (since / while)

     6.   _____

Jane   Good for you! Thank you for sharing your story with us.

B 🔊 Listen to the interview and check your answers.

Exercise 2.3 Using Adverb Clauses

Group Work   What are some ways to avoid bad shopping habits? Write five sentences using adverb clauses. Use the ideas in the unit and your own ideas. Decide as a group which two ideas are the most effective and give reasons.

You should take a friend with you when you shop.

3 | Reducing Adverb Clauses

▶ Grammar Presentation

Sometimes you can reduce adverb clauses to *-ing* forms. The subject of the main clause must be the same as the subject of the adverb clause.

While he was shopping, he bought things he didn't need.
While shopping, he bought things he didn't need.

3.1 Reducing Adverb Clauses

In many cases, you can reduce adverb clauses. Omit the subject, and use the verb + *-ing*.

While he was shopping, he bought a jacket.
While shopping, he bought a jacket.

3.2 Reducing Clauses That Give Reasons

You can reduce clauses that give reasons when the verb is in the simple past, present perfect, or past perfect.

For the simple past, omit the subordinator and the subject, and use the verb + *-ing*.

Because he was cautious, he didn't spend much money.
Being cautious, he didn't spend much money.

For the present perfect and past perfect, change *have* to *having*. The *-ing* forms usually begin the sentences.

Since she has gotten help, she no longer shops so often.
Having gotten help, she no longer shops so often.

3.3 Reducing Time Clauses

a. You can reduce a time clause when the verb is in the present progressive or past progressive. Omit the subject and the form of *be*.

*You can save money **while you are going** to college.*
*You can save money **while going to college**.*
*While he **was shopping**, he bought a jacket.*
While shopping, he bought a jacket

b. You can also reduce a time clause with a verb in the simple present or simple past. Omit the subject, and use the verb + *-ing*.

*She started shopping at malls **before she realized that shopping was addictive**.*
*She started shopping at malls **before realizing that shopping was addictive**.*

▶ Grammar Application

Exercise 3.1 Reducing Clauses That Give Reasons

Complete the sentences about Mike and Eric, two hoarders.[1] Rewrite the reason clauses in parentheses as reduced clauses.

1. _Buying new things all the time_ , Mike filled his apartment with useless items.
   (because he bought new things all the time)

2. _____ , he took action.
   (because he understood that he had a problem)

3. _____ , he had no savings.
   (because he had spent so much money on clothes)

4. _____ , Eric is now able to keep his apartment
   (since he has received treatment)
   much cleaner.

5. _____ , he no longer feels anxious.
   (because he has worked with a therapist)

6. _____ , he no longer hoards useless items.
   (since he has gotten help)

[1]**hoarder:** a person who collects large supplies of things, usually more than he or she needs

Exercise 3.2 Reducing Time Clauses

Complete the sentences about a compulsive spender. Rewrite the time clauses in parentheses as reduced clauses.

1. _While shopping online_ , Amy was ecstatic.
   (while she was shopping online)

2. _____ , she was in an altered state.
   (while she was spending money)

3. Amy had spent over $30,000 _____ .
   (before she got treatment)

4. _____ , Amy decided to join Debtors
   (before she spent more money)
   Anonymous (DA).[1]

5. _____ , Amy learned how to budget.
   (after she joined DA)

6. She also got help with her credit _____ .
   (after she started DA)

7. Amy has changed her behavior _____ .
   (since she received treatment)

[1]**Debtors Anonymous (DA):** an organization that helps compulsive spenders

4 Subordinators to Express Purpose

▶ Grammar Presentation

Some subordinators can express a purpose.	*He got help for his shopping addiction **so that** he could feel better.* (= He got help for the purpose of feeling better.)

4.1 Using Subordinators to Express Purpose

a. Use *so* or *so that* to show a reason or purpose. Clauses with *so that* usually come after the main clause.	*People go to psychologists **so that** they can talk about their problems.* *I keep track of my money **so** I don't spend too much.*
b. You can also show a reason or purpose with *in order to* or *to* when the subject of the main clause and the adverb clause are the same. Do not repeat the subject.	*Shopping addicts buy things they don't need **to** feel good.* (= Shopping addicts buy things they don't need so that they feel good.) *Shopping addicts may get help **in order to** stop shopping.* (= Shopping addicts may get help so that they stop shopping.)

▶ Grammar Application

Exercise 4.1 Using Subordinators to Express Purpose

A Complete the sentences from the book *Consumer World*. Put the subordinators in parentheses in the right place in the sentences.

1. Psychologists have shown that we actually need very little ^*in order to* feel happy. (in order to)

2. Some people buy things feel good about themselves. (to)

3. Some people acquire things they have a sense of who they are. (so that)

4. It's also possible that people acquire things feel secure. (in order to)

5. They buy a lot feel that they are financially secure. (in order to)

6. They buy a lot they are prepared for any emergency. (so that)

7. Find out how little you really need, think about what you would do if you had to move. (to)

8. I think that have true peace of mind, you should have as little as possible. (in order to)

B *Group Work* Discuss the questions with your group. Use *in order to*, *so*, *so that*, and *to* in your discussion.

- Does owning things make people happy?

- What are some of the problems that owning things can cause?

- What do people have to do to be truly happy?

- What are some ways to live with less?

A In order to be truly happy, you should focus on people, not things.
B I agree, but to have a happy life, you need some possessions.

C Write sentences about your five best ideas in B. Use subordinators to express purpose.

In order to be truly happy, you should focus on people, not things.
Pretend you are moving so you can decide what to get rid of.

5 | Avoid Common Mistakes ⚠

1. Remember that *even though* is two words, not one.

  even though
I bought a computer bag ~~eventhough~~ I do not own a computer.

2. Use *even though*, not *even*, to create an adverb clause.

Even though
~~Even~~ it was late, the store was open.

3. Do not start a new sentence with *because*, *whereas*, or *although* when the clause refers to the previous sentence.

                store because
I returned the camera to the ~~store. Because~~ I did not really need it.

4. Remember to use the verb + *-ing* in reduced clauses after words like *after*, *before*, *while*, and *when*.

     watching
When ~~watch~~ ads on TV, some people feel a strong urge to buy the products.

Editing Task

Find and correct eight more mistakes in the paragraphs about addictions.

After ~~look~~ *looking* at research, we see clearly that alcohol and drug addictions are serious physical conditions. Psychologists are now considering adding shopping to the list. Eventhough these experts say that shopping is as addictive as drugs, I disagree that it should be considered a serious addiction.

5 People who argue that shopping is addictive have good reasons. While shop, many people get a good feeling. They like spending money even they may not need to buy anything. However, after go home, they feel regret. They have spent money on something they did not want or need. Because buying something makes them feel a sense of power.

10 However, after examine the situation of over-shopping closely, one can see that many people are victims of advertising. Even they may not plan to buy something, a powerful advertisement can change their mind. If people did not watch so much TV, they would not feel the urge to shop as strongly. In this way, shopping addiction differs from drug and alcohol addictions, which create a chemical change in the body that is 15 very difficult to resist.

Eventhough shopping too much is a serious problem, it should not be considered an addiction. If advertisements disappeared, society would not have this problem called shopping addiction.

6 Grammar for Writing ✏

Using Adverb Clauses to Give More Information About Main Clauses

Adverb clauses give more information about main clauses. Writers often use them to show contrasting ideas, reasons, or purposes. However, the main clause always contains the most important information. Read these examples:

Since having more than one credit card often leads to debt, financial advisers often advise people to cut up all but one credit card.

Some people are able to effectively use only one credit card even though they have many.

Recovering shopaholics should not carry credit cards with them so that they don't overspend.

A credit card feels like an infinite amount of money, while a wallet full of cash does not.

Pre-writing Task

1 Read the paragraph below. Why don't you need money for the kind of shopping that the writer describes?

Shopping for Free

Although shopping usually requires money, it has not always, and it does not have to now. In the past, instead of paying for things that they needed with money, people swapped skills and homemade items so that they could "buy" the things they wanted or needed. For example, a baker might trade freshly baked bread for coal or wood for

5 the bakery oven. This was called bartering, and it used to be done between neighbors and friends. The Internet has helped bring back this form of shopping, but this time with a modern twist. Since the Internet is worldwide, it is no longer necessary to find someone in your community to barter with. Now, you can barter with people all over the world. Bartering on the Internet not only saves people money but also solves the

10 problem of how to get rid of unwanted things without creating more garbage. Instead of throwing things away, you can find homes for the things you no longer want or need. Because there are so many websites that make this an easy thing to do, more and more people are participating. Some websites require a token membership fee of a dollar or two, while others simply require that you have something to give away before you can

15 "buy" something for yourself. Anyone can do this, provided that they can afford postage

to send the things they are giving away. After you have made a bartering agreement with someone, all you have to do is sit back and wait for the things you have ordered to arrive. Internet bartering sites have made shopping both easy and painless, and they could even be helpful for shopaholics.

2 Read the paragraph again. Underline the subordinators and the adverb clauses that follow. Notice that in each sentence, the most important information is in the main clause. Double underline the subordinators that show contrasting ideas. Put a check (✓) over the subordinators that signal reason or cause and effect. Put an ✗ over the subordinator that expresses purpose.

Writing Task

1 *Write*   Use the paragraph in the Pre-writing Task to help you write about some aspect of consumerism. You can write about one of these topics or use your own ideas.

- garage sales
- shopping on the Internet
- shopping on TV
- shopping at thrift stores
- using what you have instead of buying more

2 *Self-Edit*   Use the editing tips to improve your paragraph. Make any necessary changes.

1. Did you use adverb clauses with subordinators to modify main clauses?
2. Did you put the most important information in the main clause?
3. Did you use the correct subordinators to show cause-and-effect relationships, express purpose, show reasons, or show contrasting or opposite ideas?
4. Did you avoid the mistakes in the Avoid Common Mistakes chart on page 374?

1 | Grammar in the Real World

A How are video games today different from the games of 5 or 10 years ago? Read the web article about a kind of animation technology that is being used in games today. How has it changed the look of video games?

 ## *Motion Capture Technology*

Computer animation was first introduced in the late 1970s; **however**, today's animation is much more realistic than it was then. While the first animated video game characters moved in only two
5 directions, today's animated game heroes can jump, kick, and spin. The use of sensors[1] to record these movements is called motion capture, or "mocap."

Because of the realism that mocap gives its animated figures, a common use for mocap is in
10 video games. Video game creators use real people to help create their characters. With sports video games, for example, famous athletes are used **instead of** actors. **Consequently,** the games can feature each athlete's unique moves. How does it work? **First**, the athlete puts on a tight suit that has special markers[2] all over it. **Next**, he or she performs a sequence of actions. Video cameras record these
15 movements using the markers. **Finally**, digital information is collected from the markers and the video. This information is used to create the movements of the video character.

Another common use of mocap is in movies. *Avatar*, an epic fantasy adventure movie, used mocap to create its human-like characters. It also featured a computer-generated 3D world. **Despite** *Avatar*'s success, not all movie studios want to use mocap. **Besides**
20 **being** very expensive, mocap cannot copy every motion. **As a result**, studios must add other forms of animation.

[1]**sensor:** a device that discovers and reacts to changes in such things as movement, heat, and light | [2]**marker:** a small, reflective dot that is taped to a figure

In addition to these uses, motion capture technology is used in medicine. **For instance**, doctors have patients in mocap suits walk on treadmills. The mocap information helps doctors diagnose problems such as weak bones. **Furthermore**,
25 mocap can be used in training for jobs such as firefighting. New firefighters can use mocap games to practice moving through virtual[3] house fires. **Instead of** taking risks in a real setting, they can practice in a virtual reality.

Despite the expense, mocap technology is becoming more popular in many different areas. **Due to** its success so far, who knows what it will be used
30 for next?

[3]**virtual:** created by a computer

B *Comprehension Check* Answer the questions.

1. What is "mocap"?
2. In what areas is mocap used?
3. Why isn't mocap used more often in movies and video games?

C *Notice* Match the words in bold with their meaning.

1. **Because of** the realism that mocap gives its animated figures, a common use for mocap is in video games. _____

2. **Furthermore**, mocap can be used in training for jobs such as firefighting. _____

3. **Despite** the expense, mocap technology is becoming more popular in many different areas. _____

a. introduces additional information

b. introduces a reason

c. introduces contrasting information

2 | Connecting Information with Prepositions and Prepositional Phrases

▶ Grammar Presentation

Some prepositions and prepositional phrases can connect information to an independent clause. Like subordinators, these prepositions can be used to add information, give reasons, show contrasts, present alternatives, or give exceptions.	*Video games look realistic today **because of** improvements in computer animation.* * **Despite** the popularity of animation, most people prefer to watch live-action movies.*

2.1 Using Prepositions and Prepositional Phrases to Connect Ideas

a. One-word prepositions, such as *besides* and *despite*, and multi-word prepositions, such as *as well as*, *because of*, *in addition to*, and *in spite of*, are followed by nouns, noun phrases, or gerunds.	**Besides** <u>being</u> very expensive, animated movies can take a long time to produce. Some animated movies are also popular with adults **in spite of** <u>their appeal</u> to kids.
b. Prepositional phrases, like adverb clauses, can come before or after the main clause. Use a comma when the prepositional phrase comes first.	Video games usually use athletes **instead of actors**. **Instead of actors,** video games usually use athletes.

2.2 Meanings of Prepositions Used to Connect Ideas

a. Use *as well as*, *besides*, and *in addition to* to emphasize another idea.	I enjoy animated movies **as well as** live-action movies. This TV has 3D technology **in addition to** high definition. **Besides** being a talented director, he is an excellent actor.
b. Use *as a result of*, *because of*, and *due to* to give reasons.	**Because of** the high cost of tickets, many people don't go to the movies. **As a result of** voters' opinions, the director was nominated for an Academy Award. The movie's appeal is **due to** its special effects.
c. Use *instead of* to give alternatives.	Let's see a drama **instead of** a comedy. **Instead of** going out, they watched TV at home.
d. Use *except* or *except for* to give exceptions. When the main clause is a negative statement, you can also use *besides* to mean "except for."	This composer wrote the music for all the Alien Adventures movies **except** the first one. **Except for** their parents, the audience was mostly children. **Besides** the parents of the children, there weren't any adults in the audience.
e. Use *despite* and *in spite of* to show contrasting ideas.	**Despite** being made for children, this movie is enjoyed by adults. **In spite of** its short length, the movie was very powerful.

▶ Grammar Application

Exercise 2.1 Prepositional Phrases to Connect Ideas

Complete the paragraphs about one use of motion capture technology. Use the words in the box. Sometimes more than one answer is possible.

as well as	because of	due to	in addition to	instead of	~~in spite of~~

    In spite of the high cost of mocap, its use is expanding. For example, Ford
       (1)
Motor Company, a car manufacturer, is using mocap technology to create digital

humans.[1] _____ their human-like behavior, digital humans are used
           (2)
to study people's behavior in cars. _____ studying driver behavior,
                (3)
engineers are also studying ways to make passengers feel more comfortable. For example,

_____ using a real human, the company uses a short digital female to test
     (4)
a short driver's ability to reach the gas pedal.

    Motion capture technology helps the company improve worker safety

_____ driver safety. _____ the technology's ability to replicate
   (5)   (6)
workers' movements, the company has reduced the number of assembly line accidents.

[1]**digital human:** an electronic representation of a person

Exercise 2.2 More Prepositional Phrases to Connect Ideas

Complete the sentences about using mocap technology to help athletes recover from injuries and improve their speed. Circle the correct prepositions.

1. (**In addition to**)/ **Because of** filmmakers, physical therapists are using motion capture technology to help injured athletes.

2. **As a result of / Instead of** an injury, athletes could lose their careers.

3. An athlete's career could be destroyed **because of / instead of** injuries.

4. Analyzing an injury without motion capture technology is not always accurate, **due to / besides** being time-consuming.

5. With motion capture technology, therapists accurately see the problem **in spite of / instead of** guessing where the problem is.

6. The success of motion capture technology with Olympic athletes is **in spite of / due to** its ability to analyze the athletes' movements at high speeds.

7. **Except for / Despite** the success of motion capture technology with athletes, it cannot replace the hours of practice that athletes need to succeed.

Exercise 2.3 Using Prepositional Phrases to Connect Ideas

A Combine the ideas about the use of technology in health care. Use the prepositions in parentheses and the underlined words to create prepositional phrases.

1. Some hospitals are not using <u>paper medical records</u>. They are using electronic medical records. (instead of)

   Instead of paper medical records, some hospitals are using electronic records.

2. Everyone has <u>quick access to your records</u>. Doctors can share information with each other more easily. (Due to)

   _____

3. There are <u>many advantages to electronic records</u>. Some doctors still have serious concerns. (in spite of)

   _____

4. There should be <u>accurate information in the records</u>. The information could contain data input errors. (instead of)

   _____

5. There will be <u>a lot of security</u>. Hackers could still steal information from hospitals. (despite)

   _____

B *Group Work* Choose an area that could change because of technology. Use one of the ideas below or your own idea. As a group, write statements that explain the technology, its effects, and the possible advantages and disadvantages of using it. Use prepositional phrases.

- high speed trains
- online learning
- use of cell phones instead of money to purchase products

3 | Connecting Information with Transition Words

▶ Grammar Presentation

Transition words are words or phrases that connect ideas between sentences. They are frequently used in academic writing and formal situations.

*It's important not to judge a movie's quality by whether it is animated or not. **Furthermore,** you should not assume that a movie with human actors is superior to an animated movie.*

3.1 Using Transition Words

a. Transition words join the ideas in two sentences.	Movie stars often do the voices in animated movies. **However**, their fans don't always recognize them.
Coordinating conjunctions (*but*, etc.), subordinators (*although*, etc.), and prepositions (*in spite of*, etc.) combine two different sentences into one new sentence.	Music in movies is very important for setting the tone, **but** most people don't pay attention to it. **Although** animated movies sometimes win the best picture award, they also have their own category. **In spite of** having a lot of famous actors, the movie did not get very good reviews.
b. Most transition words occur at the beginning of the second sentence and are followed by a comma. You can also use a semicolon between the two sentences that you combine.	The studio executives choose a script. **After that**, they select a director. She is a very talented artist**; moreover**, her use of color is exceptional.
Many – but not all – transition words can go in the middle of the sentence or at the end. When the transition word comes at the end, it is preceded by a comma.	Most people**, however**, associate animation with movies. Most people associate animation with movies**, however**.
c. The short transition words *so*, *then*, and *also* are often used without a comma. *So* is used at the beginning of a sentence only in informal writing. Use more formal transition words with the same meanings in academic writing: *afterward*, *in addition*, *therefore*.	My daughter enjoys animated movies a lot. **So** we take her to them pretty often. **Then** she usually wants to stop for a snack on the way home. I am **also** usually hungry after a long movie. Children often enjoy animated movies. **Therefore**, their parents often take them to the movies. **Afterward**, it is not unusual to stop for something to eat. **In addition**, parents often buy a book or souvenir connected to the movie for their children.

3.2 Meanings of Transition Words

a. To show a sequence or the order of events or ideas, use *first*, *second*, *then*, *next*, *after that*, and *finally*.	How do animators capture an athlete's movement? **First**, the athlete puts on a special suit. **Then** the athlete performs the action. **Next**, the computer collects digital information.
b. To summarize ideas, use *in conclusion*, *to conclude*, and *to summarize*.	**In conclusion**, technological innovations will change many fields, including animation.
c. To give additional information, use *also*, *furthermore*, *in addition*, and *moreover*.	Animation is used in movies, video games, and other entertainment industries. **In addition**, it is used in sports medicine.

3.2 Meanings of Transition Words *(continued)*

d. To give alternatives, use *instead*.	*I had expected the movie to be boring.* **Instead**, *I thought it was quite entertaining.*
e. To give contrasting ideas, use *on the other hand* and *in contrast*.	*The story was not very original.* **On the other hand**, *the animation was impressive.*
f. To give a result, use *as a result, consequently, therefore,* and *thus*.	*The game was designed with animation.* **Therefore**, *the characters were very lifelike.*
g. To give examples, use *for example* or *for instance*.	*Many animated movies are very popular.* **For example**, *Kung Fu Panda and* Shrek *were huge box office hits.*

Data from the Real World

The most common transition words in writing are:	The most common transition words in conversation are:
however, so, then, therefore, thus	*anyway, so, then, though*

▶ Grammar Application

Exercise 3.1 Transition Words to Show Sequence

A *Pair Work* Look at the steps involved in computer game design. Can you put them in the correct order? Make guesses with your partner and try to number the steps in order from 1 to 6.

_____ a. Make a prototype (a model or "first draft") of the game and test it.

_____ b. Work with the marketing team to get the game ready to sell.

___1___ c. Decide on the theme and environment of the game.

_____ d. Do research on the theme.

_____ e. Figure out the goal of the game and the rules.

_____ f. Make any necessary changes to the game.

B ◀)) Now listen to a game designer describing her job. Were your answers correct?

C 🔊 Listen again and complete the sentences. Use the sequence words in the box. Add commas when necessary.

after that	finally	first	next	second	then

1. _____*First,*_____ I decide on an overall concept for a game.
2. _____ I figure out the goal of the game and the rules.
3. _____ I do research on the theme.
4. _____ I use software to make a prototype of the game.
5. _____ I go back to the computer and make any necessary changes.
6. _____ I work with the marketing people.

Exercise 3.2 Transition Words for Academic Writing

Complete the paragraph about the differences between computer animation and traditional animation. Circle the correct transition words.

Computer-generated animation (CGA) is very popular today. The spectacular effects of CGA in big-budget movies impress many people. **Therefore /(However)**, in my opinion, CGA is not as pleasant to look at as
(1)
traditional animation (TA). **First / Afterward**, CGA does not require the
(2)
same skill as TA. Traditional animators draw by hand, and the resulting images look complex and rich in style. **Instead / To summarize**,
(3)
computer animators use software to produce images. These images often have a cold, hard look to them. **To conclude / Furthermore**, with CGA,
(4)
objects are often overly bright. This adds to the unnaturalness of their appearance. **In contrast / Thus**, the images from TA are often soft
(5)
and appear more natural. **In conclusion / Moreover**, TA produces
(6)
better-looking images that have more style as well as a lifelike appearance;
on the other hand, / therefore, it is better than CGA.
(7)

Computer-Generated
Animation

Traditional
Animation

Exercise 3.3 Using Transition Words

A Look at the brainstorming notes a student made for a paragraph comparing two movies. Use the words to write sentences to summarize the ideas. Use the notes to help you.

War of the Aliens	The Magical Forest
excellent computer graphics	poor animation
dull plot[1]	interesting story
unappealing characters	likeable characters
bad dialog	good dialog

[1]**plot:** story

1. excellent computer graphics / in contrast / poor animation

   War of the Aliens had excellent computer graphics. In contrast, The Magical Forest had poor animation.

2. excellent computer graphics / however / dull plot

   _____

3. furthermore / unappealing characters

   _____

4. on the other hand / interesting story

   _____

5. in addition / likeable characters

   _____

6. moreover / good dialog

   _____

7. in contrast / bad dialog

   _____

8. in conclusion / a better movie than

   _____

B *Over to You* Think of two movies you have seen that have animation or special effects. Which one was better? Why? Write four to six sentences comparing the two movies. Use transitions to add ideas and show contrasts.

Cowboys in Space *was very popular.* On the other hand, Cowboys in Space II *didn't do very well.*

4 Avoid Common Mistakes ⚠

1. The prepositional expressions *as well as*, *in spite of*, *despite*, and *in addition to* are followed by a noun phrase or a gerund, not a subject + verb.

the high costs
Despite ~~the costs are high~~, 3D TVs are becoming very popular.

using
The filmmakers used mocap in addition to ~~they used~~ digital technology.

2. Use *on the other hand*, not *in the other hand*, when contrasting points of view.

on
The movie industry has many career opportunities; ~~in~~ the other hand, it is very competitive.

Editing Task

Find and correct four more mistakes in the paragraph about the filmmaking industry.

the slow economy
Filmmaking is a durable industry. Despite ~~the economy is slow~~, the movie industry is doing well. People always seem to find money for entertainment. As a result, movie production companies often hire people because it takes many professionals to create a movie. In addition to they hire actors and directors, they hire tens of thousands of other
5   professionals that are not well known – for example, grips (people who set up and tear down the sets), production assistants, and camera operators. The jobs can be exciting and challenging; in the other hand, some can be low paying. As with most other careers, it is necessary to work hard and be ambitious to succeed. The work can also be especially tough for production crews – for example, camera operators, production
10 assistants, and makeup artists – who work up to 18 hours a day. Despite they have long hours, these jobs can be difficult to find because there is a lot of competition for them. In general, moviemaking is seen as a glamorous profession, and some people want to be a part of that glamour more than anything else. Movies often require celebrities and artists; in the other hand, they also rely on many people with other skills. It is a growing
15 industry, too. The Bureau of Labor Statistics states that employment opportunities for people in the filmmaking industry will increase 14 percent between 2008 and 2018. In short, this industry is competitive, but young people should pursue it if they have an interest in movies.

5 Grammar for Writing ✏️

Using Prepositions and Transition Words to Support an Argument

Writers often need to argue their opinions in persuasive writing. Good arguments in academic writing have logic that is easy for the reader to follow. Prepositions and transition words help to clarify the steps in the writer's logic as they link ideas together in meaningful relationships. Read this example paragraph:

> *In the future, I think all special effects will be computer-generated. First, audiences seem to prefer the effects from computer-generated animation. Second, computer-generated effects are cheaper due to their not requiring real life models of the sets. Also, it's safer to use them than to use actors and stuntmen. Therefore, movies made with this technology are likely to make more money.*

Pre-writing Task

1 Read the paragraph below. What is the writer's opinion about 3D technology?

Is 3D Technology Here to Stay?

Movies that are in 3D can be a lot of fun and are becoming much more common. However, the technology should not be used too much because it is not good for all types of movies. First, 3D technology can be good for adventure, science fiction, and animated movies. However, it does not seem to work well for serious dramas and art

5 films, where the plot and the characters are very important. Instead of getting involved in the plot and the characters, people tend to watch the special effects of the 3D technology when they watch a 3D movie. As a result, the plot and characters fade in importance. Thus, the 3D technology distracts the audience from the more important elements of the movie. Second, many people cannot watch 3D movies for health

10 reasons. Some people cannot physically see 3D technology because of an eye problem. There are others who get headaches or feel nauseated when they watch 3D movies. Third, tickets for 3D movies are more expensive than tickets for regular movies. If more movies are made with 3D technology, people who do not want to spend a lot of money may have fewer movie choices. As a result, people may go out to the movies less often. If

15 moviemakers start making more 3D movies, they will be making movies that entertain only rather than enrich, which will be a terrible loss for the art of moviemaking. In conclusion, I hope that 3D technology is used primarily for animated or science-fiction movies, and not for all types of movies.

2 Read the paragraph again. Circle the prepositions and transition words that are used to link ideas. Underline the prepositions and transition words that begin sentences. Notice how they link to the information in the previous sentences.

Writing Task

1 *Write* Use the paragraph in the Pre-writing Task to help you write about your opinion of some aspect of technology in entertainment. You can write about one of these topics or use your own ideas.

- 3D technology on TVs
- HD TV
- satellite radio

- video gaming
- video streaming on TV
- watching TV shows on the computer

2 *Self-Edit* Use the editing tips to improve your paragraph. Make any necessary changes.

1. Did you use prepositions, prepositional phrases, or transition words to show the relationships among ideas?
2. Did you add prepositions, prepositional phrases, or transition words to clarify the logic in your paragraph?
3. Did you avoid the mistakes in the Avoid Common Mistakes chart on page 387?

Appendices

1. Irregular Verbs

Base Form	Simple Past	Past Participle	Base Form	Simple Past	Past Participle
be	was / were	been	hide	hid	hidden
become	became	become	hit	hit	hit
begin	began	begun	hold	held	held
bite	bit	bitten	hurt	hurt	hurt
blow	blew	blown	keep	kept	kept
break	broke	broken	know	knew	known
bring	brought	brought	leave	left	left
build	built	built	lose	lost	lost
buy	bought	bought	make	made	made
catch	caught	caught	meet	met	met
choose	chose	chosen	pay	paid	paid
come	came	come	put	put	put
cost	cost	cost	read	read	read
cut	cut	cut	ride	rode	ridden
do	did	done	run	ran	run
draw	drew	drawn	say	said	said
drink	drank	drunk	see	saw	seen
drive	drove	driven	sell	sold	sold
eat	ate	eaten	send	sent	sent
fall	fell	fallen	set	set	set
feed	fed	fed	shake	shook	shaken
feel	felt	felt	show	showed	shown
fight	fought	fought	shut	shut	shut
find	found	found	sing	sang	sung
fly	flew	flown	sit	sat	sat
forget	forgot	forgotten	sleep	slept	slept
forgive	forgave	forgiven	speak	spoke	spoken
get	got	gotten	spend	spent	spent
give	gave	given	stand	stood	stood
go	went	gone	steal	stole	stolen
grow	grew	grown	swim	swam	swum
have	had	had	take	took	taken
hear	heard	heard	teach	taught	taught

Base Form	Simple Past	Past Participle	Base Form	Simple Past	Past Participle
tell	told	told	wake	woke	woken
think	thought	thought	wear	wore	worn
throw	threw	thrown	win	won	won
understand	understood	understood	write	wrote	written

2. Stative (Non-Action) Verbs

Stative verbs do not describe actions. They describe states or situations. Stative verbs are not usually used in the progressive. Some are occasionally used in the present progressive, but often with a different meaning.

Research shows that the 25 most common stative verbs in spoken and written English are:

agree	dislike	hope	love	see
believe	expect	hurt	need	seem
care (about)	hate	know	notice	think
cost	have	like	own	understand
disagree	hear	look like	prefer	want

Other stative verbs:

appear	deserve	mean	smell
be	feel	owe	sound
belong	forgive	recognize	taste
concern	look	remember	weigh
contain	matter		

Stative verbs that also have action meanings:

be	have	look	taste
expect	hear	see	think
feel	hope	smell	weigh

Using the present progressive form of these verbs changes the meaning to an action.
*Can you **see** the red car?   (= use your eyes to be aware of something)*
*I**'m seeing** an old friend tomorrow.   (= meeting someone)*
*I **think** you're right.   (= believe)*
*Dina **is thinking** of taking a vacation soon.   (= considering)*
*I **have** two sisters.   (= be related to)*
*We**'re having** eggs for breakfast. (= eating)*
*He **is** in his first year of college.   (= exist)*
*She **is being** difficult.   (= act)*

3. Modals and Modal-like Expressions

Modals are helper verbs. Most modals have multiple meanings.

Function	Modal or Modal-like Expression	Time	Example
Advice less strong	could *Podrías* → might (not) *podría* →	present, future	He **could** do some puzzles to improve his memory. You **might** try some tips on improving your memory.
stronger	ought to *debería* should (not) "	present, future	We **ought to** take a memory class next month. Greg **should** improve his memory.
	had better (not) *tener mejor*	present, future	You**'d better** pay attention now.
Past Advice, Regret, or Criticism	ought to have should (not) have	past	She **ought to have** tried harder to improve her memory. You **should have** made an effort to improve your memory. He **shouldn't have** taken that difficult class.
Permission	can (not) may (not)	present, future	You **can** register for the class next week. You **may not** register after the first class.
	could (not)	past	You **could** ask questions during the lecture yesterday, but you **could not** leave the room.
formal →	be (not) allowed to be (not) permitted to	past, present, future	He **was not allowed to** talk during the test, but he **was allowed to** use his books. Students **will not be permitted to** refer to notes during examinations.
Necessity / Obligation	have to need to be required to be supposed to	past, present, future	I **have to** study tonight. She **needs to** quit her stressful job. You **won't be required to** take a test. He **is supposed to** tell you his decision tomorrow.
	must (not)	present, future	You **must** have experience for this job.
Obligation not to / Prohibition	must not be not supposed to	present, future	You **must not** talk during the exam. Students **are not supposed to** take their books into the exam room.

Modals and Modal-like Expressions *(continued)*

Function	Modal or Modal-like Expression	Time	Example
Lack of Necessity / Choices or Options	*not have to* *not need to* *be not required to*	past, present, future	You **didn't have to** bring your notes. You **don't need to** study tonight. You **are not required to** bring your books.
Ability	*can (not)*	present, future	We **can** meet the professor at noon tomorrow.
	could (not)	past	I **could** understand the lecture, but I **could not** remember it.
	be (not) able to	past, present, future	She **wasn't able to** see very well from her seat.
	could have	past	I **could have** done well on that memory test.
	could not have	past	I **couldn't have** taken the test yesterday. I was in another state!
Probability	*can't* *could (not)* *(not) have to* *must (not)*	present	Hackers **can't** be interested in my data. He **could** be online now. She **has to** be at work right now. He **must not** be worried about data security.
	may (not) *might (not)* *ought to* *should (not)*	present, future	Your computer **may** be at risk of hacking. That software **might not** be good enough. That password **ought to** be strong enough. It **shouldn't** be difficult to find good software.
	could *will (not)*	future	The company **could** start using cloud computing next month. My sister **will** probably get a new computer soon.
	can't have *could (not) have* *may (not) have* *might (not) have* *must (not) have*	past	I **can't have** entered the wrong password! The expert **could not have** given you good advice. The company **may have** been careless with security. I **might have** written the wrong password down. Someone **must have** stolen all the passwords.

A4

4. Noncount Nouns and Measurement Words to Make Noncount Nouns Countable

Category of noncount noun	Noun Examples	Measurement Words and Expressions
Abstract concepts	courage, luck, space, time	a bit of, a kind of *You had **a bit of** luck, didn't you?*
Activities and sports	dancing, exercise, swimming, tennis, yoga	a game of, a session of *They played **two games of** tennis.*
Diseases and health conditions	arthritis, cancer, depression, diabetes, obesity	a kind of, a type of *She has **a type of** diabetes called Type 2.*
Elements and gases	gold, hydrogen, oxygen, silver	a bar of, a container of, a piece of, a tank of *We have **tanks of** oxygen in the storage room.*
Foods	beef, broccoli, cheese, rice	a bottle of, a box of, a bunch of, a can of, a grain of, a head of, a loaf of, a package of, a piece of, a pinch of, a serving of, a slice of, a wedge of *I'll take **a serving of** rice and beef.*
Liquids	coffee, gasoline, oil, tea	a bottle of, a cup of, a gallon of, a glass of, a quart of *I would like **a cup of** tea.*
Natural phenomena	electricity, rain, sun, thunder	a bolt of, a drop of, a ray of *There hasn't been **a drop of** rain for three months.*
Particles	pepper, salt, sand, sugar	a grain of, a pinch of *My food needs **a pinch of** salt.*
Subjects and areas of work	construction, economics, genetics, geology, medicine, nursing	an area of, a branch of, a field of, a type of *There are a lot of specialty areas in **the field of** medicine.*
Miscellaneous	clothing, equipment, furniture, news	an article of, a piece of *I need **a piece of** furniture to go in that empty corner.*

5. Order of Adjectives Before Nouns

When you use two (or more) adjectives before a noun, use the order in the chart below.

Opinion	Size	Quality	Age	Shape	Color	Origin	Material	Nouns as Adjectives
beautiful	big	cold	ancient	oval	black	American	cotton	computer
comfortable	fat	free	antique	rectangular	blue	Canadian	glass	evening
delicious	huge	heavy	new	round	gold	Chinese	gold	government
expensive	large	hot	old	square	green	European	leather	rose
interesting	long	safe	young	triangular	orange	Japanese	metal	safety
nice	short				purple	Mexican	paper	software
pretty	small				red	Peruvian	plastic	summer
rare	tall				silver	Thai	silk	training
reasonable	thin				yellow		silver	
shocking	wide				white		stone	
special							wooden	
ugly							woolen	
unique								

Examples:

*That was a **delicious green Canadian** apple!* (*opinion before color before origin*)

*I saw the **shocking government** report on nutrition.* (*opinion before noun as adjective*)

*Wei got a **small oval glass** table.* (*size before shape before material*)

6. Verbs That Can Be Used Reflexively

allow oneself	challenge oneself	hurt oneself	remind oneself
amuse oneself	congratulate oneself	imagine oneself	see oneself
ask oneself	cut oneself	introduce oneself	take care of
be hard on oneself	dry oneself	keep oneself (busy)	talk to oneself
be oneself	enjoy oneself	kill oneself	teach oneself
be pleased with oneself	feel sorry for oneself	look after oneself	tell oneself
be proud of oneself	forgive oneself	look at oneself	treat oneself
behave oneself	get oneself	prepare oneself	
believe in oneself	give oneself	pride oneself on	
blame oneself	help oneself	push oneself	

7. Verbs Followed by <u>Gerunds</u> Only

admit	keep (= *continue*)
avoid	mind (= *object to*)
consider	miss
delay	postpone
defend	practice
deny	propose
discuss	quit
enjoy	recall (= *remember*)
finish	risk
imagine	suggest
involve	understand

[handwritten margin notes: HW; two forms ← I. enjoy doing it or I enjoy to do it]

8. Verbs Followed by <u>Infinitives</u> Only

[handwritten: + to + sn]

afford	help	pretend
agree	hesitate	promise
arrange	hope	refuse
ask	hurry	request
attempt	intend	seem
choose	learn	struggle
consent	manage	tend (= *be likely*)
decide	need	threaten
demand	neglect	volunteer
deserve	offer	wait
expect	pay	want
fail	plan	wish
forget	prepare	would like

[handwritten: I want to do it]

9. Verbs Followed by Gerunds or Infinitives

begin	like	regret*
continue	love	start
forget*	prefer	stop*
get	remember*	try*
hate		

*These verbs can be followed by a gerund or an infinitive, with a difference in meaning.

10. Expressions with Gerunds

Use a gerund after certain fixed verb expressions.	
Verb expressions spend time / spend money waste time / waste money have trouble / have difficulty / have a difficult time	*I **spent time helping** in the library.* *Don't **waste time complaining**.* *She **had trouble finishing** her degree.*
Use a gerund after certain fixed noun + preposition expressions.	
Noun + preposition expressions an excuse for in favor of an interest in a reason for	*I have **an excuse for not doing** my homework.* *Who is **in favor of not admitting** him?* *He has **an interest in getting** a scholarship.* *He has **a reason for choosing** this school.*

11. Verbs + Objects + Infinitives

advise	force	remind	ask*
allow	get	request	choose*
cause	hire	require	expect*
challenge	invite	teach	help*
convince	order	tell	need*
enable	permit	urge	pay*
encourage	persuade	warn	promise*
forbid			want*
			wish*

* These verbs can be followed by an object + infinitive or an infinitive only, with a difference in meaning.
Examples: *My boss **advised me to go** back to school.* *They **urged the advertisers not to surprise** people.* *My department **chose* Sally to create** the new ads.* *My department **chose* to create** the new ads.*

12. *Be* + Adjectives + Infinitives

be afraid	be delighted	be encouraged	be lucky	be sad
be amazed	be depressed	be excited	be necessary	be shocked
be angry	be determined	be fortunate	be pleased	be sorry
be anxious	be difficult	be fun	be proud	be surprised
be ashamed	be easy	be happy	be ready	be upset
be curious	be embarrassed	be likely	be relieved	be willing

13. Verbs + Prepositions

Verb + *about*	Verb + *by*	Verb + *of*	Verb + *to*
ask about	be affected by	be afraid of	admit to
care about	be raised by	approve of	belong to
complain about	Verb + *for*	be aware of	confess to
be excited about	apologize for	consist of	listen to
find out about	apply for	dream of	look forward to
forget about	ask for	be guilty of	refer to
hear about	care for	hear of	talk to
know about	look for	know of	be used to
learn about	pay for	take care of	Verb + *with*
read about	be responsible for	think of	agree with
see about	wait for	✳ be warned of- *about*	argue with
talk about	Verb + *from*	Verb + *on*	bother with
think about	graduate from	concentrate on	deal with
worry about	Verb + *in*	count on	start with
be worried about	believe in	decide on	work with
Verb + *against*	find in	depend on	
advise against	include in	insist on	
decide against	be interested in	keep on	
Verb + *at*	involve in	plan on	
look at	result in	rely on	
smile at	show in		
be successful at	succeed in		
	use in		

14. Adjectives + Prepositions

Adjective + *about*	Adjective + *by*	Adjective + *in*	Adjective + *to*
concerned about	amazed by	high in	accustomed to
excited about	bored by	interested in	due to
happy about	surprised by	low in	similar to
nervous about	Adjective + *for*	Adjective + *of*	Adjective + *with*
pleased about	bad for	accused of	bored with
sad about	good for	afraid of	content with
sorry about	ready for	ashamed of	familiar with
surprised about	responsible for	aware of	good with
upset about	Adjective + *from*	capable of	satisfied with
worried about	different from	careful of	wrong with
Adjective + *at*	safe from	full of	
amazed at	separate from	guilty of	
angry at		sick of	
bad at		tired of	
good at		warned of	
− successful at			
surprised at			

15. Verbs and Fixed Expressions that Introduce Indirect Questions

Do you have any idea…?	I'd like to know…	I don't know…
Can you tell me…?	I wonder / I'm wondering…	I'm not sure…
Do you know…?	I want to understand…	I can't imagine…
Do you remember…?	Let's find out…	We don't understand…
Could you explain…?	Let's ask…	It doesn't say…
Would you show me…?	We need to know…	I can't believe…

16. Tense Shifting in Indirect Speech

Direct Speech	Indirect (Reported) Speech
simple present *She said, "The boss **is** angry."*	**simple past** *She **said** (that) the boss **was** angry.*
present progressive *He said, "She **is enjoying** the work."*	**past progressive** *He **said** (that) she **was enjoying** the work.*
simple past *They said, "The store **closed** last year."*	**past perfect** *They **said** (that) the store **had closed** last year.*
present perfect *The manager said, "The group **has done** good work."*	**past perfect** *The manager **said** (that) the group **had done** good work.*
will *He said, "The department **will add** three new managers."*	**would** *He **said** (that) the department **would add** three new managers.*
be going to *She said, "They **are going to hire** more people soon."*	**be going to** (past form) *She **said** (that) they **were going to hire** more people soon.*
can *The teacher said, "The students **can work** harder."*	**could** *The teacher **said** (that) the students **could work** harder.*
may *Their manager said, "Money **may not be** very important to them."*	**might** *Their manager **said** (that) money **might not be** very important to them.*

* Note: *should, might, ought to,* and *could* do not change forms.

17. Reporting Verbs

Questions	Statements				Commands and Requests	
ask inquire question	admit announce assert assure claim comment complain confess	convince exclaim explain find indicate inform mention note	notify observe promise remark remind reply report shout	show state suggest swear yell	advise ask command demand order	request say tell urge warn

18. Passive Forms

	Active	Passive
present progressive	People are speaking English at the meeting.	English is being spoken at the meeting.
simple present	People speak English at the meeting.	English is spoken at the meeting.
simple past	People spoke English at the meeting.	English was spoken at the meeting.
past progressive	People were speaking English at the meeting.	English was being spoken at the meeting.
present perfect	People have spoken English at the meeting.	English has been spoken at the meeting.
past perfect	People had been speaking English at the meeting.	English had been spoken at the meeting.
simple future	People will speak English at the meeting.	English will be spoken at the meeting.
future perfect	People will have spoken English at the meeting.	English will have been spoken at the meeting.
***be going to* (future)**	People are going to speak English at the meeting.	English is going to be spoken at the meeting.
Questions	Do people speak English at the meeting? Did people speak English at the meeting? Have people spoken English at the meeting?	Is English spoken at the meeting? Was English spoken at the meeting? Has English been spoken at the meeting?

19. Relative Clauses

	Identifying	Nonidentifying
Subject Relative Clauses	Many people **who / that support the environment** recycle.	My sister, **who lives in Maine**, loves being outside.
	Electricity **that / which saves energy** is a good thing.	People power, **which is a way to create energy**, is popular.
	They are the scientists **whose research has won awards**.	Brad Pitt, **whose movies are well known**, gives a lot of money to environmental causes.
Object Relative Clauses	Detectives are people (**who / whom / that) I respect tremendously**.	The character Sherlock Holmes, who / **whom Arthur Conan Doyle created**, was a fictional detective.
	Evidence (**which / that) criminals leave at the crime scene** is called forensic evidence.	Evidence from criminals, **which we call forensic evidence**, can help police solve cases.
	The person **whose car the thieves stole** was a friend of mine.	Arthur Conan Doyle, **whose medical clinic not many patients attended**, had time to write his stories.
Object Relative Clauses as Objects of Prepositions	There's the police officer (**that / who / whom) I spoke to**. (informal) There's the police officer **to whom I spoke**. (formal)	There's Officer Smith, **who / whom I spoke to yesterday**. (informal) There's Officer Smith, **to whom I spoke yesterday**. (formal)
	Police found evidence from the crime scene under the chair (**that / which) I was sitting on**. (informal) Police found evidence from the crime scene under the chair **on which I was sitting**. (formal)	The door, **which I entered through**, had been broken during the robbery. (informal) The door, **through which I entered**, had been broken during the robbery. (formal)

	Identifying	Nonidentifying
Relative Clauses with *Where* and *in Which*	It's a city **where you can find Wi-Fi almost everywhere**. It's a city **in which you can find Wi-Fi almost everywhere**.	The city of Atlanta, **where my sister lives**, is very large. The city of Atlanta, **in which my sister lives**, is very large.
Relative Clauses with *When* and *During Which*	Night is a time **when many students study for exams**. Night is a time **during which many students study for exams**.	Joe prefers to study at night, **when his children are asleep**. Joe prefers to study at night, **during which his children are asleep**.
Participle Phrases	Students **concerned with the environment** should get involved in environmental groups on campus.	Millennials, **raised in the era of technology, cell phones, and the Internet**, understand technology very well.
	The expert **giving tomorrow's talk on Millennials** is very well known.	The movie Twilight, **starring Millennials**, is based on a book by Gen Xer Stephenie Meyer.
Prepositional Phrases	The computers **in our classroom** are fast. Young workers **low in self-esteem** are unusual.	
Appositives		Jan Smith, **the president of Myco**, will be speaking at noon today. Jan Smith (**the president of Myco**) will be speaking at noon today. (formal writing)

20. Conditionals

Situation	Tense	*If* clause	Main clause	Example
Real Conditionals	present	simple present	simple present	*If a website **is** popular, people **talk** about it.*
	future	simple present	future	*If you only **listen** to one station, you **will hear** only one opinion.*
Unreal Conditionals	present	simple past or past progressive	*would, could, might* + base form of verb	*If I **studied** every day, I **would pass** all my tests.* *If I **weren't dreaming** all day, I **would pass** all my tests.*
	future	simple past	*would, could, might* + base form of verb	*If our school **closed** next year, we **wouldn't have** a place to learn.*
	past	past perfect	*would have, could have, might have* + past participle	*If the city **had hired** more teachers, the schools **might have improved**.*
Wishes	**Tense**	***that* clause**		**Example**
	present	simple past, past progressive, could		*I wish (that) schools **were improving**.*
	future	*were going to, would, could*		*I wish (that) the teachers **were going to** give us a party.*
	past	past perfect		*I **wish** (that) I **had studied** more.*

21. Academic Word List (AWL) Words and Definitions

The meanings of the words are those used in this book. ([U1] = Unit 1)

Academic Word	Definition
academics (n) [U25]	the subjects that you study in high school or college
access (n) [U5] [U6]	the opportunity or ability to use something
access (v) [U8]	get information, especially when using a computer
accurate (adj) [U22]	correct and without any mistakes
adapt (v) [U2] [U26]	change something so that it is suitable for a different use or situation
adequately (adv) [U20]	good enough but not very good
adult (n) [U4] [U8] [U9]	someone (or something such as a plant or animal) grown to full size and strength
affect (v) [U5] [U10] [U14] [U15] [U17] [U19] [U20] [U24] [U27]	have an influence on someone or something
aid (n) [U12]	help or support, especially in the form of food, money, or medical supplies
aid (v) [U9]	help or support
alter (v) [U20]	change a characteristic, often slightly; cause something to happen
alternative (adj) [U21]	available as another choice
alternative (n) [U18]	something that is different, especially from what is usual; a choice
analyst (n) [U24]	someone who studies or examines something in detail, such as finances, computer systems, or the economy
analyze (v) [U22]	study something in a systematic and careful way
appreciation (n) [U17]	being grateful for something
approach (n) [U2] [U15]	a method or way of doing something
approximately (adv) [U19]	almost exact
area (n) [U19] [U26] [U28]	a particular part of a country, city, town, etc.
attitude (n) [U1] [U15]	the way you feel about something or someone, or a particular feeling or opinion
author (n) [U7] [U9] [U17]	a writer of a book, article, etc.; a person whose main job is writing books
automatically (adv) [U22]	done in a manner as a natural reaction or without thinking
available (adj) [U14] [U18]	ready to use or obtain
aware (adj) [U8] [U21]	knowing that something exists; having knowledge or experience of a particular thing
beneficial (adj) [U10] [U20]	tending to help; having a good effect
benefit (n) [U11] [U20]	a helpful service given to employees in addition to pay; a helpful or good effect

Academic Word	Definition
challenge (n) [U8]	something needing great mental or physical effort in order to be done successfully
challenge (v) [U7]	test someone's ability or determination
challenging (adj) [U23]	difficult in a way that tests your ability or determination
chemical (n) [U20] [U27]	any basic substance that is used in or produced by a reaction involving changes to atoms or molecules
cite (v) [U20]	mention something as an example or proof of something else
civil rights (n) [U3]	the rights of every person in a society, including equality under law
classic (adj) [U10]	having a traditional style that is always fashionable
colleague (n) [U23]	one member of a group of people who work together
communication (n) [U5]	the exchange of messages or information
complex (adj) [U8] [U17]	having many, but connected, parts making it difficult to understand
computer (n) [U5] [U6] [U8] [U9] [U22] [U23] [U28]	an electronic device that can store, organize, and change large amounts of information quickly
computing (n) [U6]	the use of computers to complete a task; the study or use of computers
concentrate (v) [U7] [U12]	direct your attention and thought to an activity or subject
conclude (v) [U24]	cause something to end; end
conclusion (n) [U24]	a decision made after a lot of consideration
consequently (adv) [U16] [U28]	as a result; therefore
consist of (v) [U12] [U20]	be made up or formed of various specific things
constant (adj) [U5]	not changing
constantly (adv) [U1]	nearly continuously or very frequently
consumer (n) [U13] [U26]	a person who buys goods or services for their own use
contact (v) [U4]	have communication with a person or with a group or organization
contribute (v) [U3] [U10]	help by providing money or support, especially when other people or conditions are also helping
controversial (adj) [U4]	causing or likely to cause disagreement
convert (v) [U21]	change the character, appearance, or operation of something
convince (v) [U13] [U15] [U24]	cause someone to believe something or to do something
corporation (n) [U3]	a large company
create (v) [U1] [U2] [U7] [U15] [U17] [U20] [U21] [U26] [U28]	cause something to exist, or to make something new or imaginative
creation (n) [U16] [U19]	something that is made
creative (adj) [U13] [U18]	producing or using original and unusual ideas
creatively (adv) [U18]	done in a new or imaginative way

Academic Word	Definition
creator (n) [U28]	a person who creates something
crucial (adj) [U7] [U10]	extremely important because many other things depend on it
cultural (adj) [U15] [U19] [U26]	relating to the way of life of a country or a group of people
culture (n) [U2] [U14] [U19] [U26]	the way of life of a particular people, especially shown in their ordinary behavior and habits, their attitudes toward each other, and their moral and religious beliefs
data (n) [U6]	information collected for use
debate (n) [U4] [U20]	a discussion or argument about a subject
demonstrate (v) [U1]	show how to do something; explain
depressed (adj) [U27]	unhappy and without hope
design (v) [U18] [U20]	make or draw plans for something
despite (prep) [U28]	used to say that something happened or is true, although something else makes this seem not probable
device (n) [U5] [U6] [U8]	a piece of equipment that is used for a particular purpose
distribution (n) [U20]	the division of something among several or many people, or the spreading of something over an area
dominant (adj) [U4]	more important, strong, or noticeable
dominate (v) [U19]	control a place or person, want to be in charge, or be the most important person or thing
dramatically (adv) [U10]	suddenly or noticeably
economic (adj) [U14] [U21] [U24]	connected to the economy of a country
eliminate (v) [U6]	remove or take away
energy (n) [U9] [U21]	the power to do work and activity
environment (n) [U4] [U10] [U13] [U17] [U20] [U21]	the conditions that you live or work in, and the way that they influence how you feel or how effectively you can work; the air, water, and land in or on which people, animals, and plants live
error (n) [U23]	a mistake, especially in a way that can be discovered as wrong
ethnic (adj) [U3]	relating to a particular race of people who share a system of accepted beliefs and morals
evidence (n) [U16] [U22]	something that helps to prove that something is or is not true
expert (n) [U6] [U7] [U9] [U18] [U19] [U22] [U23] [U25]	a person with a high level of knowledge or skill about a particular subject
external (adj) [U17]	relating to the outside part of something
facility (n) [U11]	a place where a particular activity happens
file (n) [U6]	a collection of information in a computer stored as one unit with one name
final (adj) [U7]	last

Academic Word	Definition
finally (adv) [U4] [U12] [U16] [U18] [U20] [U28]	at the end, or after some delay
financial (adj) [U11] [U12] [U16] [U27]	relating to money
flexible (adj) [U18]	able to change or be changed easily according to the situation
focus (v) [U11] [U17] [U21]	direct attention toward someone or something
found (v) [U3]	start an organization, especially by providing money
foundation (n) [U3]	an organization that provides financial support for activities and groups
furthermore (adv) [U6] [U15] [U28]	also and more importantly
generate (v) [U6] [U21]	produce
generation (n) [U23]	all the people within a society or family of about the same age
global (adj) [U2] [U3] [U19] [U20]	relating to the whole world
globalization (n) [U26]	the increase of business around the world, especially by big companies operating in many countries
globally (adv) [U26]	pertaining to the whole world
goal (n) [U3] [U4]	an aim or purpose, something you want to achieve
grade (n) [U17]	the measure of the quality of a student's schoolwork
grant (n) [U12]	money that a university, government, or organization gives to someone for a purpose, such as to do research or study
guarantee (v) [U8]	promise that a particular thing will happen
identical (adj) [U4]	exactly the same
identify (v) [U22]	recognize or be able to name someone or something; prove who or what someone or something is
identity (n) [U19]	who a person is, or the qualities of a person, thing, or group that make them different from others
image (n) [U2] [U7] [U22]	an idea, especially a mental picture, of what something or someone is
immigrant (n) [U26]	a person who has come into a foreign country in order to live there
impact (n) [U4] [U10]	the strong effect or influence that something has on a situation or person
implicit (adj) [U1]	suggested but not communicated directly
inappropriate (adj) [U2] [U25]	unsuitable, especially for the particular time, place, or situation
inconclusive (adj) [U22]	not leading to a definite result or decision; uncertain
individual (n) [U4] [U18]	a person, especially when considered separately and not as part of a group
individualism (n) [U15]	the quality or state of being different from other people

Academic Word	Definition
innovation (n) [U11]	something new or different
institute (n) [U9] [U11]	an organization where people do a particular kind of scientific, educational, or social work
internal (adj) [U17]	happening inside a person, group, organization, place, or country
investigate (v) [U1] [U4] [U22]	try to discover all the facts about something
investigation (n) [U22]	the search for facts
investigator (n) [U22]	a person who examines the particulars of an event in an attempt to learn the facts
isolated (adj) [U24]	separated from other things
issue (n) [U11] [U12] [U14] [U20] [U24]	a subject or problem that people are thinking and talking about
job (n) [U11] [U12] [U14] [U19] [U23] [U24] [U28]	the regular work that a person does to earn money
legislator (n) [U25]	a member of an elected group of people who has the power to make or change laws
link (n) [U9] [U24]	a connection; a word or image on a website that can take you to another document or website
link (v) [U20]	make a connection
locate (v) [U26]	put or establish something in a particular place
location (n) [U6]	a place or position
maintain (v) [U7]	make a situation or activity continue in the same way
maintenance (n) [U23]	the work that is done to keep something in good condition
major (adj) [U2] [U9] [U21]	more important, bigger, or more serious than others of the same type
media (n) [U24]	newspapers, magazines, television, and radio considered as a group
mental (adj) [U7]	relating to the mind, or involving the process of thinking
method (n) [U18] [U22]	a way of doing something
minority (n) [U3]	a part of a group that is less than half of the whole group, often much less
modify (v) [U20]	change something in order to improve it
motivate (v) [U17]	cause someone to behave in a certain way, or to make someone want to do something well; give a reason for doing something
motivation (n) [U17]	enthusiasm to do something
negative (adj) [U23]	not happy, hopeful, or approving
nondominant (adj) [U7]	not as important, strong, or noticeable
nonetheless (adv) [U6] [U25]	despite what has just been said or referred to
occupy (v) [U4]	fill or use

Academic Word	Definition
occur (v) [U8] [U22] [U23] [U24]	happen
option (n) [U12]	a choice
participant (n) [U18]	a person who becomes involved in an activity
percent (adv) [U11] [U14] [U21] [U27]	for or out of every 100
physical (adj) [U9]	relating to the body
plus (conj) [U12]	added to
policy (n) [U24] [U25]	a set of ideas or a plan of what to do in particular situations that has been agreed on by a government or group of people
portion (n) [U9]	the amount of food served to, or suitable for, a person
pose (v) [U6]	cause a problem or difficulty
positive (adj) [U13] [U15] [U17] [U23] [U24]	happy or hopeful
potential (adj) [U20]	possible but not yet achieved
predict (v) [U5] [U16]	say that an event will happen in the future
prediction (n) [U24]	events or actions that may happen in the future
principle (n) [U3]	a rule or belief which influences your behavior and is based on what you think is right
prior (adv) [U25]	existing or happening before something else
priority (n) [U7]	something that is considered more important than other matters
process (n) [U1] [U18]	a series of actions or events performed to make something or achieve a particular result, or a series of changes that happens naturally
professional (adj) [U18] [U21] [U27]	relating to the workplace; engaging in as a career; relating to a skilled type of work
project (n) [U7] [U16]	a piece of planned work or activity that is completed over a period of time and intended to achieve a particular aim
psychologist (n) [U1] [U17]	someone who studies the mind and emotions and their relationship to behavior
range (n) [U24]	the level to which something is limited, or the area within which something operates
react (v) [U1] [U13]	feel or act in a way because of something else
refined (adj) [U9]	made more pure by removing unwanted material
relaxed (adj) [U10]	comfortable and informal
relaxing (adj) [U10]	feeling happy and comfortable because nothing is worrying you
reliable (adj) [U6]	to be trusted or believe
relocate (v) [U14]	move to a new place
rely (v) [U24]	need or trust someone or something
require (v) [U18]	need something, or to make something necessary

Academic Word	Definition
research (n) [U1] [U2] [U4] [U5] [U10] [U14] [U15] [U16] [U17]	the detailed study of a subject or an object in order to discover information or achieve a new understanding of it
research (v) [U1]	study a subject in order to discover information
researcher (n) [U3] [U4] [U5] [U15] [U17]	a person who studies something to learn detailed information about it
reveal (v) [U1]	allow something to be seen that had been hidden or secret
role (n) [U4]	the duty or use that someone or something usually has or is expected to have
route (n) [U7]	the roads or paths you follow to get from one place to another place
schedule (n) [U16]	a list of planned activities or things to be done at or during a particular time
secure (adj) [U6]	safe
seek (v) [U27]	search for something
sequence (n) [U28]	a series of related events or things that have a particular order
series (n) [U2]	several things or events or the same type that come one after the other
similar (adj) [U2] [U3] [U4] [U24]	looking or being almost the same, although not exactly
similarity (n) [U4]	when two things or people are almost the same
similarly (adv) [U10]	in almost the same way
site (n) [U6] [U11] [U13] [U24]	a place where something is, was, or will be; a place on the Internet with one or more pages of information about a subject
source (n) [U21] [U24]	origin or beginning of something
specific (adj) [U20]	relating to one thing and not others; particular
specifically (adv) [U1]	for a particular reason or purpose
strategy (n) [U11] [U13] [U26]	a plan for achieving something or reaching a goal
stress (n) [U11]	a feeling of worry caused by a difficult situation
style (n) [U10] [U13]	a way of doing something that is typical to a person, group, place, or time
sum (n) [U6]	an amount of money
survey (n) [U6]	a set of questions to find out people's habits or beliefs about something
survive (v) [U15]	continue to live, especially after a dangerous situation
team (n) [U12] [U22] [U23]	a group of people who work together, either in a sport or in order to achieve something
technique (n) [U7] [U18] [U22]	a specific way of doing a skillful activity
technological (adj) [U8]	relating to or involving technology

Academic Word	Definition
technology (n) [U5] [U6] [U20] [U21] [U22] [U23] [U28]	the method for using scientific discoveries for practical purposes, especially in industry
tradition (n) [U15]	a custom or way of behaving that has continued for a long time in a group of people or a society
traditional (adj) [U13] [U18] [U22] [U25]	established for a long time, or part of a behavior and beliefs that have been established
traditionally (adv) [U15]	relating to or involving tradition
transfer (v) [U12]	move someone or something from one place to another
trend (n) [U9]	the direction of changes or developments
unbiased (adj) [U24]	not influenced by personal opinion
unique (adj) [U28]	different from everyone and everything
uniquely (adv) [U26]	in a manner that is unusual or special
variation (n) [U18]	a change in quality, amount, or level
varying (adj) [U10]	different
version (n) [U18]	a form of something that differs slightly from other forms of the same thing
virtual (adj) [U28]	created by a computer
visualization (n) [U7]	an image in your mind of someone or something
visualize (v) [U7]	create a picture in your mind of someone or something
voluntary (adj) [U11]	done or given because you want to and not because you have been forced to

22. Pronunciation Table International Phonetic Alphabet (IPA)

Vowels	
Key Words	**International Phonetic Alphabet**
cake, mail, pay	/eɪ/
pan, bat, hand	/æ/
tea, feet, key	/iː/
ten, well, red	/e/
ice, pie, night	/ɑɪ/
is, fish, will	/ɪ/
cone, road, know	/oʊ/
top, rock, stop	/ɑ/
blue, school, new, cube, few	/uː/
cup, us, love	/ʌ/
house, our, cow	/aʊ/
saw, talk, applause	/ɔː/
boy, coin, join	/ɔɪ/
put, book, woman	/ʊ/
alone, open, pencil, atom, ketchup	/ə/

Consonants	
Key Words	**International Phonetic Alphabet**
bid, jo**b**	/b/
do, fee**d**	/d/
food, sa**f**e	/f/
go, do**g**	/g/
home, be**h**ind	/h/
kiss, ba**ck**	/k/
load, poo**l**	/l/
man, plu**m**	/m/
need, ope**n**	/n/
pen, ho**p**e	/p/
road, ca**r**d	/r/
see, re**c**ent	/s/
show, na**ti**on	/ʃ/
team, mee**t**	/t/
choose, wa**tch**	/tʃ/
think, bo**th**	/θ/
this, fa**th**er	/ð/
visit, sa**v**e	/v/
watch, a**w**ay	/w/
yes, on**i**on	/j/
zoo, the**s**e	/z/
bei**g**e, mea**s**ure	/ʒ/
jump, bri**dg**e	/dʒ/

Glossary of Grammar Terms

action verb a verb that describes an action.
> I **eat** breakfast every day.
> They **ran** in the 5K race.

active sentence a sentence that focuses on the doer and the action.
> **Jorge played** basketball yesterday.

adjective a word that describes or modifies a noun.
> That's a **beautiful** hat.

adjective clause see **relative clause**

adverb a word that describes or modifies a verb, another adverb, or an adjective. Adverbs often end in -ly.
> Please walk **faster** but **carefully**.

adverb clause a clause that shows how ideas are connected. Adverb clauses begin with subordinators such as *because*, *since*, *although*, and *even though*.
> **Although it is not a holiday**, workers have the day off.

adverb of degree an adverb that makes other adverbs or adjectives stronger or weaker.
> The test was **extremely** difficult. They are **really** busy today.

adverb of frequency an adverb such as *always*, *often*, *sometimes*, *never*, and *usually* that describes how often something happens.
> She **always** arrives at work on time.

adverb of manner an adverb that describes how an action happens.
> He has **suddenly** left the room.

adverb of time an adverb that describes when something happens.
> She'll get up **later**.

agent the noun or pronoun performing the action of the verb in a sentence.
> **People** spoke English at the meeting.

appositive a reduced form of a nonidentifying relative clause. Appositives are formed by removing the relative pronoun and the verb *be*, leaving only a noun phrase.
> Jan Smith, **an expert on Millennials**, will be speaking at noon today.

article the words *a / an* and *the*. An article introduces or identifies a noun.
> I bought **a** new MP3 player. **The** price was reasonable.

auxiliary verb (also called **helping verb**) a verb that is used before a main verb in a sentence. *Do*, *have*, *be*, and *will* can act as auxiliary verbs.
> **Does** he want to go to the library later? **Have** you received the package? **Will** he arrive soon?

base form of the verb the form of a verb without any endings (-s or -ed) or *to*.
> **come**   **go**   **take**

clause a group of words that has a subject and a verb. There are two types of clauses: **main clauses** and **dependent clauses** (*see* **dependent clause**). A sentence can have more than one clause.

MAIN CLAUSE   DEPENDENT CLAUSE   MAIN CLAUSE

I woke up when I heard the noise. It was scary.

common noun a word for a person, place, or thing. A common noun is not capitalized.

mother   building   fruit

comparative the form of an adjective or adverb that shows how two people, places, or things are different.

*My daughter is **older than** my son.* (adjective)

*She does her work **more quickly** than he does.* (adverb)

conditional a sentence that describes a possible situation and the result of that situation. It can be a real or unreal condition / result about the present, past, or future.

If a website is popular, people talk about it. (present real conditional)

If I had studied harder, I would have passed that course. (past unreal conditional)

conjunction a word such as *and*, *but*, *so*, *or*, and *yet* that connects single words, phrases, or clauses.

*We finished all our work, **so** we left early.*

Some more conjunctions are after, as, because, if, and when.

consonant a sound represented in writing by these letters of the alphabet: ***b, c, d, f, g, h, j, k, l, m, n, p, q, r, s, t, v, w, x, y,*** and ***z.***

count noun a person, place, or thing you can count. Count nouns have a plural form.

*There are three **banks** on Oak Street.*

definite article *the* is the definite article. Use *the* with a person, place, or thing that is familiar to you and your listener. Use *the* when the noun is unique – there is only one (*the sun*, *the moon*, *the Internet*). Also use *the* before a singular noun used to represent a whole class or category.

***The** movie we saw last week was very good.*

***The** Earth is round.*

***The** male robin is more colorful than **the** female.*

dependent clause a clause that cannot stand alone. A dependent clause is not a complete sentence, but it still has a subject and verb. Some kinds of dependent clauses are adverb clauses, relative clauses, and time clauses.

***After we return from the trip**, I'm going to need to relax.*

determiner a word that comes before a noun to limit its meaning in some way. Some common determiners are *some*, *a little*, *a lot*, *a few*, *this*, *that*, *these*, *those*, *his*, *a*, *an*, *the*, *much*, and *many*.

***These** computers have **a lot** of parts.*

*Please give me **my** book.*

direct object the person or thing that receives the action of the verb.

*The teacher gave the students **a test**.*

direct question a type of direct speech (see **direct speech**) that repeats a person's question.

The president asked, ***"Who were your best employees last month?"***

direct speech (also called **quoted speech**) repeats people's exact words. A direct speech statement consists of a reporting clause and the exact words of a person inside quotation marks.

The manager said, ***"Workers need to use creativity."***

factual conditional *see* **present real conditional**

formal a style of writing or speech used when you don't know the other person very well or where it's not appropriate to show familiarity, such as in business, a job interview, speaking to a stranger, or speaking to an older person who you respect.

Good evening. I'd like to speak with Ms. Smith. Is she available?

future a verb form that describes a time that hasn't come yet. It is expressed in English by *will, be going to,* and present tense.

*I'**ll meet** you tomorrow.*

*I'**m going to visit** my uncle and aunt next weekend.*

*My bus **leaves** at 10:00 tomorrow.*

*I'**m meeting** Joe on Friday.*

future real conditional describes a possible situation in the future and the likely result. The *if* clause uses the simple present. The main clause uses a future form of the verb.

***If** you only **listen** to one station, you **will hear** only one opinion.*

future unreal conditional describes an imaginary situation in the future. The *if* clause uses the simple past. The main clause uses the modals *would, could,* or *might.*

***If** teachers **prepared** students better for exams, more students **would pass**.*

gerund the *-ing* form of a verb that is used as a noun. It can be the subject or object of a sentence or the object of a preposition.

*We suggested **waiting** and **going** another day.*

*Salsa **dancing** is a lot of fun.*

*I look forward to **meeting** you.*

habitual past a verb form that describes repeated past actions, habits, and conditions using *used to* or *would.*

*Before we had the Internet, we **used to** go to the library a lot.*

*Before there was refrigeration, people **would** use ice to keep food cool.*

helping verb *see* **auxiliary verb**

***if* clause** the condition clause in a conditional. It describes the possible situation, which can be either real or unreal.

***If it rains tomorrow**, I'll stay home.*

imperative a type of clause that tells people to do something. It gives instructions, directions to a place, and advice. The verb is in the base form.

***Listen** to the conversation.*

***Don't open** your books.*

***Turn** right at the bank and then **go** straight.*

indefinite article *a/an* are the indefinite articles. Use *a/an* with a singular person, place, or thing when you and your listener are not familiar with it, or when the specific name of it is not important. Use *a* with consonant sounds. Use *an* with vowel sounds.

*She's going to see **a** doctor today.*

*I had **an** egg for breakfast.*

indefinite pronoun a pronoun used when the noun is unknown or not important. There is an indefinite pronoun for people, for places, and for things. Some examples are *somebody, anyone, nobody, somewhere, anywhere, nothing, everything*, etc. Use singular verb forms when the indefinite pronoun is the subject of the sentence.

***Everybody** is going to be there. There is **nowhere** I'd rather work.*

indirect object the person or thing that receives the direct object.

*The teacher gave **the students** a test.*

indirect question (also called **reported question**) tells what other people have asked or asks a question using a statement. There are two kinds of indirect questions: *Yes/No* and information questions. Indirect questions follow the *subject-verb* word order of a statement.

*Mia **asked whether** we **would begin** Creative Problem Solving soon.*

*The president asked **who** my best employees **were** last month.*

indirect speech (also called **reported speech**) tells what someone says in another person's words. An indirect speech statement consists of a reporting verb (see **reporting verb**) such as *say* in the main clause, followed by a *that* clause. *That* is optional and is often omitted in speaking.

*He **said** (that) she **was enjoying** the work.*

infinitive *to* + the base form of a verb.

*I need **to get** home early tonight.*

infinitive of purpose *in order* + infinitive expresses a purpose. It answers the question *why*. If the meaning is clear, it is not necessary to use *in order*.

*People are fighting **(in order) to change** unfair laws.*

informal is a style of speaking to friends, family, and children.

Hey, there. Nice to see you again.

information question (also called **Wh- question**) begins with a *wh*-word (*who, what, when, where, which, why, how, how much*). To answer this type of question, you need to provide information rather than answer *yes* or *no*.

inseparable phrasal verb a phrasal verb that cannot be separated. The verb and its particle always stay together.

*My car **broke down** yesterday.*

intransitive verb a verb that does not need an object. It is often followed by an expression of time, place, or manner. It cannot be used in the passive.

*The flight **arrived** at 5.30 p.m.*

irregular adjective an adjective that does not change its form in the usual way. For example, you do not make the comparative form by adding *-er*.

good → *better*

irregular adverb an adverb that does not change its form in the usual way. For example, you do not make the comparative form by adding *-ly*.

badly ➞ *worse*

irregular verb a verb that does not change its form in the usual way. For example, it does not form the simple past with *-d* or *-ed*. It has its own special form.

go ➞ *went*   *ride* ➞ *rode*   *hit* ➞ *hit*

main clause (also called **independent clause**) a clause that can be used alone as a complete sentence. In a conditional, the main clause describes the result when the condition exists.

*After I get back from my trip, **I'm going to relax**.*

*If I hear about a good story, **I move quickly to get there and report it**.*

main verb a verb that functions alone in a clause and can have an auxiliary verb.

*They **had** a meeting last week.*

*They have **had** many meetings this month.*

measurement word a word or phrase that shows the amount of something. Measurement words can be singular or plural. They can be used to make noncount nouns countable.

*I bought **a box** of cereal, and Sonia bought **five pounds** of apples.*

modal a verb such as *can, could, have to, may, might, must, should, will*, and *would*. It modifies the main verb to show such things as ability, permission, possibility, advice, obligation, necessity, or lack of necessity.

*It **might** rain later today.*

*You **should** study harder if you want to pass this course.*

non-action verb *see* **stative verb**

noncount noun refers to ideas and things that you cannot count. Noncount nouns use a singular verb and do not have a plural form.

*Do you download **music**?*

noun a word for a person, place, or thing. There are common nouns and proper nouns. (*see* **common nouns, proper nouns**)

COMMON NOUN   PROPER NOUN

*I stayed in a **hotel** on my trip to New York.*   *I stayed in the **Pennsylvania Hotel**.*

object a noun or pronoun that usually follows the verb and receives the action.

*I sent **the flowers**. I sent **them** to **you**.*

object pronoun replaces a noun in the object position.

*Sara loves exercise classes. She takes **them** three times a week.*

participle phrase a reduced form of an identifying relative clause. Participle phrases are formed by removing the relative pronoun and the verb *be*. Participle phrases can be used when the verb in the relative clause is in the form verb + *-ing* (present participle) or the past participle form.

*He is the person **using the Internet too much at work**.*

particle a small word like *down, in, off, on, out,* or *up.* These words (which can also be prepositions) are used with verbs to form **two-word verbs** or **phrasal verbs**. The meaning of a phrasal verb often has a different meaning from the meaning of the individual words in it.

passive sentence a sentence that focuses on the action or on the person or thing receiving the action. The object is in the subject position.

__English was spoken__ at the meeting.

past participle a verb form that can be regular (base form + *-ed*) or irregular. It is used to form perfect tenses and the passive. It can also be an adjective.

I've __studied__ English for five years.

The __frightened__ child cried.

past progressive a verb form that describes events or situations in progress at a time in the past. The emphasis is on the action.

They __were watching__ TV when I arrived.

past unreal conditional describes a situation that was not true in the past. Past unreal conditionals describe something that was possible but did not happen. The *if* clause uses the past perfect. The main clause uses the modals *would have, could have,* or *might have* and the past participle form of the verb.

If we __hadn't had__ a hurricane, the schools __wouldn't have closed__.

phrasal verb (also called **two-word verb**) consists of a verb + a particle. There are two kinds of phrasal verbs: separable and inseparable. (*see* **particle, inseparable phrasal verbs, separable phrasal verbs**)

       VERB + PARTICLE

They __came back__ from vacation today. (inseparable)

Please __put__ your cell phone __away__. (separable)

phrase a group of words about an idea that is not a complete sentence. It does not have a main verb.

__across the street__   __in the morning__

plural noun a noun that refers to more than one person, place, or thing.

__students__   __women__   __roads__

possessive adjective *see* **possessive determiner.**

possessive determiner (also called **possessive adjective**) a determiner that shows possession (*my, your, his, her, its, our,* and *their*).

possessive pronoun replaces a possessive determiner + singular or plural noun. The possessive pronoun agrees with the noun that it replaces.

My exercise class is at night. __Hers__ is on the weekend. (hers = her exercise class)

preposition a word such as *to, at, for, with, below, in, on, next to,* or *above* that goes before a noun or pronoun to show location, time, direction, or a close relationship between two people or things. A preposition may go before a gerund as well.

I'm __in__ the supermarket __next to__ our favorite restaurant.

The idea __of__ love has inspired many poets.

I'm interested __in__ taking a psychology course.

prepositional phrase a reduced form of an identifying relative clause. Prepositional phrases are formed by removing the relative pronoun and the verb *be,* leaving only a prepositional phrase.

*The computers **in our classroom** are fast.*

present perfect a verb form that describes past events or situations that are still important in the present and actions that happened once or repeatedly at an indefinite time before now.

*Lately scientists **have discovered** medicines in the Amazon.*

*I**'ve been** to the Amazon twice.*

present perfect progressive a verb form that describes something that started in the past, usually continues in the present, and may continue in the future.

*He **hasn't been working** since last May.*

present progressive a verb form that describes an action or situation that is in progress now or around the present time. It is also used to indicate a fixed arrangement in the future.

*What **are** you **doing** right now?*

*I**'m leaving** for Spain next week.*

present real conditional (also called **factual conditional**) describes a situation that is possible now and its result. Present real conditionals describe general truths, facts, and habits. The *if* clause and the main clause use the simple present.

*If you **control** the media, you **control** public opinion.*

present unreal conditional describes an imaginary situation in the present. The *if* clause uses the simple past or past progressive. The main clause uses the modals *would, could,* or *might.*

*If I **studied** every day, I **could pass** all my tests.*

pronoun a word that replaces a noun or noun phrase. Some examples are *I, we, him, hers, it.* (*see* **object pronoun, subject pronoun, relative pronoun, possessive pronoun, reciprocal pronoun, reflexive pronoun**.)

proper noun a noun that is the name of a particular person, place, or thing. It is capitalized.

Central Park** in **New York City

punctuation mark a symbol used in writing such as a period (.), a comma (,), a question mark (?), or an exclamation point (!).

quantifier a word or phrase that shows an amount of something. In addition to measurements words, some other quantifiers are *much, many, some, any, a lot, plenty, enough,* etc.

*We have **three bottles** of juice and **plenty of** snacks.*

quoted speech *see* **direct speech**

reciprocal pronoun a pronoun (*each other, one another*) that shows that two or more people give *and* receive the same action or have the same relationship.

*Mari and I have the same challenges. We help **each other**. (I help Mari, and Mari helps me.)*

reflexive pronoun a pronoun (*myself, yourself, himself, herself, ourselves, yourselves, themselves*) that shows that the object of the sentence is the same as the subject.

*I taught **myself** to speak Japanese.*

regular verb a verb that changes its form in the usual way.

live ⟶ live**s**

wash ⟶ wash**ed**

relative clause (also called **adjective clause**) defines, describes, identifies, or gives more information about a noun. It begins with a relative pronoun such as *who, that, which, whose,* or *whom*. Like all clauses, a relative clause has both a subject and a verb. It can describe the subject or the object of a sentence.

*People **who have sleep problems** can join the study.* (subject relative clause)

*There are many diseases **that viruses cause**.* (object relative clause)

relative pronoun a pronoun (*who, which, that, whose, whom*) that connects a noun phrase to a relative clause

*People **who** have sleep problems can join the study.*

*There are many diseases **that** viruses cause.*

reported question *see* **indirect question**

reported speech *see* **indirect speech**

reporting verb a verb used to introduce direct speech or indirect speech. *Say* is the most common reporting verb. Other such verbs include *admit, announce, complain, confess, exclaim, explain, mention, remark, reply, report, state,* and *swear,* and *tell*.

*The president **said**, "We will change our system of rewarding employees."*

*The president **stated** that they would change their system of rewarding employees.*

result clause *see* **main clause**

sentence a complete thought or idea that has a subject and a main verb. In writing, it begins with a capital letter and has a punctuation mark at the end (. ? !). In an imperative sentence, the subject (*you*) is not usually stated.

This sentence is a complete thought.

Open your books.

separable phrasal verb a phrasal verb that can be separated. This means that an object can go before or after the particle.

***Write down** your expenses.*

***Write** your expenses **down**.*

simple past a verb form that describes completed actions or events that happened at a definite time in the past.

*They **grew up** in Washington, D.C.*

*They **attended** Howard University and **graduated** in 2004.*

simple present a verb form that describes things that regularly happen such as habits and routines (usual and regular activities). It also describes facts and general truths.

*I **play** games online every night.* (routine)

*The average person **spends** 13 hours a week online.* (fact)

singular noun a noun that refers to only one person, place, or thing.
*He is my best **friend**.*

statement a sentence that gives information.
Today is Thursday.

stative verb (also called **non-action verb**) describes a state or situation, not an action. It is usually in the simple form.
*I **remember** your friend.*

subject the person, place, or thing that performs the action of a verb.
***People** use new words and expressions every day.*

subject pronoun replaces a noun in the subject position.
***Sara and I** are friends. **We** work at the same company.*

subordinator a conjunction that connects a dependent clause and an independent clause. Some common subordinators include *although, because, even though, in order to, since,* and *so that*.
***Although** many people like to shop, some people shop too much.*

superlative the form of an adjective or adverb that compares one person, place, or thing to others in a group.
*This storm was **the most dangerous** one of the season.* (adjective)
*That group worked **most effectively** after the disaster.* (adverb)

syllable a group of letters that has one vowel sound and that you say as a single unit.
There is one syllable in the word lunch *and two syllables in the word* breakfast. (Break *is one syllable and* fast *is another syllable.)*

tag question consists of a verb and pronoun added to the end of a statement. Tag questions confirm information or ask for agreement. The tag changes the statement into a question.
*They don't live in Chicago, **do they?***   *Geography is interesting, **isn't it?***

tense the form of a verb that shows past or present time.
*They **worked** yesterday.* (simple past)
*They **work** every day.* (simple present)

third-person singular refers to *he, she,* and *it* or a singular noun. In the simple present, the third-person singular form ends in *-s* or *-es*.
***It looks** warm and sunny today. **He washes** the laundry on Saturdays.*

time clause a phrase that shows the order of events and begins with a time word such as *before, after, when, while,* or *as soon as*.
***Before** there were freezers, people needed ice to make frozen desserts.*

time expression a phrase that functions as an adverb of time. It tells when something happens, happened, or will happen.
*I graduated **in 2010**. She's going to visit her aunt and uncle **next summer**.*

transitive verb a verb that has an object. The object completes the meaning of the verb.
*She **wears** perfume.*

two-word verb *see* **phrasal verb**

verb a word that describes an action or a state.

*Alex **wears** jeans and a T-shirt to school. Alex **is** a student.*

vowel a sound represented in writing by these letters of the alphabet: ***a, e, i, o,*** and ***u.***

***Wh-* question** *see* **information question**

***Yes/No* question** begins with a form of *be* or an auxiliary verb. You can answer such a question with *yes* or *no.*

*"**Are** they going to the movies?" "**No,** they're not."*

*"**Can** you give me some help?" "**Yes,** I can."*

Index

Art Credits

Illustration